AfroLatinas and LatiNegras

CRITICAL AFRICANA STUDIES: AFRICAN, AFRICAN AMERICAN, AND CARIBBEAN INTERDISCIPLINARY AND INTERSECTIONAL STUDIES

Series Editor: Christel N. Temple, University of Pittsburgh

Series Editorial Board: Martell Teasley, Kimberly Nichele Brown, Jerome Schiele, Marquita M. Gammage, and Bayyinah S. Jeffries

The Critical Africana Studies book series features scholarship within the emerging field of Africana studies, which encompasses such disciplines as African studies, African diasporan studies, African American studies, Afro-American studies, Afro-Asian studies, Afro-European studies, Afro-Islamic studies, Afro-Jewish studies, Afro-Latino studies, Afro-Native American studies, Caribbean studies, Pan-African studies, Black British studies and, of course, Black studies. The Critical Africana Studies book series directly responds to the heightened demand for monographs and edited volumes that innovatively explore Africa and its diaspora employing cutting-edge critical, interdisciplinary, and intersectional theory and methods.

Recent Titles in the Series

AfroLatinas and LatiNegras: Culture, Identity, and Struggle from an Intersectional Perspective, edited by Rosita Scerbo and Concetta Bondi

African Sovereigns: The Workings of Diaspora in Jamaican Maroon Communities, by Mario Nisbett

Race, Identity, and Privilege from the US to the Congo, by Brenda F. Berrian

Ama Mazama: The Ogunic Presence in Africology, by Molefi Kete Asante

The Afrocentric Pan Africanist Vision: Afrocentric Essays, by Molefi Kete Asante

Branches of Asanteism, by Abdul Karim Bangura

Transcendence and the Africana Literary Enterprise, by Christel N. Temple

Strategies for Success among African-Americans and Afro-Caribbeans: Overachieve, Be Cheerful, or Confront, by Chrystal Y. Grey and Thomas Janoski

Rastafari Reasoning and the RastaWoman: Gender Constructions in the Shaping of Rastafari Livity, by Jeanne Christensen

AfroLatinas and LatiNegras

Culture, Identity, and Struggle from an Intersectional Perspective

*Edited by Rosita Scerbo
and Concetta Bondi*

LEXINGTON BOOKS
Lanham • Boulder • New York • London

Published by Lexington Books
An imprint of The Rowman & Littlefield Publishing Group, Inc.
4501 Forbes Boulevard, Suite 200, Lanham, Maryland 20706
www.rowman.com

86-90 Paul Street, London EC2A 4NE, United Kingdom

British Library Cataloguing in Publication Information Available

Library of Congress Cataloging-in-Publication Data

Names: Scerbo, Rosita, editor. | Bondi, Concetta, editor.
Title: Afrolatinas and Latinegras: culture, identity, and struggle from an intersectional
    perspective / edited by Rosita Scerbo and Concetta Bondi.
Description: Lanham: Lexington Books, 2022. | Series: Critical Africana studies:
    African, African American, and Caribbean interdisciplinary and intersectional studies |
    Includes index.
Identifiers: LCCN 2022041048 (print) | LCCN 2022041049 (ebook) | ISBN
    9781666910339 (hardcover) | ISBN 9781666910346 (epub)
Subjects: LCSH: Women, Black—Latin America. | Intersectionality (Sociology)—Latin
    America. | Power (Social sciences)—Latin America.
Classification: LCC HQ1910.5 .A37 202 (print) | LCC HQ1910.5 (ebook) | DDC
    305.4896/098—dc23/eng/20220901
LC record available at https://lccn.loc.gov/2022041048
LC ebook record available at https://lccn.loc.gov/2022041049

Contents

Acknowledgments

This edited book was born from inspiring and engaging conversations we have been having in academic, professional, and personal spaces and with intersectional feminist collectives. This project would not have been possible without all the strong women of color in my life. From mentors, senior colleagues, former advisors, friends, and family members, I wouldn't be here today without your constant, tireless, and genuine support.

To Concetta, my dear friend, colleague, and coeditor/author in this volume, thank you for being one of my strongest pillars of support. Thank you for always believing in me even in my moments of deepest doubt.

Above all, I would love to express my gratitude to all the outstanding contributors to this book for their enthusiasm, dedication, and commitment to social justice. From professors, writers, scholars, artists, and activists, each of you is deeply engaged in our communities and use your positions to advocate for gender, racial, and cultural equity.

Special thanks to Mexiafricana poet Natasha Carrizosa for granting us permission to include four of her original wonderful poems in this book: "six (wishbone)," "the richest poor people," "black rock," and "holy mother." Thanks also to Afro-Dominican poet Jasminne Mendez for allowing us to reprint sections of her interview that you can find in chapter 10. I would also like to acknowledge with gratitude Brooklyn-based Dominican-born multimedia artist Fanesha Fabre for contributing to this book cover with the digital art piece *Together*.

To my students, thank you for making me a better person every day, for teaching me to don't be so hard on myself and to never give up. Thank you for showing me that there is still hope in this world because tomorrow it will be in your compassionate and empathetic hands.

To my daughter, Sol, you are just three, but you are already a little fearless feminist and multicultural warrior, and I keep learning from you every day. I'm forever grateful for the light you brought into my life.

Y a todas las que siguen luchando o se juntarán a nosotras en la lucha . . . GRACIAS.

—Rosita Scerbo

I am forever indebted to the powerful collective of women that stand behind this project. This volume is a testament to the strength, courage, and resilience of generations of Afrolatina women both past and present, who will continue to inspire and influence generations to come. Thank you for sharing your hearts and your histories; this volume is dedicated to you.

Rosita, my dear friend and one of the women I most admire—thank you for allowing me to share in this special project.

I am nothing and could do nothing without the network of strong women who have stood by my side over the course of my life. In particular, the generations of women in my family who arrived to a new country as immigrants and were forced to give up their dreams so I could have my own. Thank you.

To all of these women, I am lucky to have met you and am proud to know you.

Gracias de corazón.

—Concetta Bondi

Introduction

Centering Black Women/Challenging Latinidad and Hegemonic Discourses

Rosita Scerbo and Concetta Bondi

six (wishbone)

wish i was on the porch
drinking brandy and slowly smoking clove
praying. taking time to listen. breathe
witness birds fly. watch me sit
remember when momma and granny said
breathe dream weep write drown live
heavy light back porch sage until
i am blue in the face
burn sage inside of a seashell
swallow everything up like a whale
two fish and five loaves sit
deep in my belly. burning church.
holy hell. i been setting myself
on fire ever since they left
i ain't nobody. wish i was.
more than ash. more than embers.
wish i could see they face
wish i was more than. remember:
when our hands was so holy?
we could make salt taste like
sugar. we could turn water into
wine. remember when we didn't no
jesus? it was just us three.
and, we didn't have to wait
on nobody. no god. tuh know.
how tuh build no altar. oar.

ark. ask no questions. tell me
no lies. we beyond. devil. we
is. black woman. shaking that six
one palm. roll. time. we divine.

—Natasha Carrizosa

INTRODUCTION: CENTERING BLACK
WOMEN, CHALLENGING LATINIDAD

In recent years, numerous instances of anti-Black violence have brought to light a long, complex history of institutional racism and violence in the United States and in different countries of Latin America and the Caribbean. At the same time, these events have inspired collective action and consciousness across the globe, prompting communities to recognize their own histories of racism, racial inequality, and discrimination as well as their manifestations in contemporary society. In the Latin American context, the effects of conquest and colonization have played an especially significant role in the shaping of social and cultural histories and identity construction/representations.

This edited volume offers a close examination of texts produced by or about people of African descent with identity connections to Latin America. Through the study of cultural expressions of Blackness throughout the Americas, the authors consider the relationship that social and historical processes such as sovereignty and colonialism have on narrative and cultural production. We aimed to analyze a vast range of power dynamics as represented in different cultural texts of the Afro-Latinx community. Moreover, with this work we wish to acknowledge that racial and gender equity cannot exist without Intersectionality. This volume serves as a much-needed academic reference, providing a window into the challenges inherent to the Afro-Latina experience in the Americas with a specific focus on Black women generally unrepresented in literary, scholarly, and cultural discourses. We use this opportunity to reaffirm our support and commitment to Black, Brown, and other minoritized community coalitions in an effort to combat anti-Blackness sentiments in our own communities.

All the chapters in this edited collection are tied together by the employment of an intersectional approach to multiple cultural representations of Blackness that have at the center the unique experience of the Black Latina woman. It is then worth mentioning what we mean when we use the notion "intersectional." Intersectionality as a critical framework has attracted a lot of scholarly attention in the past few decades. The term Intersectionality was first coined by Black scholar of critical race theory and civil rights activist Kimberlé Crenshaw[1] in 1989. Crenshaw used the term to describe how gender, race, sexuality, class, and many other factors play a role in the oppressions faced by an individual. Intersectionality, then, recognizes that multiple forms of identities do not exist independently of each other. Instead, each aspect of a person identity informs the others, creating a complex convergence of oppression. Black feminism has always been the primary site where intersectional approaches developed. Even decades before the theorization of Crenshaw's ideas, the same concepts can be found in the work of other prominent Black women scholars such as Truth (1851), Wells (1892), and Cooper (1892). One of the benefits of applying an intersectional approach relates to the fact that we can examine a social justice issue from a holistic point of view. Intersectionality is exponentially becoming a topic of consideration for equity work and initiatives and is arguably the only way to develop effective strategies to address inequality issues. Crenshaw first used this term to describe how Black women experience different forms of discrimination at the intersection of race, gender, and other social factors simultaneously.

Intersectionality contributes to better outcomes in the process of seeking equity, as people are considered as a whole and not just with one part of their identity. An intersectional approach would put specific social justice issues in context, considering what specific barriers are experienced by particular groups of women, such as differently abled women; Black women; women from minoritized ethnic or racial groups; bisexual, transgender, lesbian, and genderqueer women; immigrant women; uneducated women; younger and older women; and pregnant women, just to mention a few. All our social identities, as an intertwined combination, play a role in our privilege even if we struggle to acknowledge this reality. We should all work daily to understand and carefully reflect on how these aspects of our identity impact the various forms of discrimination we do or do not experience. As Audre Lorde perfectly pointed out in February 1982, when she delivered the address, "Learning from the 60s" as part of the celebration of the Malcolm X weekend at Harvard University, "there is no such thing as a single-issue struggle because we do not live single-issue lives."[2] Whether in research, teaching, advocacy or any other social practices, an intersectional approach allows us as scholars, educators, and activists to focus on systems and contexts and notice whose voices have been historically silenced and connect what we discover as researchers to larger systematic issues. Intersectionality is about a constant learning, listening, and understanding of different experiences that are not our own, making space for and centering stories of individuals who have been systematically pushed aside in the context of the dominant power structure of an "imperialist white-supremacist capitalist patriarchy."[3]

Intersectionality as a method of inquiry is deeply rooted in critical race theory and Black feminism. In her 1989 essay, Crenshaw talks about "intersectionality" as the intersection and interconnectedness of identities, such as race, gender, ethnicity, and sexuality. Crenshaw focused on three legal cases that dealt with the issues of both racial discrimination and sex discrimination: *DeGraffenreid v. General Motors*, *Moore v. Hughes Helicopter, Inc.*, and *Payne v. Travenol*. In each of these cases, courts did not allow Black female plaintiffs to allege discrimination on the basis of both race and gender. The judges could not see and understand the reality of this specific form of oppression, because there was no word at the time to describe this problem. Nowadays, we should all aim to apply Crenshaw's work to our own social activism and exploration of identity, as Intersectionality is the only way to achieve real equity. Crenshaw states that viewing antidiscrimination through a single-axis framework is problematic and argues that the antidiscrimination framework disregards and complicates Intersectionality. Finally, using the three court cases mentioned above, Crenshaw explains how Black women are pushed to the margins in (Anti)discrimination doctrine, the feminist movement, and the fight for Black liberation. Therefore, Crenshaw's work is fundamental because it provides guidance on how feminist and antiracist movements can better include Black women and embrace Intersectionality. Two years later, Crenshaw published a second essay,[4] "Mapping the Margins: Intersectionality, Identity Politics, and Violence Against Women of Color" in which the critical race theory scholar employs Intersectionality to explore how social movement organizations around violence against women completely omitted the vulnerabilities of women of color, particularly those from immigrant and socially disadvantaged communities. Following Crenshaw's guidelines, as we are both scholars of Afro-Hispanic/Latinx studies, intersectional feminists, and activists in our own marginalized communities, we decided to place Black women at the center of our book project as we strongly believe this is the only way to advance antiracist work in our discipline.

Our edited volume is completely innovative in its field because no existing/published work exists that focuses on the Afro-Latina experience from an intersectional perspective. All the chapters explore cultural and historical themes such as music, dance, photography, religion, poetry, spirituality, power dynamics, and colonialism through the lens of Black Latina women. The term "LatiNegra" in the book's title comes from the article published by Marta I. Cruz-Janzen in 2001 in which the author describes LatiNegras as "Latinas of obvious black ancestry and undeniable ties to Africa, women who ancestral mothers were abducted from the rich lands that cradled them to become and bear slaves, endure the lust of their masters, and nurture other women's children" (168). AfroLatinas or LatiNegras as a subject of scholarship have been woefully underrepresented. In this context, this collection is an important and timely intervention. It starts with the examination of several contemporary works and then offers a deep analysis of historical texts to reflect the long history those contemporary texts emerge from, returning then to the present and suggesting the future by the end. The attention to contemporary works makes this very appealing as a teaching text, and the inclusion of activist voices broadens its reach and links theory to praxis. The consistent attention to AfroLatinas' agency across all the chapters is not superficially empowering; it is attentive to the difficult circumstances in which that agency is asserted, and the tremendous breadth of what agency can look like, from a silent look to coded language and practices to full-throated assertions. The range of texts examined includes photography, colonial inquisition records, dance, fiction, nonfiction, poetic memoir, and religious expressions. This is connected to the range of modes of expressing agency and reflects the complexity of AfroLatinas' humanity. It ensures this project resists re-essentializing AfroLatinas. We aimed to focus on the analytical power of the concept of Intersectionality. With this perspective we wish to acknowledge the hegemonic pressures on AfroLatinidad and the essentializing moves that an intersectional approach enables evading, resisting, and overthrowing. Our volume seeks to fill a scholarly and investigative gap by adopting an intersectional approach based on recognizing whose voices are the most marginalized in the context of Latin American Studies. The three sections of the book explore different power dynamics as represented in different cultural productions, but they all look at these topics from the lens of the Black Latina Woman or AfroLatina/LatiNegra. All chapters apply an intersectional theory perspective that analyzes how these experiences are unique and distinctive when taking into consideration the intersection of race and gender.

From a historical standpoint, the start of the Atlantic slave trade, initiated by Portuguese traders along the West African coast in the early fifteenth century, would mark the beginning of a global system that would change the history of not only the region but also humanity itself.[5] Between the period from 1490 to 1850, it is estimated that 12.5 million Africans were forcibly transported to the New World, including almost 2 million who perished during the crossing known as the Middle Passage.[6] The largest long-distance forced movement in history, the transatlantic slave trade would lead to the greatest concentration of people of African descent outside Africa. Its full impact to the economic, social, and cultural development of the regions within its reach is impossible to fully discern.

Though the concept of slavery was not exclusive to the Americas, its origins rooted in the earliest of human civilizations spanning almost all corners of the globe,[7] researchers have drawn special attention to the Latin American context for several reasons. In *The Black Experience in Colonial Latin*

America, Ben Vinson III and Greg Graves maintain: "What distinguishes colonial Latin America from other places in the Western Hemisphere is the degree to which the Black experience was defined not just by slavery but by freedom."[8] It is estimated that by the end of the eighteenth century, over a million Africans and people of mixed African and European descent lived as freed women and men in the New World, either as part of European colonial society or in autonomous communities established by runaway slaves. In their respective communities, they actively participated in different capacities, from the Afro-Iberian men who traveled to the Americas as soldiers and sailors to enslaved African women who worked as street vendors.

Today, the presence, influence, and contribution of members of the African diaspora[9] and their descendants in the cultures and modern nations of the Americas and the Caribbean are undeniable. Yet, perhaps somewhat ironically, for decades the topic remained vastly unacknowledged in both academic scholarship and national ideologies. In response, in recent years there has been a renewed interest in recovering and reclaiming the forgotten histories and voices of the Afro-Latinx population, both historic and contemporary. As a result, an astonishing growing body of scholarship on the topic has expanded the scope of research and led to the development of a concentrated field of study.[10]

These works offer significant counternarratives that challenge stereotypes and destabilize dominant hegemonic narratives surrounding the African diaspora in the New World. Their subject matter ranges from the reevaluation of historical documents including royal archives and colonial texts to the analysis of contemporary expressions of diasporic culture in artistic and cultural production. Though early investigations focused on examples from specific national contexts, several contemporary studies take a more holistic approach that extends physical borders. In this new critical space, some distinct branches of study can be defined including those with a historical focus, those focusing on the experience of Blackness, and the celebration of the contributions of the African diaspora and their descendants. In the following section, we will provide a brief review of some fundamental contributions to the field that bring to light the lived experience of the African diaspora. Our review of the existing literature does not intend to represent an exhaustive list, but rather a selective one outlining some pieces of work and concepts that inform our methodology.

Echoing the diversity of the geographic region itself, the identities[11] and experiences of Afro-Latinx populations both past and present are difficult to synthesize without running the risk of overgeneralizing; Gwendolyn Midlo Hall has noted, "Nothing in the realm of slavery stood still. Patterns changed over time and place in both Africa and the Americas."[12] In part, this diversity is rooted in the regional nature of the transatlantic slave trade and the vast ethnic and geographic origins of this population. Though early forced migrations initiated along the coast of West Africa, Congo, and Angola, as the trade system expanded, it expanded into parts of Central Africa. The arrival of millions of people to the New World with distinct linguistic, cultural, and ethnic backgrounds created new alliances and divisions among these groups. In colonial Spanish and Portuguese society, these distinctions were amplified within a complex hierarchical caste system that ensured European superiority and placed those of indigenous and African descent at the bottom.[13] As McKnight and Garfalo note, this caste system was not only race-based but also distinguished between generation and birthplace, as well as social status, religious affiliation, language, profession, cultural and social practices, and even marital status.[14] They go on to note that "race and ethnicity operated as social constructions rooted in a particular place at a particular historical moment."[15]

Among the most prominent works to trace the history of the Afro-Latinx population in the Americas and Caribbean from the early fifteenth century to the present is Leslie Rout Jr.'s *The African Experience in Spanish America: 1502 to the Present Day*. Originally published in 1976, it is considered one of the founding texts of African diaspora studies. The first general history on the people of African descent in the Spanish Americas, it examines the history of slavery in each country. Rout also interrogates perceptions of Spanish America as a "racial paradise" and the idea that "we have no discrimination in our country."[16, 17]

As the first modern history of the experience of African slaves in the European colonies of the Americas, the volume spans the entire history of slavery across Latin America and the Caribbean from its establishment to abolition. Notably, Klein and Vinson compare and contrast the implementation and trajectory of slavery throughout the different regions, ranging from 1500s Latin America to 1800s Brazil and Guyana. They emphasize the ethnic diversity and differing lived realities of the African diaspora. The chapter "Freedmen in a Slave Society" examines the social, political, and economic structures of free communities throughout Latin America.[18]

George Reid Andrews expands on the continent's complex geographic, social, and political reality in his volume *Afro-Latin America (1800–2000)*, noting: "Afro-Latin America is not a fixed or immutable entity; rather, it ebbs and flows, though the tendency has clearly been for it to contract over time."[19] Spanning two hundred years of histories, the text calls attention to the significant role played by the African diaspora in colonial and modern Spanish America, Brazil, and the Caribbean. Specifically, he underscores Afro-Latinx activism and contributions to the economic and social spheres (both local and national) including political reform and organization.

While earlier investigations provided us with a more limited perspective located within specific geographic regions and communities, our intersectional approach has led us to adopt a more holistic view of Afro-Latina histories and experiences in their many forms. In doing so, we are able to contextualize individual lived experiences within larger, often interlocking systems of oppression based on race, class, and gender.[20] The politics and boundaries of difference in any society are rarely static and are in constant evolution; influenced by place and time. In order to understand more about how the politics of difference have shaped the Afro-Latina experience over time, we must consider the multilayered cultural dimensions of day-to-day life in colonial and modern Latin American society. When we talk about highlighting the voices of AfroLatina women, it is important to mention the book *Women Warriors of the Afro-Latina Diaspora*, a collection of eleven essays and four poems in which Latina women of African descent share their stories in the form of testimonios and address issues such as inequality, racism, and social justice in their respective countries. However, *Women Warriors* represents an assembly of personal stories because of its autobiographical content and for that reason has a different scope if compared with our volume that aims to provide a critical, theoretical, and literary analysis of different cultural expressions of Blackness that put at the center the experience of AfroLatinas.

Among the most recent publications to address issues of culture, discourse, and representation in Spanish colonial society, we wish to underscore the significance of *Afro-Latino Voices: Narratives from the Early Modern Ibero-Atlantic World, 1550–1812*. Edited by Kathryn Joy McKnight and Leo J. Garofalo, this is the first book-length collection of Afro-Latinx narratives from the early modern Ibero-Atlantic world.[21] The extensive list of translated documents includes juridical, ecclesiastical, and administrative records from the sixteenth and seventeenth centuries. The diverse nature of the subject matter is echoed in its list of contributors, bringing together researchers from several fields including Latin American studies, African history, and Spanish American and Luso-Brazilian literature. The nature and breadth of this volume of work is exemplary of the richness of theoretical perspectives that interdisciplinary collaborations provide.

The translated documents paired with their analysis recover lost Afro-Latinx voices from the archives of Latin America and Europe.[22] They are a testament to the crucial roles the African diaspora—both free and enslaved—played in Spanish and Portuguese colonies. As McKnight and Garofalo outline:

> In these texts, people of African descent speak about war and politics; they define and support their families and communities; they reveal a broad gamut of spiritual beliefs and practices; and they claim and defend their rights against the cruelties of enslavement and the discrimination of a racialized society.[23]

Part I of the volume leads with a royal inquiry from 1550, ordered by Dom Diogo I, King of Kongo, into treason against him by Dom Pedro Njanga a Mvemba, former king of Kongo. This was an important internal legal document retrieved from the Portuguese archives, and John K. Thornton and Linda Heywood note that it gives insight into the complex political and legal structure of the Kingdom of Kongo, while providing evidence that European kingdoms were not the only ones to keep written archives.[24] In the same section, we wish to draw attention to the chapter "Queen Njinga Mbandi Ana de Sousa of Ndongo/Matamba: African Leadership, Diplomacy, and Ideology, 1620s–1650s." In it, Linda Heywood and Luis Madureira (translator) present translated letters written by Queen Njinga to several Portuguese governors. Queen Njinga was the first woman to rule Ndongo. In 1622, she was sent to Luanda, the capital of the Portuguese kingdom of Angola, on behalf of her brother, Ngola a Mbandi, King of Ndongo, to negotiate a peace treaty with the Portuguese. She was known as a brilliant, resilient leader, and her letters—albeit mediated—give insight into the tact and diplomacy she employed over months of negotiations.[25] The chapter is only one example of Black agency[26] reflected throughout the entire collection; as editors McKnight and Garofalo affirm: "The Afro-Latinos in this volume formed and exercised control within religious societies, autonomous communities, and states. They used the languages, institutions, and literate practices of the Ibero-colonial enterprise to improve their situations."[27]

Moreover, we underscore the significance of this collection in its representation of the Black female experience in its many forms. The voices and histories of Afro-Latinas permeate the text and cover almost all sectors of society and both sides of the Atlantic. The examples range from royals to members of religious communities like Sister Chicaba (1676–1748) and from Palenque residents to the female relatives of Afro-Iberian men who traveled to the Americas as soldiers and sailors.[28] The representation of gendered relationships and the Black female experience is the subject of at least nine chapters.[29] The documents illuminate the integral role Afro-Latinas played in Spanish and Portuguese colonial society, not only in the domestic sphere, charged with household tasks and rearing children, but also outside the home. For example, Afro-Latina women played important roles in religious and spiritual rituals and belief systems, as well as the economic realm, with some holding urban occupations such as public street vendors.

Ironically, even though nearly all early studies[30] on the topic of the transatlantic slave trade and the Afro-Latinx experience in the New World featured discussions on family dynamics, marriage/intermarriages, and other religious and social relations that are clearly gendered, few studies have represented the Black female experience to the same extent as McKnight and Garofalo's volume. If we consider that Afro-Latinx history has been vastly overlooked up until the last few decades, its important leaders and events absent from the pages of Latinx Studies and Spanish textbooks and popular nationalist ideologies alike, representations of the Afro-Latina experience have been almost nonexistent until recently. Some notable exceptions include María Elisa Velázquez's book, published in Spanish, *Contemporary Historical Debates: Africans and Afro-descendants in Mexico and Central America* (my translation).[31] Her chapter "The Female Slave Experience: Africans, Afro-descendants, and Indigenous in Viceregal Mexico" (my translation)[32] presents specific cases of enslaved women employing legal and cultural strategies to survive, negotiate, and in many cases, successfully improve their conditions living in Spanish colonial society. Some examples are the 1643 testimony of Magdalena de la Cruz, an African slave living in Mexico City, who publicly denounced the abuse she suffered at the hands of her master, Martín de Ortega, and defended her legal right to see her husband at least once per week.[33] The volume gives us a glimpse into the diverse conditions and day-to-day life of enslaved African women in New Spain.

In the contemporary context, *Women Warriors of the Afro-Latina Diaspora*, as mentioned in a section above, provides an important contribution to the documentation of the Afro-Latina lived experience. An anthology consisting of personal essays and poems by Black women from all over Latin America, the collection sheds light on the complexities of Afro-Latina identity set within various national and cultural contexts. Their stories open up a discursive space that not only addresses the interplay of racism, sexism, and social inequalities faced by the women both within and outside of their own communities but highlights their strength to overcome these barriers. Similarly, *Black Social Movements in Latin America: From Monocultural Mestizaje to Multiculturalism* also attests to Afro-Latina strength and leadership in the modern era. In it, a comprehensive collection of essays examines the role of Afro-Latino social movements from the 1970s, rejecting romanticized versions of mestizaje that privilege whiteness and reproduce the erasure of Afro-Latinx history and identity. The book was inspired by the 2011 International conference titled "Afro Latino Social Movements: From Monocultural *Mestizaje* and 'Invisibility' to Multiculturalism and State Corporatism/Co-optation" held at Florida International University. Though it does not focus on the topic of gender, the inclusion of two first-person accounts of the Afro-Latina experience in the political realm are significant. Rahier includes the transcripts of two separate interviews; in part III, María Alexandra Ocles Padilla, former Minister-in-Charge of Ecuador's Secretariat of the Peoples, Social Movements, and Citizens' Participation recounts her experience as an Afro-Latina in an entirely white-mestizo cabinet. Part IV moves to Brazil, with an interview with Maria Inês Barbosa, former Vice-Minister of the Federal Special Secretariat for the Adoption of Policies that Promote Racial Equality (SEPPIR). The fact that these two Afro-Latina political figures are the only direct, firsthand voices from any of the government agencies and organizations discussed in the volume is powerful.[34] In fact, Ocles Padilla's interview points to a long history of female-led social and political organization in Ecuador, describing her hometown of El Comité del Pueblo, Quito, as "a neighborhood with a very strong history of social organization. And my mother was always involved in a variety of social issues."[35]

Other recent studies continue to expand the scope of Afro-Latinx studies, many examining how this population has helped shape the modern nations of the Americas and the Caribbean. Early research on the topic had focused to a great degree on its contribution to artistic and cultural production in the form of music, dance, and theater. Since then, several authors have sought to address gaps in established anthologies by mapping out the work of Afro-Latinx art and culture producers from a wider range of mediums. For example, in the case of literary production, notable examples include Margaret Lindsay Morris's *The Afro-Latino Voice in World Literature*. Here, Morris compares and contrasts literature of the the Afro-Latino diaspora, featuring the work of female writers and poets such as Alzira Rufino (Brazil), Andrea Cristina Rio Branco (Brazil), and Eulalia Bernard (Costa Rica). Other notable contributions to this field include: *Daughters of the Diaspora: Afra-Hispanic Writers, Literary Passion, Ideological Commitment: Toward a Legacy of Afro-Cuban and Afro-Brazilian Women Writers, Voices Out of Africa in Twentieth-Century Spanish Caribbean Literature,* and *Writing the Afro-Hispanic: Essays on Africa and Africans in the Spanish Caribbean;* the latter presents a collective view of Afro-Latinx literature that pays tribute to the significant contributions of Black female voices. Among them, Afro-Cuban poetry reciter and actress Eusebia Cosme (1911–1976)[36]—the only Cuban woman to participate in the art of declamation, performing poetry on the topic of Black racialized identities internationally—along with Nancy Morejón (1944–) who wrote on the use of culture as commodity from an African-centered perspective.

The recent period has seen the publication of new synthetic texts that bring innovative approaches to the study of contemporary Afro-Latinx cultural and artistic production; notable examples include López Oro's "Refashioning Afro-Latinidad: Garifuna New Yorkers in Diaspora" and *Being La Dominicana: Race and Identity in the Visual Culture of Santo Domingo*. Part III, "Africa in the Arts: Migration, Improvisation, Exchange" of *African Diaspora in the Cultures of Latin America, the Caribbean, and the United States* is comprised of an original, wide variety of examples of Afro-Latinx artistic and cultural production ranging from visual depictions of African slaves working as pearl divers in the Caribbean to the Cuban animated film *Vampiros en La Habana* to the musical genre of reggaeton.

The list of contributors also echoes its diverse nature; musicologists and DJs, anthropologists, and academics among them.

Jerome Branche's edited collection *Black Writing, Culture, and the State in Latin America* examines poetry and narrative alongside film and popular theater (and even a segment of rap and hip-hop). In breaking with "the standard genres of the lettered traditions,"[37] Branche challenges existing colonial, hegemonic ideologies surrounding literature and the concept of writing itself:

> A definition of "writing," in the canonical sense, is amplified in order to allow for the range of expression reflected herein, so that varying registers of orality (or "oral literature"), of literacy, and of artistic technique and convention of the kind that guides critics and anthologizers must be encompassed.[38]

With this, Branche situates himself within the context of current trends in cultural and literary studies to adopt postcolonial criticism and decolonize existing research paradigms. For our purposes, we identify an element of Intersectionality in this methodology, as the analysis of literature and language can serve as a vehicle for discussions of race, class, and gender inequalities that are at once individual/collective and local/global.

Decolonial Diasporas: Radical Mappings of Afro-Atlantic Literatures continues to expand the scope of Afro-Latinx and Latinx literary studies by including works from female authors from Spanish-speaking Equatorial Guinea in dialogue with the Hispanophone Caribbean. Yomaira C. Figueroa-Vásquez develops a theoretical framework in which select Afro-Atlantic literary and cultural texts are studied through the lens of women of color feminism. In particular, she introduces her concept of "destierro,"[39] which she uses to describe the nuances and complexities of the notion of "home" and the impossibility of ever truly finding it in decolonial settings. This framework serves as an important analytical tool for examining the intersections between Black, Latinx, and Hispanic female identities and effecting social change.

Other recent publications have explored the untold histories of Afro-Latinx communities and their contributions to the intellectual, social, and political realms of Latin American society. Among the examples, *Afro-Descendants, Identity, and the Struggle for Development in the Americas* includes a discussion on activist organization and mobilization in the Afro-Colombian population in the quest for independence and equality.

The Afro-Latin Diaspora: Awakening Ancestral Memory, Avoiding Cultural Amnesia also focuses on the contributions of Afro-descendants in political and cultural work. Taking a comparative approach, the study examines Afro-Latin communities in over twenty-two Latin American countries and the United States; its chapters highlight the stories of Afro-Latino leaders and freedom fighters, while dialoguing with issues of ethnic, cultural, and linguistic identity.[40]

Among the recent studies, some have chosen to shed light on these silenced voices and histories in specific cultural and national contexts. They include, for example, *Finding Afro-Mexico: Race and Nation after the Revolution, Colonial Blackness: A History of Afro-Mexico,* and *Afro-Mexico: Dancing Between Myth and Reality,* which explore Afro-Mexican identity and influence. Others have instead opted to go beyond material borders and draw transnational connections; among the notable examples are: *Afro-Latin@s in Movement: Critical Approaches to Blackness and Transnationalism in the Americas*, *The Afro-Latin@ Experience in Contemporary American Literature and Culture: Engaging Blackness*, *The Afro-Latin@ Reader: History and Culture in the United States*, *Afro-Latinx Digital Connections* and *Afro-Latinos in the U.S. Economy,* which explores the economic contributions and status of the US Afro-Latinx population.

Though our list of works is far from comprehensive, the above-mentioned studies provide valuable findings that have expanded the scope of Afro-Latinx research and have allowed us to rethink the ways in which the African diaspora and their descendants have helped shape contemporary cultures in the Americas. Surprisingly, despite the impressive growth in publications and their commitment to recovering these forgotten histories, the Afro-Latina voice remains severely underrepresented. This is the first book-length scholarly study dedicated entirely to Afro-Latina histories, experiences, and influences. Informed by an intersectional approach, we draw on feminist scholarship of women of color in the United States and in developing nations to help deconstruct existing hegemonic ideologies and representations surrounding Afro-Latinas, many times shaped by Eurocentric, patriarchal worldviews. With this, we challenge the attempted erasure and frequent misrepresentation of Afro-Latina identities and lived experiences in their many forms. The following chapters are a testament to the resilience, agency, and perseverance of the Afro-Latina woman across time.

This edited volume represents a physical and metaphorical collection of Afro-Latina voices, histories, and experiences across the Americas, spanning from the colonial period to the present. Echoing the expansive cultural, geographic, and linguistic diversity of the African diaspora itself, this collection takes a comprehensive, intersectional approach that is reflected in the list of contributors. An expansive community of female authors/women from across multiple backgrounds, disciplines, and corners of the globe, each chapter presents a unique contribution to the field of Afro-Latinx studies. Most of the chapters selected are authored by women of color, among them both well established and emerging voices in this inclusive and interdisciplinary field.

It is impossible to speak of historical or contemporary mediums of cultural and artistic expression in the Americas without recognizing the impact and contribution of the African diaspora to nearly all its forms. We have structured the collection in three sections. We have dedicated the first part of the volume to chapters that study the intersection of race and gender in different cultural expressions of Blackness, from music, dance, and photography. The second section deals with issues of visibility and representation as well as examples of Black female leadership in the sphere of religion and spirituality, educational resources, and social activism. Finally, the third section offers a reflection on the processes of re-learning our history while putting at the center the legacy of Afrodiasporic intergenerational trauma, and it does such work while dialoguing with colonial analyses as well as new critical evaluations of contemporary texts.

Within this scope, our collection opens with a series of innovative scholarly works on the topic of Afro-descendant music, dance, and photography and its connection to race and gender. In the first chapter, Lesley Feracho's "Opening Up Black Spaces, Female Spaces" examines selected works by female Afro-Brazilian singer-songwriters Luedji Luna and Xênia França as cultural and visual texts. The site of one of the first and largest ports of the transatlantic slave trade in the Americas, the state of Bahia and its capital, Salvador da Bahia, are particularly significant in the history of Afro-Brazil. Rooted in the Bahia region, Feracho centralizes the relationship between the material and symbolic spaces of Afro-Brazil as articulated in these works through connections with African ancestry and spirituality. Engaging with theorists at the intersections of race, gender, and place, Feracho points to the capacity of these musical texts to serve as vehicles for the creation and representation of female Afro-Brazilian identity, as well as a space for female agency, solidarity, and resistance.

Algris Xiomara Aldeano's chapter "The Black Woman as Leader in the Bunde and Bullerengue" continues with the topic of Afro-descendant music and dance, this time shifting focus to the bundle and bullerengue in Darién, Panama. Identifying as a Black woman from Darién herself, Aldeano presents a careful analysis of not only the mechanics and aesthetics of the bundle and bullerengue as musical genre and dance, but as representative of oral literature and cultural promotion in their communities. In her chapter, Aldeano engages with the theory of Intersectionality within the framework of Africology, arguing that those framed within the Aryan model fall short in their ability to fully comprehend and analyze Black artistic expressions in Latin America. Instead, Aldeano opts for an Afrocentric or Afrological approach, drawing special attention to these two genres as examples of classical African artistic expression. Central to her study is the principal role played by women in the bundle and bullerengue, which extends the performative aspect; Aldeano traces the motif of the powerful Black woman exhibited in these artistic forms from ancient African civilizations to the contemporary context, translated into the Black Girl Magic movement.

This section of the book continues its intersectional analysis with a focus on Black female leadership in its various forms, focusing on its representation in photographic and spiritual expressions. In her chapter, "No me llames trigueña, soy negra," Meaghan Coogan examines the work of Adriana Parrilla, an Afro-Puerto Rican photographer and photojournalist. Parilla is based between Paris and Puerto Rico, and much of her work is informed by her personal experiences; she interrogates notions of race, gender, and identity construction, as seen from a transnationalist perspective. Coogan's study is centered on Parrilla's most recent photographic project, a series entitled *No me llames 'trigueña,' soy negra*, that was exhibited in New York City in the summer of 2020. In it, Parrilla explores the complexities of Black identity in Puerto Rico; its title, a powerful rejection of the attempted erasure of Afro-Puerto Rican identity and a message of empowerment for the Afro-Puerto Rican community. Coogan presents a detailed analysis of the individual photographs featured in the series, paying close attention to the role of Eurocentric concepts surrounding body image and beauty standards that have influenced the racialization of Afro-Puerto Rican women. In particular, she highlights the importance of Black hair and its connection to Puerto Rican landscape and identity. Coogan's study addresses the exclusion and invisibility of Black Puerto Rican women from a feminist intersectional perspective, informed by a transnational connection to the mainland United States, Puerto Rico, and France.

Kerry Green continues the discussion of the photographic portrayal of Afro-Latina women and resistance in her chapter, "The Resistance in the Photographic Indexical Portrayal of Afro-Latina Women in Manuel González de la Parra's *Luces de raíz negra*," this time through the lens of Mexican photographer Manuel González de la Parra. Green explores González de la Parra's photographic work as presented in his book *Luces de Raíz Negra*, published in 2004. In it, González de la Parra juxtaposes images of Afro-descendant populations in the towns of Coyolillo, Veracruz, Mexico, and Tumaco, Colombia. Her chapter includes a detailed review of introductory essays by Sylvia Navarrete and Odile Hoffmann and Adriana Naveda as well as an analysis of several of the photographs themselves. Engaging with scholars including Adriana Pena Mejía on the topic of the hyper sexualization and the continued stereotyping of Afro-Latina populations in domestic roles, Green argues that the images continue to present a one-dimensional representation of Afro-Mexicans and Afro-Colombian women. Despite this, in her analysis of the corporeal and spatial elements of the images, Green maintains that the subjects reflect a sense of Black female agency that rejects the authority of the (white, male) ethnographic gaze. In doing so, Green identifies a possible paradigm shift in power, where the Afro-Latina subject can break with the colonizing gaze of the camera and play an active role in communicating with the spectator in an act of resistance.

Part II of the book, in line with the discussion of Black female agency and leadership, expands on the topics of expressions of Blackness, Black social activism, and gendered visibility in educational resources. Jamie Lee Andreson's chapter "Representing Candomblé in the Public Sphere" examines the role of Black Candomblé priestesses' authorship in Brazilian cultural production. The Candomblé region is African diasporic religion that developed in Brazil following the abolition of slavery at the end of the nineteenth century; Andreson outlines the central role played by women there. Her chapter provides an overview of the history and trajectory of the role of priestesses from possessors of hidden knowledge, reliant on the aid of writers and academics to transcribe documents to the end of the twentieth century, when a far greater number were producers of their own texts and cultural production. The chapter also includes detailed records of the lives and accomplishments of several known Mães, as well as a notable geneal-ogy of major works published by Candomblé priestesses. Their histories are contextualized within Brazil's social and political landscape over the course of the twentieth century, during which they have been "recognized as prominent, cultural, intellectual, and political leaders." Despite this, Jamie Lee Andreson notes that their contributions have been, for the most part, left out of the national Brazilian literary canon. Through their strong engagement in the public sphere, Andreson maintains that Candomblé priestesses have participated as knowledge and culture producers, actively shaping the per-ception of their role and their religious practice. In the contemporary context, Andreson pinpoints the significance of the digital age in enabling new tools for self-representation including digital storytelling and audiovisuals, as well as advocacy for education, freedom, and increased opportunities.

The fight for equal representation in the United States is more prevalent now than it was years ago. Recent demonstrations and protests regarding police brutality and the treatment of Black people have brought movements such as "Black Lives Matter" and "Say Her Name" to national and inter-national attention. In the light of this growing call for equity and inclusion, chapter 7, "The Invisible Women," by Lillie Padilla contributes to the ongo-ing discussions by examining the representation of people of Afro-Latinx her-itage in Spanish-language textbooks. Despite the abundance of research on textbook materials, specifically, Spanish textbooks, there has been no study that has examined the representation of Afro-Latinx individuals in beginner-level Spanish textbooks and in particular the visibility in these texts of the AfroLatina woman. These books are fundamental because they are the first contact most students have with college-level Spanish and thus, they play an important role in familiarizing students with the Spanish language and culture. The theoretical framework that guided this study is Fairclough's (1995) framework for critical discourse analysis (CDA). The analysis was conducted on three of the most popular Spanish books used by the most popular publishers in the United States. Consequently, in examining the visual portrayal of AfroLatina life and culture, the present chapter builds on previous language textbook studies. It not only examines elements that appear in these textbooks concerning AfroLatinas but also the elements that do *not* appear. In light of the results, the study provides suggestions for teachers and educators for including the AfroLatina experience in their classroom instruction.

In their chapter, "Writing and Activism," Renata Dorneles Lima, Yoiseth Patricia Cabarcas, and Lindsay Gary discuss the fact that to embrace the Black identity is to embrace the territory where they belong. It is also to narrate and poeticize from those places reviled by the establishment and marginalized by institutional contempt and racism. Thus, the voices of AfroLatina women who resist in the territories resonate like Maroon drums, defying the hegemonic canons, to confront them with their presence and outrage. Their writing is in itself a political act, so powerful that it has reached the gates of the academy, to return like a boomerang to its original settings and explode with more vigor. Therefore, in Colombia, Brazil, and the Caribbean, AfroLatina women have used writing as a visible force and a political scene connected to their territories and, in turn, with the movements of women poets and storytellers who use the word as a source of memory, collective meeting, place of enunciation, and scene of local power. The chapter analyzes specific cases such as the one of Mayra Santos-Febres and Nelly Rosario, who have exposed racism in the literary field and in Caribbean society. Adelaida Fernández is one of the figures behind a entire wave of Afro-Colombian women writers agitating in the marginalized corners of the country; they are women who narrate their territory as a militant political act that seek to situate the empowerment of the word as resistance, but also spaces of ancestral and cultural connection. Luz Ribeiro, Mel Duarte, and Kimani are voices of resistance and empowerment of Black women in Brazil who keep the voices of the poetry slam shaking in the outskirts of São Paulo and reaching other cities of the country. Ultimately, this chapter seeks to make visible this force that goes beyond writing, to analyze the political, social, and cultural impacts of this phenomenon, from an interdisciplinary and Afrocentric perspective.

    The last section of the book brings together four chapters with the objective of rewriting and relearning the Black history and past of Latin America. Karen S. Christian's chapter, "Repairing the Broken Strands of Afro-Latina History in Mayra Santos-Febres's Fiction," analyzes how memory, history, and identity are intricately woven together, enabling us to know (or think we know) who we are. Yet for marginalized communities like Afro-descendants, identity is fragmented through a process of forgetting that takes place when cultural/historical memory is silenced or erased. Saidiya Hartman explores this process in depth in *Lose Your Mother: A Journey Along the Atlantic Slave Route*, discovering that the slave trade left a devastating absence of a complete, unbroken narrative of African American history. The writing of Afro-Puerto Rican author Mayra Santos Febres resists this erasure by creating alternate archives of history stored in and on the bodies of her female characters. In this essay, the author focuses on the subversive potential of these alternate archives in two short stories from Santos Febres's 1995 collection *Pez de vidrio*, "Hebra rota" ("Broken Strand") and "Marina y su olor" ("Marina's Fragrance"). In "Hebra rota," the legacy of intergenerational trauma, violence, and colonialism is literally inscribed on the bodies of the characters, clients of a beauty salon that specializes in straightening Black women's hair. By bringing visibility to this legacy, Santos Febres inserts AfroLatina voices into the narrative of Caribbean history. "Marina y su olor" rewrites history even more audaciously. The protagonist is a young Afro–Puerto Rican woman who discovers that her body can produce odors that influence the emotions and actions of others. Marina's evocative "fragrances" ultimately become acts of resistance that summon the intersectional power of her femininity and her Blackness to overcome her oppressors. Through this chapter we learn that by changing the historical narrative to celebrate Black bodies, Santos Febres's writing works to repair the broken strands of AfroLatina history.

    In her chapter, "Afro-Mexican Women in the Northern Frontier" Brenda Romero analyzes how the field of Latin American studies has historically relegated, silenced, and ignored AfroLatinx voices. In the Mexican context, the invisibility of AfroMexicans is deeply rooted in the country's colonial past, a period when African slaves and their descendants where relegated to the bottom of the complex racial hierarchy known as Sistema de Castas. This chapter rescues the voices and stories of AfroMexican women living in the northern village of Cuencamé (currently a town in the state of Durango) during the seventeenth century. In contrast to metropolitan and more populated colonial towns such as Mexico City and Puebla, the remoteness of settlements near the northern frontier fostered a more permissive environment in terms of gender and race boundaries. This study examined the inquisitorial confessions and accusations collected by Alonso de Benavides, Commissary of New Spain's Holy Office, during his visit to Cuencamé in 1625 and 1626. The firsthand accounts found in these thirty-five files provide us with a rare glimpse into the power dynamics of this marginal colonial society where AfroMexican women acquire a voice and lose their anonymity despite of their intersectional marginalization. Among the stories of these *negra, criolla, mulata,* and *ladina* women, we encounter tales of bigamy, witchcraft, cross-dressing, and even bullfighting. This investigation scrutinized statements given by and about Black women to identify the ways in which they took advantage of their subaltern position in society to have an active role in the peripheral culture of Cuencamé. These documents are analyzed from a postcolonial theoretical perspective framed by the concepts of subalternity, mimicry, and transculturation.

"Blurring Genres, Blurring Borders" by Dr. Melissa Castillo Planas explores how in 2016, *Daring to Write: Contemporary Narratives by Dominican Women*, edited by Erika M. Martinez, brought together twenty-four narratives written by Dominican women and women of Dominican descent living in the United States, demonstrating a new spotlight on the work of Dominicanas after decades of literary neglect. Fiction and nonfiction by writers like Angie Cruz, Nelly Rosario, Sophia Quintero, and others reflect the emergence of a strong female narrative in the Dominican diaspora. Meanwhile, recent publications by Elizabeth Acevedo and Peggy Robles Alvarado represent a new Dominican American poetic voice. Amid this literary renaissance, within the past five years, Afro-Dominicanas Jasminne Mendez and Amanda Alcántara have each published books exploring a different genre: the poetic memoir. Blending themes of race, heritage, and ancestral knowledge in poetics alongside very personal narratives about their upbringing, *Blooming Jasminne* (2018) and *Chula* (2019) are a new form of Afro-Dominican expression. Although poetic memoirs are not novel in Latinx literary history, the exploration of this blurred genre by Mendez, Alcántara, and Marte are an emerging trend in Afro-Dominican womens' writing in the diaspora embodying an opening into the personal and literary lives of Afro-Dominicanas in the United States. Through an analysis of both the poetics and the memoir writing of these three writers, this piece discussed what it means to be a US-based Black Dominican woman writer in contemporary times.

Finally, the last chapter of the collection, "Papi's Bridge" by Keturah Nichols analyzes how on November 12, 2001, two months and one day after the September 11 attacks, American Airlines flight 587 bound for Santo Domingo, Dominican Republic, departed from JFK international airport as scheduled. Minutes after takeoff it fell from the sky and crashed in Queens. All 260 people aboard the flight were killed on impact as were five people on the ground. This is the second deadliest aviation accident in US history, where most victims were Dominican immigrants returning to their homeland. Due to the harsh realities of US life after 9/11, the author reflects on the reasons why this disaster has fallen out of the wider cultural memory and explores in which ways Dominican Americans shape narratives of survival, memory, and visibility in a world dominated by anti-Blackness. In this chapter Keturah

Nichols argues that *Clap When You Land*, a novel by AfroDominican American author Elizabeth Acevedo, addresses the aftermaths of slavery, where the devaluation of all Black life describes the realities of its diverse characters. It is worth pointing out that this novel is written from two different perspectives, that of Yahaira Rios, residing in New York City, and Camino Rios, who is in the Dominican Republic. These two protagonists, who are teenage girls, are drawn together after the plane crashes and discover that they shared a late father. After discussing how anti-Bblackness manifests in the Dominican Republic and in diasporic Dominican culture and consciousness, the author of this chapter also worked on the ways the main characters' double consciousness as Dominican and Black negotiates forms of racialization and invisibility. Finally, the chapter explores the politics of care employed by Haitian, Dominican, Dominican American, and Black American characters in deference to those who have already passed and those who continue.

It is worth pointing out that this book serves also as an opportunity to highlight and display the work of emerging and well-established AfroLatina artists. For instance, each part of the book opens with and features original poetry by AfroMexicana poet, writer, and creative writing teacher Natasha Carrizosa. Raised as the daughter of a fierce African American mother and a Mexican father, her writing reflects the dichotomy of these two rich cultures. The original poetry by Carrizosa included in the volume is dedicated to the two strongest women in her life, her mother, and her grandmother. Moreover, the book cover art was another space in which we were able to showcase authentic work, such as the digital art piece titled "Together" created by Fanesha Fabre, a Brooklyn-based, Dominican-born multimedia artist. In her illustrations Fabre celebrates her experiences as a Latina living in New York City. Her digital images capture and elevate her everyday surroundings with vibrant colors as well as the different shapes, shades, and complexions that reveal what it means to be an AfroLatina. Ultimately, the main objective of our book was to put at the center of our analysis the specific and unique experiences lived by Black Latina women in Latin America, the Caribbean, and the United States. All the authors, artists, and activists included in the book belong themselves to one or more marginalized social groups, with some of them residing in the United States and others living and working in different regions of Latin America. We focus on the institutional discrimination that women of color face based on their race and gender. These two factors simultaneously play a role in the distinctive oppression they experience. We wanted to offer some reflections on the ways in which the intersection of these combined systems of oppression determines and conditions the socioeconomic, political, and cultural position of Afro-descendant women in various societies in the Americas, which is structurally and systematically expressed as ethnic-racial and gender discrimination. By reviewing these multiple inequalities, we acknowledge that not all women face the same level of discrimination, domination, or privilege for that matter. We adopted an intersectional approach because we strongly believe this remains the only effective method to reach real equity in our society. This perspective provides a lens that allows us to examine the policies, practices, structures, and power dynamics that play roles in the establishment of the peculiar disadvantages or discriminations that are uniquely experienced by Black Latina women because of their intersecting identities. As young scholars in our fields of study coming from different marginalized groups and populations, we recognize that whether in our research, teaching, serving, and mentoring practices, an intersectional lens empowers us to focus on contexts and entire systems, noticing whose voices have been silenced or erased, and working together as a community to alter the hegemonic narrative.

BIBLIOGRAPHY

Alves, Miriam, and Carolyn Richardson Durham, eds. *Enfim . . . Nós/Finally Us: Escritoras Negras Brasileiras Contemporaneas/Contemporary Black Brazilian Women Writers.* Colorado Springs: Three Continents, 1994.

Andrews, George Reid. *Afro-Latin America (1800–2000).* New York: Oxford University Press, 2004.

———. *Afro-Latin America: Black Lives, 1600–2000.* Cambridge: Harvard University Press, 2016.

———. *The Afro-Argentines of Buenos Aires, 1800–1900* Madison: University of Wisconsin Press, 1980.

———. *Blacks & Whites in São Paulo, Brazil, 1888–1988* Madison: University of Wisconsin Press, 1991.

———. *Blackness in the White Nation a History of Afro-Uruguay.* Chapel Hill: University of North Carolina Press, 2010

Arrelucea Barrantes, Maribel, and Joseph P. Sánchez, Angelica Sánchez-Clark, and Larry D. Miller (trans). "Slavery, Writing, and Female Resistance: Black Women Litigants in Lima's Late Colonial Tribunals of the 1780s." In *Afro-Latino Voices: Narratives from the Early Modern Ibero-Atlantic World, 1550–1812*, edited by Kathryn Joy McKnight and Leo J. Garofalo, 285–301. Cambridge, MA: Hackett, 2009.

Arriaga, Eduard, and Andrés Villar, eds. *Afro-Latinx Digital Connections.* Gainesville: University of Florida Press, 2021.

Ball, Erica L., Tatiana Seijas, and Terri L. Snyder, eds. *As If She Were Free: A Collective Biography of Women and Emancipation in the Americas.* Cambridge, UK: Cambridge University Press, 2020.

Bennett, Herman L. *Colonial Blackness: A History of Afro-Mexico.* Bloomington: Indiana University Press, 2009.

Bostoen, Koen, and Inge Brinkman. *The Kongo Kingdom: The Origins, Dynamics and Cosmopolitan Culture of an African Polity*. Cambridge, UK: Cambridge University Press, 2018.

Braham, Persephone. *African Diaspora in the Cultures of Latin America, the Caribbean, and the United States*. Lanham, MD: Rowman & Littlefield, 2014.

Branche, Jerome, ed. *Black Writing, Culture, and the State in Latin America*. Nashville: Vanderbilt University Press, 2015.

Butler, Judith. *Gender Trouble: Feminism and the Subversion of Identity*. New York: Routledge, 1999.

Cohen, Theodore W. *Finding Afro-Mexico: Race and Nation after the Revolution*. New York: Cambridge University Press, 2020.

Cooper, A. J. *A Voice from the South*. Xenia, OH: The Aldine Printing House, 1892.

Crenshaw, Kimberlé. "Demarginalizing the Intersection of Race and Sex: A Black Feminist Critique of Antidiscrimination Doctrine, Feminist Theory and Antiracist Politics." *University of Chicago Legal Forum*, no. 1 (1989): 139–67.

———. "Mapping the Margins: Intersectionality, Identity, and Violence Against Women of Color." *Stanford Law Review* 43, no. 6 (1991): 1241–1300.

Cruz-Janzen, Marta I. "Latinegras." *Frontiers* (Boulder) 22, no. 3 (2001): 168.

Cuervo Hewitt, Julia. *Voices Out of Africa in Twentieth Century Spanish Caribbean Literature*. Lewisburg, PA: Bucknell University Press, 2009.

DeCosta-Willis, Miriam, eds. *Daughters of the Diaspora: Afra-Hispanic Writers*. Miami: Ian Randle, 2003.

Duke, Dawn. *Literary Passion, Ideological Commitment Toward a Legacy of Afro-Cuban and Afro-Brazilian Women Writers*. Lewisburg, PA: Bucknell University Press, 2008.

Eltis, David, Stanley L. Engerman, K. R. Bradley, Paul Cartledge, Craig Perry, David Richardson, and Seymour Drescher, eds. *The Cambridge World History of Slavery*. Cambridge, UK: Cambridge University Press, 2011.

Figueroa-Vásquez, Yomaira C. *Decolonial Diasporas: Radical Mappings of Afro-Atlantic Literatures*. Evanston: Northwestern University Press, 2021.

FitzPatrick Sifford, Elena. "A Fly in Milk: Fear and Black (In)visbility in New Spanish Painting." In *Emotions, Art, and Christianity in the Transatlantic World, 1450–1800*, edited by Heather Graham and Lauren G. Kilroy-Ewbank, 345–73. Boston: Brill, 2021.

Flores, Juan, and Miriam Jiménez Román. *The Afro-Latin@ Reader: History and Culture in the United States*. Durham, NC: Duke University Press, 2010.

Fuente, Alejandro de la, and George Reid Andrews. *Afro-Latin American Studies: An Introduction*. Cambridge University Press, 2018.

Gonzalez, Anita. *Afro-Mexico Dancing Between Myth and Reality*. Austin: University of Texas Press, 2010.

Hall, Gwendolyn Midlo. *Slavery and African Ethnicities in the Americas: Restoring the Links*. Chapel Hill: University of North Carolina Press, 2005.

Heywood, Linda M. *Njinga of Angola: Africa's Warrior Queen*. Cambridge: Harvard University Press, 2017.

Heywood, Linda M., and Luis Madureira (trans.). "Queen Njinga Mbandi Ana de Sousa of Ndongo/Matamba: African Leadership, Diplomacy, and Ideology, 1620s-1650s." In *Afro-Latino Voices: Narratives from the Early Modern Ibero-Atlantic World, 1550–1812*, edited by Kathryn Joy McKnight and Leo J. Garofalo, 38–51. Cambridge, MA: Hackett, 2009.

Hoetink, Harmannus. *Slavery and Race Relations in the Americas: Comparative Notes on Their Nature and Nexus*. New York: Harper & Row, 1973.

Holder, Michelle, and Alan A. Aja. *Afro-Latinos in the U.S. Economy*. Lanham, MD: Lexington Books, 2021.

Hooks, Bell. *The Will to Change: Men, Masculinity, and Love*. New York: Atria Books, 2004.

James, Conrad, ed. *Writing the Afro-Hispanic: Essays on Africa and Africans in the Spanish Caribbean*. London: Adonis & Abbey, 2012.

Klein, Herbert S., and Ben Vinson III. *African Slavery in Latin America and the Caribbean*. New York: Oxford University Press, 2007.

López Oro, Paul Joseph. "Refashioning Afro-Latinidad: Garifuna New Yorkers in Diaspora." In *Critical Diálogos in Latina and Latino Studies*, edited by Ana Y. Ramos-Zayas and Mérida M. Rúa, 223–40. New York: New York University Press, 2021.

Lorde, Audre. "Learning from the 60s." *SOS—Calling All Black People*, edited by John H. Bracey, Sonia Sanchez, and James Smethurst. Amherst: University of Massachusetts Press, 2015.

Maguire, Emily. "The Eusebia Cosme Show: Translating an Afro-Antillean Identity." In *Writing the Afro-Hispanic: Essays on Africa and Africans in the Spanish Caribbean*, edited by Conrad James, 77–98. London: Adonis & Abbey, 2012.

McKnight, Kathryn Joy, and Leo J. Garofalo, eds. "Introduction." In *Afro-Latino Voices: Narratives from the Early Modern Ibero-Atlantic World, 1550–1812*, edited by Kathryn Joy McKnight and Leo J. Garofalo, ix-xxii. Cambridge, MA: Hackett, 2009.

Medina, Jameelah Xochitl. *The Afro-Latin Diaspora: Awakening Ancestral Memory, Avoiding Cultural Amnesia*. Bloomington: AuthorHouse, 2004.

Moreno Vega, Marta, Marta Moreno-Vega, Marinieves Alba, and Yvette Modestin. *Women Warriors of the Afro-Latina Diaspora*. Houston: Arte Público Press, 2012.

Morris, Margaret Lindsay. *The Afro-Latino Voice in World Literature*. New York: Edwin Mellen Press, 2003.

Oboler, Suzanne, and Anani Dzidzienyo, eds. *Neither Enemies nor Friends: Latinos, Blacks, Afro-Latinos*. New York: Palgrave Macmillan, 2005.

Quinn, Rachel Afi. *Being La Dominicana: Race and Identity in the Visual Culture of Santo Domingo*. Champaign: University of Illinois Press, 2021.

Rahier, Jean Muteba, and Mamyrah A. Dougé-Prosper. "Interview with María Alexandra Ocles Padilla, Former Minister, *Secretaría de Pueblos, Movimientos Sociales y Participación Ciudadana*, Ecuador." In *Black Social Movements in Latin America: From Monocultural Mestizaje to Multiculturalism*, edited by Jean Muteba Rahier, 169–84. New York: Palgrave Macmillan, 2012.

————. "Interview with Maria Inês Barbosa, Former Vice-Minister, *Secretaria Especial de Políticas de* Promoção *da Igualdade Racial* (SEPPIR), Brazil." In *Black Social Movements in Latin America: From Monocultural Mestizaje to Multiculturalism*, edited by Jean Muteba Rahier, 213–24. New York: Palgrave Macmillan, 2012.

Ramsay, Paulette A., and Antonio D. Tillis, eds. *The Afro-Hispanic Reader and Anthology.* Kingston, Jamaica: Ian Randle Publishers, 2018.

Richardson, Jill Toliver. *The Afro-Latin@ Experience in Contemporary American Literature and Culture: Engaging Blackness*. Cham: Springer, 2016.

Rivera-Rideau, Petra R., Jennifer A. Jones, and Tianna S. Paschel, eds. *Afro-Latin@s in Movement: Critical Approaches to Blackness and Transnationalism in the Americas*. New York: Palgrave Macmillan, 2016.

Rout, Leslie B., Jr. *The African Experience in Spanish America: 1502 to the Present Day*. Princeton, NJ: Markus Wiener, 2003.

Simmons, Kimberly Eison, and Bernd Reiter. *Afro-Descendants, Identity, and the Struggle for Development in the Americas*. East Lansing: Michigan State University Press, 2012.

Slavevoyages.org. "Trans-Atlantic Slave Trade Database." https://www.slavevoyages .org/voyage/database (accessed December 1, 2021).

Tannenbaum, Frank. S*lave and Citizen: The Negro in the Americas*. New York: Knopf, 1947.

Thornton, John K., and Linda Heywood. "The Treason of Dom Pedro Nkanga a Mvemba against Dom Diogo, King of Kongo, 1550." In *Afro-Latino Voices: Narratives from the Early Modern Ibero-Atlantic World, 1550–1812*, edited by Kathryn Joy McKnight and Leo J. Garofalo, 2–29. Cambridge, MA: Hackett, 2009.

Truth, S. "Ain't I a woman." Speech delivered at Women's Convention, Akron, Ohio, 1851.

Vega, Marta Moreno, Alba Marinieves, and Yvette Modestin. *Women Warriors of the Afro-Latina Diaspora*. Houston: Arte Público Press, 2012.

Velázquez, María Elisa. "Experiencias de esclavitud femenina: africanas, afrodescendientes e indígenas en el México virreinal." In *Debates históricos contemporáneos: africanos y afrodescendientes en México y Centroamérica*, edited by María Elisa Velázquez, 243–66. México: Instituto Nacional de Antropología e Historia, 2011.

Vinson, Ben, III, and Greg Graves. "The Black Experience in Colonial Latin America." *Latin American Studies*. Oxford: Oxford University Press, 2011.

Wells, I. B. *Lynch Law in All Its Phases*. New York: The New York Age Print, 1892.

NOTES

1. Kimberlé Crenshaw, "Demarginalizing the Intersection of Race and Sex: A Black Feminist Critique of Antidiscrimination Doctrine, Feminist Theory and Antiracist Politics" *University of Chicago Legal Forum*, no. 1 (1989): 139–67.

2. Audre Lorde, "Learning from the 60s." In *SOS—Calling All Black People*, edited by John H. Bracey, Sonia Sanchez, and James Smethurst (University of Massachusetts Press, 2015): 656.

3. Bell Hooks, *The Will to Change: Men, Masculinity, and Love* (New York: Atria Books, 2004): 17.

4. Kimberlé Crenshaw, "Mapping the Margins: Intersectionality, Identity, and Violence Against Women of Color." *Stanford Law Review* (1991): 1241–1300.

5. During their travels, Portuguese traders and merchants travelling through West Africa established the African slave trade; the traders "bought and sold kola nuts, cattle, salt, ivory, gold, and enslaved people (McKnight and Garofalo, xvi). Though slavery was already being employed in several African societies at the time, this would mark the beginning of the largest forced migration known to humankind. For more information on the early stages of the African slave trade see the section "African Demographics in the Ibero-Atlantic World" (McKnight and Garofalo, xvi–xix).

6. The Middle Passage refers to the voyage across the Atlantic that African slaves were forced to endure; chained together and packed into cramped spaces in the lower ship decks, they risked disease and malnutrition. It is estimated that 12–13 percent of African slaves died during the voyage (Slavevoyage.org). For the most up-to-date estimates see the online Trans-Atlantic Slave Trade Database (Slavevoyage.org).

7. For a comprehensive review on the history of slavery throughout the world see: David Eltis, Stanley L. Engerman, K. R. Bradley, Paul Cartledge, Craig Perry, David Richardson, and Seymour Drescher, eds. *The Cambridge World History of Slavery.* Cambridge: Cambridge University Press, 2011.

8. Vinson, Ben, and Greg Graves. "The Black Experience in Colonial Latin America." *Latin American Studies*. Oxford University Press, 2011.

9. The term "African diaspora" is used to refer to the descendants of people from Africa.

10. For a review of the history of Afro-Latinx American studies, see Alejandro de la Fuente and George Reid Andrews, *Afro-Latin American Studies: An Introduction.* Cambridge University Press, 2018. The collection is the first book-length survey of the history of the field.

11. Here we align with the definition of *identity* as outlined by Judith Butler: "any voice and the identity it constructs are not essential or fixed qualities or a person or culture, but rather performances that are fluid and changing, as they respond to social structures, relationships, and circumstances" (177).

12. Hall, xvi.

13. On the topic of the Spanish colonial caste system, we must draw attention to the production and use of *casta* paintings. These paintings, normally produced in sets of sixteen images of a mother, father, and child, depicted different inter-ethnic combinations listed according to race and social status (accompanied by the appropriate term). Elena FitzPatrick Sifford comments on their significance and influence in social constructs and perceptions surrounding the female body, womanhood, and Blackness: "While the earliest casta paintings tended to be idealized views of racial harmony, as the genre developed, they came to contain negative stereotypes of the casta (non-Spanish) figures [. . .] in these later iterations African women began to be

depicted as belligerent and abusive. Violence occurs in casta sets particularly when a Black person is involved, whether with a Spanish or Indigenous spouse" (368).

14. McKnight and Garofalo, xxi.

15. Mcknight and Garofalo, xxi.

16. Rout, 317. Although Rout does not provide bibliographical information for this citation, we can assume that it was a common belief he encountered during his travels throughout Latin America. Unfortunately, this myth persists amongst some people in Latin America today.

17. His analysis also outlines important political and socio-racial terminology used in colonial society along with its definition, helping readers to understand this complex system and its implications. Also worth noting are the appendixes, as they include important historical records such as numerical tables listing the prices of African slaves.

18. Among them, Klein and Vinson examine the importance of Maroonage, inter-marriages, and religious affiliations.

19. George Reid Andrews, "Afro-Latin America (1800–2000)," 5. The author has since then published a more extensive edition: George Reid Andrews, *Afro-Latin America: Black Lives, 1600–2000.* Cambridge: Harvard University Press, 2016.

20. Here we align ourselves with the notion that the categories of race, gen-der, social class, and sexuality co-construct each other (Crenshaw, "Mapping the Margins").

21. McKnight and Garofalo outline the difficulty in locating texts from the period written by Afro-Latinx persons: "Although some Afro-Latinos in the early modern world did read and write and many engaged with literature culture, almost none composed texts that were considered publishable at the time. Consequently, the writ-ten sources in which their voices survive are primarily juridical, ecclesiastical, and administrative documents located in the archives of Europe and Latin America" (xiii).

22. In the introduction to the volume, editors McKnight and Garofalo provide an in-depth discussion on the topic of voice and mediation. They call attention to the issue of "voice" in these documents: "These words have been modified after they were spoken by at least three processes of writing. First, the European scribe tran-scribed the speaker's utterance into an early modern (often bureaucratic) genre. Sec-ond, the contributors to this volume copied the handwritten transcription, interpreting occasionally enigmatic script. Third, the contributors translated the transcription from Spanish or Portuguese to English" (xxiii). Nevertheless, they underscore their value: "These highly mediated documents allow modern readers to approach voices of these distant speakers and glimpse the way in which Afro-Latinos saw, understood, and presented themselves and their worldviews in early modern Ibero-Atlantic world" (McKnight and Garfalo, xxii). These compelling arguments should be considered when interpreting any colonial text.

23. McKnight and Garofalo, xiii.

24. John K. Thornton and Linda Heywood, "The Treason of Dom Pedro Nkanga," *Afro-Latino Voices: Narratives from the Early Modern Ibero-Atlantic World, 1550–1812.* Ed. Kathryn Joy McKnight and Leo J. Garofalo (Cambridge, MA: Hackett, 2009): 8. Linda Heywood provides an in-depth study of the life of Queen Njinga in

Njinga of Angola: Africa's Warrior Queen (Cambridge: Harvard University Press, 2017). For more information on the history of the Kongo Kingdom, see Koen Bostoen and Inge Brinkman, *The Kongo Kingdom: The Origins, Dynamics and Cosmopolitan Culture of an African Polity* (Cambridge: Cambridge University Press, 2018.)

25. Heywood, "Queen Njinga Mbandi Ana de Sousa," 29.

26. McKnight and Garofalo define Black agency (free and enslaved) as "actions people took against the structural and circumstantial forces arrayed against them. Actions ranged from flight and rebellion to more subtle forms of response such as negotiations with owners, altering the speed of work, or appealing to royal courts or Church authorities. At times the protagonists succeeded, at other times they failed. Most often, they created complicated and contradictory results that affected in small ways how slavery and colonial society functional" (3).

27. McKnight and Garofalo, x.

28. Heywood, "Queen Njinga Mbandi Ana de Sousa," 36.

29. Gendered relationships are the central theme of chapters 3, 5, 6, 7, 9, 11, 13, 14, 16. Additional topics outlined by McKnight and Garofalo are Afro-Latino responses to European expansion, imperialism, and colonization (chapters 1, 2, 3, 5, 8, 12, 18); Maroon communities (chapters 2, 5); racial, ethnic, and national identity: all; self-governance (chapters 1, 2, 3, 5, 8, 10, 14); slavery, slave ownership, manumission, and coartación (chapter 3, 5, 7, 8, 9, 13, 15, 16, 17); travel and movement (chapter 4, 9, 11, 12, 13, 15, 18); and violence (chapters 2, 3, 5, 8, 15, 16, 17).

30. Such early works include Frank Tannenbaum, *Slave and Citizen: The Negro in the Americas* (New York: Knopf, 1947) and Harmannus Hoetink, *Slavery and Race Relations in the Americas: Comparative Notes on Their Nature and Nexus* (New York: Harper & Row, 1973). Though some elements of early investigations have since been debated in more contemporary studies, their influence as foundational texts is undeniable.

31. The original title of the book published in Spanish is *Debates Históricos contemporáneos: Africanos y Afrodescendientes en México y Centroamérica*.

32. The original title of the chapter published in Spanish is "Experiencias de esclavitud femenina: Africanas, afrodescendientes e indígenas en el México virreinal."

33. Velázquez, 32. These accounts illustrate Arrelucea Barrantes's view of Black enslaved agency, serving to "challenge the prevalent view of colonial society as being so hierarchical and patriarchal that it prevented enslaved women from employing legal strategies on their own behalf" (285). Another important contribution to the documentation of the Black enslaved woman's voice in the colonial period is Erica L. Ball, Tatiana Seijas, and Terri L. Snyder, *As If She Were Free: A Collective Biography of Women and Emancipation in the Americas* (Cambridge: Cambridge University Press, 2020).

34. For our purposes, Ocles Padilla's account of her experience is also telling as it speaks of the lack of support from other women. Though the interviewer does not dive into many questions regarding her position as a female or feminist issues, when asked about her experience as a Black female in a white/mestizo political space she says: "the cabinet was a hard space, and this was mostly so because of the female ministers. I never had any problem with the male ministers, on the contrary, and I was very close

to several of them. But with the female ministers, it was much more complicated for a whole bunch of reasons: the way you dress, the way you talk, the way you behave as a minister in general" (Rahier and Dougé-Prosper, 178).

35. Rahier and Dougé-Prosper, 173.

36. In her chapter, Emily Maguire draws attention to the significance of the act of performing poetry saying: "by choosing to emphasize her gender in a visible way, Cosmo not only performed a black Caribbean identity through the recitation of this poetry, but performed it as a speaking black female subject" (89).

37. Branche, 1.

38. Branche, 1.

39. Figueroa-Vásquez defines the decolonial feminist concept of "destierro" as: "the ongoing event and legacy of being torn away from land" (2).

40. Among other studies that take a transnational approach to topics of Afro-Latinx identity, politics, and culture are: Bernd Reiter and Kimberly Eison Simmons, eds. *Afrodescendants, Identity, and the Struggle for Development in the Americas* (East Lansing: Michigan State University Press, 2012) and Suzanne Oboler and Anani Dzidzienyo, eds. *Neither Enemies nor Friends: Latinos, Blacks, Afro-Latinos* (New York: Palgrave Macmillan, 2005).

PART I

Diasporic Rhythms and Visual Arts

Intersecting Race and Gender in Afro-Descendent Photography, Music, and Dance

the richest poor people

God was just something we didn't do. church, either. we were black and brown people. we worked. hard. we smoked marlboro reds and kool filter kings. we drank coors light. el presidente brandy and gin with salt around the glass—when we had a little extra. extra was a luxury and so was God.

we got our lights cut off. we borrowed pennies from each other. the government paid for our groceries. a book of food stamps was a gift. paid for with our pride. when pride was low, we went to the church. not to worship. to be delivered. because the children had to eat. the church gave out boxes of food and vouchers you could take to winn-dixie. our mothers made magic with those vouchers.

we were black and brown people. our fathers made magic from tar. they were boys of sun and sweat. we rented apartments. we bathed in music. we fought and cried in color. we cursed our lot in spanish. we danced when we had nothing. we gave birth to babies that never had cribs. our elders never knew nursing homes. there were no elders. everybody worked. nobody talked of God.

God was a luxury that we could not afford.

God was never in hospital waiting rooms. God was not in the streets. God was not on the roof when my father burned himself alive, everyday. God was not in the pot of beans. God was not in my mother's tears. God was not in the pawnshops. God was not at church's chicken. God was not in the face of the children i grew up with. God was not in my grandmother's calloused hands. God was not in the rent man's frown when we got behind. God was not on the city bus. God was not in our run down shoes. God was not in our bad teeth. God was not in our everyday. God was not in our struggle. God never came for us.

we prayed in spite of sight and circumstance. we were the richest poor people.

God was in our blood.

—Natasha Carrizosa

Chapter 1

Opening Up Black Spaces, Female Spaces

Dialogues with the Orishas, the City, and the Mythic Space in "Banho de Folhas" by Luedji Luna and "Pra que me chamas" by Xênia França

Lesley Feracho

In the studies of the African diaspora—and I take as one example, those focusing on the development of African diasporic histories and historical subjects in the Americas—the twentieth and twenty-first centuries have been marked by increased focus on the role of Black women both historically and in contemporary economic, political and cultural developments. For scholars across the multilingual Americas—from seminal Black feminist theorists such as Patricia Hill Collins, Michelle Wallace, bell hooks, and Kimberlé Crenshaw, to Carole Boyce Davies and Miriam Da Costa Willis, from Mayra Santos Febres to Lélia Gonzalez, Sueli Carneiro, and Djamila Ribeiro, an understanding of the complex ways in which Black women negotiate the sociohistorical alongside a more intimate construction of subjectivity can take dual paths. On one hand one can chart the historical, political, and economic systems of dislocation, disenfranchisement, and invisibilization with its intersectional oppressions as Crenshaw discusses. Yet, on the other hand a full appreciation of how Black women navigate such systems and create tools of expression and empowerment and strategies of resistance is one that centralizes the full range of their existence and being across the African diaspora. This chapter looks at how two Black Brazilian female singer-songwriters

from Bahia, Luedji Luna and Xênia França, use specific musical texts, lyrics, and visual presentation from their 2017 debut albums to articulate a
musical-spiritual space that lays bare the historically grounded intersectional
oppressions of which scholars from Lélia Gonzalez to Crenshaw speak,
while crafting multilayered strategies of Black female empowerment. In
their musical projects, *Xênia* and *Um corpo no mundo*, respectively, I will
explore how they engage in a musical dialogue that connects two spiritualized
geographies—the geographical and symbolic space of Bahia and a mythic
Afro-Brazilian space—with the spiritual ancestry and contemporaneity of
Afro-Brazilian religious practices, such as Candombléê, through the representation of and connection to specific orishas—most notably Oxalá, Ochún,
Eleguá, Oyá, and Exu—to create a collective space of Black female agency.
In particular, the songs "Banho de Folhas"/"Bath of Sacred Leaves" and "Pra
que me chamas?"/"Why do you call me" respectively construct musical and
visual articulations of Black women in both physical and symbolic places
that connect ancestrality and the contemporary: linking the spiritual history
of (the) Afro-diasporic religions and cosmovisions, specifically Candomblé
and Santeria, and the history of slavery and resistance in Bahia—with the
contemporary assertion of Blackness, female power, and citizenship.

As Emilia María Durán-Almarza and Esther Álvarez-López have noted, the
role of Black women in the struggles for freedom against oppressive systems
of disenfranchisement and erasure is crucial as sociohistorical corrective:

> even though we agree with Gilroy (1993, 16) in his claim that "the history of the
> black Atlantic . . . continually crisscrossed by the movements of black people—
> not only as commodities but engaged in various struggles towards emancipa-
> tion, autonomy, and citizenship-provides a means to re-examine the problems
> of nationality, location, identity and historical memory," we consider that this
> goal cannot be fully achieved without a more nuanced and thorough gendered
> analysis of Afro-diasporic movements.[1]

In particular, cultural expression—through practices ranging from writing
to the visual arts, from dance to musical production—is one tool for creating projects of self-definition, empowerment, resistance, and sociopolitical
critique. Popular music in particular has been a site of not only individual
and collective expression but also the exploration and creation of collective ties that may link particularly gendered, racial, and ethnic identities, for
example, but also comment on the relationship of marginalized subjects to the
nation. In that sense, as scholars such as George Yúdice and Idelbar Avelar
have noted, music can be a representation and problematization of different
manifestations of cultural citizenship, creating dialogues with political representation yet also invested in the "maintenance and development of cultural

lineage through education, custom, language and religion and the positive acknowledgement of difference in and by the mainstream."[2]

For Black women across the diaspora, their participation in cultural production provides multiple opportunities and platforms to counter the historic invisibilities and oppressions that have worked to divest them of agency. By situating these processes in hybrid cultural practices, such as popular music, we can more fully grasp how such performances increasingly provide a space for its Black female practitioners to explore the possibilities of transformation from marginalized objects to creators and subjects of multiple, collective spaces of selfhood and agency.

Given the complex historical and cultural forces at play, one question that can be raised is in regard to the ways in which Black women negotiate dynamics of marginalization, power, subjectivity, and community. In this chapter I would like to explore this question in relation to two Black women of Brazil who use music as a tool to explore these themes while occupying social, cultural, and geographical sites and affirming their positions as historical and contemporary subjects. Within the context of the acknowledgment of the intersectional histories and identities of Black Brazilian women, I see Luedji and Xênia as two subjects positioned musically, lyrically, and visually as intermediary links of the physical and the spiritual serving as vessels that connect the histories of agency, resistance, and community of the orishas with/into the empowered Black female body. In so doing they assert their presence in different spaces in the city (for Luedji) and a constructed mythic Afro-Brazilian landscape (for Xênia) and, consequently, open up further space to explore the ways in which Black women, in response to historical and contemporary oppressions, create pathways of visibility and agency on a national level as well as local.

To emphasize the importance of Black women in this endeavor I would like to draw on Daphne A. Brooks's assessment of the need to address these silences as expressed in her comprehensive study on Black women musicians and critics, *Liner Notes for the Revolution* (2021). While focused primarily on the Black female critics in the Anglophone Americas, her articulation of the need to challenge silences and omissions is, I believe, apropos to the conditions of Black women in music throughout the Americas:

> I am also suggesting we now work toward the deep cuts and spin the long-playing record that starts with Pauline Hopkins, moves back and forth across the postbellum era, and travels into the modern centuries so as to capture the genius of Black women artists theorizing their own sound work in and through their precious bodies, the kinds of bodies that were forced to literally play the role of the gateway to the so-called New World. I am suggesting that we use a different needle to listen to the ruptures, interventions, and complexities of

the music all around us made by Black women, cultural actors but seldom heard
in high fidelity, seldom listened to with deep, rich faith in their own wisdom.[3]

In Brooks's call for a recognition of Black women's musical and equally as
important theoretical genius as "cultural actors," I would like to highlight the
corporeality that she emphasizes as part of this process, whereby the colonized bodies forced to serve as the "gateway" to the "so-called New World"
become their own creators of meaning. This use of the body as part of a
performative, decolonial act is one I will explore in the Black Bahian artists
I will analyze in this essay.

My choice of Brazil and particularly Black Brazilian women comes from
an ever-growing emphasis on the connections (and differences) between
the African diasporic communities of Brazil and the United States. Such
dialogues both accompany and expand on the ongoing attention to Brazil's
economic relationship with the United States and place on the global stage.[4]
Within this context the role of women of African descent has emerged as a
significant and continually expanding area of inquiry. For example, studies in the social sciences such as feminist anthropologist Kheisha-Khan Y.
Perry's *Black Women Against the Land Grab: The Fight for Racial Justice in
Brazil* (2013) have analyzed not only the impact of systems of oppression on
Black Brazilian women but also the ways in which they engage in developments of political and cultural citizenship in order to present a more nuanced
understanding of the full complexity of national identity as regards gender,
race, ethnicity, class, sexuality, and regional affiliations (among other markers). As Joselina da Silva declares in the preface to her collection of essays
by Black women of the Americas (Latin, Central, and North) and Africa
entitled *O Pensamento de/por Mulheres Negras* (2018) [*The Thinking of/by
Black Women*]:

> At the same time, they recognize how the history of struggle and conquests that
> we experience today, in Brazil and in the other countries of the Americas and
> of Africa, is a result, reflection and expression of the action of so many Black
> women that lived (and live) and offered themselves up (and offer themselves)
> with courage and daring to the search for social justice and for a more just,
> democratic and anti-racist society. Those Black women are a source of inspira-
> tion and strength for today's Black activists and intellectuals.[5] (translation mine)

I specifically place Luedji and Xênia in dialogue with each other not only
because of the musical-spiritual-geographical articulation of Black female
subjectivity present in their particular audio and visual texts, but in their
representation of a new generation of Bahian artists, including Black female
singer-songwriters, who, as Xênia notes "are reappropriating their own

discourse, their own way of making music, their own faces back on the cover. It is a phenomenon of independent artists sending their own message"[6] (translation mine).

Consequently, I will center my analysis of Black Brazilian women's cultural production in a transnational critical dialogue which highlights theories of race, gender, performance, and place. To begin, my analysis will foreground Black feminist diasporic thought: specifically Black Brazilian feminist theories of empowerment and voice as presented by Sueli Carneiro and Djamila Ribeiro in conversation with Crenshaw's elucidations on Intersectionality as theory and praxis and Caribbean scholar Carole Boyce Davies's migratory subjectivities. I place these in dialogue with current Brazilian scholarship on Black Brazilian women's musical production and decolonial praxis, drawing in particular on Simone Pereira Schmidt's analysis of a transnational modernity present in Luna's music as a recontextualization of negritude, and Rafael Pinto Ferreira de Queiroz's emphasis on the role of Black epistemologies in Xênia's debut single. And lastly, in order to create a more comprehensive framing of the performance of Black women's musical and spiritual subjectivity in Luedji and Xênia, I will draw on Katherine McKittrick's theories of gender, race, and place.

Specifically, I would like to situate both Luedji and Xênia as producers of cultural transcripts where the recognition of and challenge to systemic marginalizations can be placed within the project to establish a subject positionality or "place of speech" that Black diasporic feminists have expressed in different ways.[7] Such actions, in this case, reflect the types of navigations, and contestations used by Black women in Brazilian society as they navigate the codes and strictures of race, gender, class, and sexuality. As Sueli Carneiro notes, it is the ongoing systemic marginalization and silencing of Black Brazilian women, including within Brazilian feminist movements, that has continued to influence the political mobilizations of Black women in Brazil, in organizations such as Geledés (and its Instituto da mulher negra), Fala Preta, and Criola.[8] The recognition of these systemic marginalizations, the historic, cultural, and political hierarchies and invisibilities they perpetuate, and the commitment to challenge and subvert them is part of the project of a place of speech (subject positioning) that Black feminists such as Hill Collins, hooks, Lélia Gonzalez, Djamila Ribeiro, and Grada Quilomba espouse. As Ribeiro asserts,

> Speech is not restricted to the act of emitting words, but of being able to exist. We think of this subject positioning (place of speech) as refuting the traditional historiography and the structuring of knowledge that is a consequence of the social hierarchy.[9] (translation mine)

These subversions of hegemonic systems of knowledge are acts that dialogue with and serve as strategies that contest the interlocking systems of oppression that Crenshaw has established as a key characteristic of Intersectionality, whereby Black women "experience double-discrimination—the combined effects of practices which discriminate on the basis of race, and on the basis of sex. And sometimes they experience discrimination as Black women—not the sum of race and sex discrimination, but as Black women."[10] Alongside Crenshaw's theorization of intersectional identities I would like to not only acknowledge the long history of intersectional thought by Black women from Anna Julia Cooper to Combahee River Collective, Collins, and hooks, among others, but also place it in dialogue with discussions of intersectional politics in the lives of Black Brazilian women, as articulated by Black feminist scholars such as Gonzalez, Carneiro, and Ribeiro. Such expansion is important as a decentering, expansive diasporic act. As Ribeiro notes:

> It is an opportune time to decolonize hegemonic perspectives on the theory of Intersectionality and adopt the Atlantic as the locus of intersecting oppressions. . . . We can say that Intersectionality produces epistemic dislocations from Africa to the diáspora as a consequence of the fact that we do not always dedicate ourselves to the deepened intellectual work of academic reflection.[11] (translation mine)

As Black female singer-songwriters whose storytelling links the written act to what I see as a musical-visual-spiritual articulation of the individual and collective, of ancestral ties and contemporary realities, an understanding of their identities also extends to the complex journeys that traverse multiple geographies, as part of what Davies describes as "migratory subjectivities." These crossings, as part of her theorization of Black female agency, navigate the physical, psychological, structural, and temporal spaces to create strategies that challenge the multiple discourses of marginalization. As Davies asserts,

> Migratory subjects suggests that Black women/'s writing cannot be located and framed in terms of one specific place, but exist/s in myriad places and times, constantly eluding the terms of the discussion. . . . In the same way as diaspora assumes expansiveness and elsewhereness, migrations of the Black female subject pursue the path of movement outside the terms of dominant discourses.[12]

As I will expand later, Luedji and Xênia's use of the written alongside the musical to explore the complexity of their identities as Black women connect them to the process described here. Both create movements and moments of performance of the Black female subject that defy fixity as it challenges dominant (including national) discourses.

From these transatlantic considerations of Intersectionality and migration in Black women's identity I end my theoretical foundation with a consideration of McKittrick's theorizations of space in order to examine the ways in which Luedji and Xênia move through physical space as part of a larger process of articulating alternative bodies of knowledge. For McKittrick the relationship between Black populations, and particularly Black women, and geography "locates and draws on black histories and black subjectivities in order to make visible social lives which are often displaced, rendered ungeographic."[13] This visibilization—as a representation of both a counter to hegemonic systems of power and an affirmation of alternative representations of power, rooted in hybrid African diasporic cosmovisions and practices is an important outcome of these connections. As she notes, "We produce space, we produce its meanings, and we work very hard to make geography what it is . . . the interplay between domination and black women's geographies is underscored by the social production of space."[14] By understanding these geographies as mutable and impacted by subjects we can see how these spaces can work for Black women. As such, McKittrick posits that,

> the poetics of landscape allow black women to critique the boundaries of transatlantic slavery, rewrite national narratives, respatialize feminism, and develop new pathways across traditional geographic arrangements; they also offer several reconceptualizations of space and place, positioning black women as geographic subjects who provide spatial clues as to how more humanly workable geographies might be imagined. . . . Produced alongside and through practices of domination, black women's expressive acts spatialize the imperative of a perspective of struggle.[15]

For Luedji and Xênia, their personal development and production of subject positionality have intersected in important ways with their journeys through different regional, cultural, and musical spaces, engaged in what Nadja Gumes has described as "musical activism," applying the concept of Micael Herschmann and Cintia Fernandes.[16] Through the creation of cultural transcripts and their complex performance of identity and agency as Black Brazilian female singer-songwriters, they have both traveled from Salvador, Bahia, to São Paulo continually exploring and navigating cultural, historical sites that allow them to negotiate, undermine, and reshape practices of sociocultural domination (particularly marginalizing national discourses of racial democracy and whiteness) while also challenging the practices of racial and spatial domination. Such a project of critique, Black female agency, and musical experimentation put them in conversation with other twenty-first-century Black Brazilian singers such as Larissa Luz (Bahia), Tássia Reis (São Paulo), Doralyce (Recife), Karol Conká (Curitiba), Bia Ferreira (Minas

Gerais), and Helen Nzinga (Rio de Janeiro). These musical dialogues are also represented through the creations of collaborative musical partnerships, as is the case with Luedji, Xênia and Larissa—who together created the supergroup Aya Bass, who, among their many concerts together, performed on November 19–20 (which coincides with the Día da Consciência Negra) at the 2019 Afropunk Festival in São Paulo titled "Black to the Future." That year it was staged in conjunction with the Afro-Brazilian festival Feira Preta, which at the time celebrated its eighteenth anniversary. The group's name, which means Queen mother (mãe-rainha), is derived from the term used to refer to the female orishas in Yoruba ("yabas"), in particular Nanã, Iemanjá, Iansã, Oxúm, Ebá, and Euá as well as well as in reference to certain aspects of the electronic music scene.[17] One of the group's main objectives is to "represent the power of Black women with all the [*sic*] magic and flow of Bahian music, . . . to call the attention to Black singers, and occupy a prominent place instead of the one they were historically relegated to."[18] More specifically, as Gumes and Marcelo Argolô observe in their study of the group's musical activism: "The Aya Bass Project constructs a politial/aesthetic experience that places the musical work and activist discourse through the lens of Black feminism on the same level" (translation mine).[19]

I will now move on to my analysis of first Luedji then Xênia's debut singles, focusing on how each woman musically and visually presents themselves as Black Brazilian female subjects navigating the urban, symbolic space of Salvador and the larger space of Bahia, as sites of speech (a subject positioning)—and an empowering articulation of self, spirituality, and community in twenty-first-century Brazil. Both Luedji and Xênia engage in this process by drawing on Black histories and subjectivities, as McKittrick notes, through the invocation of Black Brazilian ancestries—and specifically through particular orishas of Candomblé.

I will begin with a brief introduction to Luedji's development as a Black singer-songwriter, a process informed by not only the sociocultural contexts of her life in the Northeast but also by the geographical and cultural migrations she undertakes as an adult. To begin, Luedji Luna, born Luedji Gomes Santa Rita, was born in Cabulas, Salvador, and raised in the neighborhood of Brotas, Salvador.[20] It is important to note that her political awareness began in fact as a child, as the daughter of politically engaged parents, who were part of the Movimento Negro (the shortened term for the Movimento Negro Unificado contra Discriminação Racial/Black Movement Unified against Racial Discrimination or MNU). As a movement was begun at the end of the 1970s by Black Brazilian activists, it was constructed politically and discursively as a grouping of revolutionary organizations that linked race and class as part of its anti-racist agenda, denouncing the national discourse of racial democracy while fighting to enact political, educational, and cultural strategies to better the lives of Black Brazilians.[21] Within this context, from early on Luna's valorization of her identity as a Black woman was intimately linked to a political and social awareness of the marginalizing discourses of racism and sexism historically at work in the nation, while continually seeking ways to challenge and subvert them, and subsequently create empowered spaces for the community as well as the individual. As she notes in her interview in *El País*: "The children of militants were educated to occupy spaces of power, whatever could give economic power and social position and that could move the narrative even a little"[22] (translation mine). This racial pride, for example, is seen in her name, Luedji, given by her parents in honor of the first African queen of the Lunda ethnic group at the beginning of the seventeenth century, and which means "friendship" (*amizade*), "river" (*rio*), or "moon" (*lua*) in the language of the Tchokwe ethnic group.[23] As she transitioned from the study of law at the State University of Bahia/Universidade do Estado da Bahia to the discovery of her musical and personal voice, music and songwriting became tools for affirming a collective voice, a strategy Luedji continued in the Banda Cumatê (a cultural collective dedicated to the research and transmission of traditional artistic representations of Brazilian culture), through her work as cofounder of a group of composers in Salvador and in her own songwriting, which she described as "my catharsis, my salvation, my cure"[24] (translation mine).

This connection of the lyrical and musical representation of Luedji's multifaceted subjecthood is rooted in her intersectional identity as a Black woman negotiating multiple systems of oppression in urban spaces while creating strategies of expression and collective empowerment that reflect her lived experiences.[25] When considered alongside Luedji's identification as singer-songwriter, I concur with Helen Campos Barbosa and Jorge Cardoso Filho's analysis of her performative and political project as the creation of a complex gendered, racialized "aesthetic experience" that creates a dialogue between her intersectional identity and the concept of *escrevivência* as articulated by Black Brazilian writer Conceição Evaristo that also opens up the possibilities for accessing one's experiences in the world.[26] According to Evaristo, the written expression merges the lived experiences of author and subject, particularly as Black women, as a vehicle to counter historical silences and as a continuation of the power of ancestral oralities, experience, and wisdom:

> Our *escrevivência* brings experience, the lived experience of our condition as a Brazilian of African descent, a hyphenated nationality, in which I situate myself and express myself in order to affirm my origin in the African people and celebrate my ancestrality and connect myself as much with the African people as with the African diaspora.[27] (translation mine)

Within this context I see Luedji's articulation of "an aesthetic experience" in alignment with the possibilities provided by an approach rooted in *escrevivência*. As such, Luedji's performance links her to a performance of a spiritual-corporeal mediation that allows her to respond to two main challenges faced in her personal and professional development. The first one is the navigation of Brazilian society as a Black woman, while the second entails establishing an identity as a Black female songwriter, particularly as one from Bahia who did not sing the expected musical styles of samba or axé.[28] In her album Luedji asserts a musical independence by incorporating jazz, samba, MPB, multiple Afro-Brazilian rhythms, and soukous influences to address themes of ancestrality, emigration, xenophobia, intersectional Black women's experiences, strategies of individual and collective resistance, visibility, and empowerment, connecting them as well to multiple expressions of love.[29]

In Luedji's musical and ideological vision, these examinations of Intersectionality and resistance extend beyond the borders of the national and encompass what Schmidt identifies as a diasporic and transnational representation of negritude in a post-affirmative action Brazil. This period, after the 1970s and 1980s, represents a transition in Brazilian society's discourses around race and specifically an increased challenge to its national discourse of racial democracy, signaled by the emergence of Black movements that are less focused on national projects and instead developing a more transnational profile more in dialogue with other global movements and more conscious of its own racism.[30] This shift, as Schmidt observes, is reflected in Luedji's work, in,

> the determination to assume a blackness as an extensive, transnational project, simultaneously turned inward (the urban questions, the immigrants) and outwards (the diasporic routes, the past of the Atlantic crossings, the memory of the journeys, of the cultural exchanges and slavery).[31] (translation mine)

In part inspired by her move to São Paulo and her connection with both Haitian and African immigrants from different parts of the continent, Luedji used the musical and later visual landscape to interrogate and occupy her space as a female Afro-diasporic subject: "I always say that we, the Blacks of/in the diaspora feel an ancestral longing, meeting those bodies awakened in me the desire to find out which of those Africas I could call my own."/"Eu sempre digo que nós negros da/na diáspora sentimos uma saudade ancestral, me deparar com aqueles corpos negros despertou em mim o desejo de saber qual daquelas Áfricas eu poderia chamar de minha." ("Diálogos Ausentes"; translation mine)

The geographical, historical, and symbolic importance of Bahia and specifically Salvador for complex representations of Black Brazilian (and

Afro-diasporic) collective empowerment in the face of historical systems of oppression, from enslavement and colonization to contemporary forces of economic, educational, and political disenfranchisement, is one that spans over three hundred years. As one of the first ports of arrival for the enslaved Africans in Brazil (particularly from the West Coast of Africa and the ultimately encompassing Yoruba peoples), occurring in a country with one of the largest Afro-descendant populations in the western hemisphere (larger, in fact than the United States), Salvador became not only a Brazilian capital, but also, in terms of Afro-diasporic resistance, a site of diasporic hybridity, where linguistic, filial, and cosmological ties across multiple ethnic groups defied colonial and slave systems of total cultural erasure to create syncretic religious practices, such as Candomblé, and cultural representations of Black survival, resilience, and creativity.[32] From the creation of the *blocos afros* such as Ile Ayê and Olodum in the 1970s (1974 and 1979) to diverse representations of cultural, educational, and political movements such as the Movimento Negro (MNU), Salvador continued to develop as a site of Black Brazilian cultural and political mobilization. On one hand, as Kwame Dixon observes, "while blacks are found in most of Brazil's twenty six states, Bahia and Salvador are largely recognized as a vibrant epicenter of Afro-Brazilian social identity and rich cultural traditions" (5). Such developments in part have made Brazil, and Salvador in particular, an important site for African diasporic connection and solidarity, while at the same time revealing complex economic and political inequalities at work. Nonetheless, as social inequities and systemic oppressions continued to target Black Brazilians across the nation, these communities sought and created- in cities like Salvador -new strategies of Black consciousness, racial politics, and educational initiatives that went beyond cultural representation as sole forms of community building. As Dixon attests,

> It is argued that in the 1990s, the city of Salvador represented an important site of Black grassroots mobilization and heightened social consciousness. . . . Equally important, the debates, discourses, and tactic unfolding in Salvador in the 1990s must be understood as integral to the larger "strategic puzzle," as they were central in understanding affirmative action initiatives across Brazil.[33]

For Luedji, for example, the city was an important site of belonging and representation. Only with the distance and dislocation to São Paulo did she recognize the profound significance Salvador held for her: "I began to understand that Salvador, in spite of its contradictions and violence and racism . . . was a city where I saw myself, it was a mirror for me"[34] (translation mine).

The material and symbolic significance of Salvador for Luedji (and Xênia) is intricately linked to the visual and musical representation of Afro-Brazilian religious practice as the vehicle for collective empowerment—connecting ancestral cosmovisions with contemporary Black subjectivity. In particular, the evocation of Candomblé orishas and healing practices channeled through the bodies of both Black female subjects becomes a powerful reconceptualization of space and place, to use McKittrick's terminology, and of the ability to exist ("poder de existir") that is central to an articulation of their "place of speech" (subject positioning). As a syncretic religious practice that presents orishas as the intermediaries between the human subject and the divine while also serving as agents of healing, protection, or desired behavioral influences, for Black Brazilians Candomblé was also significant in its representation of strategies of cultural and, in different ways, political empowerment in the face of their racial, economic, and political marginalizations. As Rachel E. Harding points out about its emergence in Brazil, "Candomblé became a collectivizing force through which subjugated peoples organized an alternative meaning of their lives and identities that countered the disaggregation and the imposed subalterity to which they were subjected by the dominant social structure."[35] Similarly, Sterling's analysis of ritual and the power of Candomblé for its devotees and its exercise in contemporary Brazil (in Salvador and throughout the country) highlights its strength as a "collectivizing force."[36] In their visual invocations of this religious and, in a larger sense, spiritual consciousness, the Black female subjects in both videos assert and enact a kind of Black visibility and Black power as they represent and symbolically channel the presence of the orixas, centralizing Candomblé in their musical visions, while revindicating its importance in their lived experience.[37] Just as Ferreiro de Queiroz highlights in his study of Xênia's videoclip, I would like to highlight the choice of the orishas by both Luedji and Xênia for their significance as representations of qualities that speak to the multiple, complex navigations of the Black Brazilian female subject in contemporary society, turning intersectional oppressions into strategies of empowerment.[38]

Among the orixas highlighted in Luedji's video are Oxalá, who is invoked in her song, and is particularly important in the hierarchy of Candomblé through the association with the creation of the world. Also known as Obbatalá, Oxalá is connected to the concept of the Sky Father and came to be associated with the concept of purity.[39] As occurs with many of the chief orishas, through the syncretic nature of Candomblé in the Americas, Oxalá also possesses an alter ego, the Senhor do Bonfim, the patron saint of Bahia. Female orixas (although the gendered aspect of orisha representation is more complex than male/female binaries) such as Oxún and Yemanjá, are also present and significant in both Luedji and Xênia's audiovisual visions. Associated with not only running water and its symbolic cooling effects, Ochun is a key orisha in Yoruba thought, possessing a multidimensional power that is economic, political, divinatory, maternal, natural, and therapeutic.[40] While she is connected to fresh water, especially rivers, she is also known to symbolically divide the pathways of the human and divine and is connected to nature as an herbalist. While she possesses an uncompromising femininity," she is also a warrior woman, skilled in warfare and obsessively protective in ways that reveal a darker side alongside the more "traditional" feminine attributes of beauty and wealth.[41] While Yemanjá is also connected to the water, she is by contrast associated strongly with maternity and with the ocean. Legends telling her stories repeat scenes of pain and creation where rivers flow from her breasts, in part symbolizing her ability to transcend pain and as Audre Lorde observes of the orisha, transform it into an act of creation.[42] The last scene, as I will discuss shortly, evokes this journey of pain (in this case of dislocation), as part of the Black female subject's search for answers and creation—possibly transcendence.

In Luedji's first released single, "Bath of the Sacred Leaves"/"Banho de Folhas," cowritten with Emillie Lapa, she centers a Black female subject moving through the streets of Salvador, who I see as an embodiment of the "poetics of landscape." She is a subject in search of an encounter that, although unrealized, opens up the possibility for a union with the orishas as a representation of the connection with ancestrality and the guidance they provide in a modern world. In so doing, she "develops new pathways across traditional geographic arrangements."[43] From the very title, the reference to the sacred leaves used not only in collective ritual ceremonies but also in individual petitions brings the spiritual practice to the contemporary space and individual journey. As a brief reflection on this journey I will highlight parts of the process, represented by significant types of images or image sequences in the video. They establish the centrality of the journey as a respatialization and development of her subjectivity– highlighting the arc of this Black female subject: from the positioning of the subject within Salvador (with all its accompanying historical and cultural significance) to the doubt and dislocation, to the constant verbal and spatial invocation of the power of ancestrality for cultural, individual, and collective affirmation.

From the beginning of the video, directed by Joyce Lapa, before the Black female subject is present, the spectator is presented with two geographical and spatial elements that will be important in this journey: Bahia de Todos os Santos and specifically Salvador and the complexity and multiplicity of nature. As the music plays—highlighting a soukous-like guitar line without words—the camera establishes the city as a principal character in the journey: it pans over the water (presenting a force of nature whose significance as a historical and cultural conduit and ancestral force becomes evident later), then over the coastline of Salvador and finally over the city from different angles. Referring back to the historical and cultural import of Salvador for representations of Black Brazilian and Afro-diasporic cultural and political

development, this establishes the primacy of these histories for our protagonist. Within quick succession, the space is populated even further—through
images that imply and as a result amplify the connection to ancestrality—and
Afro-Brazilian religious elements from Candomblé: from alternating images
of beads and plants (that connect as the video progresses with the sacred and
ritualistic), to objects such as a chair (alluding to use in a religious ceremony),
animals (a goat), and food (spices and fruit). Within the alternating images
there is a quick presentation of a partially covered sign—that indicates
Candomblé—possibly a *terreiro*—establishing even further the cultural and
religious space that will be the focal point of the musical and visual journey.

When the lyrics begin—it is part of a joint process of subjectivity—the
expression of doubt and dislocation of the Black female subject within a city
of such enormity that the desired connections only result in her further marginalization. The visuals emphasize this initial focus on the individual—with
close-ups of the subject in different closed street sites—highlighting not only
the colors that characterize the city, but also marking these spots as older—
and thus highlighting the idea of a protracted wandering. While she identifies
the journey through the city by a specific day—"It was a Thursday"/"Foi em
uma quarta-feira" these images and the later repetition of the verse link it to
a larger, deeper, sense of doubt and questioning.[44] While the video represents
a fictional creation—I would like to further contextualize this process by
drawing on links to the singer-songwriter's own reflections on her place as
a Black woman in both Southeastern spaces such as São Paulo and native
spaces such as Salvador as examined earlier. This autobiographical sense of
unease and dislocation is in fact an emotion that Luedji weaves into several
songs on her debut album, most notably "A body in the world"/"Um corpo
no mundo," which gives the debut its name and relates her complicated journey to situate herself in a city (São Paulo) where she feels like an outsider.
As Schmidt observes, "And so, speaking of the body and of not belonging,
of crossings and memories, that we find in Luedji Luna the staging that syn-
thesizes the contemporary urban Brazil. The body in the world, unleashed in
the city, sings the loneliness of the diaspora"[45](translation mine). While the
sentiments expressed in this song are in reference to that particular experience
in São Paulo, it is also relevant for the subject's anxiety in Salvador expressed
in this song, and the ways in which her journey through the city weave its
own "poetics of landscape" and connect with spiritual items connected to
Candomblé that both ground her and open her up to African diasporic memory and cultural legacies.

A second element of the journey that surfaces therefore is the response to
this dislocation—for this subject this response is the call to the orisha/patron
saint (already alluded to in the opening visuals). As the subject lyrically calls
out to Oxalá for guidance: "I am going to ask Oxalá/Oxalá who guides" ("Vou

pedir a Oxalá/Oxalá quem guia") she highlights the importance of ancestral-ity as a guiding force—from the spiritual to the everyday. The last line of this appeal: "Oxalá who sent you" ("Oxalá quem te mandou") highlights the bond to the orixá as both for the individual, in the most personal way, and also as a force to aid in the production of collective bonds. As these initial questions seem to yield few answers, the visual representation highlights a respatializa-tion and subjectivity: moving through the city, actively traversing multiple physical spaces and their cultural implications as part of her query. Without delving into detailed analysis of each individual frame I would like to there-fore emphasize this next "step" in her journey: the reinforcement of ances-trality in the urban, contemporary space, connecting the spiritual—personal and collective. Lyrically, this is represented by the transition from anxiety to valorization and visibility of the ancestral as sources of protection. The first two lines: "No answer/but a fistful of sacred leaves" ("Nenhuma resposta/ Mas um punhado de folhas sagradas") begins by linking the emotional and the spiritual. The initial frustration of a request for help seemingly denied or unheard is immediately challenged not just by the physicality of the leaves she has collected but more importantly by their spiritual significance and the promise they could hold. By following with the lines: "to cure me, to separate me from all evil" ("Pra me curar, pra me afastar de todo mal") she assures herself of the sacred power for healing and protection that is in fact at her dis-posal. The visual juxtaposition of the personal—focusing on the Black female subject—to the larger historical, cultural import of the city—then gives way to the emphasis on the connection to the sacred, urban spaces. As the camera pans across the sacred leaves and colorful beads, the community that is part of these processes is highlighted: from the market woman picking leaves to the supplicant walking through the market in search of the items and the spiritual and emotional support they represent.

I see in these sequences a centralization of the Black female subject as the intermediary, conduit one may say, between the ancestral and the sacred in the urban space. As the initial wanderer seeking a resolution to doubt, she here visibilizes an engagement with the sacred in the cityscape—she will not only ask Oxalá for guidance but will assert her agency to locate it in these multiple sites. As the visuals of the religious alternate with sequences of celebration—it affirms the Black female subject's "place of speech" (subject positioning)—affirming an existence in spaces that affirm the cultural Afro-descended practices. This is reinforced by the specificity of the chorus—various sacred leaves ("folhas sagradas") or Folhas de Orô, which are sacred plants and leaves (but also seeds and roots) used in religious ceremony. In this first listing, "Para-raio, bete branca, assa peixe," the song moves from Chinaberry to Bétis branco or Ewê boyi fun-fun to assa-peixe or ironweed, which is a leaf associated with Ogún that "produces a white floral display that suggests Oxalá's color preference."[46] The second set that follows these: "abre caminho/patchouli . . . ," link these leaves to patuás or protective amulets historically used (particularly in the late nineteenth century) by devotees to protect the body from evil.[47]

The last part of this phase of the journey, albeit an ongoing one on a larger scale, and represented by the repetitions of the subject's arc –of searching without resolution, represent what I see as akin to M. Nourbese Philip's concept of the "public genealogy of resistance" that centralizes histories, names, and places of Black pain, language, and opposition, which are "spoken with the whole body and present to the world, to our geography, other rhythms, other times, other spaces."[48] In these last moments the connection of the female and the sacred is heightened as both individual journey of the Black female subject and as symbolic representation of the possibilities for the collective (a collective space of union). The final sequences of images moves the female and the sacred out of the specificity of the cityscape and returns to the sea. In a scene evocative of a passage through the "Door of no return" on Gorée Island, the Black female subject walks toward the bay dressed in a blue dress with shades of white, linking her to Yemanjá—the orisha of the ocean. As she enters the water, she enters a space that is not only of historical, cultural, and religious significance of enslavement, survival, physical, cultural, and economic transport but also of spiritual cleansing and revival—thus completing—within this musical and visual cycle—the work of the sacred leaves and the spatial and spiritual renewal of the Black female subject.

I would like to now briefly turn to Xênia and the music video for her single—"Why do you call me"/"Pra que me chamas?," cowritten with Lucas Cirillo, a comember of the group Aláfia, and directed by Fred Ouro Preto.[49] As a musical and visual celebration of ancestrality and Black female empowerment, I see Xênia's single and video in dialogue with Luedji's work as an application of a poetics of landscape that helps her create a "site of speech" (subject positioning) through which she expresses the complexity of her identity. At the same time, another important element of note in Xênia's musical and visual text is that of cultural critique, calling out those in society guilty of cultural appropriation and an exploitation of African cultural forms for personal interest. As Anderson Hebreu observes: "the track deals with questions related to cultural appropriation, where the symbols of the Black population are adopted without the necessary foundation, reflection, values and meanings, but a culturally dominant and opposing group"[50] (translation mine).

Similar to Luedji, Xênia's personal and professional development of her Black female subjectivity is shaped by the confluence of the historical and cultural context that surrounded her in Bahia, together with the opportunities for a greater political consciousness facilitated by her move to the Southeast, specifically to São Paulo. For Xênia, the move to São Paulo, initially to

pursue modeling, opened her up to possibilities to be a part of collective affirmations of Afro-Brazilian cultural pride, which she began through collaborations with the rapper Emicídio and emphasized as part of the group Aláfia
from 2011 to 2015. The objective of the group drew on images and concepts
that reflected their places as Black Brazilians, "of what it is today to be a
Black artist in Brazil without fear of being neither Black, nor pop or critic.
. . . That word came to us through Candomblé. There when people confirm
something we say aláfia."[51] As Eduardo Breschó, one of three singers in the
group, explained of the Afrodiasporic roots of the band's name,

> That word came to us through Candomblé. When people confirm something we
> say aláfia. It is one of the results of cowrie-shell divination, the mythological
> stories [odu] of happiness, of prosperity, of what you will be able to achieve or
> what you desire are also called aláfia.[52] (translation mine)

For Ferreira de Queiroz, it is in fact the link with the symbolic, ancestral
power of reinvention through Candomblé, available to Black women, alongside the agential, contestatory self-naming discourses embodied by Cleonora
Hudson-Weem's Africana Womanism that serve as a key to understanding
the narrative power of Xênia's video and song, encompassing qualities such
as "genuine sisterhood, strength, spirituality, unity with the Black man in
the struggle, respect for elders, as well as the maternal, nourishing role"[53]
(translation mine).

It is this affirmation of the power of roots—including African ancestrality as cosmovision and guide, in dialogue with the spiritual and geographic
routes she traversed, that became for Xênia a key element of the personal
and musical development as a Black woman from the Northeast that she
infused into her debut album, a process that incorporated a recognition of her
intersectional identity, channeled through the narration of lived experience
embodied in Evaristo's *escrevivência*. As she notes, "it is an album about
emotion, ancestrality, intimacy, faith, restlessness and identity. It is about how
I affirmed myself in the city of São Paulo. . . . For a Black person a voice is a
very powerful tool. And *Xênia* is an essay about having a voice"[54] (translation
mine). Musically, similar to Luedji's rejection of any singular musical vision,
Xênia's álbum would draw on multiple Afro-Brazilian and Afro-diasporic
musical influences, which included Yoruba influenced rhythms (and imagery), samba-rock, R&B and neo-soul, and jazz, in order to affirm strategies
of empowerment and connection.[55]

In my discussion of the music video and song I would like to highlight
three categories of images and image sequences that relay Xênia's linking of
ancestrality and empowerment, both personal and collective, that also foreground a diasporic and transnational vision that highlights a cultural, musical,

and spiritual dialogue between Brazil and Cuba. These are the images of the sea, the communal encounter of Black women and Xênia's transcendent climb to the top of the mythic space as the embodiment of the orisha Eleguá. As Xênia observes regarding the song's beginning, which is also indicative of themes running throughout: "I start my disc at the beginning, referencing my ancestors, because I know that my history does not begin with me"[56] (translation mine). Inspired by a trip to Cuba that opened her up to the connection with multiple diasporas[57] the song's title is a reference to the *orikí* (parable of an orixáa) used in Santeria to call on Eleguá (the equivalent of Exu in Candomblé) that states "Why do you call me if you don't know me?"[58] In this opening track Xênia starts with this salution to Eleguá/Exu, the one to whom the *ebo* (a ritual practice) is offered and who in turn takes the offering to the other orishas. This transnational gesture is the beginning of the musical-visual pairing that Xênia creates that on one hand includes a musical landscape that combines the ancestral influences of Yorubá cultures, the sacred drums of Run, Rumpi e Lé used in Candomblé rituals, and sacred batá drum of the Cuban Santeria with twenty-first-century electronic instrumentation.[59] On the other hand, Xênia's video treatment of the song presents the singer-songwriter in various moments wearing a long red dress representing Oyá (the orixáa that is the queen of the wind, lightning, and storms), in a geographical space, that while set on a piece of land in urban São Paulo, is digitally revised in postproduction to symbolize a mythic spiritual site, interspersed with images that include the orisha Exu at the crossroads, the Ibeji twins, and various Black women reading significant African-diasporic texts in communion together.[60] In its totality, the video serves as a visual resignification of the cultural and spiritual space of the Black female subject and addresses the power of the intermediary connection with the orishas, together with the valorization of a Black female sisterhood. This mixing of the spiritual with contemporary Afro-diasporic knowledge is ultimately part of a larger narrative of affirmation, celebration, and challenge to both cultural appropriation and national discourses of racial whitening.

In the song and its video, Xênia opens with both a sense of affirmation and critique. As Ferreira de Queroz notes, the song's structural use of a musical prologue and epilogue, incorporating sounds of African-descended rituals, is reflective of Yoruba cosmogony.[61] Through the opening ritual where the name Elegbara (alternate name for Exu used by the fons for vodun) can be heard, to the closing song for Exu, pronounced in the midst of a series of call-and-response and accompanied by African-derived drumming, Xênia affirms an African diasporic spiritual foundation and framing for her message.[62] As critique, she begins by challenging restrictive, limiting presentations of Black Brazilian religious culture by the dominant culture (by including the reference to Ibeji—the Yoruba twins and Aganju—the manifestation of Eleguá) through the reference to the pejorative terminology used. By also noting how African diasporic culture and Blackness have been culturally inscribed and relegated to its greatest visibility during Carnival February, Xênia not only brings awareness to the marginalizing discourses at play, but also makes the spectator aware of the many ancestral roots and geographical and cultural routes of collective Black Brazilian survival, resistance and agency that are in fact present.

As she observes, "Not even ibeji/For o ibge is a twin . . ." (translation mine), this reference to the Yoruba twins immediately marks the African diasporic presence as a central touchstone in the commentary that will follow. In continuation the observation of: "The baiana, the baiano/That are [only] remembered in revelry in February" (translation mine) begins the verse with the condemnation of the stereotypical representation of Black Brazilian culture only at the height of Carnival, which hides the complexities of its global imagery of unfettered excess, alongside its presentation of possibilities for transformation but also for a masking of "the poverty and social misery that mars the Brazilian sociopolitical body."[63] Yet, together with this critique is that of the invisibilizing of *baiano* and their existence as historical and contemporary subjects in their own right throughout the year(s). When Xênia continues: "Aruanda, Aganjú, Azondô, Ajayô/Ancient words, far from just onomatopoeia"[64] (translation mine), this listing of terms challenges the cultural and historical distortions, presenting names that correspond to sites, communities, and spiritual figures important to Afro-Brazilian religious and cultural life-from Aruanda, the mythic home of the orixas, the divine spirits of Brazilian cosmology and Congo cosmology, to Aganjú, the son of the orisha Obatalá (the sky god).[65]

This critique of those who want to reap the benefits of Black culture without any acknowledgment of its historical and cultural roots becomes an even more pointed protest of cultural appropriation repeated at several moments throughout the video but particularly from the third stanza leading into the chorus. The first line of this section directly challenges the outsider: "From time to time/One opens their mouth without being native born" (translation mine), and establishes the geographical and cultural decontextualization that occurs. The verses that follow (a few of which I cite here) ending in the title phrase: "To take for themselves the banner of beauty, of the struggle, of the gift. . . . Why do you call me if you don't know me?"[66] highlight the depth of this act, as an appropriation of the complexity of the pain and beauty of the experiences of Afro-descendants.

Similar to Luedji's visual representation of the historical and cultural power of the sea, the video begins with an inversion in which these historical to spiritual contextualizations, from Middle Passage and social death to the transmission of African cosmovisions and possibilities of rebirth, are given primacy. In this journey to the New World, one of the ideological and discursive challenges—to the sublimation of African identities below discourses of racial whitening (*branquitude* in Portuguese)—is represented by the burning of a White, blonde female doll (an image later repeated near the end of the song) and the later image of the doll's head being broken off. This image in part responds to the intersectional oppressions under which Black girls (in many parts of the African diaspora—including Brazil and the United States) and later Black women operate. In addition, as Ferreira de Queiroz notes, it directly challenges the dominant discourses of racial whitening, of which Fanon among others speaks, that condition Black children to self-hate and identification with their oppressor (8). The imagery of fire that engulfs the doll can be seen as dual in function: serving as both destruction of these discourses and as a cleansing force. In particular the burning doll serves as a visual allusion to and subversion of the historic 1963 Clark doll experiment of racial socialization where Black children presented with dolls of different racial features and skin color (Black and White in particular) preferred the White one, demonstrating the privileging of a dominant discourse of Whiteness over the perceived ugliness of Blackness and to the scarcity of positive images of Black dolls for little girls in Brazil.[67]

This cultural critique is soon overlaid with visual affirmation of the ancestral and its representation through the power of the collective. What results is a visual representation of the poetics of landscape that McKittrick describes. While developing new, Afro-diasporic centered pathways across these multiple geographic sites, Xênia's imagery respatializes feminism in dialogue with ancestrality –centralizing Black female bodies as intermediaries of the spiritual-terrenal link. An initial image linked to the Orisha Oxalá (the oldest orisha, related to the act of creation) extending an invitation to enter this kingdom (and enter into communion) is followed by a Black female sisterhood representing African heritage and a collective response to the struggles faced by Black women through the use of African-inspired clothing and masks that for Ferreira de Queiroz allude to archetypes of *yabás and* the traditions of female African warriors from the kingdom of Kush to Daomé.[68] The images of the community of Black women in various forms of solidarity—from celebration to reflection, is repeated in multiple spaces throughout the video: initially in the midst of nature, but later in a private, domestic space.[69] This image of the collective is then alternated with the individual—the single Black female representative of Oyá (in this case Xênia) dressed in red, with an African inspired head piece and followed by alternations between the three images in rapid succession. In a later adaptation of this sequence a representation of an orisha is holding a baby—representing new birth and the connection of ancestrality to the future generation.

The link of ancestrality to the present is further represented by the placement of Black women in private interior spaces, engaged in acts of solidarity, and communion. The first I would like to reference occurs in a healing bath (in which we later see Xênia, wearing an African turban), creating a link with the sacred leaves (folhas sagradas) highlighted in Luedji's video, in a room that evokes a domestic space of spiritual communion and the sharing of knowledge. The women in the first of these scenes wear the masks alluding to Black female warrior traditions while in another Xênia's video persona is having her hair braided as a physical and symbolic representation of sisterhood and the affirmation of the African-influenced natural hair styles (along with the larger cultural affirmation it represents), while in yet another, Xênia's video persona extends hands to another Black woman in a physical and symbolic representation of spiritual communion and unity.

In a separate scene the video shifts presents a linking of sisterhood to a counter narrative to hegemonic discourses, creating a connection of the ancestral/spiritual (through the evocation of Candomblé and Santeria seen and heard throughout) and the logocentric. This is presented through the image of several Black women reading texts that represent a sample of Afro-diasporic and particularly Afro-Brazilian knowledge production (fictional and non-fictional), including: *Um Defeito de Cor/A Color Defect* by Ana María Gonçalves (2006), *Quem Tem Medo do Feminismo Negro/Who is Afraid of Black Feminism* by Djaimila Ribeiro (2019), and *Na Minha Pele/In My Skin* by Lázaro Ramos (2017). I would like to call particular attention to the novel by Gonçalves that highlights the journey of a freed African woman returning to Brazil (the site of her former enslavement) in search of her missing son and then returning again to Africa, alongside the Black feminist autobiographical essay by Ribeiro that challenges the history of silencing that impacted her and many other Black women in Brazil. I see these examples of Black women's writings specifically, along with the identification of singer-songwriter made by Xênia (and Luedji) as yet another example of the expansive, contestatory migratory subjectivity of which Davies speaks—highlighting texts by Black women that "pursue the path of movement outside the terms of dominant discourses" (37). Ultimately, the reference to both ancestral—and written discourse as generators of knowledge and sources of guidance is symbolically paired with the multiple images of Exu (here represented by a Black female figure) dancing at the crossroads.[70] While not occurring in the urban space of Bahia as Luedji's video—the interweaving of nature and the private, of Black female subjects and the orishas also centralizes the connections of ancestrality, and the power of female collectivity and mediation with the spiritual, what Ferreira de Queiroz also identifies as a representation of the principles of Africana Womanism and the strength of matrifocality throughout the African diaspora, including Brazil:

In the clip, there is an imagetic constitution of strength and power through Black women: this is connected to their important position in Yoruba society and in Afrodescendant rites, that, wraps itself in the principles of Africana Womanism. Those spaces of knowledge reiterate the woman's role of birthing knowledge as something central, just like the African matrilineal characteristic. In Brazil, the socioeconomic situation produced by slavery forced Black women to exercise matrifocaliy, an aspect that united with matrilinearity when they constructed the first *terreiros* (Candomblé houses of worship) in the country.[71]

I would like to end with the conclusion to Xênia's visual treatise connecting ancestrality and Black female subjectivity, solidarity and agency. Amidst alternating images once more of the guiding force of Exu at the crossroads the camera presents an overhead shot of a strip of land leading to a visual representation (or allusion to) a baobab tree (the natural representation of the symbolic dwelling of the orishas). This constructed sacred space (using the power of technology to create a mythic space in the midst of an urban landscape) in its minimalism also serves to highlight the image of the sole Black female (Xênia)—dressed in the red robes of Oyá—wearing her crown and walking toward this summit. This confluence is a final visual embodi-ment of the potentiality of the Black female subject—embodying the divine in an act that can symbolically, when placed within the totality of the video, provide a final symbolic representation of her capacity for self-affirmation and transcendence. The final image, highlighting the divine Black female subject on the strip of land—continuing on the terrestrial journey toward the mythic—in the midst of a vast body of water—brings me back to the image in Luedji's "Sacred Leaves Bath." In one sense, here too the juxtaposition of the Black female subject, the orisha Oyá, and the ocean emphasize the multiple strategies of ancestrality and spiritual connection found in both Luedji and Xênia's visual compositions and representations of the Black female body's movement through their carefully constructed poetics of landscape. For both women, the musical-visual articulations create collective ties and African dia-sporic counternarratives that both challenge historical marginalizations and invisibilizations of the Black Brazilian woman in the national Brazilian space and present possibilities of subject positioning (site of speech) as strategies of subjectivity, empowerment and resistance.

BIBLIOGRAPHY

"Afropunk & Feira Preta Present 'Black to the Future,'" *Afropunk*, November 11, 2019, https://afropunk.com/2019/11/afropunk-feira-preta-present-black-to-the -future.

Akotirene, Carla. "Cruzando o Atlántico em memória da Interseccionalidade," in *Interseccionalidade (Feminismos Plurais).* São Paulo: Pólen, 2019.

Avelar, Idelbar, and Christopher Dunn. "Introduction: Music as Practice of Citizenship in Brazil," in *Brazilian Popular Music and Citizenship.* Durham, NC: Duke University Press, 2011, 3–4.

Barbosa, Helena Campos e Jorge Cardoso Filho. "Manifestos para Ouvir: experiência estética genderizada e racializada a partir de Luedji Luna." Compós, XXIX Encontro Anual da Compós, June 23–25, 2020 (Universidade Federal de Mato Grosso do Sul, Campo Grande—MS), 4–6.https:// Barbosa, Helena Campos and Jorge Cardoso Filho. "Manifestos para Ouvir: experiência estética genderizada e racializada a partir de Luedji Luna." Compós, XXIX Encontro Anual da Compós, June 23–25, 2020. Universidade Federal de Mato Grosso do Sul, Campo Grande—MS, 4–6. https:// d1wqtxts1xzle7.cloudfront.net/65038737/barbosa_cardosofilho-with-cover-page -v2.pdf?Expires=1640108280&Signature=H8lR13o80emckdPfwgtTYHgerva99 -JQT7TLXgl9s6vutZR2Ipr3KJT4MAareYjN3kBABrQym72jQOAQWml3SqFY SlwIu-7gWeRW43NKm6sQ9zAAoQC~j71ddXXApOnlOyJc0F9f5TVT94kNWo whs0Q3~caWrMY6D-cTNvDOI1fCksQjGEjuHyrNV2ebJdHK4nBeDs8ZkNOG 3Qc-6-SOv8oSccd66qRep~RxDLROPmFVQ1EBbJKm-9a0FnFtFLyCwONBQZ YBkyzXxpVlQOol4Ma1nbrdxGYkALoPO4ySNNOGyIsc7gSsbiQ975DyJPrym6 gn1nzUXbamvB0Z6blNlQ__&Key-Pair-Id=APKAJLOHF5GGSLRBV4ZA.

Berman, Michael, *Divination and the Shamanic Story.* Newcastle Upon Tyne, Cambridge Scholars Press, 2008.

Brooks, Daphne, *Liner Notes for the Revolution: The Intellectual Life of Black Feminist Sound.* Boston: Harvard University Press, 2021, 68.

Carneiro, Sueli, "Mulher Negra," in *Escritos de uma vida: Sueli Carneiro.* Belo Horizonte: Grupo Editorial Letramento, 2018, 13–61.

Crenshaw, Kimberle. "Demarginalizing the Intersection of Race and Sex: A Black Feminist Critique of Antidiscrimination Doctrine, Feminist Theory, and Antiracist Politics," *University of Chicago Legal Forum* 1989, no. 1, 139–67. https://chica-gounbound.uchicago.edu/cgi/viewcontent.cgi?article=1052&context=uclf

Daniel, G. Regina. *Race and Multiraciality* in Brazil and the United States: Converging Paths?. University Park: Pennsylvania State University Press, 2006.

Daniel, Yvonne. *Dancing Wisdom: Embodied Knowledge in Haitian Vodou, Cuban Yoruba and Bahian Candomblé.* Urbana: University of Illinois Press, 2005.

Da Silva, Joselina, org. *O Pensamento de/por Mulheres Negra.* Belo Horizonte: Nandyala, 2018.

Davis, Carole Boyce, *Black Women, Writing and Identity: Migrations of the Subject.* New York: Routledge, 1994.

Dixon, Kwame. *Afro-Politics and Civil Society in Salvador da Bahia, Brazil.* Tallahassee: University Press of Florida, 2016, 5.

Durán-Almarza, Emilia, and Álvarez-López, *Diasporic Women's Writing of the Black Atlantic: (En)gendering Literature and Performance.* New York: Routledge, 2014, 3.

Evaristo, Conceição. "A Escrevivência e seus subtextos," in *Escrevivência a escrita de nós: Reflexões sobre a obra de Conceição Evaristo,* org. Constância Lima

Duarte and Isabella Rosado Nunes, Rio de Janeiro: Mina, Comunicação e arte, 2020, 26–47.

Evaristo, Conceição. *Becos da memória.* Rio de Janeiro: PALLAS, 2017.

Ferreiro de Queiroz, Rafael Pinto. "A Cota é Pouca e o Corte é Fundo': Analisando o Videoclipe *Pra Que Me Chamas?* de Xênia França por meio de Epistemologias negras." *Revista Tropos: Comunicação Sociedade e Cultura* 10, no. 1 (July 2021), 1–28. https://periodicos.ufac.br/index.php/tropos/article/view/4508.

Ferreira de Queiroz, Rafael Pinto. "Cruzando a órbita prum novo mar." *Revista de Comunicação, cultura e política 21* no. 43, May 24, 2021, https://doi.org/10.46391/ALCEU.v21.ed43.2021.211

França, Xênia, "Estou curando minhas feridas acessando a minha história, diz Xênia França," interview by Kamille Viola, *Rio Adentro,* September 11, 2018, https://rioadentro.blogosfera.uol.com.br/2018/11/09/estou-curando-minhas-feridas-acessando-a-minha-historia-diz-xenia-franca/.

França, Xênia. "O sonho afro-americano de Xênia França," interviewed by Beatriz Moura, *Vice,* September 29, 2017. https://www.vice.com/pt/article/pakm7m/xenia-franca-entrevista

França, Xênia. *Xênia,* 2017.

Gumes, Nadia Vladi, and Marcelo Argolô, "Dossiê: A cor dessa cidade sou eu: ativismo musical no projeto de Aya Bass*," Revisa ecopos.eco.ufrj.br* 23, no. 1, 2020, 219–38, https://revistaecopos.eco.ufrj.br/eco_pos/article/view/27454.

Harding, Rachel, *A Refuge in Thunder: Candomblé and Alternative Spaces of Blackness,* Bloomington: Indiana University Press, 2000.

Hebreu, Anderson, "Natura apresenta 'Pra Que Me Chamas': single do novo álbum de Xênia França" *Portal Geledés,* September 16, 2017, https://www.geledes.org.br/natura-apresenta-pra-que-me-chamas-single-do-novo-album-de-xenia-franca/

Luna, Luedji, "Quería ser a Luedji Luna dos meus pais, do projeto político, mais a Luedji mesmo é cantora e compositora." interview by Joanna Oliveira, *El País,* May 11, 2019. https://brasil.elpais.com/brasil/2019/05/03/cultura/1556887397_823639.html.

———. "Luedji Luna—'Diálogos Ausentes' (2017)," November 14, 2017, Interview with Itaú Cultural, video,YouTube, 1:10, https://www.youtube.com/watch?v=agVPrvyacxI&t=352s.

McElroy, Isis, "O reino de Aruanda: de porto luso-angolano de escravos a reino mítico afro-brasileiro," *Scripta* 11, no. 20, 127–35.

McKittrick, Katherine. *Demonic Grounds: Black Women and the Cartographies of Struggle.* Minneapolis: University of Minnesota Press, 2006.

Ouro Preto, Fred, "Xênia França: Pra que me chamas (Interview for Berlin Music Awards 2019), interviewed by Noemi Berkowitz, 11-:38, https://www.dailymotion.com/video/x85ftfn?fbclid=IwAR0IGEyL6OE0vOtP6uiIotpAmh6Xn8kzg_AXckdsu4a7e5sE0Tx7xG46EME.

Pereira, Amilcar Araujo. *O Mundo Negro: Relações Raciais e a Constituição do Movimento Negro Contemporâneo no Brasil,* Rio de Janeiro: PALLAS: FAPERJ, 2013.

Perry, Kheisha-Khan. *Black Women Against the Land Grab: The Fight for Racial Justice in Brazil*, Minneapolis: University of Minnesota Press, 2013.

Ribeiro, Djamila. *Lugar de Fala (Feminismos Plurais)*, São Paulo: Pólen Livros, 2019.

Roberto, Eduardo e Araújo, Peu. "Orgulho Cismado: A Criação do Afropopfuturismo Brasileiro em 'Corpura,' Novo Disco de Aláfia." September 11, 2015. https://www .vice.com/pt/article/rnnpvx/alafia-corpura-lancamento-2015.

Santanna, Marilda. "Ancestralidade e feminismo negro nas performances d Luedji Lune e Larissa Luz: portadoras de vozes políticas," *Revista Feminismos 9, no.* 1, 87–94. https://periodicos.ufba.br/index.php/feminismos/article/view/43364.

Schmidt, Simone Pereira, "Mulheres, negritude e a construção de uma modernidade transnacional," *Revista Estudos Feministas* 27, no.1, 2019, 1–10. https://doi.org/10 .1590/1806-9584-2019v27n158957

Seigel, Micol. *Uneven Encounters: Making Race and Nation in the United States*, Durham, NC: Duke University Press, 2009.

Stampone, Caroline. "Online Conversation Series: 'A Place of Speech,' according to Djamila Ribeiro." Bergen Network for Women in Philosophy, May 4, 2021, https:// www.uib.no/en/bnwp/143973/%E2%80%9C-place-speech%E2%80%9D-accord-ing-djamila-ribeiro.

Sterling, Cheryl, *African Roots, Brazilian Rites: Cultural and National Identity in Brazil.* New York: Palgrave Macmillan, 2012.

Valdés, Vanessa K. *Oshun's Daughters: The Search for Womanhood in the Americas.* Albany: SUNY Press, 2014.

Voeks, Richard A. *Sacred Leaves of Candomblé: African Magic, Medicine and Religion in Brazil.* Austin: University of Texas Press, 1997.

Wilkinson, Doris Yvonne, "Racial Socialization through Children's toys: A Sociohistorical Examination," *Journal of Black Studies* 5, no. 1, September 1974, 96–109.

NOTES

1. Durán-Almarza, Emilia, and Álvarez-López, *Diasporic Women's Writing of the Black Atlantic: (En)gendering Literature and Performance* (New York: Routledge, 2014), 3.

2. Avelar, Idelbar, and Christopher Dunn. "Introduction: Music as Practice of Citizenship in Brazil," in *Brazilian Popular Music and Citizenship* (Durham: Duke University Press, 2011), 3–4

3. Brooks, Daphne, *Liner Notes for the Revolution: The Intellectual Life of Black Feminist Sound* (Cambridge: Harvard University Press, 2021), 68.

4. For two noteworthy studies that extend these comparative economic studies to an expansion of the role of race and nation building in the U.S. and Brazil see G. Reginal Daniel, *Race and Multiraciality in Brazil and the United States: Converging Paths?*, (University Park: Pennsylvania State University Press, 2006) and Micol Seigel, *Uneven Encounters: Making Race and Nation in the United States* (Durham: Duke University Press, 2009).

5. Da Silva, Joselina, org. *O Pensamento de/por Mulheres Negras* (Belo Horizone: Nandyala, 2018), 8.

6. Xênia França, "Estou curando minhas feridas acessando a minha história, diz Xênia França," interview by Kamille Viola, *Rio Adentro,* September 11, 2018, https://rioadentro.blogosfera.uol.com.br/2018/11/09/estou-curando-minhas-feridas-aces-sando-a-minha-historia-diz-xenia-franca/.

> estão se reapropriando do seu discurso, da sua maneira de fazer música, da sua cara de volta na capa. É un fenômeno de artistas independentes dando seu recado.

7. I use this phrase pairing "place of speech" (subject positioning) drawing on an approximation by Caroline Stampone of the Bergen Network for Women in Philosophy of the concept of "Lugar de fala" as articulated by Djaimila Ribeiro in her text *Lugar de Fala (Feminismos Plurais)* (São Paulo: Polen Livros, 2019), 63–64, discussed in more detail shortly in this chapter. The translation of this term has been a source of continuous discussion with other possibilities presented being: "locus of speech" ("Djamila Ribeiro," Wikipedia entry) and "standpoint."

8. Carneiro, Sueli, "Mulher Negra," in *Escritos de uma vida: Sueli Carneiro* (Belo Horizonte: Grupo Editorial Letramento, 2018), 15–16.

9. Ribeiro, *Lugar de Fala,* 64. "O falar não se restringe ao ato de emitir palabras, mas a poder existir. Pensamos lugar de fala como refutar a historiografia tradicional e a hierarquização de saberes consequente da hierarquia social."

10. Crenshaw, Kimberlée. "Demarginalizing the Intersection of Race and Sex: A Black Feminist Critique of Antidiscrimination Doctrine, Feminist Theory, and Antiracist Politics," *University of Chicago Legal Forum* 1989, issue 1, 149. https://chicagounbound.uchicago.edu/cgi/viewcontent.cgi?article=1052&context=uclf

11. Akotirene, Carla. "Cruzando o Atlántico em memória da interseccionalidade" in *Interseccionalidade (Feminismos Plurais]* (São Paulo: Pólen, 2019).

12. Davis, Carole Boyce, *Black Women, Writing and Identity: Migrations of the Subject* (New York: Routledge, 1994), 36–37.

13. McKittrick, Katherine. *Demonic Grounds: Black Women and the Cartographies of Struggle* (Minneapolis: University of Minnesota Press, 2006), x.

14. McKittrick, *Demonic Grounds,* xi

15. McKittrick, *Demonic Grounds,* xxiii-xxiv.

16. Gumes, Nadia Vladi, and Marcelo Argolô, "Dossiê: A cor dessa cidade sou eu: ativismo musical no projeto de Aya Bass," *Revisa ecopos.eco.ufrj.br 23, no. 1, 2020, 225,* https://revistaecopos.eco.ufrj.br/eco_pos/article/view/27454.

17. Gumes and Argôlo, "A cor dessa cidade," 220

18. "Afropunk & Feira Preta Present 'Black to the Future,'" Afropunk, November 11, 2019, https://afropunk.com/2019/11/afropunk-feira-preta-present-black-to-the-future.

19. Gumes and Argôlo, "A cor dessa cidade," 225. "O projeto Aya Bass constrói uma experiência política/estética que coloca no mesmo patamar o trabalho musical e discursivo ativista em prol do feminismo negro."

20. Santanna, Marilda. "Ancestralidade e feminismo negro nas performances d Luedji Lune e Larissa Luz: portadoras de vozes políticas," *Revista Feminismos 9, no. 1, 90.* https://periodicos.ufba.br/index.php/feminismos/article/view/43364.

21. Pereira, Amilcar Araujo. *O Mundo Negro: Relações Raciais e a Constituição do Movimento Negro Contemporâneo no Brasil* (Rio de Janeiro: Pallas: FAPERJ, 2013), 9, 40.

22. Luna, Luedji, "Quería ser a Luedji Luna dos meus pais, do projeto político, mais a Luedji mesmo é cantora e compositora." interview Joanna Oliveira, *El País,* May 11, 2019. https://brasil.elpais.com/brasil/2019/05/03/cultura/1556887397 _823639.html.

Os filhos da militância foram educados para ocupar espaços de poder, qualquer coisa que dêsse poder econômico, posição social e que mudasse um pouco a narrativa.

23. Santanna, "Ancestralidade e feminismo negro," 90.

24. Itaú Cultural, "Luedji Luna—'Diálogos Ausentes' (2017)," November 14, 2017, video,*YouTube,* 1:10, https:// https://www.youtube.com/watch?v=agVPrvyacxI &t=352s.

A escrita foi minha catarse, minha salvação, minha cura.

25. Santanna, "Ancestralidade e feminismo negro," 90.

26. Barbosa, Helena Campos and Jorge Cardoso Filho. "Manifestos para Ouvir: experiência estética genderizada e racializada a partir de Luedji Luna." Compós, XXIX Encontro Anual da Compós, June 23–25, 2020 (Universidade Federal de Mato Grosso do Sul, Campo Grande—MS), 4–6.https:// Barbosa, Helena Campos and Jorge Cardoso Filho. "Manifestos para Ouvir: experiência estética genderizada e racializada a partir de Luedji Luna." Compós, XXIX Encontro Anual da Compós, June 23–25, 2020 (Universidade Federal de Mato Grosso do Sul, Campo Grande—MS), 4–6. https://d1wqtxts1xzle7.cloudfront.net/65038737 /barbosa_cardosofilho-with-cover-page-v2.pdf?Expires=1640108280&Signature =H8lR13o80emckdPfwgtTYHgerva99-JQT7TLXgl9s6vutZR2Ipr3KJT4MAar-eYjN3kBABrQym72jQOAQWml3SqFYSlwIu-7gWeRW43NKm6sQ9zAAoQC ~j71ddXXApOnlOyJc0F9f5TVT94kNWowhs0Q3~caWrMY6D-cTNvDOI1f-CksQjGEjuHyrNV2ebJdHK4nBeDs8ZkNOG3Qc-6-SOv8oSccd66qRep ~RxDLROPmFVQ1EBbJKm-9a0FnFtFLyCwONBQZYBkyzXxpVlQOol4Ma1n-brdxGYkALoPO4ySNNOGyIsc7gSsbiQ975DyJPrym6gn1nzUXbamvB0Z6blNlQ_ _&Key-Pair-Id=APKAJLOHF5GGSLRBV4ZA.

27. Evaristo, Conceição. "A Escrevivência e seus subtextos," in *Escrevivência a escrita de nós: Reflexões sobre a obra de Conceição Evaristo,* org. Constância Lima Duarte and Isabella Rosado Nunes (Rio de Janeiro: Mina, Comunicação e arte, 2020), 30.

Nossa escreviência traz a experiência, a vivência de nossa condição de pessoa brasileira de origem africana, uma nacionalidade hifenizada, na qual me coloco e me pronuncio para afirmar a minha origem de povos africanos e celebrar a minha ancestralidade e me conectar tanto com os povos africanos, como com a diáspora africana.

Evaristo first develops the concept of *escrevivência* (a term Evaristo coined from the combination of writing/**escrita** and experience/**vivência**) which I leave in its original Portuguese, in the Introduction to her novel *Becos da memória*. There she states that:

At its base (at its core), in the foundation of the narrative of *Becos* is an experience, that was mine and of my people. Writing *Becos* was pursuing a *writexperience*. For this reason I also look for a first narration, what came before the writing. I look for the voice, the speech of whomever is speaking (telling the story), to mix with mine . . . / "Na base, no fundamento da narrativa de *Becos* está uma vivência, que foi minha e dos meus. Escrever *Becos* foi perseguir uma *escrevivência*. Por isso também busco a primeira narração, a que veio antes da escrita. Busco a voz, a fala de quem conta, para se misturar om a minha."

28. Itaú Cultural, "Luedji Luna—'Diálogos Ausentes' (2017)."
29. Santanna, "Ancestralidade e feminismo negro," 91.
30. Schmidt, Simone Pereira, "Mulheres, negritude e a construção de uma modernidade transnacional," *Revista Estudos Feministas* 27, no.1, 2019, 6. https://doi.org/10.1590/1806-9584-2019v27n158957.
31. Schmidt, "Mulheres, negritude e a construção . . . ," 7.

a determinação em assumir a negritude como projeto amplo e transnacional, voltado simultaneamente para dentro (as questões urbanas, os imigrantes) e para for a (as rotas da diaspora, o passado das travessias atlânticas, a memória das viagens, das trocas culturais e da escravidão).

32. Dixon, Kwame. *Afro-Politics and Civil Society in Salvador da Bahia, Brazil* (Tallahassee: University Press of Florida, 2016), 5.
33. Dixon, *Afro-Politics and Civil Society*, 101.
34. Itaú Cultural, "Luedji Luna—'Diálogos Ausentes' (2017)," 1:57–2:07.

Comecei a perceber que Salvador, a pesar das contradições e das violências e do racismo, . . . era uma cidade onde eu me via, era um espelho para mim.

35. Harding, Rachel, *A Refuge in Thunder: Candomblé and Alternative Spaces of Blackness* (Bloomington: Indiana University Press, 2000), 2.
36. Sterling, Cheryl, *African Roots, Brazilian Rites: Cultural and National Identity in Brazi* (New York: Palgrave Macmillan), 12.
37. Ferreiro de Queiroz, Rafael Pinto. "A Coa é Pouca e o Corte é Fundo': Analisando o Videoclipe *Pra Que Me Chamas?* de Xênia França por meio de Epistemologias negras." *Revista Tropos: Comunicação Sociedade e Cultura* 10, no. 1, 10. https://periodicos.ufac.br/index.php/tropos/article/view/4508.
38. Ferreiro de Queiroz, "A Cota é Pouca," 15.
39. Sterlin, *African Roots*, 25.

40. Valdés, Vanessa K. *Oshun's Daughters: The Search for Womanhood in the Americas* (Albany: SUNY Press, 2014), 9.

41. Valdés, *Oshún's Daughters*, 9.

42. Audre Lorde in Vanessa Valdés, *Oshún's Daughters*, 31.

43. McKittrick, *Demonic Grounds*, xxiii.

44. For both "Bath of Sacred leaves" by Luedji Luna and "Why do you call me" by Xênia França, all translations are mine.

45. Schmidt, "Mulheres, negritude e a construção de uma modernidade transnacional," 7.

É assim, falando de corpo e de não pertencimento, de travessias e memórias, que encontramos em Luedji Luna o cenário que sintetiza o Brasil urbano contemporâneo. O corpo no miundo, à solta pela cidade, canta a solidão da diáspora.

46. Voeks, Robert A. *Sacred Leaves of Candomblé: African Magic, Medicine and Religion in Brazil* (Austin: University of Texas Press, 1997), 130.

47. Voeks, Robert A. *Sacred Leaves of Candomblé: African Magic, Medicine and Religion in Brazil* (Austin: University of Texas Press, 1997), 108, 124.

48. McKittrick, *Demonic Grounds*, xvii.

49. Ferreira de Queiroz, "A Cota é Pouca 4.

50. Hebreu, Anderson, "Natura apresenta 'Pra Que Me Chamas': single do novo álbum de Xênia França" *Portal Geledés*, September 16, 2017, https://www.geledes .org.br/natura-apresenta-pra-que-me-chamas-single-do-novo-album-de-xenia-franca.

a faixa aborda questões relacionadas à apropriação cultural, onde os símbolos da população negra são adotados sem o devido fundamento, reflexão, valores e significados, por um grupo culturalmente oposto e dominante.

51. Roberto, Eduardo e Araújo, Peu. "Orgulho Cismado do Afropopfuturismo Brasileiro em 'Corpura,' Novo Disco de Aláfia." September 11, 2015. https://www .vice.com/pt/article/rnnpvx/alafia-corpura-lancamento-2015.

 do que é ser hoje no Brasil um artista negro sem medo de ser nem negro, nem pop, nem crítico.

52. Roberto, Eduardo e Araújo, Peu. "Orgulho Cismado."

Essa palavra veio até nós pelo candomblé. Lá quando a gente confirma alguma coisa falamos aláfia. Um dos resultados do jogo de búzios, o odu de felicidade, de prosperidade, de que você vai conseguir realizar o que você quer se chama aláfia também.

53. Ferreira de Queiroz, "A Cota é Pouca," 4. "irmandade genuína, fortaleza, espiritualidade, unidade com o homem negro na luta, o respeito aos mais velhos, assim como o papel maternal e nutridor."

54. Xênia França, "O sonho afro-americano de Xênia França," interviewed by Beatriz Moura, *Vice*, September 29, 2017. https://www.vice.com/pt/article/pakm7m /xenia-franca-entrevista

é um disco sobre afetividade, ancestralidade, intimidade, fé, inquietações e identidade. É como sobre como eu me autoafirmei na cidade de São Paulo. . . . A voz para a pessoa negra é uma ferramenta muito poderosa. E *Xenia* é um ensaio sobre ter voz.

55. Moura, Beatriz, "O sonho afro-americano de Xênia França."
56. Xênia França, "O Sonho afro-americano de Xênia França."

Começo o meu disco pelo começo, referenciando os meus ancestrais, porque sei que a minha história não começa comigo.

57. Xênia França, "Estou curando minhas feridas ."
58. Daniel, Yvonne. *Dancing Wisdom: Embodied Knowledge in Haitian Vodou, Cuban Yoruba and Bahian Candomblé* (Urbana: University of Illinois Press, 2005), 321. Ferreira de Queiroz, "A Cota," 4. "Pra que tu me llamas si tu no me conoces?" For information from the director regarding the creation of the mythic space see: Fred Ouro Preto, "Xênia França: Pra que me chamas (Interview for Berlin Music Awards 2019), interviewed by Noemi Berkowitz, 11-:38, https://www.dai-lymotion.com/video/x85ftfn?fbclid=IwAR0IGEyL6OE0vOtP6uiIotpAmh6Xn8kzg_AXckdsu4a7e5sE0Tx7xG46EME.
59. Ferreira de Queiroz, Rafael Pinto. "Cruzando a órbita prum novo mar." *Revista de Comunicação, cultura e política* 21, no. 43 (May 24, 2021), https://doi.org/10.46391/ALCEU.v21.ed43.2021.211
60. Ferreira de Queiroz, "A Cota é Pouca," 5.
61. Ferreira de Queiroz, "A Cota," 7.
62. Ferreira de Queiroz, "A Cota," 7
63. Sterling, Cheryl, *African Roots, Brazilian Rites,* 87.
64. Xênia França, "Pra que me chamas?," *Xênia*, 2017.

Nem mesmo ibejí/ Para o ibge é gêmio / . . . A baiana, o baiano/Que são lembrados da folia/ em fevereiro / Aruanda, Aganjú, Azonodô, Ajayô/Palavra veia, longe da onomatopeia.

65. McElroy, Isis, "O reino de Aruanda: de porto luso-angolano de escravos a reino mítico afro-brasileiro," *Scripta*, vol. 11, no. 20, 129. Berman, Michael, *Divination and the Shamanic Story* (Newcastle Upon Tyne: Cambridge Scholars Press, 2008), 170.
66. Xênia França, "Pra que me chamas."

De vez en quando/Um abre a boca sem ser oriundo/Para tomar pra si mesmo o estandarte da beleza, luta e o dom . . . Porque, tu me chamas se não me conhece . . . ?

67. Wilkinson, Doris Yvonne, "Racial Socialization through Children's toys: A Sociohistorical Examination," *Journal of Black Studies* 5, no. 1, (September 1974), 102–3.
68. Ferreira de Queiroz, "A Cota, " 19.
69. Ferreira de Queiroz, "A Cota," 5.
70. Ferreira de Queiroz, "A Cota," 5.

71. Ferreira de Queiroz, "A Cota," 9–10.

No clipe, há uma constituição imagética de força e poder através de e pelas mulheres negras: isto é conectado à posição de importância destas na sociedade iorubá e nos ritos afrodescendentes, que, por sua vez, encaixam-se nos princípios do Mulherismo Africana. Esses lugares de conhecimento reiteram o papel femenino de gestar potências como algo central, assim como o caráter matrilinear africano. No Brasil, a situação socioeconômica gerada pela escravidão forçou as mulheres negras a exercerem a matrifocalidade, aspecto que se uniu à matrilinearidade quando estas construíram os primeiros terreiros no país.

Chapter 2

The Black Woman as Leader in the Bunde and Bullerengue

Algris Xiomara Aldeano Vásquez

The bunde and bullerengue constitute an artistic "expression of Blackness in Latin America," which expression is representative of the popular oral literature from Darién, Panama. In the first place, I will demonstrate that, whereas the white supremacist mainstream of Western academe dismisses this expression as mere "folklore," the forms do, in fact, constitute a classical African artistic expression that is born of humankind's earliest literary expressions, developed by Africans from the Nile Valley; and that, indeed, "The African Origin of Civilization" is a reality. These classical literary expressions from the Nile Valley were scribal as well as oral. More pertinently, I will show that in this Black literary expression from Darién, the Black woman plays a central role. Furthermore, one of the most important distinguishing features of the civilization and culture of the ancient Africans is the preeminence of the woman. The best articulation of this centrality is "The Legend of Ra and Isis," a literary text from ancient Egypt.

Kimberlé Crenshaw's Intersectionality theory has been rightfully acclaimed by many scholars deemed to have met the standards imposed by the Western academic mainstream. When, in 1980, Molefe Kete Asante launched his theory of Afrocentricity with his *Afrocentricy: The Theory of Social Change*, his reception was not nearly as warm. Over the decades, Asante has built on his original ideas; and the concept of "Africology" has emerged as fundamental. Indeed, Ian Isidore Smart in his latest book, like Asante, sees "Africology" to be fundamental; and for this reason, his book is entitled: *"Amo a mi raza": Un enfoque africológico sobre la literatura hispanoamericana* ["I love my race": An Africological focus on Hispanic-American Literature.]. As a Black woman, I, along with scholars like Asante and Smart, see Africology as fundamental. The question of the Intersectionality of Black Latina women must take into account the Africological foundation. Unfortunately, consequent on the imposition of what Martin Bernal—on the very first page of *Black Athena*—labels the "Aryan Model" by European ideologues at the end of the eighteenth century, the irrefutable fact of the African origin of civilization has been replaced by the alternative facts that the ancient Greeks were taught the ways of high civilization by Aryan invaders. Insofar as Intersectionality per se considerably diminishes the fundamental significance of race—i.e., systemic racism—it tends to facilitate white supremacy. Every scholar has the right and the obligation to stake out her position and to defend it with rational arguments, with logic. The establishment—which is white supremacist—does not have the right, the authority, to lay out for her what should be her starting point. All that the establishment can do is assess the validity of her arguments, the logical validity.

On the very first page of his *Black Athena*, Bernal writes:

> These volumes are concerned with two models of Greek history: one viewing Greece as essentially European or Aryan, and the other seeing it as Levantine, on the periphery of the Egyptian and Semitic cultural area. I call them the "Aryan" and the "Ancient" models. The "Ancient Model" was the conventional view among Greeks and in the Classical and Hellenistic ages. According to it, Greek culture had arisen as the result of colonization, around 1500 BC, by Egyptians and Phoenicians who had civilized the native inhabitants. Furthermore, Greeks had continued to borrow heavily from Near Eastern cultures.[1]

Bernal stops short of showing how the Big Lie of the Aryan Model was invented to salve the consciences of European intellectuals for having reaped such incredible wealth from the two greatest crimes against humanity, namely, the conquest of America and the transatlantic slave trade. The Aryan Model is founded on alternative facts, which blatantly contradict the consistent and unequivocal claims by the ancient Greeks that they were introduced to the ways of high civilization by people from the heart of Africa, the land known as Cush or Nubia. This land is today's Sudan; and now, as in those ancient times, the inhabitants of this land are of a jet-black complexion; and for that reason the Greeks referred to them as Ethiopians. Furthermore, the creation account in Genesis 2 explicitly mentions Cush as within the boundaries of the Garden of Eden. It is no wonder, then, that the ancient Greeks deemed the Cushites/Ethiopians to be the most upright and beautiful of all human beings.

Since, as Bernal argues convincingly, the Academy is inescapably in the grip of the Aryan Model, I have opted for an Afrocentric—or more precisely, an Africological—analysis of an artistic "expression of Blackness in Latin America." This Africological analysis cannot be contained within the strict limits of Crenshaw's Intersectionality theory. The focus on abstruse, eclectic, esoteric theoretical discussions has been the diversionary tactic of the mainstream white supremacist academy, consuming the energy and time of the Afrocentric scholar, chasing down red herrings instead of getting to the heart of the matter—i.e., debunking white supremacy. Indeed, Smart (in unpublished conversations) holds that the case of Charles W. Mills is a perfect illustration of the point. In his pivotal *The Social Contract*, Mills presents with unsurpassed scholarship unassailable arguments exposing the outrageous fallacies concocted by the inventors of the Aryan Model. However, the guardians of the gates of academe have kept this immense wealth of knowledge and insight under tight seal within the extremely limited confines of the "ivory tower," so that all of Mills's gigantic efforts ultimately signify almost nothing.

The Africological approach requires that we "do for self" as the Honorable Marcus Mosiah Garvey recommended; or as Asante asserted: "begin from where you are, that is . . . if you are African American, begin with your own history and mythology."[2] Furthermore, there is, in fact, what Smart terms an amazing connection between the Intersectionality theory and the quintessential African intellectual tradition, which is humanity's authentic classical intellectual tradition, given, as Cheikh Anta Diop compellingly argues, and as Mercer Cook presents to the Anglophone world, *The African Origin of Civilization: Myth or Reality*. Henry Louis Gates, as we will show, connects the Signifying Monkey, the trickster, "pícaro" to Legba, the Yoruba Oricha of the crossroads, the intersection, the communicator, the door of entry. This will make Legba the divinity of the intersection (Intersectionality).

Diop's work compellingly argues for "The African Origin of Civilization." And it was the French intellectual Count Constantine Francis Chassebeuf de Volney—ironically a contemporary of Thomas Jefferson—who proclaimed in *The Ruins of Empires*: "There a people, now forgotten, discovered, while others were yet barbarians, the elements of the arts and sciences. A race of men now rejected from society for their *sable skin and frizzled hair*, founded on the study of the laws of nature, those civil and religious systems which still govern the universe"[3].

This, of course, is a confirmation of Diop's work. Gates, in *Black Literature & Literary Theory*, posits compellingly that:

> The Signifying Monkey is a trickster figure, of the order of the trickster figure of Yoruba mythology, Esu-Elegbara in Nigeria, and Legba among the fon in Dahomey, whose New World figurations—Exu in Brazil, Echu-Elegua in Cuba, Papa Legba in the pantheon of the *loa of Vaudou* in Haiti, and Papa La Bas in the *loa* of Hoodoo in the United States—speak eloquently of the unbroken arc of metaphysical presuppositions and patterns of figuration shared through space

and time among black culture in West Africa, South America, the Caribbean and the United States. These trickster figures, aspects of Esu, are primarily *mediators*: as tricksters they are mediators, and their mediations are ticks.[4]

Legba is the divinity of the crossroads, the intersection. He is the mediator, the communicator. He is Thoth, he is Hermes. He is the divinity of literature. Williams Crenshaw has demonstrated the foundational significance of the crossroads or intersection in the developing of an analytical framework. In this respect Crenshaw's theorizing dovetails with Gates in that the crossroads or intersection become central.

The evidence is overwhelming that this significance of the crossroads/ intersection is a feature that flows from the African intellectual tradition. Since, as the historical data indisputably establish, the African intellectual tradition was established "while others were yet barbarians." In fact, James P. Allen, an Egyptologist, a specialist in linguistic and cultural studies, in *Middle Egyptian: An Introduction to the Language and Culture of Hieroglyphs*, asserts on the very first page: "Egyptian first appeared in writing shortly before 3200 BC and remained a living language until the eleventh century AD." Furthermore, in chapter 14, "The Memphite Theology," he presents the powerful information and insights put forward by Diop, but in terms that are more accessible to the generalist. Allen explains that the Memphite Theology is a text from ancient Egypt that is "devoted to the role of [the god] Ptah in the creation. . . . It begins with a reference to the Heliopolitan creation account and the notion of the creative word: 'Evolution into the image of Atum occurred through the heart and occurred through the tongue.'" Allen concludes his essay as follows:

> The Memphite Theology is one of the most sophisticated texts that has survived from ancient Egypt [Kemet]. . . . By identifying Ptah as the intermediary between the creator's intellect and the physical evolution of the world, it anticipated the notion of the demiurge in Greek philosophy more than five hundred years later, a notion that eventually found its way into Christian philosophy, as expounded in the opening words of the Gospel of John:

>> In the beginning was the Word, and the Word was with God, and the Word was God. He was in the beginning with God. Through him all things came into being, and of all that has come into being not one thing came into being except through him (John 1:1–3)

Just by itself, the Memphite Theology is enough to place Egyptian thought squarely in the line, and at the beginning, of the great traditions of Western philosophy.[5]

I am a Black woman from Darién, and the artistic expression of my focus are the song and dance forms known as the bunde and bullerengue, which are representative of the popular oral literature from Darién, Panama. I fully understand that emancipation from mental slavery requires the use all the resources at our disposal, that I be as much a woman of action, a strategist as a scholar. Therefore, I am deeply engaged in the promotion of cultural activities in my native Panama, specifically in my native village of El Real de Santa María la Antigua, in the province of Darién. The crowning achievement in this regard so far was the revival of the Bunde and Bullerengue Festival. Working closely with Lesbia Aldeano, then the head of SEPRODACAN (Spanish acronym for the Secretariat for Sustainable Development of the Province of Darién and Annexed Native Territories), I organized the 2017 Bunde and Bullerengue Festival held in El Real on May 19 to 20. This was the first of the new series of festivals celebrating the cultural heritage of my native province.

Since my book, *Bunde and Bullerengue: Popular Oral Literature from My Native Region, Darién*, is the first scholarly work dedicated exclusively to the bunde and bullerengue, I am, by that very fact, the world's leading scholar in this field. Furthermore, it should be noted that since Darienites have been such a marginalized group within Panama, in spite of their Panamanian nationality, they might be deemed to have greater cultural affinity with the inhabitants of Colombia's Caribbean zone and those of northeast Chocó. For obvious reasons, then, the bunde and bulleregue can be presented as fundamentally African artistic expressions; and arguably it is legitimate to connect these artistic expressions with the fictional universe of Gabriel García Marquéz's most important novel, *One Hundred Years of Solitude*. This is significant since this universe in centered in Macondo located in García Márquez's native region, the Caribbean Zone of Colombia.

In my book, I focus on two telling points of contact between the aesthetic of the García Márquez novel and that of the bunde and bullerengue. In the first instance, the novel unfolds in a universe of magical reality which is centered on Ursula, the powerful female character, given that her memory is the axis on which the history of the family, and consequently that of Macondo itself, revolves. Secondly, I posit that the aesthetic of the bunde and bullerengue is based on rhythm. Rhythm is fundamentally repetition. One of the most vibrant scholarly voices on the matter of rhythm is that of Kofi Kissi Dompere, an Ashanti man from Ghana, who in *Polyrhythmicity: Foundations of African Philosophy,* declares that rhythm is both ontology and epistemology. I also point out that the Mexican poet and sage, Octavio Paz (1914–1998) has affirmed that poets of the modernist school (which flourished at the end of the nineteenth century) introduced a totally new element to Hispanic aesthetics, namely, the idea of rhythm as access to transcendence.

Mythical time—transcendence—is cyclical. But the very idea of transcendence as mythical time, or eternal life, as cyclical is the foundation of every philosophical system developed by Africans. And it must be borne in mind that at the very dawn of human history, when there existed neither Greek, nor Chinese, nor any other civilization, Africans from the Nile Valley had already developed a great civilization, the source of all human civilization.

Academic research is the continuation of a long chain of studies undertaken by scholars over the course of human history. However, the bunde and bullerengue have received little attention from canonical scholars. One of the few references in the scholarly literature to bunde and bullerengue is to be found in *Folklore: Cultura popular tradicional de Panamá* [Folklore: Panamanian Popular Traditional Culture]. Therein, Francisco Paz de la Rosa declares: "We could say that the bunde is the authentic Panamanian Christmas celebration"[6].

In the Hispanic world, Christmas celebrations are extremely important; and the song that is traditionally associated with these celebrations is the *villancico*. Indeed, this genre is an essential part of the repertoire of Hispanic traditional popular literature. When Paz de la Rosa declares that "the bunde is the authentic Panamanian Christmas celebration," he is simply indicating that the bunde is the Panamanian version of the *villancico*. In Trinidad, an island of the West Indies that shares a cultural heritage with Venezuela and Colombia, there is a very popular brand of Christmas music known as "parang" (a term derived from the Spanish "parranda"). Daphne Pawan Taylor authored a work entitled *Parang of Trinidad* which presents useful information on the form.

The well-known specialist in Afro-Hispanic literature Rosa E. Valdés-Cruz speaks in *La poesía negroide en América* [Negro Poetry in the Americas] of a form called the bunde, which emanates from the Caribbean region of Colombia, asserting: "In the romantic novel, *María,* the author, the Colombian Jorge Isaacs, includes a bunde or popular song in chapter lvii; two black boatmen chant a sad song." And this song, according to Valdés-Cruz, "served as the model for a later composition by Candelario Obeso, the Afro-Colombian poet. Obeso wrote a delicate boat song which he called 'The Homesick Boatman's Song.'"[7]

For the Colombian Jorge Isaacs (1837–1895)—author of the immortal romantic novel *María*, which was published in 1867, the very year of the founding of Howard University—the bunde is simply a popular song developed by Blacks from the Magdalena River Basin, while for Paz de la Rosa, it is a version of the *villancico* and would therefore, as we indicated earlier, be related to the "parang." And Manuel Zapata Olivella (1920–2004), that twentieth-century Colombian intellectual giant, agrees with Isaacs when he presents in the notes to his novel, *Changó, el gran putas* [*Chango, the Baddest SOB*], the following definition of the bunde: "A generic term used in Cartagena de las Indias (in the seventeenth century) to reference dances practiced by Blacks"[8].

For the people of Darién, the bullerengue is the song and dance form associated with the "tamborito," a drum dance assembly organized to celebrate special moments in the life of the community. It is always the woman who convokes the assembly; and it is only women who can sing at the event, although both men and women participate in the dance. Men, however, are the ones charged with the essential task of drumming. From the dawn of human history, it has been the woman who has ruled the individual household as well as the community at large. This is surely a consequence of the fact that it was the woman who discovered the science and art of agriculture, the basis of civilization itself. Thus, it could be said that Darienite society preserves intact one of human civilization's fundamental customs. With the passage of time and the changes consequent on modernity, the interest in organizing drum dances has declined; and the bullerengue was on its way to becoming just one more item in the region's folklore repertoire. Nowadays, however, there has been a resurgence of interest in drum dance assemblies and in the bullerengue as well as in other song and dance forms that are typical of the region.

Paz de la Rosa affirms that "The bullerengue is Darién's most characteristic Black dance form." This sensual dance is a symbolic representation of procreation, with both men and women participating in the dance, while only women do the singing.

> It is characterized, above all, by the air of concentration or introspection with which the woman executes her movements. She slides, rather than walks, using tiny steps (in a clockwise direction), with her soles squarely planted on the ground and her feet close together. Her legs are locked together, projecting the image of something inaccessible, of a licentious forbidden fruit. . . . The woman alternates the gliding movement of her soles with more sweeping ones at times, and reaches a climax when she executes what is known as the "bosar," which is the typical continuous movement of hips and stomach, while the male companion, as if in a trance, takes this to be a sign of approval and uses the opportunity to move in for a hit, but without any luck, for the woman slips away and evades him with a quick side step and turn.[9]

The whole question of rhythm recalls the work of the late great Fela Kuti and his Afrobeat. There is one song, "Lady," that still resonates with its irrepressible Pan-African energy. And Fela's poetic language sings the versatility of the African woman as, full of irony, he goes along with the false distinction between the African woman and the African lady. Fela sings that when the lady—as distinct from the woman—is called upon to dance: "She go dance lady dance." And he repeats when you call a lady to dance: "She go dance lady dance." But we all know that the African lady is also the African woman, and when the African woman—as distinct from the lady—is called upon to dance: "She go dance the fire dance." And again, he repeats, when you call an African woman to dance: "She go dance the fire dance."[10] The African woman/lady dances with the same sublime elegance with which Pan-African ladies/women from Darién dance the bullerengue.

Dance is fundamental to our culture. And the Dogon sage Ogotommêli, in his conversations with the French anthropologist Marcel Griaule, asserted that "the first attested dance had been a dance of divination; it had told in the dust the secrets of the Word contained in the fibres worn by the dancer."[11] In the liturgies of the traditional African spirituality systems, the devotee becomes the spokesperson of the orisha when s/he is mounted/possessed. This state of trance is achieved through dance; and, in it, the devotee makes known the will of the god. The possessed dancer, then, is the point of communication between man and the transcendental forces. And this occurs when a human being gets into a state of deeper harmony with the supernatural forces once s/he is totally in sync body and soul with the transcendental energy. For this reason, dance is as much a form a discourse as is the spoken word.

Although of late the practice and popularity of the drum dance assemblies has been rekindled, it can be said that in times past these activities took place with greater frequency and as such were part and parcel of daily life. From the point of view of outsiders, these assemblies are pure entertainment. These outsiders fail to grasp the connection between spirituality and culture; they fail to grasp that these forms of "entertainment" spring from the African cultural tradition in which the sacred and the secular are not separated. This is the same ignorance that led Thomas Jefferson to assert in *Notes on the State of Virginia* with reference to enslaved Africans: "They seem to require less sleep. A black, after hard labor through the day, will be induced by the slightest amusements to sit up till midnight, or later, though knowing he must be out with the first dawn of the morning."[12]

The Jeffersonian misunderstanding is quite a common one. Few are those who understand that bullerengue and Carnival, just like the festivities in honor of the patron saint of a community, are more than mere "amusements." They are cultural activities of great importance through which a society can come to terms with itself come to terms with its basic raison d'être.

It is interesting to consider that the plural form of the term used by the ancient Egyptians to refer to God is "*nTrw*" and that, as Allen affirms in

Middle Egyptian: "Egyptian gods and goddesses are nothing more or less than the elements and forces of the universe. The gods did not just 'control' these phenomena, like the Greek god Zeus with his lightning bolts: they *were* the elements and forces of the world."[13] It would, then, be reasonable to suggest that "*nTrw*" is the etymon of the Latin term "natura" (nature). If nature is the totality of the gods and goddesses, a human being would better be able to communicate with the gods and goddesses when he is in direct contact with nature, that is, with the earth. Clearly, then, shoes would serve as a barrier between the dancer and nature. Similarly, cutlery—especially made of metal or, even worse, of plastic—would serve as a barrier between the human being and the food she is consuming. It is for this reason that in many African cultures, even today, the hands are used to take food from plate (and frequently it is a common dish) to mouth.

The *tamborito* drum dance assemblies take place in the open air on a village street in the province of Darién. A ring is formed, and the dancers enter one couple at a time. The woman leads the way; and, when the man joins her, they both turn to face the drums to show their respect. This touch, of course, is taken directly from the established practice in Santeria rites. The Darienite *tamborito*, like all such drum dance assemblies, is not a choreographed activity; it is totally spontaneous. This very spontaneity constitutes its central feature and makes it possible for the dancers to establish contact with the transcendental forces. It must be admitted that participants in these activities, even the ones who stick most closely to the tradition, are generally unaware of the deep theological and philosophical implications of these customs. With respect to the question of the woman as leader, Fela says it with such forceful beauty: "She go say, she go say, 'I be lady, oh.'" And, to be perfectly clear: "She go say him equal to man." To sum it all up: "She go say him get power like man/She go say anything man do himself fit do."[14]

Fela the master poet is signifying at the deepest level—and remember, "signification is a nigger's occupation." He is playing on the false distinction shallow people make between "lady" and "woman." This becomes abundantly clear when one considers that in the socioeconomic order that emerged in Africa consequent on the brutal underdevelopment imposed by the conquering Aryan barbarians, the market woman is truly the most powerful force. She controls the household economy, therefore, as the golden rule dictates, she rules, notwithstanding the viciously patriarchal order imposed by the colonizers. In fact, in this perverted colonial and postcolonial world, the market woman can, indeed, declare herself to be "equal to man." The African woman/lady can legitimately declare that "him [masculine and feminine third person singular subject and object personal pronoun] get power like man/She go say anything man do himself fit do."

However, the powerful woman is a recurring theme in African philosophical and theological systems. One of the most compelling expressions of this central concept is the story recounted by the British Egyptologist, E. A. Wallis Budge, whose work was produced at the turn of the twentieth century. Budge, in his introduction to *The Egyptian Book of the Dead*, designates this account as "The Legend of Ra and Isis" and explains in a footnote: "The hieratic text of this story was published by Pleyte and Rossi, *Le Papyrus de Turin*, 1869–1876, pll. 31–77, and 131–38; a French translation of it was published by M. Lefébure, who first recognized the true character of the composition."[15]

Isis is a Greek corruption of the name Auset, hailed by the ancient Africans as the great Mother of God. Ra is the sun god. In some of the doctrines developed by the people of Kemet—and it must be remembered that Kemet existed as a unified nation for at least three thousand years—Ra is the name given to the Supreme Being. Indeed, in the first formulation of the doctrine of the Trinity, Ra was seen as one of the three persons composing the One True God. The text of the legend begins as follows: "Now Isis was a woman who possessed words of power; her heart was wearied with the millions of men, and she chose the millions of the gods, but she esteemed more highly the millions of the *khu's*. And she meditated in her heart, saying, 'Cannot I by means of the 'sacred name of God make myself mistress of the earth and become a goddess like unto Ra in heaven and upon earth?"[16]

The stage is clearly set. Auset (Isis) is a powerful woman who decides to make herself the most powerful of beings. She is not content with mere preeminence; she sets out to be the most preeminent of all. To do so, she would have to unseat Ra from his position of ultimate preeminence, and she precisely forms this resolve. Ra, the legend tells, is now an old man who dribbles. Auset (Isis) gets hold of some of this saliva, "kneaded it with earth in her hand, and formed thereof a sacred serpent in the form of a spear."[17]

The serpent stings Ra, and he becomes gravely ill. He cries out:

> "I came forth to look upon that which I had made, I was passing through the world which I had created, when lo! something stung me, but what I know not. Is it fire? Is it water? My heart is on fire, my flesh quaketh, and trembling hath seized all my limbs. Let there be brought unto me the children of the gods with healing words and with lips that know, and with power which reacheth unto heaven." The children of every god came unto him in tears, Isis came with her healing words and with her mouth full of the breath of life, with her enchantments which destroy sickness, and with her words of power which make the dead to live.[18]

The text vividly portrays Ra's powerful position as the creator. However, he is not here the One True God. The Kemites deemed Ra to be a *nTr*, a term translated as "god" with a lowercase "g." The One True God is also a *nTr*. In this context, the term *nTr* would have to be translated as "God" with an uppercase "G." The Kemetic term is, then, the exact equivalent of the Yoruba "orisha." Eschu Elegbara also called Papa Legba, one of the most important of the *nTrw* or "orishas" of the Yoruba.

Auset (Isis) is at this point also a powerful being. She is one of the four children of the sky goddess, Mut, and the earth god, Geb. Her siblings are Wosir, Set, and Nephtys. In the realm of mythology, as in the realm of poetry, the principle of non-contradiction does not apply. "A" can be what in the realm of human logic is "Non-A." So, Auset is also Wosir's faithful consort. She it was who doggedly sought out the scattered parts of her slain consort/ brother and gathered them together so that he could regain the physical integrity necessary for resurrection. She it was, in fact, who with the help of Djehuti (Thoth) breathed life back into Wosir, thereby effecting his resurrection. This action is referenced in the words of the text, "and with her words of power which make the dead to live."

It must be pointed out that when Auset made the dead Wosir live again, it was with the life of a resurrected being and as king of the afterlife. Furthermore, although the legend makes no mention of any sexual congress, it turns out that Auset becomes pregnant. The clear sense of the Kemetic doctrine is that this was a case of parthenogenesis, a further manifestation of Auset's power. For the only part of Wosir's body she was unable to find was the organ of generation. Therefore, she made him a new one; and the *txn*, [obelisk] has passed on over all these many millennia as the symbol of Auset's power. Over the many millennia during which the Kemetic theology was developed, Wosir became indistinguishable from his and Auset's son, Heru (whom the Greeks called Horus). In the realm of mythology, then, Auset is sister, wife, and mother to Wosir.

Auset (Isis) drives a hard bargain: if Ra wants to be loosed from the deadly effects of the venom, he will have to reveal to her his secret name. Ra is, naturally, loathe to do so and attempts to pull rank.

I have made the heavens and the earth, I have ordered the mountains, I have created all that is above them, I have made the water, I have made to come into being the great and wide sea, I have made the "Bull of his mother," from whom spring the delights of love. I have made the heavens, I have stretched out the two horizons like a curtain, and I have placed the soul of the gods within them. I am he who, if he openeth his eyes, doth make the light, and, if he closeth them, darkness cometh into being. At his command the Nile riseth, and the gods know not his name. I have made the hours, I have created the days, I bring forward the festivals of the year, I create the Nile-flood. I make the fire of life, and I provide food in the houses. I am Khepera in the morning, I am Ra at noon, and I am Tmu at even.[19]

Auset (Isis) is not impressed with this recitation of power. She replies with consummate cheekiness: "What thou hast said is not thy name. O tell it unto me, and the poison shall depart."[20] Auset (Isis) prevails: "Now the poison burned like fire, and it was fiercer than the flame and the furnace, and the majesty of the god said, 'I consent that Isis shall search into me, and that my name shall pass from me into her.' Then the god hid himself from the gods, and his place in the boat of millions of years was empty."[21] Ra's concession cost him his standing among the gods.

The text makes clear that Auset gained the power of Ra not for herself but for her son. "And when the time arrived for the heart of Ra to come forth, Isis spake unto her son Horus, saying, 'The god hath bound himself by an oath to deliver up his two eyes' (i.e., the sun and moon)."[22] And the closing lines of text of the legend proclaim an all-powerful Auset (Isis).

> Thus was the name of the great god taken from him, and Isis, the lady of enchantments, said, "Depart, poison, go forth from Ra. O eye of Horus, go forth from the god, and shine outside his mouth. It is I who work, it is I who make to fall down upon the earth the vanquished poison; for the name of the great god hath been taken away from him. May Ra live! and may the poison die, may the poison die, and may Ra live!" These are the words of Isis, the great goddess, the queen of the gods, who knew Ra by his own name.[23]

Consistent with the "phallocentric" orientation of so-called Western culture, an attitude of self-confidence in a poet, usually of the popular tradition, has been termed macho boastfulness. And the prime manifestation of this macho boastfulness is the use of the "I." According to this line of reasoning, Auset is employing here macho boastfulness. Auset, then, is the first womanist. She is employing the tone of supreme confidence that only a woman can use. Her confidence can thus be termed "womanist boastfulness"; and it is clearly presented as superior to any kind of macho boastfulness. It is based on demonstrated superiority, not on wishful thinking. The legend reflects a fundamental belief in the preeminence of the mother. This wins out over the patriarchal thrust of what we call Western civilization. Women of African descent born into a society fashioned by White supremacy and having been consigned to the inferior role reserved for the female by the colonizer's cultural tradition, could only rescue their preeminence by becoming "manipulative and bossy." In this, they were following the model of the Great Mother.

The Jamaican poet Lorna Goodison was born on Emancipation Day, 1947 and was appointed Poet Laureate of Jamaica in 2017. She is one of those millions of women of African descent who strive to keep the faith with the example set by their Great Mother Auset. In her collection of poems so insightfully titled, *I Am Becoming My Mother*, Goodison presents the stirring story of Nanny, a legendary African woman of the line of Auset. Nanny was the warrior par excellence chosen from childbirth and trained for her mission, to be sent over as one of the enslaved to ignite the flame of revolution, to lead her people to liberation from the barbarism of chattel slavery imposed on them by the unconscionably brutish Aryan hordes. The poem, "Nanny," is composed of seven stanzas of varying length: four of six lines, one of seven, one of four and one of two. In the opening and closing lines of the penultimate stanza, Nanny identifies her mission: "And when my training was over / . . . I was sent, tell that to history." The two lines of the final stanza ring out the message of encouragement encoded in the declaration: "Keep hope alive"; as Nanny tells us: "When your sorrow obscures the skies / other women like me will rise."[24]

Miriam DeCosta-Willis (1934–2021), a native of Memphis, served for many years as professor of Spanish at Howard University. DeCosta-Willis edited *The Memphis Diary of Ida B. Wells: An Intimate Portrait of the Activist as Young Woman*. Ida B. Wells is one of those powerful African women inspired by Auset of whom Nanny spoke when she declared: "When your sorrow obscures the skies / other women like me will rise." DeCosta-Willis opens her introduction to the book as follows:

> Those of us who live in the 1990s cannot imagine what it was like to live in the South in the 1890s, in backwater towns like Holly Springs, Mississippi, and Elaine, Arkansas, and even in urban centers like Memphis, Tennessee, capital of that vast region of flatlands and cottonfields and shotgun houses known as the Mississippi Delta. Novelists and filmmakers have captured the images of that period: night riders cloaked in white, crosses aflame on hilltops, sudden awakenings at midnight, the piercing screams of women and children, two-room plantation shacks burned to the ground, and bodies mutilated and charred beyond recognition—the strange fruit of a violent terrain.[25]

This is very region which gave birth to George G. M. James's *Stolen Legacy*, according to the Asa G. Hillard's "Editor's Notes" to the 1985 edition of that pivotal work. It was as a professor at the HBCUs of this very region that James spent the last years of his life. It is the region that gave birth to Ida B. Wells, as Miriam writes, continuing the opening paragraph of her introduction:

> That was the world into which Ida Bell Wells was born on July 16, 1862. Just four years later and forty miles to the northwest, a White mob swept through the

streets of Memphis, pillaging, burning, raping and murdering innocent people. The three-day rampage ended with

46 Black men, women, and children killed

75 wounded

5 women raped

100 robberies

91 houses burned

4 churches burned

12 schools burned (U.S. Congress 1866, 36)[26]

And the Trumpist Republicans of fall 2018 had the audacity to cast the eminently reasonable and measured response to their outrageous and now murderous White nationalist behavior as "mob" rule. Echoing and, in fact, validating the poetic imagery of Fela's composition, "Lady," Miriam writes:

> The Memphis diary describes the intimate day-to-day life of a young Black teacher and journalist, who struggles in the mid-1880s with personal, financial, and professional problems. . . . She portrays herself as a fiery, ambivalent, and fiercely independent woman, at war constantly with contrary instincts: an incipient feminism, countered by a straitlaced Victorian femininity; a desire for male companionship, but no wish for marriage; and a longing for personal freedom, checked by a sense of duty to her family.

Eventually, she chooses, instead of domesticity, an active, male-related career while following a Victorian script in her personal life. The tension between these two ways of being is apparent in the diary, as Wells struggles to be "lady," using the polite language that defines that type, without compromising her strong "unladylike" qualities, such as pride, ambition, outspokenness, assertiveness and rebelliousness.[27]

And then in 2013 CaShawn Thompson shepherded into existence Black Girl Magic to "celebrate the beauty, power and resilience of black women." The direct inspiration was the example of Michelle Obama, but the energy flows ultimately from Auset: "Thus was the name of the great god taken from him, and Isis, the lady of enchantments, said, 'Depart, poison, go forth from Ra.' . . . These are the words of Isis, the great goddess, the queen of the gods, who knew Ra by his own name."[28]

Allen writes in his essay "The Creative Word": "The link between the creator's idea of the world and its actual creation lies in the first sentence of this text: 'I made my body evolve through my effectiveness.'"[29] He goes on to explain: "The quality of effectiveness is also closely related to the concept of . . . *HkA* 'magic' . . . Magic could involve physical means, such as the use of amulets or images to ward off evil, but most often it was associated with the power of creative speech: that is, speech that is 'effective' enough to cause a desired result."[30] The concept is of profound significance for people of African descent. And, clearly, the Legend of Ra and Auset establishes that the most powerful, that is, the most effective being in the universe is the Black woman, Auset. She is recognized as the Mistress of Magic and healing. She is the original weaver of Black Girl Magic.

As we saw, the central point of the theological statement known as the Memphite Theology associated with the city of Memphis on the Nile is the power of the creative word. And as Allen asserts this theological statement developed by Africans from Memphis on the Nile "anticipated the notion of the demiurge in Greek philosophy more than five hundred years later, a notion that eventually found its way into Christian philosophy, as expounded in the opening words of the Gospel of John."[31]

One of the epicenters of this power-full Black Girl Magic movement for the 2018 midterm elections is precisely Shelby County, Tennessee, of which Memphis is the capital city. That very same Memphis of Ida B. Wells, the Memphis of the Memphite Theology.There is a most solid historical link between this Memphis, the 2018 epicenter of the Black Girl Magic movement, the original Memphis, the Memphis of Auset, the Memphis on the Nile, and Darién, Panamá, my native land. It could be reasonably argued that the Biden-Harris administration is effectively a product of Black Girl Magic; and the Biden-Harris administration has as its guiding light the slogan, "Build Back Better." The goal enunciated in the slogan will never be achieved unless humanity acknowledges the power of the woman. The white supremacist minority is desperately seeking to maintain its grip on power. The Trumpist Supreme Court of the United States (SCOTUS) is its major weapon. And SCOTUS has declared itself not only white supremacist but flagrantly patriarchal.

The Big Lie that is the Aryan Model is not just a problem for people of African descent; the Big Lie and white supremacy have manifested themselves as the legendary "chickens that have come home to roost" in the very heart of so-called Western civilization. SCOTUS seems ready to strike down the woman's right to control her own body. This is a right that as our article has argued constitutes the very bedrock of African civilization. Now more than ever humanity needs to anchor itself firmly, unrelentingly to the principle of the woman as leader, taking to heart Lorna Goodison's powerful poetic words: "When your sorrow obscures the skies / other women like me will rise."

BIBLIOGRAPHY

Aldeano Vásquez, Algris Xiomara, *Bunde and Bullerengue: Popular Oral Literature from my Native Region, Darién.* Washington, DC: Original World Press, 2010.

Allen, James P. *Middle Egyptian: An Introduction to the Language and Culture of Hieroglyphs.* 3d ed. Cambridge: Cambridge UP, 2014.

Asante, Molefi Kete. *Afrocentricity: The Theory of Social Change.* Buffalo, New York: Amulefi Publishing, 1980.

Bernal, Martin. *Black Athena: The Afroasiatic Roots of Classical Civilization.* Vol. 1, *The Fabrication of Ancient Greece 1785–1985.* New Brunswick, N.J: Rutgers UP, 1987.

Budge, E. A. Wallis. *The Egyptian Book of the Dead: (The Papyrus of Ani) Egyptian Text Transliteration and Translation.* 1895. Reprint. New York: Dover, 1967.

DeCosta-Willis, Miriam, ed. *The Memphis Diary of Ida B. Wells: An Intimate Portrait of the Activist as Young Woman.* Boston: Beacon, 1995.

Diop, Cheikh Anta. *Civilization or Barbarism: An Authentic Anthropology.* Translated by Yaa-Lengi Meema Ngemi. Edited by Harold J. Salesmanson and Marjolijn de Jager. New York: Hill, 1991.

———. *The African Origin of Civilization: Myth or Reality.* Edited and translated by Mercer Cook. New York: Hill, 1974.

Dompere, Kofi Kissi. *Polyrhythmicity: Foundations of African Philosophy.* London: Adonis & Abbey, 2006.

García Márquez, Gabriel. *Cien años de soledad.* Edición Conmemorativa Real Academia Española Asociación de Academias de la Lengua Española., 2007.

———. *El amor en los tiempos del cólera.* Bogotá: La Oveja Negra, 1985.

Gates, Henry Louis Jr., ed. *Black Literature & Literary Theory.* New York: Methuen, 1984.

———. *The Signifying Monkey: A Theory of African-American Literary Criticism.* New York:Oxford UP, 1988.

Goodison, Lorna. *I Am Becoming My Mother.* London—Port of Spain: New Beacon Books, 1986.

Griaule, Marcel. *Conversations with Ototemmêli: An Introduction to Dogon Religious Ideas.* London: Oxford UP, 1970.

James, George G. M. *Stolen Legacy: The Greeks were not the authors of Greek Philosophy, but the people of North Africa, commonly called the Egyptians.* 1954. Reprint. San Francisco: Julian Richardson Associates, 1985.

Jefferson, Thomas. *Notes on the State of Virginia.* Edited by William Peden. Chapel Hill: U of North Carolina P, 1982.

Kuti, Fela. "Lady." www.genius.com/Fela-kuti-lady-lyrics.

Maloney, Gerardo. *Juega vivo.* Washington DC: Original World Press, 2009

———. *Cuentos étnicos.* Panamá: Formato 16, 2015.

Mills, Charles W. *The Racial Contract*. Ithaca: Cornell UP, 1997.

Paz de la Rosa, Francisco. *Folklore: Cultura popular tradicional de Panamá*. Panamá: Impresora Panamá, 2000.

Smart, Ian Isidore. *Amazing Connections: Kemet to Hispanophone Africana Literature*. Washington, DC: Original World Press, 1996.

———. *"Amo a mi raza": Un enfoque africológico sobre la literatura hispanoamericana*. Washington, DC: Original World Press, 2022.

———. *Can African Americans Make America Great?* Washington, DC: Original World Press, 2017.

———. *Nicolás Guillén, Popular Poet of the Caribbean.* Columbia: U of Missouri P, 1990.

———. *Occupying Western Civilization: Debunking the White Supremacist Narrative*. Washington, DC: Original World Press, 2012.

———. *The Gunning Down of Michael Brown: An Afrocentric Response*. Washington, DC: Original World Press, 2014.

———. *The Impeachment Can Make America Great*. Washington, DC. Original World Press, 2020.

Smart, Ian Isidore, and Kimani S. K. Nehusi, eds. *Ah Come Back Home: Perspectives on the Trinidad and Tobago Carnival*. Washington, DC: Original World Press, 2000.

Valdés-Cruz, Rosa E. *La poesía negroide en América*. New York: Las Américas, 1970.

Volney, C.F. *The Ruins, or, Meditation on the Revolutions of Empires; and the Law of Nature*. Peter Eckler edition 1890. Reprint. Baltimore: Black Classic Press, 1991.

Zapata Olivella, Manuel. *Changó, el gran putas*. Bogotá: Oveja Negra, 1983.

NOTES

1. Martin Bernal, *Black Athena: The Afroasiatic Roots of Classical Civilization. Vol 1: The Fabrication of Ancient Greece 1785–1985* (New Brunswick: Rutgers UP, 1987), 1.

2. Molefi Kete Asante, *Afrocentricity: The Theory of Social Change* (Buffalo: Amulefi Publishing, 1980), 10–11.

3. C. F. Volney, *The Ruins, or, Meditation on the Revolutions of Empires; and the Law of Nature* (Peter Eckler edition 1890. Reprint. Baltimore: Black Classic Press, 1991), 16–17.

4. Henry Louis Gates Jr., ed., *Black Literature & Literary Theory* (New York: Methuen, 1984), 286.

5. James P. Allen, *Middle Egyptian: An Introduction to the Language and Culture of Hieroglyphs* (Cambridge: Cambridge UP, 2014), 205, 206.

6. Francisco Paz de la Rosa, *Folklore: Cultura popular tradicional de Panamá* (Panamá: Impresora Panamá, 2000), 88, my translation.

7. Rosa E. Valdés-Cruz, *La poesía negroide en América* (New York: Las Américas, 1970), 18–19, my translation.

8. Manuel Zapata Olivella, *Changó, el gran putas* (Bogotá: Oveja Negra, 1983), 515, my translation.

9. Paz de la Rosa, *Folklore*, 85–86, my translation.

10. Fela Kuti. "Lady" (www.genius.com/Fela-kuti-lady-lyrics).

11. Marcel Griaule, *Conversations with Ogotommêli: An Introduction Dogon Religious Ideas* (London: Oxford UP, 1970), 187.

12. Thomas Jefferson, *Notes on the State of Virginia*, ed. William Peden (Chapel Hill: U of North Carolina P, 1982), 139.

13. Allen, *Middle Egyptian*, 54.

14. Fela Kuti, "Lady."

15. E. A. Wallis Budge, *The Egyptian Book of the Dead: (The Papyrus of Ani) Egyptian Text Transliteration and Translation* (1895. Reprint: New York: Dover 1967), xci.

16. Ibid., lxxxix–xc.

17. Ibid., xc.

18. Ibid.

19. Ibid., xc–xci.

20. Ibid., xci.

21. Ibid.

22. Ibid.

23. Ibid.

24. Lorna Goodison, *I Am Becoming My Mother* (London-Port-of-Spain: New Beacon Books, 1986), 45.

25. Miriam DeCosta-Willis, ed., *The Memphis Diary of Ida B.Wells: An Intimate Portrait of the Activist as Young Woman* (Boston: Beacon, 1995), 1.

26. Ibid.

27. Ibid., 3–4.

28. Wallis Budge, *Book of the Dead*, xci.

29. Allen, *Middle Egyptian*, 194.

30. Ibid., 195.

31. Ibid., 206.

Chapter 3

No me llames triguEña, soy negra

*Claiming Puerto Rican Blackness in
Adriana Parrilla's Photography*

Meaghan Jeanne Coogan

Adriana Parrilla is a photographer and photojournalist who was born and raised in San Juan, Puerto Rico and is currently dividing her time between Paris, France, and Puerto Rico. She received her BA in Modern Languages from the University of Puerto Rico and an MA in Photojournalism and Documentary Photography from Spéos Photographic Institute in Paris. Her work explores identity construction, race, and resilience and has been exhibited in the mainland United States, Puerto Rico, and France. Her photography series *No me llames 'triguEña'; soy negra / Don't Call Me 'TriguEña'; I'm Black* was exhibited in the Bronx Documentary Center's 3rd Annual Latin American Foto Festival in the summer of 2020. Parrilla's project challenges the use of euphemistic terms such as "triguEña" utilized in an effort to distance oneself and others from Blackness through an exploration of the role of hair in the racialization of Puerto Ricans, particularly Puerto Rican women, the intimacy between Afro-Puerto Ricans and the environment, and the tendency to ascribe Blackness to a geographical and temporal "elsewhere." In claiming the term "negra," Parrilla emphasizes the importance of naming and the deconstruction of dominant terms outlined by Black US and Latin American feminists before her. Their work has exposed how the supposedly universal categories such as "woman" and "Black" exclude and invisibilize Black women and demand a more nuanced understanding of oppression which recognizes and considers the interconnecting forms of marginalization which specifically act upon women of color. Parrilla's powerful embrace of Blackness and rejection of trigueñidad highlights the intersecting systems

83

of oppression that affect Black Latin American women and Black women of Latin American descent who are erased through Puerto Rico's practice of racial distancing through the discourse of mestizaje. Furthermore, working from several geopolitical intersections, Parrilla's series challenges the normative definitions and connotations of Blackness in the mainland United States, Puerto Rico, and France. Through her visual and textual meditations on her own experience as a Black woman growing up in Puerto Rico and subsequently living in France, Parrilla's *No me llames 'trigueña'; soy negra* contests Puerto Rico's celebration of proximity to whiteness and claims Blackness as an identity with liberatory potential.

Though the term "intersectional" was coined by Kimberlé Crenshaw in her 1989 essay "Demarginalizing the Intersection of Race and Sex: A Black Feminist Critique of Antidiscrimination Doctrine, Feminist Theory and Antiracist Politics," and has gained popularity internationally as well as nationally in recent years, Black feminists in the United States and in Latin America have long highlighted how oppression does not occur along a single axis, but rather is compounded by multiple systems of marginalization. Black feminists in the Americas have also outlined the exclusionary and discriminatory practices perpetuated by mainstream feminist and anti-racist movements, that tend to center identities which occupy a more privileged space in society, such as white or mestiza women and Black or indigenous men. For example, Afro-Puerto Rican feminist Ana Irma Rivera Lassén indicates that the foundation of La Red de Mujeres Afrolatinoamericanas, Afrocaribeñas y de la Diáspora (RMAAD) in 1992 hoped to remedy the lack of space afforded to issues concerning Black women at events such as the Latin American and Caribbean Feminist Encuentro.[1] Although dominant feminism, antiracism, and other liberatory movements have been built around identification with womanhood and Blackness, they have tended to view more nuanced or intersectional categories, such as Black queer woman, as divisive and as reinforcing the logics of domination by clinging to socially constructed labels.[2] Furthermore, this logic, rather than working for liberation of the most marginalized of society, mirrors the false objectivity of white and patriarchal thinking, in which minoritized groups are significantly excluded from "universal" identities. Thus, antiracist and feminist movements center supposedly universal categories such as "woman" and "Black" respectively. An intersectional analysis urges us to unmask such "universal" language to reveal that "woman" refers to white or mestizo women and "Black" refers to Black men. I would also argue that in a US context "woman" and "Black" are interpreted as both Anglo and nonimmigrant, which would exclude most of the Afrodescendant populations in the Americas, and consequently fails to include Afro-Puerto Ricans. This has led to the goal of erasure of difference, similar to the "color-blindness" favored by the US and French governments as well as the racial democracies boasted by many Latin American nations. While the acknowledgment of identity as something that must be viewed as dynamic and constructed is stressed by Afro-Puerto Rican and Afro-Dominican feminists such as Ana Irma Rivera Lassén, Yuderkys Espinosa Miñoso, and Ochy Curiel, they also emphasize the importance of self-definition and naming in the process of liberation and as a political strategy. Curiel's discussions with Black Latin American feminists groups in Honduras, Brazil, and the Dominican Republic reveal the centrality of identity in their work and how identities "se construyen a partir de relaciones y conflictos sociales, en la necesidad de revelar hechos invisibilizados, la necesidad de autoafirmación ante la dominación cultural blanca, la necesidad de crear conciencia de ser una 'otra,' la necesidad de re-simbolizar lo que el sistema racista considera negativo en positivo, la necesidad de crear solidaridades en la lucha política y saberse semejante a otro u otra parecida."[3] It is exactly this gesture of self-affirmation Parrilla is making in her embrace of "negra" and rejection of "trigueña." By rejecting "trigueña," Parrilla is also refusing to participate in the Puerto Rican racial hierarchy that deems Black as undesirable and confronts terminology which is laced with anti-Blackness. Such affirmation of the use of "negra" or Black as a positive self-identifier has also been viewed as disruptive and divisive within a Puerto Rican or Latinx context, because it forces Puerto Ricans, a minorized and colonized community within the United States, to examine the colorism within their own community. As Black feminists in the United States and Latin America have detailed in their work, women of color are repeatedly asked to sacrifice themselves in the name of a wider movement. Thus, Afro-Puerto Rican women specifically find themselves at the center of several intersections of exclusion, as they are invisibilized among African Americans, Latinx, Latin Americans, white Americans, and Puerto Ricans.

Parrilla's transnational positionality illuminates how geopolitical intersections foster critical interventions into differing national systems of race and encourage conversations about the pervasiveness of anti-Blackness across the globe. Her work reflects what Puerto Rican scholar Juan Flores calls the "diaspora striking back," in which Afro-Latin Americans are "affirming and embracing a black identity, including unity with African Americans, and are consciously or unconsciously setting off major repercussions in their home or ancestral homelands in the Caribbean and Latin America, where such subversive ideas, values, and 'attitudes' are busy shaking up traditional notions of national culture and racial identity."[4] However, Parrilla's project offers an extension of Flores's understanding of the diaspora's intervention into Latin American national and racial identity because she does not solely intervene in mainland United Statesian and Latin American racial conceptualizations, but in those of hexagonal France as well. *No me llames 'trigueña'* stresses how these intersections contribute to collaborative strategies to deconstruct normalized racial signifiers and find constructive alternatives which embrace and affirm Blackness and African ancestry. Thus, migration helps inform and reform conceptualizations of race and identity as it challenges the "representative national subject" put forth by individual nations. Due to this positionality as an Afro-Puerto Rican living in France, Parrilla embodies these geopolitical intersections. Consequently, her project negotiates Blackness from within multiple racial hierarchies. In an interview with the Museum of Contemporary Photography in Chicago in September 2020, where her photo series *¡Santa María!* was featured in the "Temporal: Puerto Rican Resistance" exhibit, Parrilla names *No me llames 'trigueña'* as her most personal series. She explains she was motivated to start this ongoing project interrogating Black identity in Puerto Rico in conjunction with an exploration of her own identity after years of living in France.[5] In France she was confronted with a similar, though distinct, racial hierarchy which challenged her claim to Blackness. These encounters were also outlined in "Ensayo fotográfico," which won the Teodoro Torres Award at the Annual Competition of the Association of Puerto Rican Photojournalists in 2019, and in which she remarks that "[e]n Europa no era negra, pero tampoco era puertorriqueña porque [su] pasaporte decía lo contrario. Podía ser de cualquier otro país de América Latina menos de Puerto Rico. Fue entonces cuando todas las preguntas de mi identidad y mi color de piel me alcanzaron e hicieron efervescencia en mí."[6] Parrilla's reflections suggest the perception of Puerto Rico as a nonexistent space due to its status as an unincorporated US territory. A specifically Puerto Rican passport does not exist and thus, Parrilla is tied to Americanness through her US passport. However, the second sentence also reveals how skin color and Latin America are perceived in the eyes of French people. Parrilla's phrasing lends itself to ambiguity. Is it language or skin color that ties her to Latin America in these encounters?

The confrontation with her racial identity in France echoes Frantz Fanon's well-known confrontation with his own "noirceur" through the words of a French child. However, interestingly the "racial epidermal schema," to use Fanon's term, through which the French view Parrilla differs from Fanon's encounter as it endeavors to dissociate her from Blackness, though not dubbing her white either. Instead, she occupies a liminal space of ambiguity, in which others map their own interpretation of her racial identity onto her. Distancing from Blackness and avoidance of talking about race in France has manifested itself in several discursive manners. In an effort to cleanse itself of its collusion with Nazism, France has sought to construct a new image of a race-blind nation, which has led to an extreme avoidance of talking about race, a word that has become quite taboo in contemporary French society.[7] Like Puerto Ricans' tendency to avoid the use of the term "negra/o" as a self-identifier, French people—both white and of color—have avoided the term "noir(e)" to describe Black people in France. In recent years the English term "black" has been used by Black people in France as an identifier, which arguably joins Black French people in solidarity with African Americans. However, the term "les blacks," rather than confronting France's effort to bury its racist past and deny its racist present, perpetuates the taboo of articulating one's racial identity *in the French language,* and by extension, in French reality. Furthermore, French-Rwandan writer Jessica Gérondal, echoes Parrilla's experience as a Black woman of lighter complexion in France in her article "Je ne suis pas métisse, je suis une Femme Noire," (I am not mixed, I am a Black woman) whose title similarly rejects terms used specifically in the French context that often distance people of African descent from Blackness. Parrilla's experience contrasts with that outlined by many Puerto Rican writers such as Maritza Quiñones Rivera and Juan Flores, who have indicated that many Afro-Puerto Ricans found validation of their Blackness after moving to the mainland United States. Instead, France, like Puerto Rico claims to be free of racism and celebrates métissage. However, Gérondal explains that this appreciation of métissage often translates to exotification rather than acceptance where "les métisses" are admired for their beauty but continue to be excluded in French national identity. Gérondal's proclamation strongly mirrors that of Parrilla and reflects a wider movement of Afro-descendant people within mainland France and in its overseas territories to force French society to reckon with the legacies of colonialism and slavery in the present moment.

Puerto Rico similarly boasts of a racial democracy, in which Puerto Ricans are united in their Puerto Ricanness and mestizaje. National discourses beginning in the nineteenth century, which names Puerto Rico as a raceless society, positioned racism as a purely mainland phenomenon and depicts island slavery as "benevolent" in comparison with the cruelty and violence of continental US slavery,[8] which allows the island to deny culpability in the active erasure of Afro-Puerto Ricans and material consequences of slavery and racism in Puerto Rico. This nation-building project of Puerto Rico was a direct response to the US occupation of the island from 1899 to1904, a continued military presence that was justified because of the supposed primitivism of the Puerto Ricans.[9] Out of a desire to counter the US claims of primitivism, Puerto Rican elites privileged their Spanish heritage and cultivated a myth of Puerto Rico as the "whitest of the Antilles."[10]

Hilda Lloréns identifies three master narratives of Blackness in Puerto Rico that speak to the island's complicated and often contradictory relationship with Blackness. This relationship is explained by Parrilla in the beginning lines of *No me llames 'trigueña'* in which she highlights Puerto Ricans' love of Afro-Caribbean music such as Bomba and Plena, but when she was young her "only reference for this type of music was the Christmas album of José Nogueras, a white Puerto Rican singer."[11] The first master narrative outlined by Lloréns is what she calls "fugitive Blackness" which "describes the discursive and representational mechanism by which a lived black identity is often discursively located 'elsewhere': in the historical past during enslavement, or geographically circumscribed to the coast, to specific black towns or neighborhoods, or to places such as Haiti or the United States."[12] Thus, within the national discourse of mestizaje, it is often the Hispanic whiteness that is highlighted and celebrated whereas indigeneity and Blackness are downplayed or ascribed to a geographical or temporal "elsewhere." The second master narrative echoes what other theorists such as Mayra Santos-Febres and Milagros Denis-Rosario have argued in regard to the portrayal of Puerto Rican slavery as "benevolent" or "soft" in comparison to mainland US slavery.[13] The third master narrative is the belief that the proud assertion of Blackness by Puerto Ricans is due to outside influences, especially that of the United States. Consequently, as Parrilla herself and Lloréns indicate, dominant Puerto Rican society structures a racial continuum that often normalizes and encourages racial passing. This is evident in the 2010 US census data, which indicates that 75.8 percent of Puerto Ricans identify as white only while 72.4 percent of Americans on the mainland identified as white,[14] revealing the differences in interpretations and perceptions of whiteness on the US mainland and Puerto Rico. Not only do Afro-Puerto Ricans often claim Blackness within the mainland context, but "unquestionably white" people in a Puerto Rican context often "'darken' their racial self-perception when living on the US mainland."[15] As María DeGuzmán argues, the conversion of the United States into an imperial power during the Spanish-Cuban-American War in 1898 solidified white Anglo-American identity through its opposition to Spanish "off-whiteness."[16] Therefore, through the Orientalization and pejorative Africanization of Spain and "lo hispano"—and by extension Puerto Ricans, Cubans, and Filipinos—the United States justified its interventionist project and the incorporation of formerly Spanish territories, and thus established a supposedly superior Anglo-American whiteness to Hispanic "off-whiteness."[17]

The practice of racial passing in Puerto Rico is often viewed as more fluid and flexible alternative to the mainland US constraints of the black/white binary, which highly polices racial identity and excludes those with any "trace" of non-white ancestry, or "one drop" of Black ancestry, from whiteness. Consequently, articulations of mixed and biracial identities have been celebrated as a form of resistance against the United Statesian "one drop rule." However, both systems of racialization are steeped in coloniality, resulting in the perpetuation of colonial racial hierarchies. In *No me llames 'trigueña'* Parrilla highlights that in Puerto Rico Blackness is often understood as an extreme identity to which only a small number of Puerto Ricans have claim, even though many Afro-Puerto Ricans who are not described as Black still suffer microaggressions and racism.[18] Due to the desire to achieve Hispanic whiteness and distance themselves from Blackness, Puerto Ricans often refer to themselves as several different euphemistic terms such as "trigueño," "indio," "mestizo," "canela," and "jabao."[19] For example, "*la trigueñita* is a wheat-hued color Puerto Rican woman, slightly toasted by the Caribbean sun. The 'trigueñita' possesses traces of European phenotypes: hair, lips, or nose that make some of us distant from the darker-skinned women on the island. Yet, [they] are still not close enough to the European- looking women."[20] It is these euphemisms, which construct Blackness as an extreme and undesirable identity, that Parrilla rejects in *No me llames 'trigueña'* in order to cultivate and encourage an appreciation and acceptance of Blackness.

As Black feminists have highlighted, naming and reconceptualization of identity within oppressive frameworks is essential to liberation. Latinidad is an example of a new identity framework forged in solidary by people of Latin American descent and Latin American immigrants against dominant US national identities. However, as Juana María Rodríguez has indicated in regard to Latinidad, and as Black feminists have illustrated regarding Blackness and womanhood, striving for unity against a hegemonic Anglo-American culture, nuances of experience and identity are often lost. Rodríguez explains that "[t]he imposed necessity for 'strategic essentialism,' reducing identity categories to the most readily decipherable marker around which to mobilize, serves as a double-edged sword, cutting at hegemonic culture as it reinscribes nation/gender/race myths on both sides of the border."[21] Recently many Black Latin Americans and Latinxs have dubbed Latinidad to be a reit-eration of mestizaje in a US context, following the same tendency to erase or downplay the presence of Blackness and indigeneity in Latin American peoples. Thus, as US Black feminists have revealed the how "woman" and "Black" are inscribed to mean "white woman" and "Black men," Black Latin Americans have argued "Latinx" has come to mean white or mestizo Latin Americans and erases Black and indigenous peoples. Some Black Latin Americans, such as poet and writer Elizabeth Acevedo, have used "Afro-Latinx" to foreground their Blackness within the framework of Latinidad. Others, such as Quiñones Rivera, have chosen to identify as "Afro-Puerto Rican" to similarly highlight their Blackness, but from within a national identity. Some Black people from Latin America or with Latin American heritage, however—such as Alan Pelaez Lopez and Ariana Brown—have rejected the use of "Latinx/o/a" altogether and, like Parrilla, favor "negra" or Black in order to boldly claim and assert their Blackness. This gesture may also be read as essentialist and potentially harmful, as it widens the scope of Blackness in order to encompass a multitude of hues. For example, though

Curiel acknowledges the importance of identity in political organizing, she warns against essentialist identities and expresses a fear that efforts to affirm and celebrate Blackness will lead to a neglect of issues of gender, class, and sexuality. This is a legitimate fear as identity formation often falls onto the double-edged sword of "strategic essentialism." For example, while Parrilla interrogates the centering of Hispanic whiteness in Puerto Rican mestizaje, indigeneity is notably absence from Parrilla's project. Furthermore, the terms "Boricua" and "Borikén," Taíno derived words to describe Puerto Ricans and Puerto Rico which are used by many Puerto Ricans to express national pride, are also absent from the series. While the survival of Taíno culture, especially through vocabulary adopted into Spanish, is undisputed among Puerto Rican cultural critics, the survival of Taíno peoples themselves is a subject of debate. Taíno activist Tony Castanha argues that "one of the greatest myths ever told in Caribbean history is that the indigenous inhabitants of primarily the northern Antilles were extinguished by Spanish colonizers around the mid-sixteenth century"[22] instead of resisting the Spanish colonists using similar strategies as escaped enslaved Africans. The absence of indigeneity in Parrilla's photography reveals the possible limitations of her proposed widening of definitions of Blackness and the difficulty of creating identity frameworks that center the liberation of all oppressed peoples. However, Parrilla's claim to Blackness does subvert the tendency toward colorism and anti-Blackness within ethno-racial frameworks such as mestizaje or Latinidad and affirms a racialized identity that is minorized and marginalized across the globe. Rather than seeking to dilute Blackness or celebrate proximity to whiteness, the term "negra" endeavors to center and celebrate Blackness in its complexity and multitudes, including its intersections with gender.

As many writers analyzing Puerto Rican racial hierarchies and as Parrilla herself have indicated, hair plays a large role in the racialization of Puerto Ricans, especially for women and girls. Black hair has been and still is considered "pelo malo" by much of the Latin American and United Statesian community due its unconformity with dominant, white-centered standards of beauty. Conversely, straight hair is depicted as the most beautiful, professional, and appropriate.[23] Wearing specific hairstyles such as braids not only rebels against current Eurocentric conceptions of beauty, but also celebrates African heritage and continues the tradition of enslaved Africans' rebellion against slavery. In their examination of Black hair culture in the United States, Ayana D. Byrn and Lori L. Tharps note that African hairstyles were "an integral part of a complex language system [and] have been used to indicate a person's marital status, age, religion, ethnic identity, wealth, and rank within the community."[24] Consequently, the shaving of hair during slavery was a critical step in the erasure of and alienation of enslaved Africans connection from their culture.[25] The natural hair movement is also a manner in which Afro-descendent communities have fought against the discourse of "bad hair" and politics of respectability that have historically censored and disparaged Black hair.

No me llames 'trigueña' highlights Puerto Rico's participation in the perpetuation of anti-Black standards of beauty, which particularly affects Black Puerto Rican women. In her interview with the Museum of Contemporary Photography in Chicago (MoCP), Parrilla explains that her curly hair was always a marker of difference and one that connected her to Blackness. As Lloréns explains, curly hair differentiated "trigueño" from "indio," the latter's hair being "naturally straight."[26] One of the first pairings of photographs in the series is one of a palm tree next to one of a young girl, whose curly hair is pulled up into a high ponytail.[27] The text accompanying the photograph reflects on Parrilla's experiences growing as "the girl with the palm tree hair."[28] Throughout her life she would hear "'Your hair is difficult' . . . So [she] never wanted to wear [her] hair down. Having [her] hair extremely flattened without any type of volume gave [her] security growing-up because like that no one would mention [her] hair."[29] The desire to hide and flatten her hair reflects the influence of the stigmatization of Black hair as "pelo malo," ugly, and unprofessional reinforced in Puerto Rican society. However, while the little girl in the photograph wears her hair up mirroring Parrilla's own tendency to hide and tame her hair, the girl's hairstyle does not hide her hair's texture or curls. Instead, we see tight ringlets situated at the top of her head and framing her face, suggesting that Black hair cannot and should not be contained. While the caption tells us that the girl is looking at the sea in Old San Juan, the juxtaposition of the photographs also suggests the young girl is admiring the beautiful Puerto Rican landscape with the palm trees. This gesture—reinforced by Parrilla's identification as "the girl with the palm tree hair"—links Black hair with the natural landscape of Puerto Rico, troubling the notion of whiteness as natural, default, and epitome of beauty in Puerto Rican society. This comparison is further highlighted through the similar composition and colors within both photographs. The pinks and reds of the flowers and the young girl's shirt fill the bottom of the pictures while the palm leaves and curly ponytail are framed against the blue of the sky and the hair bow at the top. Moreover, Parrilla further connects Black hair with Puerto Rican national identity by drawing a parallel between Luis Lloréns Torres's poem "Madrugada," specifically the memorable line of "en el moño de una palma," with her own palm tree hair. Luis Lloréns Torres was a Puerto Rican poet who advocated for Puerto Rican independence and whose work reflected the ideology of criollismo, a nationalism which privileges white Puerto Rican identity. However, Parrilla highlights a parallel between her nickname and a line in the poem, thus positioning Blackness at the center of nationalist literature.

The next photograph shows us a picture of a young woman and man holding a baby in Loíza, Puerto Rico.[30] The image parallels Parrilla's own rejection of euphemistic terms that endeavor to negate her proximity to Blackness and of subscribing to the practice of passing in Puerto Rico. These rejections challenge the category of pure Blackness in the Puerto Rican racial continuum. As previously stated, hair texture plays a large role in the racialization of Puerto Ricans and determines where one falls in the racial hierarchy. Lloréns reveals that the "popular gendered practice of close-cropping boys' hair is one way to evade an added signifier of racial classification. In the context of Puerto Rico, where long hair is the norm for girls and an important marker of femininity, hair is a significant focus of racialization for girls in a way that is different from boys."[31] However, unlike the young boy seen in an earlier picture in the series whose hair is cut short, which consequently conceals the texture of his hair, the young man in this photograph wears his hair longer in very tight ringlets which clearly model his hair texture. Significantly, he is one of the few people in the series who is looking directly at the camera as if to confront the viewer and proclaim his presence. However, this proclamation is not without difficulty. Parrilla's interview with MoCP gives us further insight into what about this young man captivated Parrilla and why she chose to include it in *No me llames 'trigueña.'* She explains that in his face she saw strength and pain,[32] and thus, his expression reflects the difficulty of proudly claiming one's Blackness in an anti-Black world. The young woman walking beside him similarly defies Eurocentric beauty standards and Puerto Rican's societal desire to "pass" by wearing her hair in braids. Furthermore, the woman does not only emphasize her African heritage through her chosen hairstyle, but also through the colors of her extensions, which draw more attention to her hair. The yellow, red, and green signal an identification with Pan-Africanism and solidary with other African and Afro-descent people. Furthermore, in photographing young Afro-Puerto Ricans proudly asserting their African heritage, Parrilla shows us a glimpse of the possibility of a world outside the constraining and violent racial hierarchies, the possibility of a future in which the baby the young man holds in his arms can grow up knowing "negra" is not a defect or an insult or a lesser social status.

In the next pairing of photographs Parrilla continues her exploration of the disparaging rhetoric launched against Black hair in a personal reflection on her own hair and the consequences of such discourse specifically on the confidence and self-image of Black women and girls.[33] Parrilla uses the sun to produce a shadow, highlighting the texture and body of Black hair. The photograph's caption situates Parrilla in Paris, France, highlighting the global implications of the negotiation of Black identity. In the text accompanying these photographs, Parrilla reflects on her internalization of anti-Black beauty standards directed at her hair. She notes that "when [she] was younger [she] used to put long t-shirts over [her] head while [she] was playing because [she] wanted to have long straight hair. Growing up people called the texture of [her] hair many names, 'pelo duro' (hard hair), 'pelo malo' (bad hair), 'pelo como cáscara de coco' (Coconut shell hair), pelo de mapo (mop hair), pelo de palma (palm tree hair), and somehow [she] believed them as if it were true."[34] Parrilla's choice to include a shadow of her hair rather than a photograph of her face as well as her hair perhaps reveals lingering anxieties about her appearance and the difficulty of combating internalized racism. While using the shadow does indeed highlight her hair's texture, other strategies could have been used to emphasis its texture while also showing Parrilla's face. She could have positioned the sun to shine from behind her, for example. Parrilla further highlights the effects of intersections of gender and Blackness through the juxtaposition of the photograph of two young girls turning their faces from the camera with additional reflections on the implications of anti-Blackness in her childhood.[35] Parrilla writes that "growing up it was difficult for [her] to see [her]self as a young black girl because [she] was constantly reminded by other kids that black girls were ugly because of the color of their skin. [She] became extremely shy and [her] only escape was to turn away and hide."[36] The pairing of Parrilla's reflection on the consequences of anti-Black comments on her self-image and confidence as a child with the photograph of two young Black Puerto Rican girls in 2019 emphasize the persistence of the negative effects of specifically gendered anti-Blackness on young girls today. This also highlights the urgency of her project because Black girls in Puerto Rico today continue to struggle with confronting normalized notions of race and internalized colorism just as Parrilla herself did as a child. Finally, it is also important to note that besides the studio ballet photograph of Parrilla as an adolescent, one of the few subjects who boldly looks into the camera in the series is the young man, who highlights how experience of oppression is compounded by the intersections of gender and race for Black Puerto Rican women and girls.

Parrilla's visual comparison of Black hair with Puerto Rican flora, such as the young girl's ponytail and with the palm tree, speaks to a larger exploration of the intimacy between Black communities and the environment that permeates her series. Parrilla rejects colonial perspectives of land and nonhuman life, which harmfully conflate Afro-descendent and indigenous peoples with the land to dehumanize and justify exploitation and violence. Such a conflation reduced Black and indigenous peoples to objects, beasts, savages, and subhumans, and under which, "negra" continues to be wielded as a pejorative term. Parrilla's linkage, however, counters the colonial reduction of Afro-diasporic peoples achieved through association with nature. Instead, her photographs foreground what DeGuzmán calls "LatinX botanical epistemologies," reckoning with the "colossal re-organization and destruction of the natural ecosystems of colonized lands by imperially directed impositions both mixing with, appropriating, and replacing native species. The plantations and transplantations of colonization and empire involved the concomitant devaluation of the already existing knowledge-and-practice systems of the inhabitants subordinated to these colonial-imperial enterprises."[37] As DeGuzmán argues, this confrontation with colonial and imperial understandings of environment does not involve a search or "recovering" of pre-colonial purity, but rather a decolonial understanding of and informed praxis in regard to the consequences of "what happens at the crossroads of cultural encounter and also at a crossroads of crisis."[38] Specifically the use of term "trigueña" as a more desirable signifier than "negra" in Puerto Rico reveals this colonial dynamic of depreciation of native and African food and agricultural practices. As previous stated the word "trigueña," meaning "wheat-colored," is derived from "trigo," meaning wheat in Spanish. Wheat bread was among the Spanish trinity of foods along with wine and olive oil during the time of Spanish colonization and its absence in the Americas was greatly lamented by the Spanish colonists.[39] Consequently, during most of the sixteenth century imports from Spain to the colonies largely consisted of wheat flour, wine, and olive oil.[40] Due to the expense of such imports and the tendency of wheat flour to spoil during the journey, Spanish colonists quickly endeavored to transform their new territories into copies of Spain through the introduction of new plant and livestock species.[41] However, while wheat cultivation in mainland territories like Mexico and Peru was successful, the wet climate in the Caribbean colonies such as Puerto Rico prevented its success.[42] Instead, Puerto Rico, like many other Caribbean colonies, became a producer of sugar, coffee, and tobacco, which created an economic system on the island that not only hinged on ecological and human exploitation, but also created dependence on importation of food items such as rice and wheat flour first from Spain and then from the United States.[43] Despite the inability to produce wheat in Puerto Rico, the ability to eat wheat flour remained a sign of European-ness and affluence on the island from the colonial period until today.[44] Thus, the term "trigueña," etymologically derived from "trigo," metaphorically encapsulates the desire to achieve the status of a white European subject. This desire to approach the European or Western ideal by eating the foods prized by those societies as well as distance oneself from Blackness through euphemistic terms reflects what Homi Bhabha calls colonial mimicry. Through the practice of consuming "trigo," colonized subjects become "almost the same, *but not quite*,"[45] just as Puerto Ricans called "trigueño" are "*almost the same but not white*."[46] Therefore, through her confrontation of trigueñidad, Parrilla refuses to engage in such mimicry. Instead, she not only rejects the practice of racial passing in Puerto Rico, but also gestures to a rejection of European culinary and agricultural practices that have harmed and continue to harm the island.

Parrilla's ecological preoccupations are further evident in the pairing of the shadow of her hair with a photograph of dried orange peels, which she dubs "orange peel waste." Her motivation for this comparison is that to many other people her hair was always a waste that did not fit within the desired standards of beauty.[47] However, though the peels can be viewed as waste, they possess a unique beauty and interesting texture that mirror the Black ringlets featured in other photographs. Furthermore, due to the peels' darkened color and hardened texture, they are not immediately recognizable for what they are. Instead, they resemble seaweed or dried reeds. This easy misidentification can be read as a commentary on Puerto Rican society's failure to recognize the beauty and value of Blackness, which it dismisses as a burden and a waste. However, the choice of orange peels is also significant because it signals a reciprocal tie between the earth and Blackness as orange peels can be used as a highly effective fertilizer as they are the most nutrient rich part of the fruit. Their success in producing ecological revival is evident their use to restore part of the Costa Rican rain forest. Starting in 1997, the orange juice manufacturer Del Oro deposited orange peels and pulp in a barren area of land in the national park called Área de Conservación Guanacaste in Costa Rica.[48] Though the company was accused of defiling a national park by a rival company, research conducted on the plot of land fifteen years later indicate the orange peels were instrumental in creating richer soil, more tree biomass, and greater tree biodiversity.[49] Thus, the curative power of the orange peels, which can easily be misconstrued as waste, juxtaposed with Parrilla's own natural curls suggests that the acceptance of natural Black hair, and Black beauty, has a curative power in itself—a power to counter colonial logics which reduced Afro-descendant peoples to waste.

Returning to the photographs of the palm tree and the young girl, the photograph of the palm offers an ambiguous reading. The dark coloring of the photograph and the leaves covering the possible fruit make it difficult to know with certainty which type of palm is featured. However, the spindly trunk, long fronds, and the possible dark outlines of fruit suggest it is probably a coconut palm, which, significantly, is not a palm variety native to Puerto Rico.[50] While there is much debate over the origin of the coconut palm, it is thought to have originated in the Indo-Pacific region and within a century after Christopher Columbus arrival in Hispaniola, the existence of the coconut palm in Puerto Rico was documented in José de Acosta's *Historia de las Indias*.[51] Though it is unclear how the coconut palm came to Puerto Rico, its documentation in the 1500s significantly evokes the Transatlantic Slave Trade. This parallel could be viewed as problematic as it could be used to reduce Afro-Puerto Ricans to a colonial commodity and imposition that could possibility have damaged the "natural" or "native" Puerto Rican landscape. However, it could also be read as an acknowledgement of the entwined violence inflicted on both Afro-Puerto Ricans and the Puerto Rican landscape, linking both people and environment in their experience of colonial violence as well as resistance and survival in spite of such violence. Furthermore, the coconut is not only a highly important fruit in the Caribbean, but specifically important to Afro-diasporic communities. Its centrality to Afro hair care and in Afro-diasporic foodways highlights the ingenuity and skills of creative survival amid violent transplantation. However, the ambiguity of the photograph and Parrilla's choice of not specifically naming the palm variety can be interpreted as linking Afro-diasporic subjects with specifically native foliage of Puerto Rico. The implications of such linkage are complex, and perhaps problematic, due to the absence of indigeneity in *No me llames 'trigueña.'* There are many species of palm trees native to Puerto Rico which have survived the violent altering of the island with the plantation system and deforestation, imbuing the land with the resistance parallel to its Native peoples. Finally, this ambiguity provokes an interrogation of the apparently "natural" landscape of Puerto Rico, urges its viewers to reflect on the effects of coloniality on the constructions of naturalness.

Similarly, Parrilla links Afro-Puerto Rican resistance to the figure of the cimarrón, a Spanish word which has a come to mean "escaped enslaved person" and a term whose origins have been debated, in a photograph of a horse in Loíza, Puerto Rico.[52] Cimarronaje in Puerto Rico has not received much critical attention in comparison to other countries in the Americas. Up until the 1980s, it was believed that Puerto Rico was not home to any palenques or Maroon settlements, although in his *Historia de la esclavitud negra en Puerto Rico*, published in 1965, Luis Díaz Soler concedes that "[aunque] en Puerto Rico no hay noticias sobre la existencia de palenques, . . . fueron extendidas a la Isla las leyes que regían sobre ese tipo de organización."[53] Since Díaz Soler's publication Benjamin Nistal-Moret and Guillermo Baralt have expanded the scholarship on slavery and slave resistance on the island, though Nistal-Moret still reports relatively low numbers of cimarrones in comparison to other Caribbean islands. However, despite the claims of "low" incidences of cimarronaje in Puerto Rico traced in official documents, several sources agree that cimarrón communities formed in Loíza as well is in San Mateo de Cangrejos.[54] In *No me llames 'trigueña,'* Parrilla indicates she "learned about 'cimarronaje' (maroonage) and the stories of many slave men and women that revolted against the system of slavery and escaped to the forest and mangroves near the Río Grande de Loiza (Great River of Loíza) to form settlements. Cimarrón (maroons) is a Spanish word that describes a feral animal with a domesticated past."[55] Through this caption, Parrilla foregrounds enslaved peoples' resistance within Puerto Rico during slavery despite the colony's efforts to thwart rebellion and the continuity of Black Puerto Rican resistance today. The word "cimarrón" has complicated origins and several different meanings, one of which is "animal doméstico que huye al campo y se hace montaraz" according to the nineteenth edition of the Real Academia Española's *Diccionario de la lengua española*.[56] According to José Juan Arrom, several dictionaries, including la RAE and the *Diccionario manual de americanismos*, attribute the word's origin to "cima," meaning summit or peak, to which many cimarrones escaped.[57] According to these dictionaries, cimarrón also refers to wild varieties of cultivated plants as well as an adjective meaning savage or wild.[58] The first documented use of the word is in Gonzalo Fernández de Oviedo's *Historia general y natural de las Indias* to refer to indigenous peoples and wild pigs.[59] The use of the term subsequently expanded to encompass escaped enslaved Africans in the Spanish Caribbean colonies. Arrom's main intervention in the previous etymologies is his advancement of the hypothesis of the word's Taíno origins, which would significantly make the word one of the earliest Taíno words adopted into Spanish. Arrom hypothesizes cimarrón to be derived from the Taíno word "símara," meaning "arrow," which when combined with certain suffixes could have been interpreted as an "escaped or fugitive arrow," and most likely through analogy with "cima," "cimara" became favored over "símara."[60]

These etymological hypotheses have several implications for Parrilla's work. The relationship between "cima" and "cimarrón" links the escaped enslaved African, indentured indigenous person, or domesticated animal with the liberatory potential of the mountains. This encompassing term similarly illustrates the reduction and conflation of African and indigenous subjects to animals or inanimate objects by colonial powers in a violent gesture of dehumanization and depreciation of the earth. The possibility of Taíno origins is also significant, mirroring on the one hand the denial and lack of recognition Puerto Rican indigenous communities suffer today, and their enduring and persistent survival on the other. Parrilla endeavors to counter colonial acts of dehumanization of Africans and devaluation of the earth by highlighting the centrality of landscape and foliage in the resistance of enslaved peoples, in which self-freed Africans utilized their botanical knowledge and harnessed environmental obstacles to evade bondage and develop free communities. This is a point also raised by Nistal-Moret, who highlights the role of deforestation on the island in limiting the possibilities of Puerto Rican cimarronaje. The curbing of both the prosperity of ecology and free African communities once again highlights the parallel violence inflicted on environment and African bodies by colonial and imperial logics. Upon first glance the image of the horse centered among lush foliage offers a picture of optimism, exuding a feeling of freedom and safety. However, a closer look reveals a rope wrapped around the horse's nose, meaning that the horse is most likely owned. The horse could have escaped, and thus have become a cimarrón, or the horse has been allowed temporary freedom by its owner. Either possibility offers a commentary on the constraints endured by Afro-Puerto Ricans, highlighting the continuity between the past and present conditions in Puerto Rico which necessitate Black resistance.

The portrait of the horse is placed beside an image of a crowded bus in Loíza, Puerto Rico.[61] Parrilla accompanies this photograph with further reflections on the tendency among Puerto Ricans to situate of Blackness in Loíza, which she initiated in her captions for the photography of the young woman, man, and baby. Her commentary on the mapping of Blackness onto Loíza and Loízeños exemplifies Lloréns's concept of geographical and fugitive Blackness, common in Puerto Rico and many other communities in Latin America. Consequently, Blackness often becomes an otherness that is located in a geographical and temporal elsewhere. Lloréns argue that "pure Black" people are "believed to hail from specific geographic locations (in essence, Loíza, Guayama, Arroyo, Ponce)."[62] Furthermore, Blackness also is ascribed to immigrants and foreigners, such as Dominicans, Haitians, and African Americans.[63] Parrilla recalls that her "first memory of the town of Loíza was what [she] learned in school, 'los negros son todos de Loíza' . . . and that the people born in other towns of the island with a darker complexion were mixed race and not black. At that time [she] had a very mystified and far image of the people from Loíza."[64] This portrayal not only perpetuates the othering of Loízeños, but also, as Parrilla expresses throughout her project, a feeling of non-belonging among many Afro-Puerto Ricans who are not considered "real" Black subjects due to their place of birth or mixed heritage. Rather, Blackness and mixed heritage are portrayed as mutually exclusive. Parrilla specifically addresses the depreciation and folklorization of Blackness in the Puerto Rican culture, particularly in television and advertising, in which Black people are often portrayed as stereotypically uneducated, comical or criminal, or as the folkloric figure of the "mammie."[65] Parrilla indicates that the temporal mappings of Blackness often claimed that Loíza's "only contribution to Puerto Rican society was only tied to [Puerto Rican] folklore, to the heritage of [the] traditional Afro-Caribbean music, Bomba and Plena. Subsequently, the image of the Afro-Puerto Rican community in Loiza was distant and distorted."[66] This distant, distorted, mystified, and far image of Loízeños from Parrilla's youth is countered by crisp and clear pictures of Loízeños taken in 2018, in which Parrilla's positions herself close to the Loíza community through her camera. The framing of the crowded bus situates Parrilla among the Afro-Puerto Rican community, communicating an intimacy between Parrilla and the photographed Loízeños. Furthermore, the natural hairstyles of the women on the bus evokes the image of Parrilla's own hair, establishing similarities between the supposed "pure" Blackness of

Loíza and Parrilla's perceived trigueñidad. Thus, Parrilla endeavors to dispel the myth that Blackness is geographically and temporally confined to Loíza or a folkloric past by claiming as part of her own identity.

In directly rejecting the use of Puerto Rican euphemisms to encourage and naturalize the practice of racial passing in Puerto Rico, Parrilla's *No me llames 'trigueña'; soy negra* calls her viewers to confront the damaging effects of Puerto Rico's racial continuum and proposes a widening of what constitutes Blackness. Her photographs deconstruct essentialized definitions of Blackness as an extreme or as an identity located in a geographical or temporal "elsewhere," as it is often viewed Puerto Rico, or as a purely mainland US phenomenon. Therefore, her work interrupts the dominant Puerto Rican national discourse of mestizaje and privileging of Hispanic whiteness by inserting Blackness into the national narrative of Puerto Ricanness. Reflecting on the discourses directed against Black hair and its role in the racialization of Puerto Rican women, Parrilla contests the belief that Black hair is inherently inferior, unprofessional, and ugly. Furthermore, her examination of the effects of interiorization of anti-Blackness in her own life as well as those of young Afro-Puerto Rican girls highlight the continuing consequences of gendered anti-Blackness today. Her contemplations of shared experiences of colonial violence and survival between Afro-Puerto Ricans and the environment draw attention to the centrality of botanical knowledge and ingenuity in cimarronaje and the continuity of colonial violence as well as the resistance to said violence. Finally, the absence of indigeneity in Parrilla's project exemplifies the difficulties of fully avoiding essentialisms. However, Parrilla's project suggests there is liberatory potential in fully claiming Blackness and challenges its viewers to consider the implications of a future in which Blackness is celebrated in multiple and intersectional manifestations.

BIBLIOGRAPHY

Arrom, José Juan. "Cimarrón: Apuntes sobre sus primeras documentaciones y su probable origen." In *Cimarrón*, José Juan Arrom and Manuel A. García Arévalo, 13–30. Santo Domingo: Ediciones Fundación García Arévalo, 1986.

Ayala, César J., and W. Bergad. "Land Use." In *Agrarian Puerto Rico: Reconsidering Rural Economy and Society, 1899–1940,* 214–71. Cambridge: Cambridge University Press, 2020.

Bhabha, Homi. "Of Mimicry and Man: The Ambivalence of Colonial Discourse." *October* 28 (Spring 1984): 125–33.

Bronx Documentary Center. "No me llames 'trigueña'; soy negra." Accessed May 2021. https://www.laffbdc.org/adriana-parrilla.

Byrd, Ayana D., and Lori L. Tharps. *Hair Story: Untangling the Roots of Black Hair in America.* New York: St. Martin's Press, 2001.

Castanha, Anthony. "Adventures in Indigenous Caribbean Resistance, Survival, and Continuity in Borikén (Puerto Rico)." *Wicazo Sa Review* 25, no. 2 (2010): 29–64.

Crenshaw, Kimberlé. "Demarginalizing the Intersection: A Black Feminist Critique of Antidiscrimination Doctrine, Feminist Theory and Antiracist Politics," *University of Chicago Legal Forum,* (1989): 139–68.

———. "Mapping the Margins: Intersectionality, Identity Politics, and Violence Against Women of Color." *Stanford Law Review* 43, no. 6 (1991): 1241–300.

Curiel, Ochy. "Identidades esencialistas o construcción de identidades políticas: El dilema de las feministas negras." *Otras Miradas* 2, no. 2 (2002): 96–113.

DeGuzmán, María. "LatinX Botanical Epistemologies." *Cultural Dynamics* 31, no. 1–2 (2019): 108–24.

———. *Spain's Long Shadow: The Black Legend, Off-Whiteness, and Anglo-American Empire.* Minneapolis: University of Minnesota Press, 2005.

Denis-Rosario, Milagros. "Deciphering the Notion of a Raceless Nation: Racial Harmony and Discrimination in Puerto Rican Society." *Latino Studies* 18 (2020): 45–65.

———. "The Problem of Slavery in the Puerto Rican Society." *Centro Journal* 21, no. 1 (2009): 236–45.

Díaz Soler, Luis. *Historia de la esclavitud negra en Puerto Rico.* Río Piedras: Editorial Universitaria de la Universidad de Puerto Rico, 1965.

Earle, Rebecca. *The Body of the Conquistador: Food, Race and the Colonial Experience in Spanish America, 1492–1700.* Cambridge: Cambridge University Press, 2012.

Fanon, Frantz. *Peau noire, masques blancs.* Montreal: Kiyikaat Éditions, 2015. First published 1952 by Éditions du Seuil.

Fleming, Crystal Marie. *Resurrecting Slavery: Racial Legacies and White Supremacy in France.* Philadelphia: Temple University Press, 2017.

Flores, Juan. "Triple Consciousness?: Afro-Latinos on the Color Line," *Wadabagei* 8, no. 1 (2005): 80–5.

Gérondal, Jessica. "Je ne suis pas 'métisse,' je suis une Femme Noire." *Mediapart,* January 21, 2020. https://blogs.mediapart.fr/jessica-gerondal/blog/210120/je-ne-suis-pas-metisse-je-suis-une-femme-noire.

Kelly, Rose. "Orange is the New Green: How Orange Peels Revived a Costa Rican Forest." Princeton University News, August 22, 2017. https://www.princeton.edu/news/2017/08/22/orange-new-green-how-orange-peels-revived-costa-rican-forest.

Little, Jr. Elbert L., and Frank H. Wadsworth. *Common Trees of Puerto Rico and the Virgin Islands.* Washington D.C.: U.S. Department of Agriculture, 1964.

Lloréns, Hilda. "Beyond *Blanqueamiento*: Black Affirmation in Contemporary Puerto Rico." *Latin American and Caribbean Ethnic Studies* 13, no. 2 (2018): 157–78.

———. "Identity Practices: Racial Passing, Gender, and Racial Purity in Puerto Rico." *Afro-Hispanic Review* 37, no. 1 (2018): 29–47.

Nistal-Moret, Benjamín. *Esclavos, prófugos y cimarrones: Puerto Rico, 1770–1870.* Río Piedras: Editorial de la Universidad de Puerto Rico, 1984.

Ortíz Cuadra, Cruz Miguel. *Eating Puerto Rico: A History of Food, Culture, and Identity.* Translated by Russ Davidson. Chapel Hill: The University of North Carolina Press, 2013.

Parrilla, Adriana. "Ensayo fotográfico." *Afro-Hispanic Review* 37, no. 1 (2018): 145–50.

———. Interview by Dalina Aimée Perdomo Álvarez. *MoCP Behind the Lens*, 18 September 2020, https://vimeo.com/460610444.

———. "No Me Llames Trigueña; Soy Negra (2018-ongoing)." Accessed March 11, 2022. https://www.adrianaparrilla.com/triguena-ongoing#no5.

Quiñones Rivera, Maritza. "Trigueñita to Afro-Puerto Rican: Intersections of the Racialized, Gendered, and Sexualized Body in Puerto Rico and the U.S. Mainland." *Meridians: Feminism, Race, Transnationalism* 7, no. 1 (2006): 162–82.

Rivera Lassén, Ana Irma. "Afrodescendant Women: A Race and Gender Intersectional Spiderweb," *Meridians: Feminism, Race, Transnationalism* 14, no. 2 (2016): 56–70.

Rodríguez, Juana María. "Divas, Atrevidas, y Entendidas; An Introduction to Identities." In *Queer Latinidad: Identity Practices, Discursive Spaces*, 5–36. New York: New York University Press, 2003.

Santos-Febres, Mayra. *Sobre piel y papel.* San Juan: Ediciones Callejón, 2005.

Stark, David. "Rescued from Their Invisibility: The Afro-Puerto Ricans of Seventeenth-and-Eighteenth-Century San Mateo de Cangrejos, Puerto Rico." *The Americas* 63, no. 4 (2007): 551–86.

Yerebakan, Osman Can. "Photographs Exploring What It Means to Be Black in Puerto Rico." *AnOther,* August 6, 2020. https://www.anothermag.com/art-photography /12726/adriana-parrilla-puerto-rico-series-latin-american-foto-festival-new -york?fbclid=IwAR1Tg08mVOi_ezkiCBKh-YL_VDzkpYCQkpCo29x _YuTPV94mH6IxAezmjpc.

NOTES

1. Ana Irma Rivera Lassén, "Afrodescendant Women: A Race and Gender Intersectional Spiderweb," *Meridians: Feminism, Race, Transnationalism* 14, no. 2 (2016): 65.

2. Kimberlé Crenshaw, "Mapping the Margins: Intersectionality, Identity Politics, and Violence Against Women of Color," *Stanford Law Review* 43, no. 6 (1991): 1242.

3. Ochy Curiel, "Identidades esencialistas o construcción de identidades políticas: El dilema de las feministas negras," *Otras Miradas* 2, no. 2 (2002): 107.

4. Juan Flores, "Triple Consciousness?: Afro-Latinos on the Color Line," *Wadabagei* 8, no. 1 (2005): 83.

5. Adriana Parrilla, interview by Dalina Aimée Perdomo Álvarez, *MoCP Behind the Lens,* September 18, 2020, https://vimeo.com/460610444.

6. Adriana Parrilla, "Ensayo fotográfico," *Afro-Hispanic Review* 37, no. 1 (2018): 145.

7. Crystal Marie Fleming, *Resurrecting Slavery: Racial Legacies and White Supremacy in France,* (Philadelphia: Temple University Press, 2017), 6.

8. Milagros Denis-Rosario, "Deciphering the Notion of a Raceless Nation: Racial Harmony and Discrimination in Puerto Rican Society," *Latino Studies* 18 (2020): 47.

9. Mayra Santos-Febres, *Sobre piel y papel,* (San Juan: Ediciones Callejón, 2005), 147–48.

10. Santos-Febres, *Sobre piel*, 148.

11. "No me llames 'trigueña'; soy negra," Bronx Documentary Center, accessed May 2021, https://www.laffbdc.org/adriana-parrilla, since May the page has been taken down for the Latin American Foto Festival in summer 2021.

12. Hilda Lloréns, "Beyond *Blanqueamiento*: Black Affirmation in Contemporary Puerto Rico," *Latin American and Caribbean Ethnic Studies* 13, no. 2 (2018): 163.

13. Lloréns, "Beyond *Blanqueamiento*," 163.

14. "No me llames 'trigueña'"; Hilda Lloréns, "Identity Practices: Racial Passing, Gender, and Racial Purity in Puerto Rico," *Afro-Hispanic Review* 37, no. 1 (2018): 29.

15. Lloréns, "Identity Practices," 33.

16. María DeGuzmán, *Spain's Long Shadow: The Black Legend, Off-Whiteness, and Anglo-American Empire*, (Minneapolis: University of Minnesota Press, 2005), 133.

17. DeGuzmán, *Spain's Long Shadow*, 145.

18. Lloréns, "Identity Practices," 39; "No me llames 'trigueña.'"

19. Lloréns, "Identity Practices," 34.

20. Maritza Quiñones Rivera, "Trigueñita to Afro-Puerto Rican: Intersections of the Racialized, Gendered, and Sexualized Body in Puerto Rico and the U.S. Mainland," *Meridians: Feminism, Race, Transnationalism* 7, no. 1 (2006): 165.

21. Juana María Rodríguez, "Divas, Atrevidas, y Entendidas: An Introduction to Identities," *Queer Latinidad: Identity Practices, Discursive Spaces*, (New York: New York University Press, 2003), 11.

22. Anthony Castanha. "Adventures in Indigenous Caribbean Resistance, Survival, and Continuity in Borikén (Puerto Rico)," *Wicazo Sa Review* 25, no. 2 (2010), 29.

23. Lloréns, "Identity Practices," 36.

24. Ayana D. Byrd and Lori L. Tharps, *Hair Story: Untangling the Roots of Black Hair in America*, (New York: St. Martin's Press, 2001), 2.

25. Byrd and Tharps, *Hair Story*, 10–11.

26. Lloréns, "Identity Practices," 35.

27. Yerebakan, Osman Can. "Photographs Exploring What It Means to Be Black in Puerto Rico," *AnOther,* August 6, 2020, https://www.anothermag.com/art-photography/gallery/11255/don-t-call-me-triguena-i-m-black-by-adriana-parrilla/0, only the image of the young girl is included in the article.

28. "No me llames 'trigueña.'"

29. "No me llames 'trigueña.'"

30. Yerebakan, Osman Can. "Photographs Exploring What It Means to Be Black in Puerto Rico," *AnOther,* August 6, 2020, https://www.anothermag.com/art-photography/gallery/11255/don-t-call-me-triguena-i-m-black-by-adriana-parrilla/4.

31. Lloréns, "Identity Practices," 35.

32. Parrilla, *MoCP Behind the Lens*.

33. Adriana Parrilla, "No Me Llames Trigueña; Soy Negra (2018-ongoing)," accessed March 11, 2022, https://www.adrianaparrilla.com/triguena-ongoing#no5.

34. "No me llames 'trigueña.'"

35. Yerebakan, Osman Can. "Photographs Exploring What It Means to Be Black in Puerto Rico," *AnOther,* August 6, 2020, https://www.anothermag.com/art-photography/gallery/11255/don-t-call-me-triguena-i-m-black-by-adriana-parrilla/3.

36. "No me llames 'trigueña.'"

37. María DeGuzmán, "LatinX Botanical Epistemologies," *Cultural Dynamics* 31, no. 1–2 (2019): 111.

38. DeGuzmán, "LatinX Botanical Epistemologies," 120.

39. Rebecca Earle, *The Body of the Conquistador: Food, Race and the Colonial Experience in Spanish America, 1492–1700* (Cambridge: Cambridge University Press, 2012), 66–7.

40. Earle, *The Body of the Conquistador*, 68.

41. Earle, *The Body of the Conquistador*, 55, 69, 72.

42. Earle, *The Body of the Conquistador*, 71–2.

43. César J. Ayala and W. Bergad. "Land Use," *Agrarian Puerto Rico: Reconsidering Rural Economy and Society, 1899–1940* (Cambridge: Cambridge University Press, 2020), 259.

44. Cruz Miguel Ortíz Cuadra, *Eating Puerto Rico: A History of Food, Culture, and Identity,* trans. Russ Davidson (Chapel Hill: The University of North Carolina Press, 2013), 128, 215–16.

45. Homi Bhabha, "Of Mimicry and Man: The Ambivalence of Colonial Discourse," *October* 28 (Spring 1984): 127.

46. Bhabha, "Of Mimicry and Man," 130.

47. Parrilla, *MoCP Behind the Lens.*

48. Rose Kelly, "Orange is the New Green: How Orange Peels Revived a Costa Rican Forest," *Princeton University News*, August 22, 2017, https://www.princeton.edu/news/2017/08/22/orange-new-green-how-orange-peels-revived-costa-rican-forest.

49. Kelly, "Orange is the New Green."

50. Elbert L. Little Jr. and Frank H. Wadsworth, *Common Trees of Puerto Rico and the Virgin Islands (Washington D.C.: U.S. Department of Agriculture, 1964), 38.*

51. Little, Jr. and Wadsworth, *Common Trees*, 38.

52. Yerebakan, Osman Can. "Photographs Exploring What It Means to Be Black in Puerto Rico," *AnOther,* August 6, 2020, https://www.anothermag.com/art-photography/gallery/11255/don-t-call-me-triguena-i-m-black-by-adriana-parrilla/6.

53. Luis Díaz Soler, *Historia de la esclavitud negra en Puerto Rico,* (Río Piedras: Editorial Universitaria de la Universidad de Puerto Rico, 1965), 208.

54. Denis-Rosario, "Problem of Slavery," 240; David Stark, "Rescued from Their Invisibility: The Afro-Puerto Ricans of Seventeenth-and-Eighteenth-Century San Mateo de Cangrejos, Puerto Rico," *The Americas* 63, no. 4, (2007): 552.

55. "No me llames 'trigueña.'"

56. *Diccionario de la lengua española*, 19th ed., (Madrid: Real Academia Española, 1970), quoted in José Juan Arrom, "Cimarrón: Apuntes sobre sus primeras

documentaciones y su probable origen," *Cimarrón*, José Juan Arrom and Manuel A. García Arévalo (Santo Domingo: Ediciones Fundación García Arévalo, 1986), 15.

57. Arrom, "Cimarrón," 15–7.

58. Arrom, "Cimarrón," 15–7.

59. Arrom, "Cimarrón," 17.

60. Arrom, "Cimarrón," 29.

61. Yerebakan, Osman Can. "Photographs Exploring What It Means to Be Black in Puerto Rico," *AnOther,* August 6, 2020, https://www.anothermag.com/art -photography/gallery/11255/don-t-call-me-triguena-i-m-black-by-adriana-parrilla/5.

62. Lloréns, "Identity Practices," 39.

63. Quiñones Rivera, "Trigueñita to Afro-Puerto Rican," 166; Lloréns, "Identity Practices," 39.

64. "No me llames 'trigueña.'"

65. Quiñones Rivera, "Trigueñita to Afro-Puerto Rican," 166.

66. "No me llames 'trigueña.'"

Chapter 4

The Resistance in the Photographic Indexical Portrayal of Afro-Latina Women in Manuel González de la Parra's *Luces de raíz negra*

Kerry Green

The relationship between photography and the Black body in the Americas was originally developed as a colonizing tool to assimilate or to prove the inferiority of the Black race. These photographs served as a way to create an index of "otherness" from a white perspective, particularly because only those with the means in the Americas that had access to technology for photography. In his book *Photography and the Body*, John Pultz[1] points out photography's ability to delimit stereotypes that therefore created a symbolic control over the photographed bodies' subjects. This control made it so that photography became a key role in colonization and in creating the dynamics between racial and ethnic groups. Photographs of Black bodies also led to the erroneous science of Black body inferiority known as race science. Race science utilized photography to highlight differences of physique of the Black body against the white ones, establishing the white body as the backdrop, the body that all others are compared to. This is but one example of how photography served to catalog "otherness," particularly of people of color. These classifications along with the colonized history of Black populations in the Americas present an obligation to transform the existing index of photography of Black populations. In his article "The Shadow and the Substance: Race, Photography, and the Index," Nicholas Mirzoeff[2] turns precisely to photography as an opportunity that could do away with the racial indexicality, especially in the hands of rising artists in the digital age.

Indeed, with the rise of the digital age and social media, voices and photography of groups that were previously silenced or thought nonexistent have taken control of their narrative through photography. Such is the example with the Afro-Mexican population, who until 2015 were not included in the national census in Mexico. In 1929, José Vasconcelos established the national Mexican mestizaje in his book *La raza cósmica*. As an attempt to unify a country recuperating from a violent revolution, the Minister of Education José Vasconcelos[3] determines the Mexican citizen that of a cosmic race made up from primarily the combination of Indigenous origins but of Spaniard civilization. His nationalist affirmations led to the invisibility of the African descendants that made up not only Afro-Mexican identity but also heroes and examples of Afro-Mexican resistance such as Gaspar Yanga from Veracruz, Mexico. As a reaction to the erasure of Afro-Mexicans, the movement of la tercera raíz arises with the purpose of remembering and celebrating African descent as a primary part of Mexican identity. This movement also changed the way the camera's lens portrayed the Afro-Mexican population. One can see such transition between photography books like Maya Goded's *Tierra Negra* (1994) to *Luces de Raíz Negra by* Manuel González de la Parra (2004). In *Luces de raíz negra,* González combines photographs of the Afro-descendent population of the town of Coyolillo, Veracruz, Mexico, with photographs of the Afro-descendent populations of various places in Colombia

By arranging his photographs in no particular order in his photography book *Luces de raíz negra,* González breaks with the image of otherness of Afro-Latino populations in the Americas. The structure of his book and the introductory essays serve to frame Afro-Latino populations as whole and decolonized societies. However, it is imperative to recognize that these frames, which are photographed with an ethnographic lens, will contribute to the index of Afro-Latino populations. Furthermore, the catalog of the Afro-Latino women is also created in such photographs, and unfortunately, most are associated with their role within the home and family unless photographed as part of ceremonies or festivities. Yet, photographical subjects speak for themselves through their gazes, their gestures, their movements, and their noiseless sounds. That is no exception for the women subjects that appear in Manuel González de la Parra's photographs. This essay aims to identify the manner in which the Afro-Latina women resist the ethnographic camera lens through the Barthesian *punctum* in the photographs of *Luces de raíz negra* by Manuel González de la Parra.

It was previously pointed out that photography has been used to put the Black body on display, whether it was to confirm assimilation through adopted clothing or practices or to prove inferiority through scientific displays of bodies or skulls. Though the relationship between minority groups and photography has come far beyond proving racial inferiority, one must admit the problematic nature of an ethnographic approach to sharing the lived experience of minority groups. Author Trinh T. Minh-Ha[4] shares the same sentiments in her book *When the Moon Waxes Red* where she turns a critical lens on the paternalistic imposition of documentary and ethnographic texts on minority groups. She claims that by making minority communities the subjects of ethnographic cultural production, there is a demand for them to complete the impossible task of expressing themselves earnestly and holistically by snippets caught through camera lens. Such a daunting task remains impossible because of the complexity of portraying all individualities into a hegemonic snapshot that is to symbolize all members of the minority group. This in turn maintains the space of otherness intact; even if the snapshot redefines the index of the otherness, it does not dismantle it. It then becomes of utmost importance to know how to read a photograph to find the way subjects can truly communicate beyond the frames of photography.

One can turn to Ronald Barthes to understand how to identify and read the signs within a photograph. In *Camera Lucida*, Barthes[5] explains how given that subjects pose in front of a camera lens, the spectator of the photograph is never truly seeing the real versions of their subjects. In addition, everything that one sees in the photograph can never truly be seen, as what is present in the picture is no longer a reality that exists, but a glimpse into what once was. This is particularly true in photographs that have an ethnographic approach where subjects are aware and posed for the camera. Consequently, one must turn to the Barthesian *punctum* to understand the meanings of ethnographic photographs. Barthes[6] describes the *punctum* as the element in the photograph that disturbs the spectator; it is the element that captures the spectator's attention that leaves them struck by the photograph. It is precisely through the *punctum* of González's photography that the women subjects are able to tell their stories in spite of the insufficiency of the ethnographic approach. Yet, it is first essential to establish the stereotypes and the photographical index that exist of the Afro-Latina woman.

The exoticization of the Black populations in Latin America was built through the study of Afro-Latinos as primitive others, especially when referring to their dance rituals, religion, and different customs. In her book *Black Looks: Race and Representation*, bell hooks[7] questions the spectator's relationship with the body and consequently Black photography by pointing out the spectator's fixation with a primitive romantic fantasy that is always found in a dark body, whether it be a body, space, or location. This infatuation with associating Black bodies with the primitive leads to misconceptions of the Afro-Latino population. By not understanding the ceremonies practiced beyond a spectacle and a superficial knowledge, Afro-Latinos continue to be represented as primitive and posed as others rather than as an integral part of society. Peter Wade[8] highlights this phenomenon that occurs in Black communities in Colombia that are attributed powers as healers and sorcerers, which turns a common practice of healing and shamans into something out of the ordinary and into otherness. Wade mentions that this is not something uncommon for the treatment of the Afro-Latino populations of Latin America, and goes so far to include sensual dancing and music as additional parts of *negrismo*, or Black identity in Latin America. Isar P. Godreau Santiago[9] additionally explains that by not understanding these practices and, rather, posing the Afro-Latino population in exoticized practices, the Afro-Latino daily practices can become reasons to isolate them in their otherness. When these images of Black bodies and practices are decontextualized, the otherness of the Latin American Afro-descendent is reproduced and maintained.

The perception of the Afro-Latina has also depended on the primitive exoticism, particularly that of their sexuality and domesticity. Sergia Galván[10] explains how this idea was initially thought to be biologically or culturally determined. Due to the established otherness of Afro-Latinas, these women are more sexualized by their difference not only because of their race, but also by their supposed hypersexual "nature" compared to non-Afro-Latina women. This establishment of otherness is part of the consequence of the colonization of Black bodies in the Americas. Surely enough, Wade[11] points out the significance of the patriarchal gender narrative for the success of colonization and the construction of racial identities. He claims that due to colonization, there was a clear establishment of the weak, wild, seductive, silent or in danger position of others that required the help of colonizers. One can see the established progression of adjectives that fit the profile of the Afro-Latina woman.

The association of the Afro-Latina women as wild, seductive or weak makes it so that Afro-Latina women are portrayed as flat, one-dimensional people. Adriana Pena Mejía[12] affirms that this interpretation of the Afro-Latina woman is a simplification of their existence. She argues that Afro-Colombian women have been portrayed without their political and social activism that have left them as superficial second-class citizens. It is not a unique pattern pertaining only to the Afro-Colombian women, but an existing pattern in the Americas due to the ideologies of otherness that have been imposed through colonization. In addition to being hyper sexualized beings, Pena[13] explains how Afro-Latinas have also been associated with being good domestic caretakers such as cooks and maids. This profile of Afro-Latinas sheds light on the index and stereotype of the Afro-Latina woman in the modern day. This manner of misrepresenting Black women within Latin American society changes the way in which Black women are represented within the world of photography.

Apart from being seen as hypersexual and domestic beings, there is also an exoticization of women in relation to the specific dances and rites of Afro-Latino culture. Galvan[14] questions this identity that is specifically defined in relation to these practices that have been exoticized. Galvan points out that when referring to racial and ethnic identities, it is only people of color who are immediately thought of to have cultural productions of folklore, dances, rites, or festive colors. This type of discourse reveals more of the approach of those who built the speech of exoticization than the supposed exoticized population. Mirzoeff[15] also insists that because the digital age makes it so that photography can be accessed by many in a short amount of time, the photograph will lose its indexical power. Faced with this new understanding of Afro-Latinos and Afro-Latinas in particular, one sees the development of photography projects such as *Luces de raíz negra* by Manuel González de la Parra. This photography book does a good job of placing Afro-Latinos in a contextualized setting within Colombian and Mexican society, but its photographs of Afro-Latina women continue to contribute to the simplified discourse of the Black woman's experience.

The first thing you notice about the book *Luces de raíz negra* published in 2004 is its structure. The book has two introductory essays that share the experience of the Afro-Latino communities within the Colombian and Mexican world: "Negritudes americanas" by Sylvia Navarrete and "Américas negras: miradas y cruzadas a México y Colombia" by Odile Hoffmann and Adriana Naveda Navarrete's[16] first essay explains the approach that Manuel González has taken with the photographed population in the book. However, it relies on the stereotypical references that have been imposed on Black populations to situate the reader. Navarrete makes statements that imply the rowdy nature of the Afro-Latino population and insists that through photography, the atmosphere quiets in front of González's camera lens. Including such a stereotyped description of Afro-Latino subjects as an introduction simply maintains the stereotype of them being primitive or noisy. This type of stereotype also supports the continuation of the indexicality of photography of Black populations within Latin America. Likewise, Navarrete[17] insists that the photographer gets along better with women, who are more outgoing than male subjects. Unfortunately, this is not noticeable in the book, given the less-frequent appearances of female subjects in *Luces de raíz negra.*

The second article by Odile Hoffmann and Adriana Naveda gives a contextualization to Manuel González's photographs that delves deeper into the social and economic position of the Black population within the different societies of Colombia and Mexico. Although brief, Hoffmann and Naveda differentiate the ways in which each population relates to the non-Afro-descendent population within each country. They emphasize that, in Mexico, with the nationalist discourse, many of the Black populations stopped identifying as such, preferring to identify with words such as "moreno" or "mulatto."[18] They also differentiate the experience of Afro-Latinos in Colombia who had a very different trajectory from the population of Afro-Mexicans. Afro-Colombians, although they were free for a longer time, were impacted by the global commercialization of European companies[19] in Colombia. This explanation given by Hoffmann and Naveda gives a more beneficial frame to the reader and viewer of the photographs that follow.

The photographs are divided into four different parts divided by the following titles: "Imágenes de un paradigma," "La vida dúctil," "República de lo habitual," and "La fiesta y el rito." These divisions have the function of guiding the reader by framing the context of the photographs. In general, the book breaks with the history of indexicality that is present in Afro-Latino photography. It breaks with these structures because it presents them as workers, contributors to the national economy, consumers, and in various instances, includes pictures of men with power or agency through phallocentric symbols.[20] In the same way, it does not place the subjects as an otherness, since the subjects in the photographs are of primary importance, occupying the central space of the photographs' frames and with the camera's lens at eye level, producing a feeling of equality between the subjects and the spectator. The contexts in which they are taken show a variety of environments, whether they are within houses, in the field or work space or through the streets of the town, though always in low-income spaces. The photograph on page 50 shows the ties between Mexico and the United States through the Florida Gator shirt that the subject in the photo is wearing. While on page 76, the subject's agency is shown through her work and showcases modernity in Colombia by displaying trending hairstyles. The photograph is called "En la peluquería en África." These photographs establish Afro-Latino life contextualized in its historical and contemporary complexity that takes the reader hand in hand with the modern experience of Afro-Latino populations.

The introductory essays and the elements of economic integration make it possible for the viewer to approach the photographs in a contextualized and current way. In contrast, when reading the depiction of the Afro-Latina subjects, it leaves much to be desired. Each category of the book has fifteen to nineteen photographs with less than half of the photographs in each category with women as subjects, except for the chapter titled "Las fiestas y el rito." This chapter has an overwhelming amount of Afro-Latina presence which serves as a way to continue indexing Afro-Latina women as particularly susceptible to dancing and festivities. However, when looking beyond the simple number of photographs of women within the book, one must also consider what space Afro-Latinas occupy in González's photography. In this analysis, the photographs analyzed will focus on the limited presence of Afro-Latina women in the chapters other than "Las fiestas y el rito," where they are insistently portrayed in domestic spaces and involved in domestic roles and tasks. While some photographs may portray an implicit pride in such domestic tasks, two photographs in particular will showcase how the Barthesian punctum can break with the ethnographic photographic lens and will shed light into the lived experience of the Afro-Mexican and Afro-Colombian woman in González's photography.

The first two female subjects to be analyzed in the photography book determine the relationship between Afro-Latina women and their role as a caretaker. Immediately, the Afro-Latina women in González's photographs are related to children. The photo titled "Valentina y su hija Yuri" is found on page 13; Valentina is portrayed completing a domestic and maternal task: combing her daughter Yuri's hair. Yet, in the photograph, Valentina is not the main subject but rather her daughter Yuri, who accompanies her. Valentina's image is blurred, and her presence in the photograph takes a back seat as the focus is on her daughter, Yuri. This effect not only hides Valentina, but also detracts from her. In the photograph, the importance is not necessarily on Valentina nor her face, nor her body but in what she is doing, taking care of her daughter. It is a static photograph, where the motion of the comb is implied but not shown. With the attention on the task and the blurring of Valentina's image, the significance of her presence in the photograph is tied to the completion of her task.

This is also seen in the way the photograph is structured. Valentina is directly behind Yuri. Her image is blurred and the subject in focus is the daughter. This linear figure that is seen between mother and daughter is not a finite linearity, it is replicated from generation to generation, especially with a significance of the Afro-Latino identity that rests with Afro-Latino textured hair. The linearity in the picture along with Yuri's bored expression demonstrate the repetition of the task not only on a personal level, but also as a generational tradition to be passed on. It is very likely that Yuri will one day find herself in the same position as Valentina, in the background, one more Afro-Latina mother. The image perpetuates the continuity of the domestic values predetermined by being Afro-Latina. Yet, what is most striking about the photograph is the serious face and the direct contact of the camera with Yuri's gaze. Her expression can be interpreted as boredom or even discomfort perhaps not only in the practice, but having to be photographed and imposed upon during such a mundane task.

In another photograph on page 84, there are two women cooking. Unfortunately, due to a publication error, the title of the photograph is not found in the index. The photograph includes two women who are preparing tortillas, perhaps matriarchs of their community. The kitchen lacks modern technology like a stove or refrigerator. Likewise, the kitchen walls are made of clay and there is a stack of firewood on the top left corner of the photograph. While kitchen items demonstrate a scarcity of modern technology, there is no need for these technological advancements as the women seem perfectly comfortable in their space. The image shows how women prepare the typical food of the region, tortillas, without the need for the technological elements of modernity. However, again we see the representation of Afro-Latina women associated with highly domestic tasks such as cooking. Despite this, it is the first space in which the free movement of women is demonstrated.

Movement is present within the photography. This is particularly true in the motion of the woman's hands of the subject facing the camera lens. To prepare the tortilla, the clapping of hands is necessary to give the round shape to the tortilla. This is seen in the way the woman's hands are blurred from the required movement. Similarly, the light entering from above casts a blurred light that entangles itself with the hair of the subject facing the camera. It is not clear if such blur is produced by the light falling on the steam of food cooking on the stove behind the subject's body, but the blur of light seems to intertwine itself with movement, making this photograph visibly come to life. Likewise, the textures in the photograph make it so the spectator can almost reach out and feel the rough walls of the kitchen, the dry but cold touch of the hanging clay pots , and even the warmth coming off that steam. The subjects in the photograph can be seen hard at work, focused on the task at hand with no regard to the camera lens. This focus that they have can also be seen in the symmetry of the picture, the subject on the left facing the camera, and the subject on the right facing away from the camera. Since one woman is facing the camera and the other is with her back to the camera, and both are preparing the tortillas, it is inferred that the women are moving between themselves to complete the task. To the right of the woman with her back to the camera you can see the product of their work, the tortillas. Knowing about this collaboration between the two women makes it so that the spectator can visualize the movement required to complete the domestic task.

While both of these pictures lack a striking factor that could be considered the punctum of the photograph, the complete disregard for the camera in both pictures. "Valeria y su hija Yuri" along with the second picture of the women preparing tortillas demonstrate these women's pride in completing such tasks. While such photographs can be harmful in continuing the domestic space to which Afro-Latinas are so easily related, there is also a subtle sense of pride in being the agents of nurture for their community. All three female subjects completely disregard the camera, this way taking away importance from posing, from hiding their true self,[21] and focusing on the task at hand. They prioritize their duty as caretakers, in this way elevating their responsibility to more than just a mere task and showing the value these women have in their role as caretakers. In this manner, the subjects redefine the way these photographs portray the domesticity of Afro-Latinas and retake agency in their roles as caretakers.

Yet, there are photographs in *Luces de raíz negra* where the Afro-Latina subjects use the Barthesian punctum to break with the ethnographic lens that portrays the photographic scenes as accurate representations. The structure of the photograph plays a key role in reading the photograph entitled "Ana y las hijas de Noel." Like the first photograph mentioned, the title directly relates the young woman with children, whether hers or not. In the photograph, the use of frames is used to structure and demonstrate the generational expectations of young Afro-Latinas. The window that frames all three female subjects creates a contrast with light, with the interior of the window being dark and the outer side of the window reflecting the white of the building. While in this photograph the subjects are not directly engaged with a domestic chore, there is an implication of childcare and the passing of responsibility with age. Ana, the oldest of the female subjects, is equally, or if not more, hidden than Valentina. This time, Ana's image is not blurred. However, the space that Ana occupies in the photograph hides her as she is the one furthest into the building from the window. Her body is completely hidden from the camera, covered by Noel's daughters. Her face seems to be floating behind both girls who are sitting on the windowsill, a slight smile on her face. One quick glance at the photo and one could easily miss Ana's presence in the photo. The darkness inside the house makes her hair and body disappear from the camera. It should be noted that Ana's space is clearly inside the house. While the two daughters are literally on the border between the house and the space outside, Ana is not only inside the house, but hidden and almost swallowed by the darkness and the domestic space. Although different from Valentina's silence, this position takes away her focus and represents her as a young Afro-Latina in relation to children.

The value of women and their relationship with children and, consequently, the role of being a mother is clearly defined using the frame and light of the photograph. From the title it can be inferred that the girls are not Ana's daughters. However, Ana is clearly not labeled a daughter, as she is the subject that takes responsibility for the younger girls, old enough to start playing her role as a future mother. While Ana is obviously still a young woman herself, one can see that she has responsibilities expected of her, such as watching over Noel's daughters. This progression of growing into the expectations of an Afro-Latinas is seen in the generational linearity between the three subjects. It can be seen first in the space occupied by the subjects. The younger girls occupy a space on the border, balancing themselves on the edge of the house, playing with the border between the domestic space, the inside where Ana stays and the outside space, where the sun hits and light is dispersed. In comparison, Ana is already deep inside the house, almost unnoticed. Ana's age means that she already inhabits the space of the house as the keeper of Noel's daughters. Similarly, this reproduction is seen in the position of the subjects' hands. The youngest girl is the only one with her hands loose and without restraint. Her sister's hands, although one is explicitly positioned on her skirt, the other is seen on her little sister, as a way to reassure her and in a way, to take care of her. Both of Ana's hands are on the youngest girl's waist, obviously out of necessity, since without holding her, the little girl would most likely fall and hurt herself. One can see the transition of different ages and how the expectation of childcare grows with the passing of age.

The two older subjects, Ana and the young child to her left, stand perfectly posed and static. The oldest of Noel's daughters gives a restrained smile with slightly scrunched eyebrows, a playful if somewhat forced smile. Similarly, Ana's smile though seemingly more genuine holds note of shyness, again demonstrating her restraint or discomfort at being photographed. Yet, when looking at the youngest daughter, she seems to be the only one who does not hold back on expressing her true self, disregarding the posing that Barthes[22] insists is portrayed in photography. If the Barthesian posing is equal to hiding the true self from the camera, the crying child in this picture breaks precisely that and shows the spectator a precise version of herself. This cry that one can witness is what pierces and stands out most in the photograph, making the physical manifestation of her cry the punctum of the frame. With her cry, the youngest daughter is the subject that disrupts the continuity of the photograph, immediately calling attention to her discomfort, breaking the beautifully structured frame of not only the photograph but also the light that represents the window frame. She opens her mouth freely and expresses her disgust or discomfort, whether it be directed at the camera lens or not. Likewise, she is the only subject who can be seen expressing herself without filter, as opposed to her sister's and Ana's cryptic and poised smiles. Similarly, her cry makes it so that her perfectly chosen outfit and bow look out of place, a resistance to the perfectly shaped still of her life. This cry can be seen as a sign of resistance, intentional or not, to the ethnographic gaze that insists on indexing the Afro-Latina female as purely domestic beings.

The last photograph analyzed is titled "Neneu y su novia," found on page 79 of the photography book *Luces de raíz negra.* The photograph frames a man named Neneu and his girlfriend who remains nameless. It is very important to highlight that the female subject is stripped of her identity since her name is left out from the title of the photograph. They are in a bedroom atop of a bed. However, the position in which they were photographed is extremely uncomfortable, especially for the Afro-Latina girlfriend. Their positions are posed and unnatural, especially in the way they are poised atop the bed, the way their bodies relate with each other, and the position of their arms. The hands of the female subject are not relaxed but perfectly placed on Neneu's arm and leg. Likewise, Neneu's arms are placed unnaturally around his girlfriend, seemingly caging her across her upper chest. She is between his legs, and the arm that crosses her entire chest makes it so that she has minimal movement as she is pressed up against Neneu's arm and his chest. But her lack of movement in the photo is also highlighted by the image of a dancing man displayed on the wall above the couple. This man in the image creates a contrast with the couple on the bed, as he is a still representation of movement, emphasized even more by the waves of the sea, yet another element of movement, and more so, powerful freedom. The way this image is held behind an uncomfortable and immobile couple makes this lack of movement of the couple stand out even more, particularly for the female subject. Much like the linearity pointed out in the previous photographs, there is a particular linearity going from stillness present with the girlfriend and movement displayed by the dancing dreaded man. The position of the dancing man is behind Neneu which functions as an extension of Neneu's existence. Neneu acts as a buffer between a place of zero mobility to one of free mobility; he also functions as a gatekeeper for such mobility. However, the girlfriend has nothing in the photograph to imply her ability to move; even her fingers are positioned unnaturally. This photograph demonstrates the immobility of the Afro-Latinas compared to her male counterparts.

Nonetheless, more noticeable still are the expressions that both subjects hold. Neneu is not looking directly at the camera, yet this action seems to be intentional as Neneu's expression seems to be distracted away from the camera. In contrast, the girlfriend is looking directly at the camera, but her expression serious and piercing. It is precisely in her gaze that the Barthesian punctum can be found, this piercing gaze transmitting the resistance of the Afro-Latina girlfriend. While her hands and body seem to be perfectly poised and controlled, the very opposite can be seen in the way her eyes pierce the camera. The corners of her lips turned slightly downward and lips barely ajar, along with her eyebrows slightly furrowed, her expression conveys her discomfort whether with the position or the presence of the photographer. Through her gaze, the female subject is able to communicate with her spectator, disregarding her immobile pose and showing her resistance through her piercing gaze. If her body is completely controlled by her pose, it is her eyes that transmit her resistance to simply becoming one more subject model. Her gaze becomes a commentary on the camera lens that cannot possibly begin to embody her lived experiences as an Afro-Latina woman, especially when posed in such an unnatural manner. Yet, it can capture the moments in between, where her discomfort becomes a resistance in front of the ethnographic lens.

The role of women within the home and their space is different in all photographs, but the indexicality of the photographs remain the same, the Afro-Latina woman finds her work and value as domestic caretakers. Pena Mejía[23] warns against the invisibility that this continuing catalog of Afro-Latina women in photography can have, especially at the hands of patriarchal values that insist on portraying women in domestic spheres. Yet, as spectators, one must be vigilant in looking for the signifiers that speak far beyond the four borders of each photograph. The Afro-Latinas displayed in the first two pictures do this in their lack of acknowledgment of the camera, where they defy the ethnographic gaze by being engrossed and finding significance in their domestic duties as caretakers. Their lack of posing in front of the camera shows the seriousness with which they take their domestic responsibilities and their role within the community.

While in a different manner, the Afro-Latinas in the third and fourth photographs also demonstrate resistance to the ethnographic photograph by producing the photographic Barthesian *punctum.* Through signs like the noiseless cry of the child or the intense gaze of the female subjects, they guarantee communication with the spectator in a fashion that implies their multiplicity in a still photograph. In each photograph, there is a linearity that stages different experiences of being an Afro-Latina. With the photograph "Ana y las hijas de Noel," the linearity of the female conditioning from crying toddler to well-behaved caretaker is ruptured precisely through the cry of the young girl. Similarly, the girlfriend's piercing gaze in "Neneu y su novia" also breaks with the scale of mobility presented in the photograph. While the photographs were intentionally staged to better produce documentary-style photographs, it is what is *not* staged that amplifies the voices of the Afro-Latina women in González's photography.

As a whole, the photography book would gain more by firstly including more women. By reducing the number of photographs of Afro-Latinas in *Luces de raíz negra*, the importance and role that women have within Black populations in Latin America is diminished. Including more photographs of women in the variety of roles that these women have would help to change the indexicality that is created of Afro-Latina women. The problem with the way Manuel González de la Parra chooses to include Afro-Latinas in his ethnographic photography is that it follows the pattern of domesticity that has been previously imposed on those women. Taking into consideration the history of indexicality that Afro-descendant photography has and its relationship with the creation of Afro-Latino otherness, it is important to consider all these aspects when creating an ethnographic photography book. By not including women in places outside the home, the indexicality of Afro-Latinas will continue to be simplified as good mothers and exceptional caretakers. Yet, the Afro-Latina women subjects are not voiceless, even behind the ethnographic camera lens. They find their resistance in the spaces between the poised positions and the camera lens. Their resistance lies in the silences, their noiseless cries, or their piercing gazes that puncture the perfectly framed ethnographic photographs. When faced with the ethnographic lens, the spectator must welcome the Barthesian *punctum* that will communicate the subjects' resistance in spite of the persistence of indexical photography.

BIBLIOGRAPHY

Barthes, Roland. *Camera Lucida: Reflections on Photography.* New York: Hill and Wang, 1981.
Fusco, Coco. "Racial Time, Racial Marks, Racial Metaphors." In *Only Skin Deep: Changing Visions of the American Self,* edited by Coco Fusco and Brian Wallis, 13–48. New York: Harry N. Abrams, 2003.
Galvan, Sergia. "El mundo étnico-racial dentro del feminism latinoamericano." *África América Latina, Cuadernos: Revista de ánalisis sur-norte para una cooperación solidaria*, no. 19 (1995): 33–38.
Godreau Santiago, Isar P. "Dinámicas de género en la representación del folclor puertorriqueño negro." *Identidades Revistas Interdisiplicinarias de Estudios de Género* 1, no. 1 (August 2003): 88–96.
Gonzalez de la Parra, Manuel. *Luces de raíz negra.* Veracruz: Universidad Veracruzana, 2004.
Hoffmann, Odile, and Adriana Naveda. "Américas negras: miradas cruzadas a México y Colombia." In *Luces de raíz negra*, by Manuel González de la Parra, 12–25. Veracruz: Universidad Veracruzana, 2004.
hooks, bell. *Black Looks: Race and Representation.* Boston: South End Press, 1992.
Mirzoeff, Nicholas. "The Shadow and the Substance. Race, Photography, and the Index." In *Only Skin Deep*: *Changing Visions of the American Self,* edited by Coco Fusco and Brian Wallis, 111–127. New York: Harry N. Abrams, 2003.
Molina, Óscar L., and John Pultz. *La fotografía y el cuerpo.* Madrid: Akal Ediciones, 2003.
Navarrete, Sylvia. Negritudes americanas. In *Luces de raíz negra*, by Manuel González de la Parra, 8–11. Veracruz: Universidad Veracruzana, 2004.
Pena Mejía, Alejandra. "Negra mente: Por un reconocimiento a la mujer afrocolombiana." *Artelogie*, no. 9 (June 2016): https://doi.org/10.4000/artelogie.322.
Vasconcelos, José. *La raza cósmica.* Madrid: Aguilar, 1966.
Wade, Peter. *Race and Ethnicity in Latin America*. London: Pluto Press, 2010.

NOTES

1. John Pultz, *Photography and the Body*, trans. Óscar L. Molina (Madrid: Akal Ediciones, 2003), 20.

2. Nicholas Mirzoeff, "The Shadow and the Substance. Race, Photography, and the Index," in *Only Skin Deep: Changing Visions of the American Self*, ed. Coco Fusco and Brian Wallis (New York: Harry N. Abrams, 2003), 112.

3. José Vasconcelos, *La raza cósmica* (Madrid: Aguilar, 1966), 28–32.

4. Trinh T. Minh-Ha, *When the Moon Waxes Red* (New York: Routledge, 1991), 60.

5. Barthes, Roland, *Camera Lucida: Relfections on Photography* (New York: Hill & Wang, 2010), 10–11.

6. Barthes, *Camera Lucida,* 26–27.

7. bell hooks, *Black Looks: Race and Representation* (Boston: South End Press, 1992), 33.

8. Peter Wade, *Race and Ethnicity in Latin America* (London: Pluto Press, 2010), 93.

9. Isar P. Godreau Santiago, "Dinámicas de género en la representación del folclor puertorriqueño negro," *Identidades: Revista interdisciplinaria de estúdios de género* 1, no. 1 (October 2003): 93.

10. Sergia Galván, "El mundo étnico-racial dentro del feminism latinoamericano," *Africa América Latina, Cuadernos: Revista de ánalisis sur-norte para una cooperación solidaria*, no. 19 (1995): 34.

11. Wade, *Race and Ethnicity in Latin America*, 81.

12. Alejandra Pena Mejía, "Negra mente: Por un reconocimiento a la mujer afrocolombiana," *Artelogie*, no. 9 (June 2016): https://doi.org/10.4000/artelogie.322.

13. Pena Mejía, "Negra mente," https://doi.org/10.4000/artelogie.322.

14. Galván, "El mundo étnico-racial," 34.

15. Mirzoeff, "The Shadow and the Substance. Race, Photography, and the Index," 125.

16. Sylvia Navarrete, "Negritudes americanas," in *Luces de raíz negra* ed. by Manuel González de la Parra (Veracruz: Universidad Veracruzana, 2004), 10.

17. Navarrete, "Negritudes americanas," 11.

18. Odile Hoffmann and Adriana Naveda, "Américas negras: miradas cruzadas a México y Colombia," in *Luces de raíz negra* ed. by Manuel González de la Parra (Veracruz: Universidad Veracruzana, 2004), 21.

19. Odile Hoffmann and Adriana Naveda, "Américas negras: miradas cruzadas a México y Colombia," 24.

20. See the photographs *Braulio León* (55), *Son of Isidro and Felipa* (92), *Remo de hombre* (93), *Reparando la canoa* (95), *Silvano* (97).

21. Barthes, *Camera Lucida,* 11–12.

22. Barthes, *Camera Lucida*, 10.

23. Pena Mejía, "Negra mente," https://doi.org/10.4000/artelogie.322.

PART II

Challenging Hegemonic Spaces

*Female Leadership and Visibility in
Social Activism, Educational Resources,
and Spiritual Expressions of Blackness*

holy mother

of God

seated in stone cloud red and white prayers slow burning embers
dripping from mouth
leaden lagrimas nailed sun bloodstains salvation and sacrifice suspended glory
her eyes brimming purgatory
es una lástima

where will her poor children run when it rains blood fire in the
streets?

what happens to a rich man's soul when an angel folds her wings?

holy mother
of wolf and lamb
el lobo se traga a los pobres elite read
from milton translation glass mansion retreat paradise lost
the good book of retiro

no one here knows of ghent everyone here will testify beyond poverty line
del grupo mondongo milagro

it reads
como red words in bible
it binds como red chord famine corrugated sheet metal congregation
barren barrio choir singing oraciones below black wires

wicked men like poor women never sleep
preachers like politicians
sell souls for babylonian dreams

holy mother
of labyrinthine alleys blind faith y guitarra of scavenged bricks y las
jarras

oh my god

holy mother
of cocaine paste paco y pintar de negros
of plastilina cera y alquitrán acero e hilos de algodón sobre madera

holy mother of slum altar
of violence and rebellion
of entrapment and innocence of rags and salt water
eye of Ra

holy mother of villa 31 nuestra patria
del espejo y del humo

cierre el ojo open the sky

—Natasha Carrizosa

Chapter 5

Representing Candomblé in the Public Sphere

Black Priestesses' Authorship in Brazilian Cultural Production

Jamie Lee Andreson

"O que não se registra, o tempo leva / What you don't record, time will take away." This iconic statement from Maria Stella de Azevedo Santos (Mãe Stella)[1] in her groundbreaking text *Meu Tempo é Agora / My Time is Now* (1993) dictates a clear justification for Candomblé priestesses' authorship. In this book she presents the history and rites of her temple to a public audience with appropriate detail. Candomblé is a religion of secrecy—not all ritual knowledge is available to all initiates, who are organized hierarchically, and even less may be disclosed to an uninitiated public.[2] As the high authority of the temple Ilê Axé Opô Afonjá in Salvador, Bahia, throughout her life Mãe Stella recorded what she deemed appropriate to preserve through the time capsule of the written form. From her abundant writings, she then selected what to publish and disseminate to a broader public with the intention of defending Candomblé against historic discrimination and representing herself as a religious authority requiring no mediation. By the end of her life at ninety-three years of age in 2018, Mãe Stella had published four books, wrote a column for the local newspaper, was nominated as a member of the Bahian State Academy of Letters, and gained an honorary doctorate from the State University of Bahia (UNEB) in 2009, to mention just a few of her accomplishments. Her works, together with the body of literature and cultural products produced by and with Black women leaders of the Candomblé religion in Brazil, featured their roles as authoritative figures in Brazilian history and placed them at the forefront of national conversations on race, religion, and culture.

As leaders of Afro-Brazilian religion based in oral traditions, Black Candomblé priestesses are the keepers of ancestral knowledge in their communities. For most of the religion's history—from Africa to the Americas—the myths, stories, rites, and teachings of Candomblé were not primarily recorded through written texts. Transmission of ritual knowledge during the initiation process is both oral and corporal. The wisdom of Candomblé cannot be learned from a book; it is an experiential religion passed through generations of *convivência* [coexistence] in the temple territory of the *terreiro*. Given the primacy of orality in Candomblé, many leaders throughout the twentieth century formed partnerships with writers, artists, and scholars to corroborate in the documentation and dissemination of their wisdom in the Brazilian public sphere. Toward the end of the twentieth century, select priestesses "appropriated the academics' tools"[3] and took the initiative to record their own stories on their own terms. In the twenty-first century, practitioners and practitioner-scholars have increased their methods of self-representation through written and audiovisual projects given advancements in education, technology, and cultural capital in Brazil. Despite these many engagements in the public sphere, Candomblé priestesses are rarely included in the canon of Brazilian literary and cultural production, as Black women's contributions to the Brazilian nation are often overlooked. This chapter offers a brief genealogy of the most prominent written and published works by Candomblé priestesses, placing their works centrally within Brazilian cultural production as ancestral wisdom inherited from generations of Black communities.

TWENTIETH-CENTURY PRIESTESSES: POLITICS AND CULTURE

At least since the 1930s, Candomblé leaders have selectively articulated religious knowledge in the public sphere and negotiated for religious freedom in Brazilian society. Throughout the twentieth century, select Candomblé priestesses were recognized as prominent cultural, intellectual, and political leaders. Through media appearances and collaborations produced with artists and scholars, highly regarded priestesses of historic temples created lasting legacies and contributed to public dialogue that defended Candomblé as a religion. Contrary narratives had historically discriminated against Afro-Brazilian religious practices through common racist tropes such that it was "black magic," sorcery or diabolical through a Euro-centric Christian perspective dominant in Brazilian society. Priestesses including Mãe Aninha, Mãe Senhora, and Mãe Menininha from historic temples in Salvador shared select religious knowledge in the public sphere to represent their religious practice and African heritage from their perspective, gaining international notoriety and respect as prominent cultural figures.

With the proliferation of the Candomblé religion following the abolition of slavery in Brazil in 1888, the prominent priestess Mãe Aninha (Eugênia Anna Santos, 1869–1938) founded the Ilê Axé Opô Afonjá temple in 1910 in Salvador and crowned the city the "Black Rome." Discursively locating Bahia as the epicenter of Black religions in the Americas, Mãe Aninha propagated this vision widely, and it continues to reverberate in characterizations of Salvador's place in the Afro-American diaspora.[4] Mãe Aninha was born to African parents of the Grunsi ethnicity in Salvador in 1869.[5] She was a financially successful merchant, facilitating the importation of African ritual materials as a commercial trader with shipments between Bahia and West Africa. Her commercial success contributed to her financial independence and allowed her to legally buy the large piece of land in the São Gonçalo neighborhood of Salvador where she built her temple of 39,000 square meters that still stands today.[6] As the founder of Ilê Axé Opô Afonjá, Mãe Aninha was the first in a prominent lineage of head priestesses that transformed public discourse on race, gender, and African heritage through the Candomblé religion in Brazil.

Oral histories contend that Mãe Aninha negotiated with politicians to protect the future of her religious practice. She was monumental in influencing the 1934 federal law that guaranteed freedom of religion, credited to her lobbying the president Getúlio Vargas.[7] She was also the primary informant for Donald Pierson, a US sociologist who conducted research on race in Bahia in the 1930s. Mãe Aninha was one of the central collaborators in the Second Afro-Brazilian Congress organized in Salvador in 1937, which brought together scholars and religious leaders to represent Candomblé as a religion in civil society in the face of historic discrimination and persecution.[8] She organized the Congress with the Bahian journalist and ethnographer Edison Carneiro, whom she had granted the ritual title of *ogã*—reserved for men to represent the temple in public relations.[9] The Congress Annals include written articles by prominent scholars and religious leaders including Edison Carneiro, Martiniano do Bonfim, Melville Herskovits, Donald Pierson and a piece written by Mãe Aninha on the culinary traditions from the Candomblé temples. At that time, she also proposed the creation of the Union of Afro-Brazilian Religious Sects as a body of leaders to represent Candomblé and self-organize the community.[10] The Union of Afro-Brazilian Religious Sects served to defend the fifth item of Article 113 of the 1934 Constitution, which granted "the liberty of consciousness, belief and guarantee of free exercise of religious cults."[11] Although the 1934 Brazilian constitution gave nominal freedom to African religion in a declaration of religious equality, the

Bahian state continued persecutory policies from the colonial period, requiring temples to pay for licenses to conduct their ceremonies and subjecting temples to police raids until 1976.

Mãe Aninha was a public figure in Salvador and considered throughout the nation to be a prominent leader of African religion. She was so popular and beloved that her death in 1938 at sixty-eight years of age caused great commotion in the city of Salvador. Edison Carneiro published Mãe Aninha's obituary and described her burial with a front-page article entitled "There goes the most popular Bahian *Mãe de Santo* [Priestess]" in the local newspaper *O Estado da Bahia*. In this article he eulogized Aninha, celebrating her leadership and popularity through initiatives including the Second Afro-Brazilian Congress and the Union of Afro-Brazilian Sects. The article described the flurry of people mourning their collective loss at Aninha's funerary scene:

> nearly three thousand people crying, struggling to carry her coffin, yelling desperately so that she might resuscitate, running over each other to put their hands on Aninha's coffin, lamenting and scorning her death, singing lugubrious African songs to accompany her last steps in this world.[12]

In 1945 the priestess Mãe Senhora (Maria Bibiana do Espírito Santo, 1890–1967) became the head priestess of the Ilê Axé Opô Afonjá Temple. Mãe Senhora continued her predecessor's public engagement through collaborations with famous artists and scholars including Bahian novelist Jorge Amado, the French photographer and anthropologist Pierre Verger, and the Argentinian visual artist Héctor Julio Páride Bernabó (Carybé). The cultural products that these men produced in collaboration with Mãe Senhora dictated public knowledge of the religion from the priestess as a primary source. Like Aninha's initiation of journalist and scholar Edison Carneiro, Mãe Senhora initiated the novelist Jorge Amado as a male representative of the temple to negotiate the temple's affairs in the public sphere. Jorge Amado, in turn, represented Candomblé and Mãe Senhora through his writings as the most prolific novelist of Afro-Bahia in the twentieth century, including *Jubiabá* (1935), *Capitães da Areia* (1937), *Bahia de Todos os Santos* (1944), *Dona Flor e Seus Dois Maridos* (1966), and *Tenda dos Milagres* (1969). During a time when most of what was considered national literature came from the Southern areas of Brazil with European influence, Jorge Amado's collaboration with Mãe Senhora was a powerful transgression of national hierarchies of power and representation that placed Brazil's African heritage as central to national culture.

Mãe Senhora, like Mãe Aninha, was also an independent businesswoman who sold African products through commercial networks in the historic center of Salvador.[13] Senhora ran a food vendor's tent called the Vencedora (the

Winner) at the Mercado Modelo, a central public market in the lower city of Salvador, where she became acquainted with the Bahian intelligentsia, including Jorge Amado.[14] As acting head priestess from 1942 to 1967 at the Opô Afonjá temple, Mãe Senhora received international visitors, particularly from Africa, Europe, and North America. At the turn of the 1960s Mãe Senhora was sought out by international artists, local intelligentsia, and politicians as a living legend of African heritage in Brazil, even crowned the "Mãe Preta" (Black Mother) of Brazil by the national folkloric director in Rio de Janeiro in 1965.[15] Mãe Senhora was widely sought out as the source of African religious knowledge in Brazil, though her perspective was mediated primarily through the collaboration of white men who, particularly in the mid-twentieth century, had greater access to resources, platform, audience, and the tools of representation.

The same Bahian intelligentsia, artists, and politicians w had encircled Mãe Senhora also frequented the Gantois Temple led by the head priestess Mãe Menininha (Maria Escolástica da Conceição, 1894–1986). Mãe Menininha often appeared within scholarship, the media, and popular culture as the head priestess of the historic Gantois Temple (Ilê Axé Iyá Omin Iyamassê) since 1922. She figured prominently in Ruth Landes's ethnography *The City of Women* (1947)*,* which portrayed the religion as a matriarchy, based on oral histories of Mãe Aninha and ethnographic research with prestigious priestesses including Mãe Menininha and Mãe Flaviana in Candomblé temples in Salvador from 1938 to 1939. Toward the end of her lifetime Mãe Menininha also appeared heavily in print media. An analysis of photographs taken and archived by journalists at the biggest newspaper in the state of Bahia, *A Tarde*, reveals just how much media attention was given to Mãe Menininha as an iconic Candomblé priestess in the late twentieth century. The archive holds five separate folders of materials including 189 photographs of her and seventy-four articles published about her in that newspaper alone.[16] Her public visibility heightened in popular culture and the media after she was about eighty years old as part of the growing initiatives to celebrate African heritage in Brazil. During the 1970s, she reached iconic status in the Tropicalia cultural movement, revered by famous artists in Brazil who included her and her temple in Brazilian cultural products exported widely.[17] For example, the samba musician Dorival Caymmi wrote the song "Oração de Mãe Menininha," which describes her as the grand Mother of Brazil, "the most beautiful star . . . the brightest sun. . . . the beauty of the world . . . the sweetest mother . . . the people's consolation."[18] The famous singer Clara Nunes also produced the hit song with Clementina de Jesus "Embala Eu," which featured the priestess' name in the chorus.

Mãe Menininha was also sought out by local politicians, including the Bahian Governor, Antônio Carlos Peixoto de Magalhães (known as ACM), photographed in 1976 in her private room within the Gantois temple quarters. The multigenerational ACM family represents the oligarchy of Brazilian politics as politically important families establish patronage relationships with the majority poor and Black constituents. The governor's relationship to Mãe Menininha constituted a strategic alliance in his broader project of connecting with "the people" (*o povo*) through authoritarian government. Antonio Carlos Magalhães "was said to be an initiate, or at least a client of Mãe Menininha, and this mutual client-patron relationship often came to the public eye."[19] From this alliance, ACM benefited from being recognized as a true Bahian who identified with the religious traditions of his people. In exchange, Mãe Menininha received government protection, widespread respect, and public recognition that sometimes translated into material resources. That ACM was instrumental to ending the state persecution of Candomblé with a Bahian state law in 1976 demonstrates how consequential such alliances could be for the entire Afro-Bahian religious community. Through the cultivation of these public relationships, Black priestesses reaffirmed their authoritative position as leaders of their communities and engaged with politicians, scholars, and artists to protect their autonomy and guarantee the future of their religious practices against discrimination and persecution.

The decree that eliminated the Bahian state's control of Candomblé in 1976 instigated a shift in the public engagement of Candomblé leaders and initiates, who no longer had to hide their ritual practices for fear of police persecution.[20] This new opening also allowed for unprecedented public representation of the religion in popular culture, as representative of the Brazilian nation. To navigate these cultural shifts, artists and the media turned especially to Candomblé priestesses as the public authorities and cultural brokers of the Candomblé community. The priestesses took on this role with the same approach, epistemologies, and perspectives with which they had historically led their own communities. They used their position to publicly represent and disseminate information about Candomblé on an unprecedented scale to various audiences.

The public representations of Candomblé priestesses in the early to mid-twentieth century were largely mediated through collaborations with primarily male journalists, artists, and politicians who increasingly turned to them as leaders of their communities and cultural representatives of African heritage in Brazil. Mãe Aninha engaged intellectually through her participation in the Second Afro-Brazilian Congress alongside prominent scholars including Edison Carneiro, Melville Herskovits, and Donald Pierson and negotiated with politicians to publicly legitimize her religious practice. Mãe Senhora collaborated with writers such as Jorge Amado and photographers such as Pierre Verger to further disseminate the historical importance of her temple as a conduit between Brazil and Africa. Mãe Menininha was heavily

represented in Brazilian cultural exports including samba music and used her fame to advocate for greater protection of the religion in Brazilian society. This generation of priestesses collaborated with coconspirators to influence the public's perception of Candomblé but were largely framed as the subjects of cultural commentary rather than the producers of cultural products. As such, their contributions as authors and sources of public knowledge were minimized as part of a broader trend that has erased Black women's agency and political strategies throughout history. Approaching the twenty-first century, the next generation of priestesses changed these dynamics toward
greater self-representation and public confrontation amidst political, cultural, and technological transformations within Brazilian society.

CANDOMBLÉ WRITINGS IN DEMOCRATIC BRAZIL

The year 1985 marked the end of a twenty-year military dictatorship that had censored political dissent and education in Brazil. Grand shifts in education, politics, and media addressed racial inequalities in public discourse and transformed policies in favor of Black and indigenous communities for the first time in Brazilian history. The Brazilian Black movement in conversation with Candomblé leaders were central to crafting the democratic federal constitution implemented in 1988. Key advancements included new federal laws that required the teaching of African and Afro-Brazilian history and subjects in school, as well as land rights for quilombo communities descended from formerly enslaved African populations in Brazil. Cultural consciousness shifted to recognizing and celebrating African heritage through concrete measures, like the protection of historic temples through their designation as federal heritage sites. Given these shifting political and cultural contexts, select Candomblé priestesses developed their public engagement through works of single authorship, moving beyond the prior mediation that had facilitated the representation of their religious communities through scholarly texts, media, and cultural products from a more restrictive period. Notable publications by the Bahian-born priestesses Mãe Beata and Mãe Stella transformed wisdom from oral traditions into timeless written works that captured their experiences and stories as inherited from prior generations of Africans in Brazil who did not have the same means of representation.

The most prolific Candomblé priestess author the world has yet seen, Mãe Stella (Maria Stella de Azevedo Santos, 1925–2018), continued the traditions established by her lineage of priestesses Mãe Aninha and Mãe Senhora at the Ilê Axé Opô Afonjá temple in Salvador. Over the course of her lifetime Mãe Stella promoted transatlantic educational and religious connections between African leaders and her temple, established the Ohun Lailai Museum to preserve the legacy of her predecessors, and became a vanguard as the first published Candomblé writer in a religion of oral traditions. Building on the foundation built by previous priestesses and taking advantage of new openings in the politics of culture and education in Brazil, her published books, writings as a newspaper columnist and self-representation through documentaries and public interviews transformed the notion that the Candomblé religion be represented and propagated by white mediators, educated outsiders, elite artists, or society's established "intellectuals" and "experts."[21] Her religious leadership and public pedagogy made her an authoritative public figure of Candomblé in Brazil until her recent passing into the *orun* (heaven) in 2018.

Meu Tempo é Agora/My Time is Now (1993) was the first book published by a Candomblé priestess. With the work, Mãe Stella became "the first primary source to offer us ancestral knowledge without an intermediary," communicating beyond the traditional orality of African cultures.[22] In the book she addresses the lineage of priestesses that founded and led the temple before her, detailing the community's history and organization. She then provides basic information regarding the initiation process and the kin relationships and hierarchies established among initiates, as well as the rituals and customs practiced at her temple. The final chapters address "some polemic subjects" regarding the religion's contemporary practice in Brazil, making clear her approach in maintaining the strict hierarchy of access to ritual knowledge.

> The essence of our religion is the Àṣẹ (the magic that makes everything happen), transmitted in secret practices by those who receive it. Practice and theory complete one another, but the force transmitted, what happens to it? Those who have not received Àṣẹ cannot pass it on (I insist on repeating this), no matter how much practical and theoretical knowledge they may have. It's as if somebody were to take a recipe book and make a very beautiful cake, but the dough had poison in it. In Candomblé you cannot skip steps. Everything must happen at the right time.[23]

Mãe Stella often defended the practice of writing about Candomblé against critics (mostly internal to the religion), who worried that the publication of ritual knowledge and information would divulge secret ritual information and corrupt religious practice. Through the above passage and the book's title, Mãe Stella makes clear that if in her religion everything happens at the right time, *her time is now*, and she will disseminate what she deems important based on her authoritative position as the head priestesses of one the most historic and prestigious Candomblé temples in Brazil.

Following this first seminal work, Mãe Stella published three additional books of single authorship, two collections of Yoruba proverbs, and a collection of newspaper articles with the local newspaper.[24] Given her established success as an author, from 2011 to 2012 Mãe Stella wrote the Opinion column for *A Tarde,* the largest newspaper circulated in the city of Salvador and the state of Bahia. It was the first time that a Candomblé priestess had regularly published texts of her own authorship in a paper with wide circulation.[25] Like the justification she had made for writing *Meu Tempo É Agora,* her first column made clear her motives for writing in this venue, "here it is fitting to reveal a bit of the wisdom of Candomblé, not with the intention of making the sacred profane, but so that the respect this millennial religion deserves is conquered in fair measure."[26] The collection of column articles address themes such as her temple's 101st anniversary, narratives of annual seasonal changes, human relationships with the natural environment, children's games, the passing of prominent figures, rituals including the Waters of Oxalá, celebrations of Christmas and other local holidays, and general reflections on life and society. When publishing the compilation, the editors included comments from readers sent to the *A Tarde* newspaper responding to Mãe Stella's articles as they came out. The book's introduction reflects on this decision, recognizing how Mãe Stella "wanted a communal book. After all, that is how she sees life: everyone with a common objective—to live with dignity in all senses."[27] It is clear from the readers' comments that the public enjoyed Mãe Stella's writings, which gave them new perspectives and topics to consider in their daily lives.

Mãe Stella was not the only priestess writing during this period. Mãe Beta de Yemanjá (Beatriz Moreira Costa, 1931–2017), located in Rio de Janeiro, published her first book of stories, *Caroço de Dendê: A Sabedoria dos Terreiros / Palm Oil Seed: The Wisdom of the Temples* in 1997, using her ritual name. Mãe Beata was born in 1931 in Cachoeira, Bahia, as the great granddaughter of an enslaved Nigerian man and the niece of a Candomblé priest (babalorixá).[28] Even though she only went to school until the third grade, during her life she wrote two books and several articles that preserve the ancestral knowledge transmitted through the Candomblé terreiros. She established her temple in Rio de Janeiro in the 1960s and gained many recognitions including prizes, honorary diplomas, and head positions at leading organizations associated with the Black Brazilian movement.[29] Due to the social and educational projects she promoted as head priestess, her temple Ilê Omiojuaro was recognized as a federal cultural heritage site by the national agency IPHAN (Instituto do Patrimônio Histórico e Artistico Nacional) in 2015. This national recognition meant that her temple would remain on its sacred land and receive protection and support from the state to continue functioning permanently. According to Geledes—the Institute of Black Women in Brazil—"the strength of Mãe Beata's stories are in her ancestrality, as a paper record of the teachings transmitted by generations in the day to day, story circles, and in the advice from mothers to the youth in the temples."[30]

Mãe Beata's first book offered a written record of oral stories from the African cultural tradition in which she grew up among the descendants of ex-slaves.[31] It is a fictional account of myths together with religious beliefs from Candomblé. Consider the translation of the following excerpt from one of the myths, recounting a creation story for the world and two deities, the Orixá of planting, Oko, and the Orixá of iron, Ogum.

> When the world was created, there still wasn't anything planted. . . . One day, Olorum [the creator] called on the old man [Oko] and said: — I created the world, but there are no plantations, and I don't know how to make them, how to plant. You are going to be charged with this task. Oko stayed seated on the ground, thinking –what a large mission Olorum gave me! He thought, and thought, and then he remembered that from his walks along the roads he had encountered a palm tree, and that underneath this palm tree there was always a boy. . . . [Oko] went back to the same place and met the boy sitting underneath the palm tree, digging in the soil. . . . "Keep digging"—Oko said. But as he was digging, the little piece of wood he was using broke. He fought with it and rubbed it on the ground, making a point with the wood. In that moment, the boy was discovering a tool when he scraped wood on the ground. And with it he went back to digging together and took out a sliver from the soil, which was a stone. . . . The next day when Oko returned, the little boy had a fire lit and many pieces of stone on fire. . . . As those stones were melting, they would slide down and the boy created sheets. That is how iron was created. And do you know who that little boy was? He was Ogum, the creator of iron. And from then on, the Orixá Oko, the great prayer and planter, with his ideas on farming, harvest, and tillage, and Ogum, with his tools to help till the earth, the plough, the ax, the sickle, and the hoe, continued to work together in the plantations that have great importance for the creation of the world.[32]

Mãe Beata's writing of historic myths of the Orixás—the deities worshipped by Candomblé practitioners—documented in a new medium: stories passed orally through generations from West Africa to Brazil that had persisted within families and temples despite the violence and ruptures of the trans-Atlantic slave trade and Brazilian slavery. Her work made these myths available to new audiences at a larger scale, bringing humanity, images and texture to the creation stories as understood by generations of Afro-Brazilian religious communities. In 2004, Mãe Beata published another book in the same genre, *Histórias que a minha avó contava/The Stories my Grandmother Told* (Terceira Margem, 2004).[33] She continued to be an active and outspoken leader, appearing in documentaries and interviews and at seminars and events until death.

Both Mãe Stella and Mãe Beata were innovative in their publication of stories, myths, and teachings from their roles as head priestesses of Candomblé temples. They were the sole authors of their works, in that they did not need mediation from external collaborators, and they reached new audiences, including circulation in newspapers. Yet the wisdom they shared from the Candomblé context was not only theirs. They published small portions of the ritual and historical knowledge inherited from generations of ancestors that survived from Africa to Brazil for pedagogical and consciousness-raising purposes. As Mãe Stella reminds us, all knowledge is collective. The many recognitions these two women received throughout their lives helped elevate the traditions they came from and disseminate them further through the genre of national literature. Their bodies of works offered perspectives inherited orally from generations of Africans and their descendants in Brazil through textual mediums, making themselves visible as prominent authors of Afro-Brazilian culture on the national stage.

SELF-REPRESENTATIONS IN THE
TWENTY-FIRST CENTURY

The works, initiatives, and writings from generations of priestesses in the twentieth century transformed the public's perception of Candomblé and offered more first-hand information regarding the religion's history and practice in Brazilian society. Democratic mobilization during the PT (Worker's Party) government led to the implementation of the first affirmative-action policies in Brazilian history in the early 2000s, opening space for Black, indigenous, and low-income students to attend public universities and develop research projects in service of their own communities. Advancements in access to education, technological equipment, and media platforms opened even more space for Candomblé priestesses and temples to write, organize, and disseminate information in the public sphere.

In a campaign to finance the publication of her second book, *Reflexões*, in 2019, Mãe Val de Ayrá (Valnizia Bianch, referred to as Mãe Val) of the historic temple Terreiro do Cobre in Salvador recalled the moment that pushed her to write: "A few years ago, a French historian came here [to the temple] wanting to speak about our religion. And afterwards I thought about how I had told my whole history to this man who I didn't even know, and I thought jeez, I am going to start to tell my own story." Fed up with the expropriation of her ancestral knowledge, particularly by white foreigners, Mãe Val articulated a sentiment that drives much of the current self-representation of Candomblé leaders and practitioners in Brazilian cultural products including documentaries, songs, videos, photographs, artwork, and writings. In cutting out the intermediaries in the process of representation and dissemination, Candomblé priestesses have taken greater control of the information circulated about them, their communities, and their religion. Mãe Val says that she always has a notepad close by to write down "a message she wishes to convey to her readers, who are beyond the universe of followers of African-based religions."[34] Reaching new audiences is a technique to address the widespread misinformation about Candomblé in Brazilian society, particularly by Christian ideologies that interpret their deities and ritual system as diabolical—a discourse that has contributed to the marginalization, persecution, and discrimination of Candomblé since the Brazilian colonial era.

Mãe Val is now one of the most prolific authors among living Candomblé priestesses, having published three books to-date, including *Resistência e Fé / Resistance and Faith* (2009), *Aprendo Ensinando / I Learn Teaching* (2011) and *Reflexões / Reflections* (2019), which is a collection of fifteen articles published from her time as the columnist for the *A Tarde* newspaper from December 2014 to August 2016. Mãe Val was born the biological great granddaughter of the head priestess of the Terreiro do Cobre, Mãe Flaviana. Mãe Val wrote that her great grandmother "came from Africa when she was still a small girl with her mother, Margarida de Xangô," who founded the temple where she now serves as head priestess.[35] Following Mãe Flaviana's passing, the temple did not have a successor and was closed for the next fifty years. According to oral histories, when Mãe Flaviana was dying, she said the person who would take over as Mãe-de-santo had not been born yet. Mãe Val was then born on May 10, 1959 (serendipitously Mother's Day), and initiated into Candomblé at about twenty years of age. She found out she would be the head priestess and reestablish the Terreiro do Cobre when she was just 28 years old and took on the position in the early 1990s.[36] Taking on the role at a young age, she reestablished the temple's physical structures that had been in disuse and reconnected the religious ties with the community, as well as created new ones.[37]

Mãe Val became the second priestess to write the Opinion column for *A Tarde* following Mãe Stella. The themes analyzed in the collection include subjects involving citizenship, the environment, identity affirmation, religiosity, and her general attitudes toward life. *Reflexões* was translated into English by the African American historian and initiate of the Terreiro do Cobre, Rachel Harding. In the translator's note, Harding presents Candomblé as "a religion of mothering," in which "Black women are the pinnacle of leadership," carrying wisdom "imbedded in ancestral strength."[38] This ancestral strength and wisdom are shared through the public writings of Candomblé priestesses, offering teachings that reach far beyond the religious sphere. Harding mentions how Mãe Val is part of a growing number of leaders who are transmitting knowledge about their own lives, communities, and religion on their own terms, "not allowing their narratives to be usurped and structured by others, well-intentioned or not."[39]

In honor of Mother's Day, Mãe Val published stories from her childhood in which elders used herbal medicine to treat children's ailments,

> I remember that when children were born with bowed legs, what they called 'cangalha,' the mother would wait until her child began to walk and then, for seven Fridays in a row, she would take the child to the beach. There, she covered the baby's legs with damp sand for a couple of hours then bathed them in sea water. It worked. If the baby wouldn't sleep, the mother made a tea with herbs, like Melissa and erva cidreira. Another method was to place a bowl with an infusion of the herbs close to where the child slept, so that she or he inhaled the scent. It was very rare for us to use patent medicines.[40]

Through this passage and others, Mãe Val articulated ancestral Afro-Indigenous knowledge, particularly as connected to the natural world, which in Candomblé is animated with divine forces. She also shared stories of her own background and upbringing, such that her mother birthed thirteen children, and her father died when she was just eleven years old. Given these challenging circumstances, she shared how "my mother carried water, worked as a laundress, as a domestic [worker] and made cookies (bolachinhas de goma) and sweet coconut crackers (sequilhos) to sell and supplement her income."[41] Her writings offer a portrait of generations of Black women of Candomblé who endured through poverty, racism, and discrimination, sustained by the ancestral wisdom of Candomblé women.

Another article in Mãe Val's collection reflects on "the power of the word," as Mãe Val considers the impact of writing and how words have been weaponized against Black populations in Brazil: "Words are very powerful. They can create, destroy, make us happy, make us sad, shelter us, expose us, counsel, bring joy as well as misery. Words also have the power to kill or to save; to teach and to train."[42] Through her public writings, Mãe Val took control of the word to use it in service of her community. She wrote intentionally as a political tool to transform public opinion and direct popular understandings of Candomblé and Black Brazilian experiences toward greater acceptance, tolerance, and respect.

Other temples have also taken this initiative, though not exclusively through the written form. The Terreiro São Jorge Filhos da Gomeia led by Mãe Lúcia (Maria Lúcia Santana Neves Santos) has been prolific in the production of audiovisual material including campaigns, interviews, conferences, and symposia on themes related to Candomblé and society.[43] Virtual audiovisual initiatives have expanded during the pandemic. For instance, the Terreiro Tumba Junçara has organized the public symposium "Rediscovering Our History" annually at their temple, and this year's edition is available on YouTube with support from local government grants and initiatives.[44]

Given the primacy of oral storytelling, Candomblé priestesses have appeared in numerous documentaries produced by the Candomblé community including "A Cidade das Mulheres" (2006), "100 Anos do Bate Folha" (2016), and "Cá Te Espero no Tumbenci" (2019), to mention just a few.[45] The prominence of audiovisual storytelling and self-representation among Candomblé practitioners has grown immensely with increased access to video cameras, training, and free virtual platforms that have increased the dissemination of information about Candomblé by leaders and practitioners on their own terms. These new tools alongside the publication of written works by Candomblé priestesses has transformed access to public knowledge of Candomblé, where the religious leaders are the sole authors.

Since the twentieth century prominent priestesses have influenced popular discourse and culture, but were often working in collaboration with scholars, politicians, and artists external to their communities. The cultural products about their religion were not made exclusively by the religion's practitioners or leaders, even if they were consulted throughout the process. Black Candomblé's priestesses have sought formal education and occupied public positions as authors uniquely situated to respect the sacred context while educating the public toward greater racial, political, and environmental consciousness. The cultural productions by Candomblé leaders offer educational materials and African epistemologies to the Brazilian public, informed by ancestral wisdom guarded by the priestesses, who speak beyond the ritual sphere to new audiences. The publication of single authorship written works by prominent priestesses in post-democratic Brazil transformed knowledge production about the religion toward greater self-representation and autonomy, dictated by Black women as the authoritative representatives of their religious communities. The priestesses selectively share ritual and historical knowledge from Afro-Brazilian communities, acting as key figures in the nation's development and offering potential pathways to social and environmental change informed by Afro-indigenous epistemologies and generations of inherited knowledge and wealth.

BIBLIOGRAPHY

A Tarde. "Mãe Menininha do Gantois, a mãe ecumênica." Salvador, May 28, 1977.

Adinolfi, Maria Paula, and Van de Port, Mattijs. "Bed and Throne: The 'Museumification' of the Living Quarters of a Candomblé Priestess." *Journal of Material Religion* 9(2013): 282–303.

Alberto, Paulina. *Terms of Inclusion: Black Intellectuals in Twentieth-Century Brazil.* Chapel Hill: University of North Carolina Press, 2011.

Bianch, Valnizia. *Reflexões: escritas de Mãe Valnizia Bianch*, translated by Rachel Harding. Salvador: Edição do Autor, 2019.

Carneiro, Edison. "O Congresso Afro-Brasileiro da Bahia." *Ladinos e Crioulos: Estudos Sôbre o Negro no Brasil,* edited by Edison Carneiro. Editôra Civilização Brasileira S.A. Rio de Janeiro, 1964.

Carneiro, Edison. "Apresentação." In *O Negro no Brasil: Trabalhos Apresentados ao 2° Congresso Afro-Brasileiro.* Civilização Brasileira, Rio de Janeiro, 1940.

Carneiro, Edison. "Era a mais popular mãe-de-santo da Bahia." *O Estado da Bahia* (Jan 5, 1938). Accessed at the Biblioteca Barris, Salvador, Brazil.

Castillo, Lisa Earl. *Entre a oralidade e a escrita: a etnografia nos candomblés da Bahia.* Salvador: Editora UFBA, 2008.

Costa Lima, Vivaldo da. "O candomblé da Bahia na década de 1930" In *Cartas de Edison Carneiro a Artur Ramos: De 4 de Janeiro de 1936 a 6 de Dezembro de 1938,* edited by Waldir Freitas Oliveira and Vivaldo da Costa Lima. São Paulo: Corrupio, 1987.

Diário de Notícias. "Orixás em festa por Menininha." February 25, 1971. Accessed at the Fundação Gregório de Mattos, Salvador, Brazil.

Duarte, Assis, org. Literatura e afrodescendência no Brasil: *antologia crítica.* Belo Horizonte: Editora UFMG, 2011.

Dunn, Christopher. "Black Rome and the Chocolate City: The Race of Place." *Callaloo* 30, no. 3 (Summer 2007).

Filho, Renato Simões, and Cleidiana Ramos. "Apresentação." In *Opinião: Mãe Stella de Azevedo Santos*, organized by Renato Simões Filho and Cleidiana Ramos. Salvador, Brazil, 2012.

Harding, Rachel. "Translator's Note: Black Women's Wisdom and Bridgework" in Valnizi Bianch, *Reflexões: escritas de Mãe Valnizia Bianch*, translated by Rachel Harding. Salvador: Edição do Autor, 2019.

Hartikainen, Elina Inkeri. "Candomblé and the Academic's Tools: Religious Expertise and the Binds of Recognition in Brazil." *American Anthropologist* 121, no. 4 (December 2019): 816–829.

Johnson, Paul Christopher. *Secrets, Gossip and Gods.* Oxford: Oxford University Press, 2002.

Landes, Ruth. *The City of Women.* New York: The Macmillan Co., 1947.

Martins, Cléo, and Lody, Raul, orgs. *Faraimará: Mãe Stella 60 anos de iniciação.* Rio de Janeiro: Pallas, 1999.

Matory, J. Lorand. *Black Atlantic Religion: Tradition, Transnationalism and Matriarchy in the Afro-Brazilian Candomble.* Princeton University Press, 2005.

Oliveira, Waldir Freitas. "Os estudos Africanistas na Bahia dos anos 30." In *Cartas de Edison Carneiro a Arthur ramos: De 4 de Janeiro de 1936 a 6 de Dezembro de 1938*, edited by Waldir Freitas Oliveira and Vivaldo da Costa Lima. São Paulo: Corrupio, 1987.

Pierson, Donald. *Negroes in Brazil: A study of race contact at Bahia.* Chicago, Il: University of Chicago Press, 1942.

Ramos, Cleidiana. "Especial 20 de Novembro: Celebração da Escrita de Ialorixás," translated by Rachel Harding, *Flor de Dendê,* November 20, 2019, http://flordedende.com.br/especial-20-de-novembro-celebracao-da-escrita-de-ialorixas/.

Romo, Anadelia. *Brazil's Living Museum: Race, Reform and Tradition in Bahia.* Chapel Hill: The University of North Carolina Press, 2010.

Santos, Deoscóredes Maximiliano. *História de um Terreiro Nagô.* São Paulo: Max Limonad, 1988.

Santos, Jocélio T. *O poder da cultura e a cultura no poder: A disputa simbólica da herança cultural negra no Brasil.* Salvador: EDUFBA, 2005.

Santos, José Félix dos, and Cida Nóbrega, orgs. *Mãe Senhora: saudade e memória.* Salvador: Corrupio, 2000.

Santos, Maria Stella de Azevedo. *Meu tempo é agora.* São Paulo: Editora Oduduwa, 1993.

Santos, Maria Stella de Azevedo. *Òsòsi: o caçador de alegrias.* Salvador: Secult— Secretaria de Cultura da Bahia, 2006.

Santos, Maria Stella de Azevedo. *Òwe.* Salvador: Sociedade Cruz Santa do Ilê Axé Opô Afonjá, 2007.

Santos, Maria Stella de Azevedo. *Epé Laiyê terra viva.* Salvador: Sociedade Cruz Santa do Axé Opô Afonjá, 2009.

Santos, Maria Stella de Azevedo. *Meu tempo é agora.* 2ª edição, Assembleia Legislativa do Estado da Bahia, 2010.

Santos, Maria Stella de Azevedo. *Abrindo a arca.* Salvador: Edição da autora, 2014.

Santos, Maria Stella de Azevedo. *O que as folhas cantam: para quem canta folha.* Salvador: Edição da autora, 2014.

Talento, Biaggio, and Luiz Alberto Couceiro. *Edison Carneiro: O mestre antigo: Um estudo sobre a trajetória de um intelectual.* Assembleia Legislativa da Bahia, 2009.

Yemanjá, Mãe Beata de. *Caroço de dendê: a sabedoria dos terreiros.* 2. ed. Rio de Janeiro: Pallas, 2002.

Yemanjá, Mãe Beata de. *Histórias que a minha avó contava.* São Paulo: Terceira Margem, 2004.

Yemanjá, Mãe Beata de. "Tradição e religiosidade." In *O livro da saúde das mulheres negras,* organized by Jurema Werneck. Rio de Janeiro: Pallas, 2000.

NOTES

1. Throughout this chapter I use the title "Mãe" in Portuguese to refer to the head priestesses with the term "Mother" as they refer to themselves. In the context of Candomblé, the head priestesses are called the Mães-de-santo, or the Mothers-in-saint. They are the ultimate authorities of the Candomblé ritual family constituted through initiation in the temples.

2. Paul C. Johnson, *Secrets, Gossip and Gods. The Transformation of Brazilian Candomblé* (Oxford University Press, 2002).

3. Makota Valdina in Elina Inkeri Hartikainen, "Candomblé and the Academic's Tools: Religious Expertise and the Binds of Recognition in Brazil," *American Anthropologist 121, no. 4 (December 2019): 820.*

4. Mother Aninha first mentioned the term "Roma Negra" to Donald Pierson during his fieldwork. Donald Pierson, *Negroes in Brazil: A Study of Race Contact at Bahia* (Chicago: University of Chicago Press, 1942). Ruth Landes also highlighted this in *The City of Women* (New York: Macmillan Co., 1947). The term was then taken up in popular culture, including in works by Jorge Amado and the song "Reconvexo" by Maria Bethania, a famous singer and initiate of the Gantois temple. See also Christopher Dunn, "Black Rome and the Chocolate City: The Race of Place," *Callaloo30, no. 3 (Summer 2007): 849–50.*

5. Deoscóredes Maximiliano Santos, *História de um Terreiro Nagô* (São Paulo: Max Limonad, 1988): 9.

6. Santos, *História.*

7. The details of this assertion have been discussed and disputed in the following works: Lisa Earl Castillo, *Entre a oralidade e a escrita: a etnografia nos candomblés da Bahia* (Salvador: Editora UFBA, 2008); J. Lorand Matory, *Black Atlantic Religion: Tradition, transnationalism and matriarchy in the Afro-Brazilian Candomble* (Princeton University Press, 2005).

8. Edison Carneiro, "O Congresso Afro-Brasileiro da Bahia" in *Ladinos e Crioulos: Estudos Sôbre o Negro no Brasil,* ed. Edison Carneiro (Editôra Civilização Brasileira S.A. Rio de Janeiro, 1964); Anadelia Romo, *Brazil's Living Museum: Race, reform and tradition in Bahia* (The University of North Carolina Press, 2010); Waldir Freitas Oliveira, "Os estudos Africanistas na Bahia dos anos 30" In *Letters de Edison Carneiro a Arthur ramos: De 4 de Janeiro de 1936 a 6 de Dezembro de 1938,* orgs. Waldir Freitas Oliveira and Vivaldo da Costa Lima (São Paulo: Corrupio, 1987).

9. Ruth Landes, *The City of Women*: 35, 72.

10. Edison Carneiro, "Apresentação" in *O Negro no Brasil: Trabalhos Apresentados ao 2º Congresso Afro-Brasileiro* (Civilização Brasileira, Rio de Janeiro, 1940).

11. Biaggio Talento and Luiz Alberto Couceiro, *Edison Carneiro: O mestre antigo: Um estudo sobre a trajetória de um intelectual* (Assembleia Legislativa da Bahia, 2009): 61.

12. Edison Carneiro, "Era a mais popular mãe-de-santo da Bahia" (*O Estado da Bahia,* Jan 5, 1938 accessed at the Biblioteca Barris, Salvador, Brazil).

13. José Félix dos Santos and Cida Nóbrega, orgs., *Mãe Senhora: saudade e memória* (Salvador: Corrupio, 2000).

14. Santos and Nóbrega, *Mãe Senhora*: 21, 22. Mother Senhora had significant ties with the local elite and international intelligentsia including the French photographer and ethnographer Pierre Verger, Argentinian painter Carybé, ambassadors from Ghana, Senegal, and Dahomey, among other Brazilian politicians, writers, and artists including Vinícius de Moraes, Dorival Caymmi, Mário Cravo, Milton Santos, among many others. For a more comprehensive list see Santos, *História*: 27.

15. Mãe Senhora was visited by Jean-Paul Sartre and Simone de Beauvoir, for example, at her temple in 1960. For more on the Mãe Preta, see Paulina Alberto, *Terms of Inclusion: Black Intellectuals in twentieth-century Brazil* (Chapel Hill:

University of North Carolina Press, 2011), 77, 69. See also Jamie Lee Andreson, "Mothers in the Family of Saints: Gender and Race in the Making of Afro-Brazilian Heritage" (PhD dissertation, University of Michigan, 2020).

16. Photographic collection from the newspaper *A Tarde* located at the headquarters in Salvador, Bahia.

17. Some examples include Dorival Cayammi's "Oração de Mãe Menininha," Clara Nunes and Clementina de Jesus' "Embala Eu," as well as covers, renditions and mentions of her in the songs by Caetano Veloso, Maria Bethania, and Gilberto Gil.

18. "Oração de Mãe Menininha" by Dorival Caymmi, published in "Mãe Menininha do Gantois, a mãe ecumênica" (*A Tarde,* May 28, 1977).

19. Maria Paula Adinolfi and Mattijs Van de Port "Bed and Throne: The 'museumification' of the living quarters of a candomblé priestess," *Material Religion* 9, no. 3 (2013): 293–94.

20. Jocélio T. Santos, *O poder da cultura e a cultura no poder: A disputa simbólica da herança cultural negra no Brasil* (Salvador: EDUFBA, 2005).

21. Cléo Martins and Raul Lody, orgs., *Faraimará: Mãe Stella 60 anos de iniciação* (Rio de Janeiro: Pallas, 1999); Hartikainen, "Candomblé and the Academics' Tools."

22. Oscar Dourado Ogã in *Meu Tempo é Agora* (2nd edition, Assembleia Legislativa do Estado da Bahia, 2010). Original in Portuguese: "a primeira fonte primária a oferecer-nos conhecimento ancestral sem intermediário."

23. Santos, *Meu Tempo É Agora*: 141.

24. Maria Stella de Azevedo Santos, *Òsòsi: o caçador de alegrias* (Salvador: Secult—Secretaria de Cultura da Bahia, 2006); *Epé Laiyê terra viva* (Salvador: Sociedade Cruz Santa do Axé Opô Afonjá, 2009); *O que as folhas cantam: para quem canta folha* (Salvador: Edição da autora, 2014); *Òwe* (Salvador: Sociedade Cruz Santa do Ilê Axé Opô Afonjá, 2007); *Opinião* (Salvador: EGBA—Empresa Gráfica da Bahia, 2012); *Abrindo a arca* (Salvador: Edição da autora, 2014). Prior to her first book *Meu tempo é agora* (São Paulo: Editora Oduduwa, 1993), she had published a coauthored book with her partner Cléo Martins, *E daí aconteceu o encanto* (Salvador: Edição independente, 1988). Posthumously an additional eight books have been published from her writings.

25. Renato Simões Filho and Cleidiana Ramos, eds., *Opinião: Mãe Stella de Azevedo Santos* (Salvador, Brazil, 2012).

26. Filho and Ramos, *Opinião:* 11. Original in Portuguese: "E aqui cabe revelar um pouco dos conhecimentos do Candomblé, não com a intenção de profanar o sagrado e, sim, para que o respeito que essa religião milenar é merecedora seja conquistador na justa medida."

27. Ângela Botelho, "introdução" in: Renato Simões Filho and Cleidiana Ramos, eds., *Opinião: Mãe Stella de Azevedo Santos* (Salvador, Brazil, 2012).

28. Pallas Editorial, "Adeus, Mãe Beata," May 27, 2017, https://www.pallaseditora.com.br/blog/Adeus__Mae_Beata_/30.

29. Fábio Marques, "Mãe Beata: Contos da guerreira," *Portal Geledés,* May 28, 2012, https://www.geledes.org.br/mae-beata-contos-da-guerreira/.

30. Marques, "Mãe Beata."

31. Literafro: O portal da literatura afro-brasileira, "Mãe Beata de Yemonjá," July 7, 2018, http://www.letras.ufmg.br/literafro/autoras/591-mae-beata-de-yemonja.

32. Caroço de dendê: 115. Translation by the author. Available at http://www.letras .ufmg.br/literafro/autoras/24-textos-das-autoras/584-mae-beata-de-yemonja-oko.

33. Additional works by Mãe Beata include a contribution to an anthology, *Literatura e afrodescendência no Brasil: antologia crítica*, Assis Duarte, org. (Belo Horizonte: Editora UFMG, 2011, v. 2,) and the article "Tradição e religiosidade" in *O livro da saúde das mulheres negras*, organized by Jurema Werneck (Rio de Janeiro: Pallas, 2000).

34. Valnizia Bianch, *Reflexões: escritas de Mãe Valnizia Bianch*, trans. Rachel Harding (Salvador: Edição do Autor, 2019): 11.

35. Bianch, *Reflexões:* 30

36. Oral history relayed to me by Cleidiana Ramos. I also want to thank Cleidiana for conversations and prior writings on the subject of Candomblé priestesses' written works, including the article translated into English by Rachel Harding, "Especial 20 de Novembro: Celebração da Escrita de Ialorixás," *Flor de Dendê,* November 20, 2019, http://flordedende.com.br/especial-20-de-novembro-celebracao-da-escrita-de -ialorixas/.

37. Bianch, *Reflexões:* 8.

38. Harding, "Translator's Note": 15.

39. Harding, "Translator's Note": 14 – 15.

40. Bianch, *Reflexões:* 38 – 39.

41. Bianch, *Reflexões*: 31.

42. Bianch, *Reflexões*: 53.

43. See the YouTube Channel with all vídeos produced by Terreiro São Jorge Filho da Gomeia, https://www.youtube.com/c/TerreiroS%C3%A3oJorgeFilhodaGomeia.

44. See the recorded seminar "Redescobrindo nossa história" organized by the Terreiro Tumba Junçara at https://www.youtube.com/watch?v=ZBE8f7YEwM0.

45. All these titles are available on YouTube.

Chapter 6

The Invisible Women

An Analysis of the Representation of Afro-Latinx Women in Spanish-Language Textbooks

Lillie Padilla

INTRODUCTION

Language textbooks are one of the essential components of many language classes. They provide the students with grammar, vocabulary, effective language models, and various learning resources. For language educators they are equally beneficial; they may provide the structure together with the syllabus, standardize instruction, and are usually visually appealing. According to Bábara Cruz, "the textbook still enjoys a primary role in the delivery of content information and, in many cases, in the development of curriculum and instructional strategy."[1] Moreover, beyond the language benefits, textbooks influence the social reality of their users. Who/what is included in these textbooks is just as important as who/what is excluded. As agents of socialization, they reflect what is acceptable or not in the target culture.

However, textbooks cannot be accepted as neutral purveyors of knowledge despite the advantages that they provide to both learners and educators.[2] Ryan Cragun[3] calls textbooks a "necessary evil" because, despite the advantages they provide to both students and educators, they also come with certain obstacles. Specifically, according to Patrick Heinrich, textbooks can be one of the most salient agents of transmitting political and social agendas to promote the interests of dominant groups in society at the expense of minority groups.

143

One of such minority groups is the people of African descent in the Spanish-speaking world and the Caribbean, Afro-Latinx.

According to the World Banks 2018 report, Afro-Latinx are one of the most excluded groups in Latin America and the Caribbean. During the era of colonialization, the Spaniards implemented a caste system in the countries they controlled. According to Kurt Organista, with this system, the phenotypically born whites were at the top of the pyramid, followed by offspring of the Spaniards (criollos), the mestizos, mulatos, zambos, indigenous people, and then the Africans. The hierarchy was rooted in phenotype and skin color. Thus, being Black and at the bottom of the pyramid meant no access to social and economic mobility.

According to the Economic Commission for Latin America and the Caribbean, to date, Afro-Latinx make up one-quarter of the population of Latin America, and they are overrepresented among the poor in every Latin American country. As argued by Roman and Flores, anti-Blackness still plays a vital role in Latino identity. Moreover, research by Michael Dumas has shown that Afro-Latinx face rejection both in schools and educational settings, whereas the results of Marta Cruz-Janzen and Carla Shedd's studies show that they face rejection in their societies as well. Peter Wade posits that this discrimination is rooted in the ideology of *mestizaje,* mixing races, which is still prominent in certain parts of Latin America. This ideology originates from notions of "bettering the race," and it is an effort to eradicate Black identity.[4]

Afro-Latinx women, in particular, suffer from multiple forms of oppression rooted in gender and race-based discrimination. Interestingly, despite the abundance of research conducted on language textbooks and women, no study has examined Afro-Latinx women's textual and visual representation in Spanish-language textbooks. Yet, Harrison, Yang, and Moyo find that these representations present a social reality to viewers and play an important role in identity formation. Moreover, this analysis is crucial because in the words of van Leeuwen, visuals particularly "are able to 'disguise' power structures and hegemony as 'objective' representations because to the uncritical eye, visuals are transparent and universally understood."[5]

Furthermore, examining the representation of Afro-Latinx women is a step in removing some of the educational obstacles and inequalities faced by these women. For instance, the National Center for Educational Statistics in 2016 pointed out that the college completion rate of Latinas was 12.5 percent in the 2014–2015 academic year, while white females' graduation rate was 65 percent. Although there are no statistics on Afro-Latinx women's graduation rate, this number could even be lower. In this regard Joseph Graci attests that "pedagogy inevitably involves the transmission, exchange, and initiation of ideas. When subtle or blatant sexism is present in the curriculum, that information is then conveyed to the learners."[6]

The study chooses to investigate beginner-level Spanish textbooks for several reasons. Firstly, beginner textbooks are foundational textbooks, as well as the most widely used Spanish-language textbooks. These are the textbooks that provide the formative experience to textbook users. Secondly, they are targeted at second-anguage learners of Spanish in the United States. These speakers may or may not have had contact with the Spanish language and culture before using these books. Thirdly, these books are used by a broad group of students; heritage language Spanish speakers, second-language speakers, and in some cases, native speakers taking the Spanish class to get an easy A.

By examining the textual and visual representation of Afro-Latinx women in these books, the study aims at increasing the visibility and recognition of Afro-Latinxs, contribute to the improvement of language textbooks, and finally, contribute to the works of Black feminists such as Kimberlé Crenshaw, Vigoya Viveros, and Patricia Collins. With this research, the present study advances the understanding of the issues affecting Afro-Latinx students in the Spanish classroom.

THE INTERSECTIONAL EXPERIENCES OF AFRO-LATINX WOMEN

The term "Intersectionality" was developed by Kimberlé Crenshaw to critique the failure of the US antidiscrimination laws to consider the unique experiences that Black women face concerning sexism, racism, and social class. According to Leslie McCall, "Intersectionality is one of the most significant theoretical contributions that women's studies, in conjunction with related fields, has made thus far."[7] Crenshaw reechoed the need to understand the "intersecting patterns of racism and sexism"[8] in political, economic, and legal structures. Although this perspective initially was focused on the experiences of Black women, it can be applied to the social experiences of all minorities, for instance, issues of poverty, immigration, social class, sexuality, and disabilities, among others.

It is noteworthy that although minority groups in society suffer similar instances of injustice and dominance, Afro-Latinx women experience forms of discrimination that distinguish them from that of other minority groups. During the slave trade, not only did women suffer from the long gruesome hours of work, but also, they were deemed as sexual objects to be enjoyed by men, as well as reproduction tools for farm labor. Even after slavery, this race-gender oppression did not cease. Afro-Latinx women still face the same discrimination they endured as slaves in now more sophisticated ways. Men are given better jobs, education, and privileges in society that elevate them to a higher status than women, especially Afro-descendant women.

As reported by Alicia Bárcena and Winnie Byanyima, to date, Latin America has one of the highest rates of inequality and discrimination in the world, and in countries such as Peru, Colombia, Ecuador, Brazil, and Honduras, Afro-Latinx women are the poorest among the poor. Intersectionality theory thus is vital to the present study because it challenges the tendency to examine these experiences through one lens. Particularly, in the case of Afro-Latinx women, it demonstrates that the multiple forms of discrimination and oppression that these women face are consequences of intersecting identities, resulting in unique experiences for these Afro-Latinx women.

LITERATURE REVIEW

Language Textbooks and Ideologies

Susan Gal argues that language ideologies are "those cultural presuppositions and metalinguistic notions that name, fame and evaluate linguistic practices linking them to political, moral and aesthetic positions of the speakers, and to the institutions that support these positions and practices."[9] Language ideologies are hardly about language per se. As such, Erin Mackiney explains that ideologies are often not recognized and hardly ever challenged by members of society. They are rooted in political, social, and moral stances in the communities in which they are located. According to Kroskrity, language ideologies usually (1) protect the interests of the dominant groups in society, (2) represent multiple perspectives, (3) may or may not be recognized by members of the society, and (4) they can mediate social structures and linguistic forms. Language ideologies thus benefit dominant groups in society who use various institutions to legitimize their power (e.g., the church, school, courts, etc.). Moreover, the social environment plays an important role in the formation and dissemination of these ideologies.

Irvine, Gal, and Kroskrity explain three ways by which ideological representations of linguistic differences are constructed: *iconization, fractal recursivity*, and *erasure*. *Iconization* is the linking of specific linguistic forms or features to the social identity of the speakers. In other words, these linguistic forms are presented as icons of their speakers. *Fractal recursivity* is when the differences that are presented as iconic are used to create a dichotomy of "us" versus "them." Both iconization and fractal recursivity result in the *erasure* of minority groups. In other words, the significant differences that exist between these groups are made invisible.

Several language ideologies have been uncovered in language textbooks; Padilla and Vana uncovered ideologies in Spanish textbooks, Shardakova and Pavenko and Azimova and Johnston also found Russian textbooks with underlying ideologies. With respect to English textbooks, the studies of Cortez, Dendrinos, and Gray highlight the prevalence of language ideologies in English textbooks. French textbooks are no exception, Chapelle's findings reecho the dominance of several language ideologies in language textbooks. Of interest to the present study nonetheless is the presence of the *standard language ideology*, *raciolinguistic ideologies*, and *tourism discourse* uncovered in these previous studies.

The standard language ideology is defined by Rosina Lippi-Green as a "bias toward an abstracted, idealized, homogenous spoken language which is imposed and maintained by dominant bloc institutions."[10] This type of ideology imposes a one-size-fits-all approach and fails to recognize the variation that exists within a language. Thus, the rules concerning how language should be spoken are enforced by the educated in society through educational institutions. According to James Milroy, these institutions tend to describe their chosen varieties as more prestigious than varieties that deviate from the "so-called standard."

Rosa and Flores argue that the standard language ideology is linked to language and race. In other words, certain races are equated with "linguistic deficiency" while others are not. Rosa and Flores thus created the term "raciolinguistic ideologies" to refer to this connection, where the language by minoritized groups or races is seen through white subjects' eyes as a linguistic deficiency. Interestingly, when white subjects use these exact linguistic features, they are not considered deficient or unmarked, according to the authors. The examination of raciolinguistic ideologies help understand why Afro-Latinx women are underrepresented in these textbooks.

Coupled with the raciolinguistic ideologies are *tourism discourse* and the ideology of the *tourist gaze*. According to John Urry, the tourist gaze is when important cultural practices of local populations are reduced to commodities, with some being regarded as more valuable than others. These findings are supported by studies such as Uzum, Yazan, Zahwri, Bouamer, and Malakaj's study of Arabic and French textbooks, as well as Padilla and Vana's study of Spanish textbooks. These studies show that languages provide an avenue for the tourist gaze to function, and language learners are viewed as potential tourists ready to consume the products they have been provided. For instance, it is now prevalent to see language textbooks filled with tourist guidebooks, travel vocabulary, television shows, and various ads. John Gray argues that tourism discourse is so prevalent in language textbooks because tourism is considered one of the "safe topics" by textbook publishers. With this biased view, the cultural practices that cannot be understood, consumed, or deemed unattractive by the tourists are regarded as less valuable practices.

Second, while not the only topic of interest, describing and understanding the potentially destructive view of the "tourist gaze" (Urry, 1996; Urry and Larsen, 2011) and additional perspectives of the tourist gaze as more benign concepts provide foundational support for this particular issue. Originally, Urry (1996) introduces the tourist gaze as the set of expectations that tourists place on local populations when they participate in heritage tourism, in the search for having an authentic experience. Responding to tourist expectations and often cultural and racial stereotypes, local populations reflect the "gaze" of the expectations of tourists to benefit financially (Stronza, 2001). This gaze often is described as a destructive process, reducing important local cultural expressions to commodities, and causing these traditions to fall out of favor with local populations. Gaze serves as a destructive process as local populations become consumed by an economic process that values certain cultural expressions over others, and cultural themes that cannot be commoditized easily fall out of favor and eventually become lost (MacCannell, 1984, 1992).

Language Textbooks and Female Representations

For decades now, researchers have been interested in gender representation in various textbooks. Notable studies are the studies of Lydia Namatende-Sakwa, the studies of Jane Sunderland, Benjamin Rifkin, and John Gray. Studies that have focused on the written representations have examined the dialogues between speakers, the cultural information provided, vocabulary, and the notes presented. In contrast, the studies that have examined the visual representation have considered the number of visual representations of women presented, how they are presented, their position in the picture (for instance whether they are foregrounded or in the background), the roles they are engaged in, the occupations associated with them, and their ages, among others.

Several studies have brought to light the fact that textbooks tend to underrepresent women in society. For example, in Amy Achison's study of ten introductory political science American government textbooks, the author found that women were hardly represented in these books. In these books, the author found that information related to women was relegated to chapters that concerned theory and ideologies, movements, and elections. The author argues that these reflections of women not only reinforce certain stereotypes but also, they marginalize women in society. Similar findings were uncovered in history textbooks. For example, in Angela Leslie's study of the representation of Latinas in history textbooks, the author found that Latinas only represented 0.0063 percent of the individuals mentioned in historical content. Moreover, very few pictures of these pictures were of successful Latinas.

Concerning second-language textbooks, Jackie Lee examined three Japanese English Foreign Language textbooks to determine whether the government's endeavor to promote gender equality was reflected in these books. On the one hand, the results showed the prevalence of gender-neutral vocabulary and a balanced distribution of men and women. However, on the other hand, the author observed the underrepresentation of women and their achievements in these textbooks. Other observations were the portrayal of men in a broader range of social roles than women and men being portrayed as more physically and cognitively developed than women. Similarly, Sunderland found erasure/invisibility, stereotyping, and degradation of females in the books examined. These results were corroborated by Budi Seyton's study that analyzed EFL textbooks. The author found discourses that promoted gender bias on the one hand and, on the other hand, discourses that represented constructive images of women.

The previous studies mentioned above reecho Apple and Smith's assertion that textbooks are more than just pedagogical materials. They are a means to legitimize the power of particular groups of people to the detriment of others. Unfortunately, to date, no study has specifically examined the representation of Afro-Latinx women in Spanish-language textbooks. The closest study in this direction is Lillie Padilla and Rosti Vana's forthcoming study on the representation of Afro-Latinx in Spanish textbooks. In this study, the authors found that Afro-Latinx are underrepresented in these language textbooks. Moreover, in the few instances where Afro-Latinx were represented, the authors found colorism, stereotypes, superficiality, and impersonalization.

The present study fills critical gaps in research by focusing on the representation of Afro-Latinx women in Spanish-language textbooks and the underlying ideologies surrounding this representation. The following research questions thus guide the present study: 1) How are Afro-Latinx women represented (in the texts and visuals) in beginner-level Spanish-language textbooks? 2) What are the ideologies behind these representations?

THEORETICAL PERSPECTIVES

The theoretical framework for this chapter is a comprehensive framework grounded in critical discourse analysis (CDA) by Norman Fairclough, the grammar of visual design by Gunther Kress and Theo van Leeuwen, and Intersectionality theory by Kimberlé Crenshaw. CDA is the core of the framework, focusing on how dominance and power are mirrored in discourse. The grammar of visual design, together with CDA, provides key dimensions for understanding unequal relations in society. Finally, the Intersectionality framework reflects the multiple identities and dominance according to race, sex, social class, disability, ethnicity, etc. In the following sections, we elaborate on how these theoretical perspectives have informed the present study.

Critical discourse analysis (CDA) is an important discipline and framework in the humanities and social sciences. van Dijk posits that CDA "primarily studies the way social power abuse, dominance, and inequality are enacted, reproduced, and resisted by text and talk in the social and political context. . . . Critical discourse analysts take an explicit position, and thus want to understand, expose, and ultimately resist social inequality."[11] Similarly, Fairclough describes CDA as a form of discourse analysis that is aimed at uncovering opaque relationships, discursive practices, and texts and how these are a product of the power relations in society. Moreover, van Dijk argues that to establish control, dominant groups use institutions and positions of power to legitimize their authority. These groups then determine what can be said, who can say it, when, and how. CDA thus questions the positioning of the text, whose interests are being, whose interests are being denied, and the effects of the position being taken.

In the analysis of the text, Fairclough proposes three interdependent stages. These stages are summarized as description, interpretation, and explanation. At the description stage, the focus is on the formal properties of the text. Thus, there is a need to closely read the text and analyze the linguistic features, structure, and grammar. The second step, interpretation, examines the text as a discursive practice, focusing on the relationship between the text and interaction. Since the text is a product of the society in which it was produced, in this step, there is the need to examine speech acts, intertextuality, and discursive styles, among other factors. Finally, the third step, explanation, looks at the society as a whole to understand power and dominance and the consequences of this control.

Like the text, the understanding and interpretation of visuals are based on the power relations and dominance in society. van Leeuwen argues that in general, visuals "are able to 'disguise' power structures and hegemony as 'objective' representations" (4) because to the uncritical eye, language used in visuals is "transparent" and "universally understood."[12] In order to understand the hidden ideologies with respect to visuals, Kress and van Leeuwen provide a way to analyze the relations between objects, people, and places.

Kress and van Leeuwens's analysis is grounded in Michael Halliday's theory of metafunctions. This theory argues that language performs three metafunctions; ideational, interpersonal, and textual. These functions have been expanded by Kress and van Leeuwen to visual semiotics and are now known as *representational*, *interactive*, and *compositional* metafunction. Representational metafunction refers to the representation of entities.

According to Kress and van Leeuwen, "any semiotic mode has to be able to represent aspects of the world as it is experienced by humans. In other words, it has to be able to represent objects and their relation in a world outside the representational system."[13] The interactive metafunction focuses on the relationship between the producer and the viewer. It is thus essential to examine gestures, gazes, facial expressions, and points of view. With respect to the compositional metafunctions, the emphasis is on the layout of the visuals and the verbal elements.

The Intersectionality framework complements CDA and visual analysis to understand how power can be constructed by combining various minoritized identities of Afro-Latinx women in beginner-level Spanish textbooks. In conducting any research using Intersectionality as a tool, Collins argues that researchers should concentrate on "a concrete topic that is already the subject of investigation and . . . find the combined effects of race, class, gender, sexuality, and nation, where before only one or two interpretive categories were used."[14] This is made possible by focusing on a specific marginalized social dimension, according to McCall. In the case of the present study, Afro-Latinx women. Overall, the theoretical perspectives discussed above inform the analysis in the present study and addresses the need to explore the representation of historically marginalized groups, such as Afro-Latinx women in these textbooks. Moreover, these perspectives highlight the ideological nature of textbook materials and how dominant groups maintain their power in society.

DATA COLLECTION AND ANALYSIS

To examine the representation of Afro-Latinx women in beginner-level Spanish textbooks, the researcher did an internet search of the most widely used Spanish textbooks in the universities in Arizona, California, New Mexico, and Texas. The researcher searched on the websites of various Spanish departments and located their syllabus to find the textbooks that were used in their institutions. Six beginner-level Spanish textbooks were selected from the list of textbooks obtained. These books are *Puntos de Partida* (published by McGraw-Hill), *Unidos* (by Pearson), *Plazas* (by Cengage), *¿Cómo se dice?* (by Cengage), *Portales* (by Vista Higher learning), *Nexos* (by Cengage), and *Aventuras* (by Vista Higher Learning). The six textbooks are produced by major publishers in the United States, and due to their prominence, they have dominion over the type of information that beginner-level Spanish students are exposed to. In table 6.1, the list of these books and their years of publication are presented.

The six textbooks examined all had a similar type of organization. Each textbook had chapters arranged according to different themes and countries.

Table 6.1. Textbooks Analyzed in the Present Study

Title	Publisher	Year of publication
Puntos de partida	McGraw-Hill	2017
Unidos	Pearson	2013
Plazas	Cengage	2017
¿Cómo se dice?	Cengage	2015
Portales	Vista Higher Learning	2016
Nexos	Cengage	2017
Aventuras	Vista Higher Learning	2014

Some books also came with an online component/e-book, videos, audios, student supplementary workbooks, and graded activities. However, the study only focused on the hard-copy textbooks of the student editions because the supplementary materials the books came with were not uniform across the textbooks.

ANALYSIS

Textual Analysis

In the text, we paid attention to the description of speakers, dialogues, and cultural readings. For the visuals, all people were examined, whether they took the form of drawings, animations, or photographs. To avoid using phenotypical assumptions to determine the race of the women in the text, the researcher relied on the explicit reference in the textbook to Afro-Latinx women. Thus, in coding both the text and visuals, an image was only coded as an Afro-Latinx woman when it was clearly labeled as such. For instance, "a Garifuna woman" or "an Afro-descent woman." Moreover, to ensure inter-rater reliability, the identified codes were shown to other researchers to ensure that the codes accurately reflected the representation of Afro-Latinx women in these textbooks. Disagreements on the coding were resolved with further discussions.

Fairclough's three-step model for conducting CDA was used in analyzing the text: description, interpretation, and explanation. At the first step, the description stage, the focus was on the formal properties of the language; choice of pronouns, passive voice, active voice, and grammatical constructions, among others. Moreover, Reisigl and Wodak argue that in the examination of texts that concern race and identity, it is important to focus on discursive strategies to uncover how the ideologies are embedded in the texts, particularly, nominative (how they are named or referred to), predication (the attributes they are given), argumentation (the justification of these attributes), perspectivization (the perspective from which they are presented), and mitigation and intensification strategies (the use of vague expressions hesitations, indirect speech, etc.).

In the second step, the focus was on the interpretation of the text. According to Collins, when conducting an intersectional analysis, one should focus on "a concrete topic that is already the subject of investigation and . . . find the combined effects of race, class, gender, sexuality, and nation, where before only one or two interpretive categories were used."[15] Thus, at this stage, the goal was to uncover patterns that were found in the texts, the intersection with race and gender, and how these were related to the setting in which the text was produced, the audience, and the textbook authors.

With the third step, explanation, we examined the dominant ideologies and power relationships in society. For instance, the role of Afro-Latinx women, their access to social and economic mobility, and the historical and social facts concerning people of color in the United States.

Visual Analysis

In conducting the visual analysis, all images of people, instead of buildings or scenery, were examined. As previously mentioned, to avoid using phenotypical assumptions, as well as assumptions based on gender, the study relied on the description of the surrounding text to determine if the image was an Afro-Latinx woman or not.

Moreover, following Kress and van Leeuwen, the visuals' representational, interactive, and compositional meanings were coded. The visual's representational meaning involved identifying the represented participants, the type of activity they are involved in, and the setting in which it is performed. Thus, in the present study, the focus was on how many Afro-Latinx women were represented in the visuals, as well as how they were portrayed. For instance, did the image represent an upper-class Afro-Latinx woman, a celebrity, were they presented as a group or individually, were they together with men, do the images depict stereotypes, etc. To determine the interactive meaning, Kress and van Leeuwen argue that one must examine the relationship between the image and the audience. Thus, in the present study, we examined the view (whether they looked directly or away from the viewer), the facial expressions, the type of distance they maintained from the audience, gestures, and the gaze were examined. The type of interaction with the viewer indicates the power relations that exist between the participants and viewers. Finally, with respect to the compositional meaning, the study examined the layout of the pages to determine how the verbal and visual complement each other and give coherence (for instance, the placement of images, the framing, the placement of elements to the left or right, the size, among others).

RESULTS AND DISCUSSION

This section is dedicated to the presentation of the results derived from the analysis. It would begin with the findings with respect to the text and then the findings of the visuals.

The Representation of Afro-Latinx in Beginner Level Spanish Textbooks

The first research question addressed the representation of Afro-Latinx women in beginner-level Spanish textbooks. Interestingly, the analysis of both the text and the visuals were similar; there was hardly any representation of Afro-Latinx in general. Out of the six books analyzed, there were only twenty-two textual representations of Afro-Latinx. Out of this number, there were seventeen references to Afro-Latinx men and ten references to Afro-Latinx women. This information is presented in table 6.2. From the table, it is evident that not only is there a scarce representation of Afro-Latinx in general, but Afro-Latinx women particularly have little or no representation in some of the textbooks examined.

With respect to the visuals, out of the six books examined, there were 1,507 images of people, as opposed to buildings or nature. Out of this number, there were sixteen images that indicated that the image was that of an Afro-Latinx. Out of the sixteen images of Afro-Latinx, there were eleven images of Afro-Latinx men and seven images of Afro-Latinx women. Three of these books have no visual representation of Afro-Latinx women in any of the images. This information is presented in Table 6.3.

Moreover, the roles that Afro-Latinx women were engaged in were examined, both in the text and then visuals. The analysis brought to light that Afro-Latinx women were presented engaging in some type of

Table 6.2. Number of Textual Representations with Clear Reference to Afro-Latinx

Title	Number of textual representations of Afro-Latinx	Number of textual representations of Afro-Latinx men	Number of textual representations of Afro-Latinx women
Puntos de partida	6	4	4
Unidos	3	2	2
Plazas	2	1	0
¿Cómo se dice?	5	3	0
Portales	1	3	2
Nexos	5	4	2
Total	22	17	10

Table 6.3. Number of Visual Representations with Explicit Reference to Afro-Latinx Women

Title of Textbook	Total number of visual images with explicit reference to Afro-Latinx	Total number of visual images with explicit reference to Afro-Latinx men	Total number of visual images with explicit reference to Afro-Latinx women	Total number of pages with pictures of people
Puntos de Partida	6	4	2	333
Unidos	4	2	2	243
Plazas	1	1	0	235
¿Cómo se dice?	0	0	0	205
Portales	2	2	0	240
Nexos	3	2	1	251
Total	16	11	7	1507

entertainment-dancing, singing, or playing an instrument. This type of representation was evident in five out of seven images.

The Ideologies behind this Representation

The second research question examined the ideologies behind the representation of Afro-Latinx women. The ideologies uncovered were erasure, superficiality/impersonalization, the standard language ideology, stereotypes, and tourism discourse. We will discuss these ideologies below.

Erasure

Erasure, according to Irvine and Gal, "renders some persons or activities (or sociolinguistic phenomena) invisible."[16] It is an ideology that has been uncovered in several textbooks in an attempt to eliminate the presence of certain minority groups in society—for instance, people with disabilities, gays, lesbians, women, etc. In the present study, erasure is manifested in the underrepresentation of Afro-Latinx women in these textbooks. There are no dialogues of Afro-Latinx women, no history or narrations, nothing to humanize the characters of these women in the few instances in which they appeared. The experiences, language practices, and culture of the Afro-Latinx women have been silenced, even though Afro-Latinx women form a substantial population in the United States, Latin America, and the Caribbean.

Moreover, we find that Afro-Latinx women are twice disadvantaged in these textbooks; not only are they are less represented than Afro-Latinx men, but also, they are less represented than white men and women in general. Consequently, Afro-Latinx women have become "the other" in Spanish textbooks, and Intersectionality as a tool shows how textbooks exclude these women. Similar findings of erasure have been uncovered in other textbook studies. For instance, Shardakova and Pavenko and Azimonova and Johnston studies found non-white Russians were invisible. In addition, other studies such as Gray's study, and Dendrino's study have found the erasure of African Americans, Asians, Native Americans, gays, and lesbians in the textbooks examined. Similarly, in Chapelles's study, the author found the exclusion of historical information in the French textbooks examined.

Superficiality and Impersonalization

In the few representations of Afro-Latinx women in the textbooks, we find instances of impersonalization and superficiality. For example, the references to Afro-Latinx women were in the third person singular/plural. This type of nomination tends to create a social distance between the reader and the text. Afro-Latinx are described with words such "Blacks," "former slaves," and "Afro-descendants." Interestingly, the only Afro-Latinx women who were given some identities were the famous ones-for instance, Susana Baca (an Afro-Peruvian singer), Celia Cruz (an Afro-Cuban American singer), and Zoe Saldana (an Afro-Dominican American actress).

The few appearances of Afro-Latinx women in these books initially give an initial impression of inclusion. However, upon closer inspection, one realizes that they are indeed excluded. There are only a few texts and pictures in which Afro-Latinx women appear, and in these texts, the focus is not on Afro-Latinx women. For instance, in the visuals, we find an Afro-Latinx woman celebrating her quinceañera, but her face is blurry. Furthermore, although the image seems to portray the celebration of the quinceañera, this is a very superficial and impersonalized view of the celebration. The most striking object in this image is the bright red car next to which she is standing. Like many other images of Afro-Latinx women in the textbook, the image offers contact, thus making no connection with the viewer. According to Kress and van Leeuwen, an image can be offering contact (gazing away from the viewer) or demanding contact (gazing at the viewer), and this has to do with the closeness and distance of the image. The portrayal of Afro-Latinx women in these visuals dehumanizes the relationship between the viewer and the visual. This is made possible by projecting images that offer contact instead of demanding contact.

The Standard Language Ideology

The standard language ideology was also evident in these texts and visuals. In this paper, we argue that the standard language ideology evident here cannot be separated from the race of these Afro-Latinx women. According to Rosa and Flores, the concept of race affects how the listening subjects perceive the utterances of the speaking subjects. Specifically, listeners "conflate certain racialized bodies with linguistic deficiency unrelated to any objective linguistic practices."[17]

The lack of voice and the nonappearance of Afro-Latinx women mirrors the racial inequalities in society. However, according to Lipski, Afro-Latinx have contributed to the linguistic enrichment of the Spanish language (for instance, the introduction of certain linguistic forms, patterns of speech, and vocabulary). Yet, there is no linguistic information regarding this population. By erasing Afro-Latinx women from these textbooks, the books send a message regarding which cultures and language varieties students need to be exposed to in the language classroom, and the erasure of Afro-Latinx women speaks volumes.

Stereotypes

The analysis of the visuals and texts also reveals the dominance of stereotypes in representing Afro-Latinx women. In the present study, we find that in the few instances in which Afro-Latinx women are represented, they provide some type of entertainment, singing, dancing, playing an instrument, etc. This representation helps to perpetuate stereotypes by consistently representing these women as sources of entertainment. This depiction also serves to sustain the stereotypes that Blacks are not smart or intellectual enough, as they only serve as entertainers for the entertainment industry. The portrayal of Afro-Latinx women in these roles frames Afro-Latinx women as the powerless in society. Moreover, these stereotypes serve to continue the marginalization of Afro-Latinx women in the educational system. Furthermore, there are no discussions on Afro-Latinx women's perspectives, neither is there a discussion of their history or the contributions Afro-Latinx women have made in Latin America, the Caribbean, and the United States.

Tourism Discourse and the Tourist Gaze

Tourism discourse appears in these texts in the form of pictures and texts emphasizing the uniqueness of Afro-Latinx culture through "exotic" elements and famous people. Out of the seven visual images of Afro-Latinx women, five out of these references revolved around the tourist gaze. As mentioned above, the only Afro-Latinx women mentioned by name are famous

Afro-Latinx singers and actresses. By showcasing only the aspects that were deemed as exotic, these textbooks prioritize the tourism industry over the lives, history, and social realities of these women.

In the textbooks, Afro-Latinx women were showcased dancing to "exotic" music, playing instruments, dancing at carnivals, and showcasing Guarani culture. These visuals could be said to be promoting Afro-Latinx culture through a tourist lens. Moreover, the promotional character of these texts is evident in the choice of words used to describe this culture in the text. For instance, the nominalization strategy used in several descriptions of this culture as "una cultura rica en ritmo, musica y baile" (a culture rich in rhythm, music and dance), and "una cultura única" (a unique culture). It can be interpreted as attempts to introduce the audience to "exotic" elements without focusing on the people, specifically, the women behind this culture. According to Byram, these representations create a difference between "us versus them" as there is no critical reflection of this culture's practices, perspectives, and products.

DISCUSSION

The results of the present study bring to light the invisibility of Afro-Latinx women in beginner-level Spanish textbooks. This invisibility, termed erasure by hooks and by Irvine and Gal, can be interpreted as a negation of the existence of Afro-Latinx women. This representation does not reflect the reality of Afro-Latinx women's representation in Latin America, the Caribbean, and the United States.

As previously stated, textbooks form one of the most critical components of the language classroom. Thus, who is included in these books, is just as important as who is erased from the textbook representation. An intersectional analysis of Afro-Latinx representation depicts that power and dominance is not only vested in gender. As argued by Elizabeth Spelman, it is also invested in racialization, in the determination of which experiences count, as well as who speaks in place of women in society. Uzum, Yazan, Zahrawi, Bouamer, and Malakaj find that "textbooks tend to foreground certain linguistic and cultural components while erasing others and tend to offer tokenistic representations of 'peripheral' dialects and cultures."[18] From these results, Afro-Latinx women are presented as "the other" in society.

Moreover, the lack of representation of Afro-Latinx women in these textbooks has potentially harmful consequences for students and educators. For instance, it may discourage Afro-Latinx students from pursuing this discipline or lose interest in their current classes. Also, this lack of representation may lead to increased imposter syndrome for educators using these books (the internal experience of feeling one is not competent).

It is thus important to consider the representation of Afro-Latinx women in these textbooks and their marginalization in society, as these are not disconnected incidents. They are both connected to the goal of maintaining the power of dominant groups in society. It promotes the erroneous idea that Latinx is a monolithic race and mirrors the hegemonic relations in society where dominant groups maintain power and control over the non-dominant groups, in this case, Afro-Latinx women.

The representation of Afro-Latinx women is distinct. It could be attributed to the overlap of various intersectional social realities; their distinct experiences of being women, African roots, racial differences, the effects of slavery, and the lower status in society. For instance, during slavery and colonization, slave owners maintained their power over the slaves by denying them access to education. Years after slavery, it is still evident that through the textbooks, dominant groups dictate what must be included and excluded in the curriculum, and the information included is at the expense of minority groups in society.

This erasure has several consequences that have been manifested in the present study. In the few instances in which we see Afro-Latinx women, we find stereotypes, impersonalization/superficiality, the standard language ideology, and tourist discourse. We realize that Afro-Latinx women are described with the third person singular pronoun and with collective categories such as "Garifunas," "Afro-descendants," and even "Blacks." In the visuals, we find images highlighting superficial elements such as the clothes of these women instead of what they stand for etc. Moreover, this erasure also has undertones of the standard language ideology. Because Afro-Latinx women are not given a voice in these textbooks, it could be implied that they are not representative enough of the Spanish language and culture. It limits the possibility of Afro-Latinx women seeing themselves as legitimate members of society.

Given these results, this chapter argues for the explicit recognition of Afro-Latinx women in beginner-level Spanish textbooks. Transforming textbooks is the first step in changing the curriculum to incorporate the history of Afro-Latinx and their social and economic contributions to Latin America, the Caribbean, and the United States, where these books are used. As uncovered by the present study, textbook authors and publishers fail to recognize the multiple forms of oppression Afro-Latinx women face (for their sex, race, and social class) and the potential negative consequences for textbook users.

CONCLUSION

This study aims not to attack textbook authors or publishers; instead, it is to ensure that Afro-Latinx women receive equal opportunities and representation in educational materials. The present study examined the representation of Afro-Latinx women in beginner-level Spanish textbooks and the underlying ideologies behind this representation. This study was conducted within the framework of Intersectionality, critical discourse analysis, and visual analysis grammar. The results depict that there is very little representation of Afro-Latinx women in these textbooks. Interestingly in the few instances in which there is some representation of these women, we find instances of stereotypes, impersonalization/superficiality, tourism discourse, and the standard language ideology. The paper argues that the representation of Afro-Latinx women in these textbooks does not paint an accurate picture of the Hispanic world. The textbooks silence minoritized groups such as Afro-Latinx women to privilege dominant groups in society. The study thus calls for a revision of these textbooks to ensure a representation of Afro-Latinx women.

BIBLIOGRAPHY

Apple, Michael, and Linda Christian-Smith, eds. *The politics of the textbook*. Routledge, 2017.

Atchison, Amy. "Where are the women? An analysis of gender mainstreaming in introductory political science textbooks." *Journal of Political Science Education* 13, no. 2 (2017): 185–99.

Azimova, Nigora, and Bill Johnston. "Invisibility and ownership of language: Problems of representation in Russian language textbooks." *The Modern Language Journal* 96, no. 3 (2012): 337–49.

Bárcena, Alicia, and Winnie Byanyima. "América Latina es la región más desigual del mundo.¿ Cómo solucionarlo." In *World Economic Forum*. 2016.

Blanco, Jose. *Portales*. MA: Vista Higher Learning, 2016.

Blanco, Jose., and Phillip. Donley. *Aventuras*. MA: Vista Higher Learning (2014).

Chapelle, Carol A. *Teaching culture in introductory foreign language textbooks*. Springer, 2016.

Collins, Patricia Hill. *Black feminist thought: Knowledge, consciousness, and the politics of empowerment*. Routledge, 2002.

Cortez, Nolvia Ana. *Am I in the book? Imagined communities and language ideologies of English in a global EFL textbook*. The University of Arizona, 2008.

Crenshaw, Kimberlé. "From private violence to mass incarceration: Thinking intersectionally about women, race, and social control." *UCLA L. Rev.* 59 (2011): 1418.

Crenshaw, Kimberlé. "Demarginalizing the intersection of race and sex: A Black feminist critique of antidiscrimination doctrine, feminist theory and antiracist politics." *u. Chi. Legal f.* (1989): 139.

Cruz-Janzen, Marta I. "Latinegras: Desired women: undesirable mothers, daughters, sisters, and wives." *Frontiers: A Journal of Women Studies* 22, no. 3 (2001): 168–83.

Dendrinos, Bessie. "The politics of instructional materials of English for young learners." In *Language, Ideology and Education*, 43–63. Routledge, 2015.

Dorwick, Thalia, M. Ana, and Anne Becher. *Puntos*. McGraw-Hill Education, 2016.

Dumas, Michael J. "Against the dark: Antiblackness in education policy and discourse." *Theory Into Practice* 55, no. 1 (2016): 11–19.

ECLA, NU. "Afrodescendent women in Latin America and the Caribbean: Debts of equality." (2019).

Fairclough, Norman. "Discourse analysis: The critical study of language." London/New York: Routledge (1995).

Fairclough, Norman. "Language and Power. " London: Longman (1989).

Fairclough, Norman. "Critical discourse analysis and the marketization of public discourse: The universities." *Discourse & society* 4, no. 2 (1993): 133–168.

Flores, Juan, and Miriam Jiménez Román. "Triple-consciousness? Approaches to Afro-Latino culture in the united states." *Latin American and Caribbean Ethnic Studies* 4, no. 3 (2009): 319–28.

Gray, John. "The branding of English and the culture of the new capitalism: Representations of the world of work in English language textbooks." *Applied linguistics* 31, no. 5 (2010): 714–33.

Guzmán, Elizabeth E., Paloma E. Lapuerta, and Judith E. Liskin-Gasparro. *Unidos Classroom Manual: An Interactive Approach*. Prentice Hall, 2015.

Halliday, Michael Alexander Kirkwood. "Spoken and written modes of meaning." *Media texts: Authors and readers* 7 (1994): 51–73.

Harrison, Philip, Yan Yang, and Khangelani Moyo. "Visual representations in South Africa of China and the Chinese people." *Journal of African Cultural Studies* 29, no. 1 (2017): 25–45.

Heinrich, Patrick. "Language ideology in JFL textbooks." (2005): 213–32.

Hershberger, Robert, Susan Navey-Davis, and Guiomar Borrás Alvarez. *Plazas*. Cengage Learning, 2016.

hooks, bell. *Representing whiteness in the Black imagination*. Duke University Press, 1992.

Irvine, Judith T., Susan Gal, and Paul V. Kroskrity. "Language ideology and linguistic differentiation." *Linguistic anthropology: A reader* 1 (2009): 402–434.

Jarvis, Ana, Raquel Lebredo, and Francisco Mena-Ayllón. *¿ Cómo se dice?*. Cengage Learning, 2010.

Kress, Gunther, and Theo van Leeuwen. "Multimodal discourse." *The modes and media of contemporary communication. (Cappelen, London 2001)* (2001).

Kroskrity, Paul V. "Language ideologies–Evolving perspectives." *Society and Language Use* 7, no. 3 (2010): 192–205.

Lackey, Madison. "The Existence of Racism in High School History Classes." (2017).

Lee, Jackie FK. "In the pursuit of a gender-equal society: Do Japanese EFL textbooks play a role?" *Journal of Gender Studies* 28, no. 2 (2019): 204–17.

Leslie, Angela Maria. "Rendering Latinas Invisible: The Underrepresentation of Latinas in K-12 History." *International Journal of Multicultural Education* 23, no. 1 (2021): 87–109.

Lippi-Green, Rosina. "The educational system." *English with an Accent. London: Routledge* (1997).

Lipski, John. *Varieties of Spanish in the United States.* Georgetown University Press, 2008.

Lipski, John. "Afro-Yungueño speech: the long-lost 'Black Spanish.'" *Spanish in context* 4, no. 1 (2007): 1–43.

Lipski, John. *A history of Afro-Hispanic language: Five centuries, five continents.* Cambridge University Press, 2005.

Long, Sheri Spaine, Maria Carreira, Sylvia Madrigal Velasco, and Kristin Swanson. *Nexos, Enhanced.* Cengage Learning, 2014.

Mackinney, Erin. "Language ideologies and bilingual realities: The case of Coral Way." In *Honoring Richard Ruíz and his work on language planning and bilingual education*, edited by Nancy Hornberger, 301–15. Bristol, UK; Multilingual Matters, 2016.

Milroy, James. "Language ideologies and the consequences of standardization." *Journal of sociolinguistics* 5, no. 4 (2001): 530–55.

Namatende-Sakwa, Lydia. "Gendering" the text through implicit citations of gendered discourses: The construction of gender and teacher talk around children's fiction." *Gender and Language* 13, no. 1 (2019): 72–93.

National Center for Educational Statistics. "Bachelor's degrees conferred by postsecondary institutions, by race/ethnicity and sex of student: Selected years, 1976–77 through 2014–15." (2016). Retrieved September 8, 2017 from https://nces.ed.gov/programs/digest/d16/tables/dt16_322.20.asp?current= yes

Organista, K. C. "The social stratification of Latino ethnicity, power, and social welfare in the United States." *Solving Latino psychosocial and health problems: Theory, practice, and populations* (2007): 39–63.

Padilla, Lillie, and Rosti Vana. "Ideologies in the foreign language curriculum: Insights from textbooks and instructor interviews." *Language awareness* 28, no. 1 (2019): 15–30.

Reisigl, Michael. and Wodak, Ruth. "The discourse-historical approach." In *Methods of critical discourse studies*, edited by Ruth Wodak and Michael Meyer, 23–61. London: Sage, 2016.

Rifkin, Benjamin. "Gender representation in foreign language textbooks: A case study of textbooks of Russian." *Modern Language Journal* (1998): 217–36.

Rosa, Jonathan. *Looking like a language, sounding like a race.* Oxford Studies in Anthropology, 2019.

Setyono, Budi, and Handoyo Puji Widodo. "The representation of multicultural values in the Indonesian Ministry of Education and Culture-Endorsed EFL textbook: a critical discourse analysis." *Intercultural Education* 30, no. 4 (2019): 383–97.

Shardakova, Marya, and Aneta Pavlenko. "Identity options in Russian textbooks." *Journal of Language, Identity, and Education* 3, no. 1 (2004): 25–46.

Shedd, Carla. *Unequal city: Race, schools, and perceptions of injustice.* Russell Sage Foundation, 2015.

Spelman, Elizabeth. *Inessential woman: Problems of exclusion in feminist thought.* Beacon Press, 1988.

Sunderland, Jane. "Issues of language and gender in second and foreign language education." *Language Teaching* 33, no. 4 (2000): 203–23.

Urry, John. "Tourism, culture and social inequality." *The sociology of tourism: Theoretical and empirical investigations* (1996): 115–33.

———. *The tourist gaze.* Sage, 2002.

Viveros Vigoya, M. "Intersectionality: A situated approach to dominance." *Debate Feminista* 52 (2016): 1–17.

Wade, Peter. "Afro-Latin studies: Reflections on the field." *Latin American and Caribbean Ethnic Studies* 1, no. 1 (2006): 105–24.

Woolard, Kathryn A., and Bambi B. Schieffelin. "Language ideology." *Annual Review of Anthropology* 23, no. 1 (1994): 55–82.

World Bank. "Afro-descendants in Latin America: Toward a Framework of Inclusion." (2018): 10–105.

NOTES

1. Cruz, Bárbara C. "Stereotypes of Latin Americans Perpetuated in Secondary School History Textbooks." *Latino Studies Journal* 1, no. 1 (1994): 51–67.

2. van Dijk, T. "Racism, discourse and textbooks: The coverage of immigration in Spanish textbooks. Paper for a symposium on Human Rights in Textbooks." History Foundation. Estambul (2004).

3. Cragun, Ryan. "The future of textbooks." *Electronic Journal of Sociology* 1, no. 1 (2007): 1–14.

4. Hordge-Freeman, Elizabeth, and Edlin Veras. "Out of the shadows, into the dark: Ethnoracial dissonance and identity formation among Afro-Latinxs." *Sociology of Race and Ethnicity* 6, no. 2 (2020): 146–60.

5. van Leeuwen, Theo. "Towards a semiotics of typography." *Information Design Journal* 14, no. 2 (2006): 139–55.

6. Graci, Joseph Peter. "Gender-role portrayal in college-level elementary Spanish language textbooks." (1993): 1430.

7. McCall, Leslie. "The complexity of intersectionality." *Signs: Journal of Women in Culture and Society* 30, no. 3 (2005): 1771–800.

8. Crenshaw, Kimberlé. "Mapping the Margins: Intersectionality, Identity Politics, and Violence Against Women of Color." *Stanford Law Review* 43, no. 6 (1991): 1241–99.

9. Gal, Susan. "Migration, minorities and multilingualism: Language ideologies in Europe." In *Language ideologies, policies and practices*, pp. 13–27. Palgrave Macmillan, London, 2006.

10. Lippi-Green, Rosina. "Language ideology and language prejudice." *Language in the USA: Themes for the twenty-first century* (2004): 289–304.

11. van Dijik, Dick, Timo Terasvirta, and Philip Hans Franses. "Smooth Transition Autoregressive models-A Survey of Recent Developments," *SSE.* No. 380. *EFI Working Paper Series in Economics and Finance*, 2001.

12. van Leeuwen, Theo. "Towards a semiotics of typography." *Information design journal* 14, no. 2 (2006): 139–55.

13. Kress, Gunther, and Theo van Leeuwen. "Reading images: the grammar of visual design." London: Routledge (1996).

14. Collins, Patricia Hill. "Moving beyond gender." *Revisioning gender* (1999): 261–84.

15. Collins, Patricia Hill. "Moving beyond gender." *Revisioning gender* (1999): 261–284.

16. Irvine, Judith., and Susan Gal. "Language ideology and linguistic differentiation.'" *Regimes of language: Ideologies, polities, and identities* (2000): 35–84.

17. Flores, Nelson, and Jonathan Rosa. "Undoing appropriateness: Raciolinguistic ideologies and language diversity in education." *Harvard Educational Review* 85, no. 2 (2015): 149–71.

18. Uzum, Baburhan, Bedrettin Yazan, Samar Zahrawi, Siham Bouamer, and Ervin Malakaj. "A comparative analysis of cultural representations in collegiate world language textbooks (Arabic, French, and German)." *Linguistics and Education* 61 (2021): 100901.

Chapter 7

Writing and Activism

A Political Perspective on Afro-Latinas' Struggle in Colombia, Brazil, and the Caribbean

Yesenia Escobar Espitia, Renata Dorneles Lima,
Yoiseth Patricia Cabarcas, and Lindsay Gary

In Colombia, Brazil, and the Caribbean, Afro-Latinas have used their writing as a visible force to consolidate a political space connected to their territories, as well as a source of memory, togetherness, place of enunciation, and scene of local power. Their writing involves more than a creative act. It is a way of showing the roots of their identity, and to retell the "herstory" to break down the stereotypes and imaginaries created about Black women for ages. Their words, both written and spoken, have become a vehicle to denounce the oppression suffered by Black women since colonialism. At the same time, these words have become a braid to strengthen their sisterhood. This is particularly relevant and revolutionary since Black women have played a repressed role historically, and they have been denied expressing themselves through writing. Hence, this rising movement of activist writers is becoming the cornerstone of social change.

Some of the approaches we adopted to analyze this phenomenon are the paradigm of Afrocentricity and the ideas of Africana womanism, Dororidade, Intersectionality, and escrevivência that emerged to organize the scene where they settle down their thoughts and targets. First, Afrocentricity is a theoretical perspective developed by Africologist Dr. Molefi Kete Asante that centers on African agency by viewing African phenomena and experiences from the lens of African people. The first full discussion of the theory was presented in his publication in 1980 *Afrocentricity: The Theory of Social Change*[1] and was expanded into a paradigm by Dr. Ama Mazama[2] which incorporates cognitive, structural, and functional aspects. It has since then been further expanded upon by numerous scholars including Karenga,[3] McDougal,[4] and Dove.[5] Dr. Nah Dove developed the theory of African Womanism, an Afrocentric theory. Building on the Africana Womanism theory of Clenora Hudson Weems,[6] Dove's contribution is "to further emphasize the concept of culture as a tool of analysis for understanding the nature of African women's experiences," addressing "culture as a weapon of resistance and a basis for defining a new world order."[7] Additionally, Cheikh Anta Diop's "Two Cradle Theory" is of paramount influence in this work. This theory was primarily emphasized in *The Cultural Unity of Black Africa: The Domains of Matriarchy and of Patriarchy in Classical Antiquity*[8] and *The African Origin of Civilization.*[9] Diop theorizes the development of and significant cultural differences between Africa and Europe/Asia in these texts. Due to Africa's environment and its abundance of resources in the Southern Cradle, a culture of justice, peace, agriculture, community, surplus, xenophilia, and matriarchy emerges. However, in the Northern Cradle, which includes Europe and parts of Asia, there were far fewer resources, infertile land, and harsh weather conditions. As a result, the culture that emerges from this is nomadic, warlike, and survivalist, which in turn led to patriarchal families and societies, the debasement and enslavement of women, xenophobia, violence, crime, individualism, pessimism, and racism. This theory provides the basis for contextualizing the ills of the Western world, which demonized and debased African women in antiquity and to continue to do so all over the world in the present.

Afrocentricity and African womanism allow us to understand how AfroLatinas build up a new perspective as Black women by describing and telling what is inside their psyches, emotions, and angles. Furthermore, this brings to the fore another issue: What does it mean to be a Black woman? What kind of struggles have Black women suffered simply on account of their racial identity?

We can attempt to answer these questions by analyzing some cultural productions pieces. We can start by looking up the poem "Me gritaron Negra," by the AfroPeruvian Victoria Santa Cruz. "On it, resides all the semantic and linguistic load of the word Black! They yelled at me Black!" This poem constitutes the multiple struggles that Black women have faced through the years while they have been fighting against race and gender discrimination. If we go back in time, and we remember the speech delivered by Sojourner Truth in 1851 at the Women's Rights Convention in Akron, Ohio, we find a voice that is rebuked and pronounced from discursive orality "Am I not a woman?" This statement vindicates and makes visible the identity of Black women while it deconstructs the hegemonic category that weighed on Black women. In other words, this discourse opens the doors to talk about the intersection between race and gender, not as two stereotyped semantic loads from the hegemonies, but on the contrary, a new way of re-signifying the concept of woman.

This idea of Intersectionality was developed by Kimberlé Crenshaw in 1989. It seeks to capture the structural and dynamic consequences of the interaction between two or more axes of subordination. Furthermore, Intersectionality deals with how specific actions and policies generate oppressions that flow along these axes, constituting dynamic or active aspects of disempowerment.[10] As Crenshaw has pointed out, AfroLatinx writers in Colombia, Brazil, and the Caribbean have remarked on how race, gender, and class are used by the power to discriminate, exclude, and make invisible the contributions of Afro-descendant women within social contexts. It involves studying and analyzing Intersectionality from two spheres: structural and political.[11] The first has to do with the interconnection between color and poverty since the experiences of many Black women have to do with socio-economic status.

Regarding the political matter, the author emphasizes how this concept locates women of color within subordinate groups linked to inequalities. These policies exclude and generate mechanisms of control and oppression, denying the validity of their subjectivities. This denial contains the most absurd violations and aberrations imposed over the bodies of Black women since slavery times. All this means that hegemony built a platform of oppression, a categorized mechanism of control referred to race and gender, and at the same time, it implemented a performance of pejorative, abusive, and violent codes to refer to the body and the history of Black women.

Keeping this in mind, the AfroLatina writers have configured new conceptions to make visible the role of Afro-descendant women in the history of Latin America and the Caribbean. Therefore, this exercise marks a new trace for Afro-Latin American literature that seeks to collect and write the history, legacy, and contributions of Afro-descendant women in the region. These Afro-Latin writers try to decode the imaginaries created about the idea of "the Black woman" and provide tools that articulate a new discourse on race, gender, and class, a discourse that reflects the necessity of modifying the rhetorical thoughts about Afro identity. Therefore, we find Black writers such as Mayra Santos Febres, Yolanda Arroyo Pizarro, and Nancy Morejón from the Caribbean; Luz Ribeiro, Mel Duarte, and Kimani from Brazil; and Alba Nelly Mina, Myriam Díaz, and Adelaida Fernández Ochoa, from Colombia, who use their writing to re-signify what it means to be a Black woman and generate reflections on the concept of liberation and empowerment of AfroLatinas.

They think about themselves from an Afrocentric perspective that accounts for movements and collective realities with their voice, a way of challenging social structures and value systems that have been imposed on race, class, and gender. They look for understanding the subjectivities of Black women and their semantic load within history, creating a new paradigm that contributes to embracing all women of color. This process frames a new paradigm of resistance and enunciation that reaffirms the existence of multiple Black women as thinking subjects and political beings. Thus, the starting point must fall on "us," on our identities, the belief that we feel Black and describe ourselves from our own experiences and pains.

These authors have also summed to their perspectives the concept of Dororidade, coined by the philosopher "Mujer Prieta," Brazilian feminist Vilma Piedade. This is a circular concept that accounts for Black and dark women. Vilma Piedade says that pain, therefore, contains the shadows, the emptiness, the absence, the silenced speech, the pain caused by racism. And that Pain is Prieto (black).[12]

The concept of Doloridade dialogues with the idea of sorority, the base of the currents of feminism. However, sorority does not account for Black and dark women. This concept comes etymologically from the word sóror-sisters, but it speaks of a sisterhood that does not cover or shelter women of color; on the contrary, it excludes them. It is here where that counterpoint of history arises, with the objective of including women of color within those silences and absences. Therefore, Dororidade is the pain that is felt, it is the pain that all women share, and it opens dialogues with other women. Pain is the empathy among Black women generated by the common pains of slavery, patriarchy, and the different types of violence that Afro-descendant women have been subjected to. Dororidade represents inclusion, it is a constant dialogue that signifies and re-signifies the role of Black women as a social and political entity. According to Vilma Piedade, the concept of Dororidade transcends and is transformed: "Does Pain unite all Women? It unites, but it also establishes itself as a Power of change, of transformation. At this point, Dororidade is established and runs the trajectory experienced by Us, Black Population, and, especially, We –Women- Black Women."[13]

It is worth noting that this concept is intimately Black, it belongs to that place of enunciation marked by historical silence, by non-place, by invisibility. As Vilma Piedade points out, Dororidade carries in its meaning the pain caused in all women by machismo, a pain coined by slavery,[14] a pain that speaks from the experiences and trajectories of Black women. Dororidade unites and breaks the borders and imposed limits. It is a pain that emerges and is transformed into narratives of the encounter and the disagreement.

The term Dororidade shares some similarities with Malungaje, coined by Jerome Branche, who took it from the word-concept Malungo. This term refers to a community that, despite being cemented throughout an experience that had pushed their physical and psychological resources to their farthest limits,[15] creates a transhistorical and transnational culture linked by the bonds of a survival experience.

Another important concept used to analyze the literary productions approached in this chapter is Escrevivência. This notion comes from the speech of Latin American Black women and from the gaze of the Black subject. Conceição Evaristo, in his text *A escrevivência e seus subtextos* (2020), uses the historiography of the Brazilian colonial period to explain the term "escrevivência" from the role of enslaved Black women. Although it is based on the Brazilian reality of this historical period, it can be linked to the reality of other Latin American countries that had Black African enslaved indoviduals. Conceição explains that the concept has "Mãe Preta" as the central figure. This Black woman resided in the Casa Grande to take care of the white children of their owners; she was the one who provided, without any other option, these children, in addition to breastfeeding, teaching the first words and the possibility of listening to stories with the aim of "putting those of the master's house to sleep" who, later, would be their masters and descendants. It is from this memory and image that Evaristo conceives the term "writing-experience."

Conceição Evaristo's proposal highlights the importance of orality in the narrative of the Black woman as a heritage from our ancestors, which is no longer used for the benefit of "La Casa Grande," but for our people. In addition, the concept emphasizes the narratives of Black women as a common experience, the experience of being Black and women at the same time. In that sense, the idea of escrevivência connects with the ideas of African womanism, Intersectionality, and Dororidade mentioned above. However, to understand how these concepts, go together, it is necessary to analyze some of the literary works created by the introduced authors.

It is worth pointing out names such as Mayra Santos Febres, Yolanda Arroyo Pizarro, and Nancy Morejón, who configure and rewrite the history of their territory from the perspective of their Afro-Caribbean female characters. Mayra Santos-Febres was born in Carolina, Puerto Rico, in 1966. She is a narrator, poet, essayist, professor, and one of the most important contemporary voices in the Caribbean. Her works embrace themes such as identity, the body, memory, the queer, and the intersection between race, class, and gender, as well as the image of the Afro-diasporic female subject. Her works are challenging artistic creations that convey a new perspective on the Black female subjects. Likewise, these literary works allow us to trace from a kaleidoscopic gaze in which the Black woman is positioned from solid foundations to resist and evade the hegemonic discourses.

For instance, in the novel *Fe en Disfraz* (2009), the reader is located in a geographical space where the past and the present bifurcate. Mayra introduces us to an intellectual Black woman, a historian who rescues the narratives of the manumitted slaves of the Lusitanian Empire:

> Algunos de aquellos papeles narraban cómo esclavas manumisas de diversas regiones del Imperio lusitano y del español lograron convertirse en dueñas de haciendas. Otros tan solo recogían testimonios de <abusos>, en los cuales las esclavas pedían amparo real. Encontró, además, documentos de condena por el Santo Oficio, declaraciones de tormentos y castigos. Mariana Di Morales, Diamantina, la mulata Pascuala, los testimonios se sucedían unos a otros. Relataban estupros y forzamientos con lujo de detalles. Su contenido sexual era particularmente violento.[16]

With this information in her possession, Fe Verdejo, the main character, re-creates the concept of oppression and violence lived by the manumitted slaves and twists the hegemonic discourse by creating an affectionate rewriting of a collective memory that has been hidden. In this sense, Fe reads the history from the lens of a Black woman historian whose objective would be to consolidate these narratives and present a female story of Black femininity in an exhibition where she would present the manuscripts of slaves, baptism certificates, mother-of-pearl missals, mantillas, jewels, photos, and the costume of the slave Xica Da Silva,[17] all of which she managed to expose in the seminary museum. Here, Fe seeks a way of redemption, a representation of the silenced body of the manumitted slaves, thus challenging patriarchy, and hegemonic institutions, thus creating a new cultural and political discourse that articulates the identity, race, and sexuality of enslaved Black bodies. Through this process, Fe Verdejo reclaims the subjectivity of these women and accomplishes this through two moments. In the first, Fe weaves the stories of these manumitted women to understand the situations they have experienced and reveal to the world the dominant scenarios built around racialized bodies, meanwhile digging deeper into the understanding of those marks of subversion:

> La Historia está llena de mujeres anónimas que lograron sobrevivir al deseo del amo desplegándose ante su mirada. Pero nunca se abrieron completas. De alguna forma, lograron sostener un juego doloroso con lo oculto. ¿Cómo hicieron que la piel se ofreciera sin traicionar lo que tenía que permanecer escondido? ¿Cómo hacer ahora para que esa piel cuente la verdadera historia de estos seres que accedieron a la esfera limitadísima de su libertad, a cambio de un asco disfrazado de ardor, de una violencia hecha devoración sagrada?[18]

The second moment refers to the body as a reading text between a violent past and a present that is established to make visible: —"¿A quiénes se habrían parecido esas mujeres? —¿No es obvio, Martín? Se parecían a mí. Me quedé mirando a Fe, en silencio. Curiosamente nunca antes me había detenido a pensar que sus esclavas se le parecieran. Que ella, presente y ante mí, tuviera la misma tez, el mismo cuerpo que una esclava agredida hace más de doscientos años."[19] Fe Verdejo, thanks to her Black body, is able to perform a performance of acts, where through rituals she shares the pain and scars of the past with the manumitted slaves, through the element of Xica Da Silva's costume as a disguise: "un ruido como de cadenas avisó la aparición de un arnés de varilla y de cuero. Fe alzó el arnés frente a mis ojos. Pude ver el metal corroído y expuesto. Acomodó el semicírculo de metal en el aire. Luego, llevó el arnés hasta su minúscula cintura. "[20] When she put on the costume and felt the pain of the harness that pierced her skin and cracked it, she shared with them the pain of a bitter past, but unlike the slaves, this pain for Fe Verdejo is pleasant, it is a sexualized pain. In other words, we observe the confrontation between the body and the erotic act as a bridge that connects the body with memory and with silenced history in the Caribbean. It is necessary to highlight this relationship between the body and memory. Santos-Febres in his book *Sobre piel y papel* had pointed out some explanation for that, "the introduction of the body and Caribbean eroticism on the page re-somatizes language, denying the difference between reason and flesh to establish another logical tradition and another option for the production of knowledge."[21] And it is here where the protagonist gives another explanation to that tradition of the pain of memory and restores the noun "Black." This word that denotes reification, degradation, darkness, violence, lack of meaning, is inverted by Fe Verdejo in another knowledge, replacing the body of the mistreated, raped and condemned Black woman in the seventeenth and eighteenth centuries, by an erotic body as an inscription of identity definitions and as the result of a process of self-knowledge and self-definition[22].

Moreover, we can mention the writer Yolanda Arroyo Pizarro (Guaynabo, Puerto Rico, 1970), and her narrative that condenses the female voices and the racialized and Black bodies of her native island Puerto Rico. She is a novelist, storyteller, essayist, and poet. Her literary voice rebukes and transgresses the discourses imposed on the category "Black woman." All her work aims to analyze the identity and political commitment of an activist, feminist, Afro Boricua, and militant woman who struggles for space and the visibility of Afro-descendant women.

Her works seek to look from an Afrocentric perspective at the image of the Black woman as an agent of history. For instance, her book *Las Negras* is part of a collection of three short stories, "Wanwe," "Matronas," and "Saeta." *Las Negras* tells the lives and histories of three enslaved Black women, whose stories intertwine with each other to show themes of identity, race, language, and slavery, that becomes part of the transnational. Yolanda Arroyo, in the dedication of *Las Negras* (2012) makes a public complaint: "To historians, for having left us out. Here we are again . . . Body present, current color." This dedication seeks to focus on the stories of many women enslaved, abused, and violated in the days of slavery. A weapon that is used from the language to position identity, race, and gender, making visible not only the pain of enslaved Black women but also their heroic acts and resistance that are part of the Caribbean history, Puerto Rican history.

In *Las Negras,* the female author narrates the lives of three women, Wanwe, Ndizi, and Tshanwe. Each of them brings a different perspective on the invisible struggles of Black women. With the story of Ndizi, a slave who is sentenced to be hanged for practicing the trade of midwife and drowning Black children at birth, the reader celebrates the importance of the "Matronas" (Midwives). Ndizi is a warrior heroine owner of ancestral wisdom who deconstructs hegemonic knowledge: the Church, the language, the body, and slavery. She is a woman capable of repealing the instruments of oppression and outwitting them, at the expense of her own life.

Through Yolanda Arroyo's narrative, we can see how the silence prevailed over women of color in the days of slavery is torn and staged from language. This fact is reflected in Ndizi, who narrates the events of her life and restores vitality to the voices silenced by history. From the first lines of the text, the reader can go through each moment of the character's life, from the moment she is locked up until the declaration of the death sentence. However, throughout this journey Ndizi lets us see the courage of the Black woman and her daring to invalidate the implanted categories. Regarding the language that during slavery and colonial times was imposed on the enslaved as unique, Ndizi transgresses this approach, she knows many languages, understands them, but keeps them secret as a weapon for her defense. "Lo entiendo, pero lo guardo como secreto (I understand it, but I keep it a secret)"[23] "Se queda de una pieza ante el descubrimiento de mi dominio lingüística (He is stunned by the discovery of my linguistic proficiency)."[24] At the same time, she ventures into all trades: healer, herbalist, sobadora (traditional healer), midwife, and cook, to use these strategies to build trust and demolish the commercialization of slaves from within. For instance, she beecones the first provider of white children while she accompanies the enslaved women in their deliveries and drowns the Black children at birth: "He impersonado todas las faenas de una esclava doméstica para acercarme primero a los niños blancos recién nacidos. Siguiendo las directrices de la gran negra bruja" "Voy ganando confianza. Todas las que hacen lo mismo que yo, y somos muchas" 'Entonces me inicio ayudando a traer al mundo a los hijos de las negras esclavas bozales. . . . Nadie sabe de lo que hablo."[25]

Thus, Ndizi attacks the roots of slavery by saving Black children from falling into the slave trade. On the other hand, she questions the sexual assaults that Black women receive from those who enter a woman's body without her permission. She makes the comparison with how in her village this assault was punished and had to be paid for with goods or with the cold-blooded removal of an organ and finally she mocks the religious establishment, as there is no confession on her part and there is no repentance of sin. Therefore, Ndizi exalts the particularities of the female subject and deinstitutionalizes the discourses of the white to apply their revolutionary ideas and of struggle from the cultural policies of gender. "Muchas me siguen. Hemos logrado un ejército (Many follow me. We have achieved an army)."[26]

In addition, we can mention Nancy Morejón (Cuba, 1944), poet, essayist, and writer, an essential figure in Latin American and Caribbean poetics. In her poem "Mujer Negra" (1975), Morejón is aware of her social and political commitment toward her sisters and materializes it through her voice. "Black Woman" is a feminist poem that focuses on the process of identifying an individual memory and on the historical reconstruction of women identity. In its first stanza, the poetic voice immerses us in the historical context of the transatlantic journey experienced from the perspective of an African woman.[27] Furthermore, slavery dehumanized her and made her work like a beast. In the following stanzas, the poetic voice explicitly portrays the testimony and oppression of the female bodies in the hands of their masters: "Su Merced me compró en una plaza/ Bordé la casaca de su Merced y un hijo/macho le parí (He bought me in a square / I embroidered his coat, and a son/male gave birth to him)"[28] a son who had no name, a son from the constant rapes to which women were subjected. This poetic voice continues spinning the drama of a woman enslaved under the yoke of an anti-humanist patriarchal society.

However, this violated woman claims a place in that same land "donde tocó la sangre húmeda" allí funda "su canto milenario" y la "esperanza" de construir su mundo, bajo sus preceptos y reglas. Entonces, esta mujer decide correr y crear procesos libertarios "en el palenque" como espacio cimarrón de lucha y libertad.[29] Each verse is the embodiment of the female struggle, it is the call to identity and the vindication of women during the diaspora and exile. It is also the voice of the survival of an African woman who overcomes obstacles and reveals herself through a Black female consciousness that seeks to delegitimize the hierarchy and build new practices to establish a cultural identity.

The Brazilian afro-female writers have also developed a revolutionary movement using her voice. To understand the base of her works it would be important to keep in mind the term outsider, coined by the Afro-American theorist Patricia Hill Collins. She used this term to name the position of the social marginality of Black women that allows a sui generis condition about herself and her environment, facilitating a different vision of social relations. Although Collins's theory focuses on American Black women, it is possible to draw some similarities with the condition of Latin American Black women. Collins writes, "this insider-outsider status has given African American women a special perspective on themselves, family, and society."[30] This concept can help us analyze the poems that deal with the social condition of Black women in societies in which racism is structural and systematic. This approach allows us to understand the annihilation that this subject suffers while fighting against daily acts of discrimination and while experiencing the denial of the Black subject as a producer of knowledge.

In this context, it is fundamental to point out the literary genre of "poetry slam," an oral poetry dispute created by Marc Smith in Chicago, in 1986, and that arrived in Brazil in 2008 thanks to Roberta Estrela D'Alva. Starting in that year, poets took the streets of various Brazilian cities to promote and participate in poetry slams, bringing to the dispute, among many topics, those related to social, racial, and gender issues. It is, in this context that the poets Mel Duarte, Luz Ribeiro, and Kimani are inserted and show all their discursive power. The three poets are Black women and come from the outskirts of São Paulo. The condition of Black women is evident in her literary productions, presenting themes related to the ancestry, religiosity, identity, and self-esteem of the Black woman, the condition of the Black subject gaze with all the social barriers that permeate this condition.

Mel Duarte, poet, cultural producer in the city of São Paulo and slammer, wrote many poems about the self-esteem of Black women and among these is the poem "Menina melanina," which deals with frizzy hair and paying attention to the importance of this phenotype as a mark of Blackness, of which it is necessary to show pride. It is indeed an invitation to develop and encourage the self-esteem of Black women. With her poetry, Duarte promotes a discussion regarding the violence inherent to the whitening process in Brazilian society and narrates the painful process of recognizing Blackness, based on the phenotype, and the self-acceptance of her image. She says about Black women:

Mulher bonita é a que vai a luta!
Porque cabelo de negro não é só resistente,
é resistência.[31]

The poet is attentive to the demands of Black women that are widely disseminated and discussed on social networks, dialoguing in her poems with current issues around Black women and the rescue of identity through other truths beyond those that start from the gaze of the Black subject. Mel, in addition to addressing the self-esteem of Black women, places, at the heart of her poetic production, the theme of the hyper-sexualization of the Black body and Black strength and ancestry.

If we analyze Lelia González's text "A political-cultural category da Amefricanidade,"[32] we can find a lot of discourses around the superiority of the white phenotype. This idealization rejects the Black identity as an identity to be proud of. The Latin American racism described by González dialogues with Mel's speech, around the whitening ideology that makes it impossible to accept a Black female identity. However, the poet calls for a sentiment of self-acceptance of her Black body including all her features, overcoming the stereotypes related to this body.

Another poet worth mentioning is Kimani, who is the champion of the Slam SP 2017, of the FLUP—Festa Literária das Periferias, which took place in Rio de Janeiro in 2017 and 2019, and winner of the Slam BR 2019, that guaranteed her a place for the Great Poetry Slam, in France, in 2020. One of the themes appraised in her literary production is the genocide of Black people in Brazil. In one of her poems, the author recites how society assumes that the assassination of Black bodies is natural. In "Conselho bom," Kimani recites the difference between a Black woman and a white woman, this time called "Sinhá"[33]] and all the violence that permeates the Black body:

Sinhá,
Por que eu vejo os meus morrendo todo dia?
Meu povo parece gado marcado, cordeiro imolado[34]

The poet, in contrast to the image of "Sinhá," describes her Black body as a body that needs to be hidden and cannot be accepted or humanized. Kimani also brings to light the story of Rafael Braga, a Black man, a collector of recyclable materials in the city of Rio de Janeiro, the only one convicted of the political demonstrations that took place throughout Brazil in 2013, although he was not part of any political group present there. Rafael was arrested because he was carrying disinfectant and bleach, which, according to police, would be used to make explosive material. Criminal selectivity is evident in this case, making it clear that Braga's conviction has only two obvious reasons: race and class.

On the other hand, we find Luz Ribeiro, poet, actress, slammer, performer, with degrees in physical education and pedagogy. She was the winner of the Slam BR 2016 and, more recently, of the Slam BR-Special Online Edition 2021 with the participation of all the winners of previous editions of the dispute. Luz Ribeiro begins her poetry "Deu (s) branco" singing the song "A carne," which was a great success for the voice of the Afro-Brazilian singer Elza Soares, and which affirms the little importance of the Black body in a society structured upon racist practices. The title of the poem is a word game that will give clues about what will be covered in the text.

[a carne mais barata do mercado é a negraaaa]
[a carne mais marcada pelo estado é a carne negra]

After singing the beginning of "A carne," Luz remains silent for a moment. Silence is a means of communication used by the poet. Therefore, it is quite significant for the understanding of her verses. The poet describes the moment she was asked about the difference between her color/skin tone and the one of other members of her family. The first verses of the poem are, then, rooted in her autobiography. In the following stanzas, Luz dialogues with God recounting different kinds of violence that she suffered throughout her life and ask why these oppressions derive from a personal experience, but which encompass simultaneously the experiences of other subjects. "Negroes," as he recites in the following lines: "But we only know how to wear a Preto or inner day" and "more years than history not mute, / that there are more than two pretos that ficam sujas de cimento, / that são as minhas equuais to take care of two filhos das sinhás."

Finally, we it is necessary to approach the Afro Colombian scene by studying the literature of Alba Nelly Mina, Myriam Diaz, and Adelaida Fernández, who become part of the plethora of artists who work in pursuit of identity strengthen and empowerment of Black women through their writing. Alba Nelly Mina was born on the Colombian Pacific Coast. She is recognized for her outstanding voice as a cantaora (traditional singer), spiritual leader, and writer. Her poetry rescues the oral tradition of African Griots and finds value in the small things of our everyday life. She separates herself from the idea of the poet as a creative genius to prove that anyone in every place can make poetry just by looking around and narrating what surrounds us. Her poems are an ode to her African roots, her territory, her struggles as a Black woman, and her social and environmental activism. For instance, in her poem "pelimaldita" (cursed hair) she rejects the pejorative name given to her hair and emphasizes its beauty and qualities, as well as the historical role it played in the liberation from slavery. In addition, she encourages other Black women to love their hair and feel proud of it. Her poem becomes part of a wave of artistic productions created by Afro Latin artists and activists who connect their works with the social struggles that aim to break down stereotypes rooted in Western culture, especially the ones about female beauty, that have such a profound impact and stigmatization on Black women. In addition, it is a poem that emphasizes the strength of Black women and their powerful contribution to their communities.

Another significant poem is "Mi África" (My Africa). This creative piece highlights the power of her ancestors who were not slaves but rather kings and queens who were enslaved. She sings to the Maroon and the resistance of her forebears. This poem also explores the importance of Palenque de San Basilio, a Maroon village located in the north of Colombia where people maintain their African culture and their language. Ultimately, "Mi África" is a song about the rebellions and the contributions of African culture to the rest of the world.

In the same way, the poem "A mis ancestors" (To my forebears) calls upon the different orishas (gods and goddess) of the Yoruba tradition as a recognition of the most ancient religion which has survived in the world until the present time, despite its demonization and persecution. This piece represents a tribute to the influence of orishas in our lives, their powers, and their characteristics. This also embodies a defiance of the predominant Christian tradition of the country and at the same time is a homage to the African legacy that remains in our culture.

Furthermore, we find the poet, teacher, and social activist Miriam Díaz, who was born on the "Palenque de San Basilio," a small town located on the Colombian Caribbean coast that isconsidered the first free village of America. She invites the readers to discover the meaning of belonging in the small land of Africa settled in the Latin American country. Her poetry is written in Spanish and Palenquero, language that embraces the double African trace in her culture. For instance, her poem "Maferefún" which means "go and pray" uses the language of her ancestors to emphasize the importance of honoring their origins. Her description of Elegguá (who opens the paths), worships the fierce warrior and illustrates his life. The female poet also demands protection and asks for permission. That's how she recognizes the superiority of orishas, the people from the diaspora. Furthermore, her poetry constitutes a cult to the different Palenquero rituals such as the lumbalúes or death ceremonies.

Díaz plays a very interesting role as a writer, but also as a teacher. She has a huge commitment to eradicating racism from our society using education. She is a real ambassador of her village who has taken the challenge of showing the world how worthy are the African cultures and the valuable role of Black women in the enrichment of these cultures. Lastly, we wish to mention the writer and professor Adelaida Fernández Ochoa, who was born in Cali, on the Colombian Pacific coast. She was awarded the prize Casa de las Americas for her novel *Afuera crece un Mundo* (A world grows outside), her first book that launched her to fame because of the meaningful story described in it. She revived the character of Nay from *María* written by Jorge Isaacs in the nineteenth century. Nay was an enslaved individual and secondary character in that novel. On the contrary, Fernández makes her a heroine who is fighting for her freedom, her son, and for returning to her homeland in Africa.

Akin to what Candelario Obeso did in *Cantos Populares de mi Tierra*, Fernández uses fluent prose to set up a scenery where African people are the main characters. She re-creates the atmosphere of the independence battles to show the pivotal role of Afro-descendants in the building of a new nation. In addition, Fernández dignifies their presence in the literature by giving them a privileged position in her stories, where they have a capacity for agency and a relevant purpose in their lives. Undoubtedly, Mina, Díaz, and Fernández's works reveal a clear interest in using literature as a vehicle to vindicate the representation of Black women in their stories. Likewise, they denounce the taunts suffered historically by them, as consequences of slavery, colonialism, and the patriarchy. They demonstrate how the repercussions of these scourges are still palpable in our society. These Afro-Colombian writers, together with the others mentioned in this chapter, adhere to the circle of female writers and activists in Latin America who have created a weave of resistance against hegemony and canonical traditions. Their works involve a mix of rebellion, research, inspiration, and struggle but, especially, the need to establish new perspectives that come from Black women who are finally able to write their own stories.

As has been noted in this chapter, the authors mentioned above represent a new generation of creators who bring to light the role of Afro-Latina writers as agents of the relocation of Black women in Latin American history. They place Black women at the center of their stories, discourses, and creations. This Afrocentric perspective involves a powerful process of liberation and consciousness that aims to understand the experiences of black women as unique and at the same time polyphonic. In summary, AfroLatinas writers have made their works a transcendental scenery for increasing the participation of Black women as intellectuals, political individuals, and creators. Without a doubt, this scenario puts in evidence the results of huge struggles but also remarks the flagrant necessity of drilling down the past and present history of Afro-Latina writers in order to broaden our collective imaginary of Latin America.

BIBLIOGRAPHY

Arroyo, Yolanda. *Las negras*, Carolina, Puerto Rico, Boreales, 2012.
.Arroyo, Yolanda *Afrofeministamente*, San Juan, Puerto Rico, Editorial EDP University, 2020.
Asante, Molefe K. *Afrocentricity: The Theory of Social Change*, Compañía Editorial Amulefi,1980.

Collins, Patricia Hill. "Aprendendo com a *outsider within:* a significação sociológica do pensamento feminista negro," *Revista Sociedade e Estado* 31, no. 1 (2016): 99–127.

Crenshaw, Kimberlé. "Mapping the Margins: Intersectionality, Identity Politics, and Violence against Women of Color," *Stanford Law Review*, 1991.

Crenshaw, Kimberlé, *Documento para o encontro de especialistas em aspectos da discriminação relativos ao gênero,* University of California, Los Angeles: Estudos Feministas, 2002.

Curiel, Ochy. *Los aportes de las afrodescendientes a la teoría y práctica feminista: desuniverzalizando el sujeto mujeres.* Buenos Aires: En Perfiles del Feminismo, Vol III, 2007.

Davis, Angela. *Mujeres, raza y clase.* Madrid-España: Akal, 2004.

Díaz, Miriam (Ed.). *Voces Ancestrales.* Bogotá: Tagigo, 2021.

Diop, Cheikh Anta. *The Cultural Unity of Black Africa: The Domains of Matriarchy and of Patriarchy in Classical Antiquity.* London: Karnak House, 1989.

Diop, Cheikh Anta. *The African Origin of Civilization: Myth or Reality.* Chicago: Chicago Review Press, 1974.

Dove, Nah. "African Womanism: An Afrocentric Theory." *Journal of Black Studies*, 1998.

Duarte, Mel. *Negra Nua Crua.* São Paulo: Ijumaa, 2016.

Evaristo, Conceição. "A escrevivência e seus subtextos'.' In: Constância Lima Duarte, and Isabella Rosado Nunes (eds.), *Escrevivência: a escrita de nós: reflexões sobre a obra de Conceição Evaristo.* 1 ed. Rio de Janeiro: Mina Comunicação e Arte, 2020.

Fernández, Adelaida. *Afuera crece un mundo.* Bogotá: Planeta Colombiana S.A., 2017.

González, Lélia. *Primavera para as rosas negras*: *Lélia González em primeira pessoa . . . , Coletânea organizada e editada pela UCPA - União dos Coletivos Pan-Africanistas.* São Paulo: Diáspora Africana, 2018.

Hudson-Weems, Clenora. *Africana Womanism: Reclaiming Ourselves.* Bedford Publishers, 1993.

Jabardo, Mercedes, ed. *Feminismos negros—Una antología*, Madrid, Traficantes de sueños, 2012.

Karenga, *Afrocentricity and Multicultural Education: Concept, Challenge, and Contribution.* The Afrocentric Paradigm, 2003.

Mazama, *The Afrocentric Paradigm*, 2003.Mbembe, Achille. *Crítica de la razón negra. Ensayos sobre el racismo contemporáneo.* París: Ediciones La Découverte, 2016.

McDougal, *Research Methods in Africana Studies*, 2014.

Mina, Alba Nelly. *Mi África. Yo soy Zaza Minyaré.* Bogotá: Tagigo, 2018.

Morejon, Nancy. *Looking Within/Mirar adentro: Selected Poems /Poemas escogidos, 1954 2000.* Ed. and Intro. Juanamaría Cordones-Cook. Detroit, MI: Wayne State UP, 2003.

Piedade, Vilma. *Doloridad, Doloridade.* São Paulo: Mandacaru, 2017.

Santiago, Ana Rita. *Vozes Literárias de Escritoras Negras.* Cruz das Almas-Bahia: Editora UFRB, 2012.

Santiago, Caballero, and Gabriela González (eds.). *Mujeres Intelectuales Feminismos y liberación en América Latina y el Caribe*, Buenos Aires, Clacso, 2017.

Santos, Mayra. Fe en disfraz. La Habana: Arte y Literatura, 2009.

———. *Sobre piel y papel*, San Juan, Puerto Rico: Ediciones Callejón, 2005.

———. *Poesía casi completa*. Mérida: La Castalia Líneaimaginaria, Impresión Digital, 2021.

Viveros, Mara. *La interseccionalidad*: una aproximación situada a la dominación, Debate Feminista, Volumen 52, (octubre de 2016): 1–17, https://doi.org/10.1016/j.df.2016.09.005

NOTES

1. Asante, Molefi. *Afrocentricity: The Theory of Social Change*, 1980.

2. Mazama, Ama. *The Afrocentric Paradigm*, 2003.

3. Karenga, Afrocentricity and Multicultural Education: Concept, Challenge, and Contribution*, The Afrocentric Paradigm,* 2003, 73–94.

4. McDougal, *Research Methods in Africana Studies*, 2014.

5. Dove, Nah. "African Womanism: An Afrocentric Theory," *Journal of Black Studies,* 1998, 515–39.

6. Hudson-Weems, Clenora. *Africana Womanism: Reclaiming Ourselves*, 1993.

7. Dove, Nah. "African Womanism: An Afrocentric Theory," *Journal of Black Studies,* 1998, 516.

8. Diop, Cheikh Anta. *The Cultural Unity of Black Africa: The Domains of Matriarchy and Patriarchy in Classical Antiquity,* 1962.

9. Diop, *The African Origin of Civilization*, 1974

10. Crenshaw, Kimberlé, *"Documento para o encontró de especialistas em aspectos da discriminação relativos ao gênero,"* University of California, Los Angeles, *Estudos Feministas*, 2002, 177. We translated it from Portuguese into English, because the original, Background Paper for the Expert Meeting on Gender-Related Aspects of Race Discrimination, was not found.

11. Crenshaw, Kimberlé. "Mapping the Margins: Intersectionality, Identity Politics, and Violence against Women of Color," *Stanford Law Review* 43 (6)(1991): 1241–99.

12. Piedade, Vilma, *Doloridad, Doloridade*, São Paulo, Mandacaru, 2017, 19.

13. Ibid., 22–23.

14. Ibid.

15. Branche, Jerome. "Introduction Malungaje: Toward a Poetics of Diaspora." *The Poetics and Politics of Diaspora: Transatlantic Musings*. Routledge, 2015, 1–18.

16. Santos, Mayra. *Fe en disfraz,* La Habana, Cuba, Arte y Literatura, 2009, 18.

17. Her first name, Francisca da Silva de Oliveira, known as Xica Da Silva or Da Silva girl. She was a Brazilian slave, later freed. The story indicates that she had an affair with Joao Fernández de Oliveira, the richest diamond exploiter. Xica Da Silva used her dress when she was first introduced to society by her lover, who had fabrics made of raw silk, rhinestones, and gold thread to Portugal. With this, Oliveira wanted

Xica to breathe luxury with the intention that that suit would scare away any memory of slavery in her lover's body.

18. Ibid., 39.

19. Ibid., 44.

20. Ibid., 46.

21. Santos, Mayra. *Sobre piel y papel*, Puerto Rico, Ediciones Callejón, 2005, 70.

22. The author Mayra Santos-Febres in her book, *Sobre piel y papel*, "On skin and paper" enunciates the use of the erotic in the Caribbean. And she highlights three conceptions of the erotic: 1. The erotic as an inscription of identity definitions, 2. The erotic such as a place where racial and class oppression is inscribed. 3. The erotic such because of a process of self-knowledge and self-definition. Santos-Febres points out that sometimes these three uses occur simultaneously, sometimes in contradiction. Perhaps there are more erotic discourses in the Caribbean, but I insistently see the presence of these three, breaking the hinges of the body and the word. Ibid., p. 64.

23. Arroyo, Yolanda. *Las negras*, Carolina, Puerto Rico, Boreales, 2012, 25.

24. Ibid., 29.

25. Ibid., 31.

26. Ibid., 32.

27. Morejón, Nancy, *Looking Within/Mirar adentro: Selected Poems/Poemas escogidos, 1954 2000*. Ed. and Intro. Juanamaría Cordones-Cook. Detroit, MI: Wayne State UP, 2003.

28. Ibid.

29. Ibid.

30. Collins, Patricia. Aprendendo com a *outsider within*: a significação sociológica do pensamento feminista negro, 2016, 100.

31. Duarte, *Negra Nua Crua*, 2016, 11.

32. González, *Primavera para as rosas negras*: Lélia Gonzalez em primeira pessoa . . . , 2018, 321–34.

33. "Sinhá" was the way in which enslaved blacks designated their mistress.

34. Kimani did not until the year 2021. The poetry presented has been transcribed from one of his presentations in a slam match.

PART III

Relearning Latin America
Black Past and Present

*Colonial Texts and the Legacy of
Afrodiasporic Intergenerational Trauma*

black rock don't dream

running from white cloud
second hands quaking
quicksand swallowing

stifling
blood moon howling
streaming
charcoal tears
quieting crashing waves
questioning: savior oar/or slaving?
i be damn/dam
burning/watering

cain't take no mo'
(offering)

got mo' holes
in muh mind than lie
got mo' cracks
in muh heart than block
got mo' rage
page cain't hold
got mo' black soul
water hose
got mo' blues
indigo

where i go?
sky cain't hold me
where i go?
hell feel so ~~lonely~~ holy
where i go?
when my gutter come out
where i go?
when my waterfall too salty

ain't nowhere tuh run
they all call me
momma?

i was taught
before i could walk

the ways of the black rock:

stay low to the ground
get high as sound
drank only from a river mouth
don't cry an' don't look back
sit in seashell
when it get too loud
iffin' yuh see hell comin'?
bet not say nothin'

hold yo' mud
cain't turn into dust
you musn't drown

rock don't dream
she become mountain
rock dry cry
she be fountain
rock been big men lullaby
she never was
(baby,)

all black rocks got
is mo' black rocks

what is life?
without a womb
a black rock

what is the world
without a black woman?
(dream.)

who is gawd?
.

where is GOD?
.

what IS she?

.

BLACK ~~dots~~ rocks

—Natasha Carrizosa

Chapter 8

Repairing the Broken Strands of Afro-Latina History in Mayra Santos-Febres's Fiction

Karen S. Christian

Communities bear scars, vestiges of historical trauma preserved through cultural memory. Intricately woven together, history, memory, and identity enable us to know (or think we know) who we are.[1] Yet for marginalized communities like Afro-descendants, identity is fragmented through a process of forgetting that takes place when cultural and historical memory is silenced or erased. Saidiya Hartman explores this process in depth in *Lose Your Mother: A Journey Along the Atlantic Slave Route*, discovering that the slave trade left a devastating absence of a complete, unbroken narrative of African American history.[2] Likewise, as Christina Sharpe points out in *In the Wake: On Blackness and Being*, the history of the descendants of enslaved people is characterized by "myriad silences and ruptures . . . accumulated erasures, projections, fabulations, and misnamings."[3]

The works of Afro-Puerto Rican writer Mayra Santos-Febres resist this erasure by creating alternate archives of history stored in and on the bodies of her female characters. Many of these characters are marked by scars; these are visible traces of personal trauma (beatings, burns, cuts) that also serve as compelling historical metaphors. Santos-Febres's alternate archives possess powerful subversive potential, as seen in "Broken Strand" from her 1997 translated short story collection *Urban Oracles*, and the author's 2009 novel *Fe en disfraz* (Faith in Disguise).[4] In "Broken Strand," the legacy of intergenerational trauma, violence, and colonialism is literally inscribed on the bodies of the characters, clients of a beauty salon that specializes in straightening Black women's hair. Santos-Febres further traces the multiple dimensions of Afro-Latina identity in *Fe en disfraz*, a dramatic novelistic effort to give a voice to the countless female slaves of the Spanish Caribbean. By altering the historical narrative to honor Black bodies, Santos-Febres's writing works to acknowledge the scars and repair the broken strands of Afro-Latina history. In so doing, her fiction foregrounds the Intersectionality that tends to render Afro-Latinas invisible, relegating their identity to what Kimberlé Crenshaw calls "a location that resists telling."[5] Drawing on untold stories and memory passed through generations, Santos-Febres thus joins Crenshaw in the ongoing struggle "to advance the telling of that location."[6]

TRAUMA, FORGETTING, AND SCARS

An integral aspect of human history—indeed, of human existence—is trauma. This experience may be physical, emotional, or psychological; it may be individual or collective; it transcends all boundaries of race, gender, class, and national origin. Trauma and its consequences have been the subject of extensive study in fields ranging from medicine and psychiatry to literary studies and law.[7] The relationship between trauma and memory is particularly complex and debated. As theorists in this field have observed, amnesia, delusions, and other forms of forgetting are frequent consequences of the rupture or "tear" in the psyche of a traumatized individual. In *The Ethics of Remembering and the Consequences of Forgetting: Essays on Trauma, History, and Memory*, psychoanalyst Marilyn Charles comments that trauma "by definition . . . eludes encoding into verbal memory. What cannot be digested and incorporated into narrative memory . . . remains inchoate."[8] This elusiveness—silences, forgetting—could potentially lead to denial that trauma occurred, particularly if survivors are unable to provide a narrative that is believable or even coherent. Claude Barbre frames the essays in *The Ethics of Remembering* by extending the concept of the "tear" to large-scale trauma. He suggests that "there can also be a tear in the collective psyche due to cultural terrors and sufferings that incur societal patches—cultural structures that obfuscate the memory of trauma, erasing the possibility of recovery by silencing trauma narration."[9]

The body, however, tends not to forget. A near-inevitable result of a traumatic experience is the formation of scars, as the body and the mind work to repair themselves. Physical scars can provide an observable record of past trauma, whereas psychological or emotional marks may be more difficult to detect or may remain hidden altogether. Visible or invisible, scars are repositories of memory and a compelling alternate archive for marginalized communities like enslaved persons and their descendants, whose voices have been unheard in the writing of history. As Silvia Molloy asserts in *At Face Value: Autobiographical Writing in Spanish America*, for slaves "the body is a form of memory, the unerasable reminder of past affronts."[10] Santos-Febres argues, in fact, that the physical self is the bearer of knowledge that defies narration, of "otros tipos de saberes que no son necesariamente lingüísticos" [other forms of knowledge that are not necessarily linguistic].[11] Indeed, Chrissy B. Arce considers Santos-Febres's writing to be a kind of "alternative epistemology" that does not insist on a clear separation of mind and body, therein challenging the traditional Western hegemony of the intellect. On the contrary, from Arce's perspective, *Fe en disfraz* "insiste una y otra vez en la experiencia del cuerpo . . . de un modo que desmonta los binomios tradicionales entre saber y sentir, al interpretar la situación de la mujer negra en el Caribe" [insists, time and again, on the experience of the body . . . in a way that dismantles the traditional binary of thinking and feeling through its interpretation of the situation of Black women in the Caribbean].[12]

Recognizing the authority of the body as alternate archive thus broadens the scope of what can and should be considered a valid historical source. Among such potential sources are the inexplicable memories possessed by the descendants of trauma survivors when the traumatic events or experiences have been shrouded in silence and denial. This is often the case, for example, with Holocaust survivors and their descendants. Essayist Elizabeth Rosner has explored connections between memory and intergenerational trauma through her work with such descendants. Rosner and other Holocaust scholars have found that the impact of the Holocaust can be in effect "passed down" to later generations, in the form of physiological manifestations and even memories. In *Survivor Café: The Legacy of Trauma and the Labyrinth of Memory*, Rosner discusses recent discoveries in the field of epigenetics that suggest potential mechanisms whereby trauma can be transmitted to subsequent generations.[13] The significance of her findings for communities whose history is marked by trauma is evident: "Slowly but surely, science is bringing descendants of Holocaust survivors as well as descendants of those who lived through other atrocities empirical proof of a legacy that many of us have already known in our bones, our dreams, and our terrors."[14]

This legacy borne through generations was first given the name "post-memory" in 1992 by Holocaust scholar Marianne Hirsch. Hirsch defines postmemory as "the relationship of the second generation to powerful, often traumatic, experiences that preceded their births but were nevertheless transmitted to them so deeply as to seem to constitute memories in their own right."[15] Hirsch has dedicated her research to works created by writers, artists, and photographers whose ancestors experienced trauma resulting from brutal dictatorship, imprisonment, exile, uprooting, and genocide. The slave trade in the Americas likewise subjected millions of people to multifaceted trauma. It should not surprise us, then, to hear the echoes of postmemory in stories told by Afro-descendants. Furthermore, postmemory collapses the distinction between thinking and feeling, thus functioning as one of the "otros tipos de saberes" to which Santos-Febres refers in *Sobre piel y papel*. When these memories—knowledge borne in/on the body—find their way into narrative, they can function as counterhistory to incomplete official history. Hirsch and collaborator Leo Spitzer argue that this postmemorial work is a necessary step toward personal and collective healing: "Each individual story helps to shape a larger history by providing it with detail, depth, and nuance. . . . Postgenerations haunted by stories that have not been worked through still find that they owe the victims this act of attentive listening, as well as this work of historical repair."[16] Marilyn Charles expresses this idea succinctly, asserting that "History haunts us to the extent that we have forgotten to remember."[17]

A thread that runs through the research of these memory scholars is the concept of *haunting*, or the persistent specter of the past in the present. In "The Time of Slavery," Saidiya Hartman proposes that for enslaved persons and their descendants, time cannot be viewed as continuity or progression. She maintains that the historical narrative of Afro-descendants in the Americas has been interrupted through erasures and silences, while the "seemingly eternal second-class status" of Blacks seems to suggest that time has stalled. Hartman's discourse is infused with language of the body as she describes Black tourists' pilgrimages to Africa in search of "stories of origin, unshakable explanatory narratives, and sites of injury—the land where our blood has been spilt . . . as if the location of the wound was itself the cure, or as if the weight of dead generations could alone ensure our progress."[18] There is implicit critique in Hartman's view of these pilgrimages: finding that location and acknowledging that weight can no more guarantee movement toward emancipation than can attempting to erase the past.

INTERSECTIONAL POSTMEMORY

Injuries and wounds leave physical and psychological scars, reminders of past trauma that can haunt survivors and communities in spite of their efforts to forget. For Black women like the Afro-Latinas in Santos-Febres's fiction, the scars are particularly significant because of the distinctive character of the violence that has been wrought against women's bodies (including female slaves) throughout history. To fully comprehend the weight of this trauma requires recognition of the intersectional identity of Afro-Latinas. As Kimberlé Crenshaw compellingly argues in her pivotal essay "Mapping the Margins:

Intersectionality, Identity Politics, and Violence against Women of Color," because of their identity "as both women *and* of color within discourses that are shaped to respond to one *or* the other, women of color are marginalized within both."[19] Viewing identity through the lens of Intersectionality requires us to understand race, gender, class, sexual orientation, and other identity categories as inseparable. Furthermore, Crenshaw seeks to expose "the processes of subordination and the various ways those processes are experienced by people who are subordinated and people who are privileged by them."[20] It is not difficult to see the layers of subordination to which Afro-Latinas have been subjected as women, as Blacks, and as Latinxs. Crenshaw acknowledges that categories have "meaning and consequences" and also values associated with them that engender social hierarchies.[21] For Afro-Latinas, these meanings and consequences stem from a long history of Blacks being portrayed as "more sexual, more earthy, more gratification-oriented" along with norms of women's sexuality used to distinguish "good" women from "bad" ones.[22] Crenshaw asserts that such sexual images that define "the allegedly essential nature of Black women" are especially damaging in the context of sexual violence, as "the very representation of a Black female body at least suggests certain narratives that may make Black women's rape either less believable or less important."[23]

To have one's story deemed unbelievable or unimportant effectively guarantees its exclusion from historical narratives. Such is the case for accounts of the sexual violence that was a constant in the lives of enslaved women. Indeed, in Latin America the historical record includes few if any first-person accounts from enslaved women, whom historian María Selina Gutiérrez Aguilera calls "las figuras femeninas más ignoradas por la historiografía tradicional" [the feminine figures that have been most ignored by traditional historiography].[24] Thus the silencing of Afro-Latinas' history cannot be characterized solely as the silencing of "women's history," or of "Afro-descendants' history," or of "Latinx history"; none of these categories is nuanced in ways that capture the complexity of this multifaceted identity. The historical disappearance of Afro-Latinas is located at the intersection of all of these silences, in what Chrissy B. Arce calls "la historia muda de la mujer esclava" [the mute history of the female slave].[25] Yet writers like Santos-Febres work to rescue this history from oblivion, through allusions and metaphors (e.g., "Broken Strand") or more directly, as in *Fe en disfraz*. Santos-Febres's narratives can be viewed as a form of mourning as understood by Saidiya Hartman: "In that it enables the aggrieved to recount the history that engendered the degradation of slavery and the injurious constitution of blackness, mourning can be considered a practice of countermemory that attends to that which has been negated and repressed."[26] The Black tourists of whom Hartman writes engage in mourning and countermemory through their travels to slave sites in Africa; in contrast, Santos-Febres's characters bear the traces of the "negated and repressed" on their bodies (as scars) and as different forms of postmemory. I propose, in fact, that what these characters experience might aptly be called *intersectional postmemory*, for the legacy of trauma that haunts them is inextricably linked to their intersecting gender, racial, and national identities. By foregrounding the alternate archive of abused, violated, scarred bodies—specifically Afro-Latina bodies—and the workings of postmemory, a less broken, more complete version of their history can begin to emerge.

THE HIGH COST OF GOOD HAIR
IN "BROKEN STRAND"

Mayra Santos-Febres's 1995 short story "Broken Strand" could be read as a case study of the multiple oppressions resulting from the intersectional identity of working-class Afro-Latinas. The story takes place in the San Juan, Puerto Rico, barrio of Trastalleres and focuses on the owner and clients of Kety's Beauty Parlor. Miss Kety specializes in hair treatments and products for Black women, her primary service being hair straightening for the local women who "want to straighten their hair so they won't be so black and so ugly and so low-class."[27] Miss Kety's life has clearly been difficult and has left her with visible scars: "[She] has a broken nose from a stray fist [and] a map of burns on her forearm."[28] Yet she is a legendary figure in Trastalleres, in part because of the meticulous care with which she maintains her own hair: "Miss Kety, so elegant—she is black, yes. 'But that beautiful head of straight hair, dyed Auburn Copper red, falling over her shoulders.'"[29] The other main character of "Broken Strand" is a thirteen-year-old girl named Yetsaida who has recently reached the appropriate age to have her hair straightened by Miss Kety. Like the other women in the barrio, Yetsaida has a broken nose ("the misguided nose," and the characteristic Black hair that requires taming by Miss Kety's red-hot comb.[30] Her dream is twofold: first to be made beautiful at the hands of Miss Kety, and eventually to enroll in the Sky Academy of Looks and Beauty in Miami.

The narrative of "Broken Strand" is quite simple: Yetsaida makes her way to Miss Kety's to have her hair straightened and, like a neophyte at the hands of a religious leader, is transformed through the beautification "ritual." The complexity of this short story is found in its vivid representation of Intersectionality, its engagement with postmemory, and the rich symbolism that links these two elements. With the exception of Yetsaida's father, all of the characters are Afro-Puerto Rican women of limited resources. The most evident sign of their Blackness is their hair, specifically the "pasas" (tight curls, but literally "raisins") that they invest time and money to eradicate at Miss Kety's. Yetsaida expresses the shame that her hair evokes, shame that she senses from her own parents: "The father doesn't even touch her curls out of disgust. Yes, disgust. Yetsaida has seen it in his face, in the jokes about his tangled hands . . . in Mama's irritation combing her hair with a broken-toothed comb."[31] The universally promoted message is that to possess "true beauty" one must have straight hair like the white women in shampoo commercials whose hair is "shining and straight as it should be,"[32] "beautiful and radiant for the west wind to play with and *make her a woman.*"[33] These standards suggest that lacking this physical appearance is grounds for exclusion from the category "women"—which implies, in turn, that one must be white to be a woman. This is a revealing example of the consequences of failing to recognize the Intersectionality of identity by viewing identity "as woman or person of color as an either/or proposition," as Crenshaw has argued, effectively rendering Black women invisible.[34] This invisibility is underscored, furthermore, by the apparent powerlessness of Santos-Febres's Afro-Latina characters to escape the recurring domestic violence of which so many of them are survivors. A particularly graphic scene illustrates how Yetsaida's nose may have been broken, when her father arrives home drunk and yells at her: "She yells back, [he] chases her to hit her and grabs her by the neck, [he] makes Mama cry and grab her nose just in case he throws a fist—'Whose nose?' All the screaming bewilders her so; the blood bewilders so, and those curls tight as snails, ah and the river that comes out of the nose, red, neon red like Miss Kety's comb."[35] We see once again how Yetsaida's father rejects her Blackness ("those curls tight as snails"), along with the implication that this is a familiar occurrence. The father is allowed to maintain his dominant position in the family in a way that mirrors the dynamic identified by Shahrazad Ali in her controversial 1989 treatise, *The Blackman's Guide to Understanding the Blackwoman*, which was incisively critiqued by Crenshaw. Ali claims that if a Black woman "ignores the authority and superiority of the Blackman, there is a penalty. When she crosses this line and becomes viciously insulting it is time for the Blackman to soundly slap her in the mouth."[36] Ali is, in effect, defending violence against Black women as necessary for the preservation of Black unity, thus naturalizing their oppression and effectively silencing them.[37]

At the same time, this violence indirectly calls attention to the ancestral trauma of slavery and the fragmented history of Afro-descendants, through postmemory experienced by characters in "Broken Strand." In the beauty shop Miss Kety shares a moment of solidarity with Yetsaida that connects both of them to a past that neither one could possibly recall firsthand:

Miss Kety and the neophyte laugh together. . . . The expert hand now rests on
Yetsaida's broken nose.

"Ah, you too."

"Yeah." And Miss Kety feels something like a tickle from the past run along the
map of the world on her forearm.[38]

Could this "tickle from the past" be a physical manifestation of postmemory?
The fact that the tickle runs along Miss Kety's map of scars is highly symbolic, as this map of the world seems to allude to the diaspora that scattered
Africans across multiple continents. This allusion is underscored by the
description of the hair straightening process as "the branding ritual,"[39] a clear
reference to slave branding that is mirrored in Miss Kety's burn scars. The
recurring history of violence against women, most visible in the characters'
broken noses, is likewise part of the legacy of trauma stemming from the
slave trade. These physical scars are linked to damaged memory in the story's
first line, "A little girl and a father and a dream and a memory broken like a
nose, at ten years old, with alcoholic breath on top of it all,"[40] an image that
evokes both violence and the incomplete—broken—historical memory of
the African diaspora. The strand in the title is a similarly powerful symbol
of interrupted history, of the disconnect from the past caused by the Middle
Passage. Saidiya Hartman examines this rupture in *Lose Your Mother*. During
her research stay in Ghana, Hartman is given a letter by an adolescent boy in
which he declares, "Because of the slave trade you lose your mother, if you
know your history, you know where you come from." Hartman reflects that
"To lose your mother was to be denied your kin, country, and identity. To
lose your mother was to forget your past."[41] Like Hartman, as descendants of
enslaved persons the characters in "Broken Strand" have inherited a history
characterized by silences and missing links.

This notion of losing one's mother is also a compelling metaphor for the
colonial status of Puerto Rico. As first a Spanish colony and then a commonwealth of the United States, the island has had limited opportunity for
self-determination. Instead, Puerto Rico has a long history of emulating
models that originate in Europe and/or the United States. Such assimilation
can be seen in Yetsaida's fantasy of one day appearing in a commercial for
the Sky Academy for Looks and Beauty in Miami, "recounting in perfect
English the trajectory of her success (*I was a small girl with a dream, a
dream of beauty that has come true. Thank you, Sky Academy!*)."[42] Not surprisingly, Black identity is not accommodated by these models. On the contrary, "Broken Strand" portrays the pervasive drive to turn Afro-Latinas into
consumers of primarily American hair and beauty products (or brands with

pseudo-European names like Tresemmé and Biolage) and hence into consumers of *whiteness*. True beauty as embraced—worshipped—by Yetsaida
and Miss Kety "is real and appears on the screens and in the ads—which we
know are there to make us buy."[43] Most importantly, "true beauty" is achieved
through adherence to white/European standards, specifically straight hair.
In effect, Miss Kety's hair treatments are a means of removing the traces of
Blackness, of losing one's mother, in an effort to advance socially. The motivation for this is understandable in a society founded upon slavery where, as
Ana Lucia Araujo points out in *Slavery in the Age of Memory: Engaging the
Past*, people of European physical appearance (fair skin and straight, light-
colored hair) have historically occupied higher social ranks.[44] Santos-Febres's
characters are simply responding to the formidable cultural and economic
forces of *blanqueamiento* (whitening) that have worked to erase Blackness in
the Americas since the advent of the slave trade.

Yet there is nothing simple about the interplay of these characters' intersectional identities and the postmemorial work achieved through their representation. These scarred Afro-Latinas with ephemerally straight hair have
the postmemory of slavery, violence, and colonialism stored in the alternate
archive of their bodies. They try in vain to escape their Black bodies and
the history attached to them, with "the sensation and the odor of something
dying, a strand that screams."[45] But in spite of their repeated performances
of whiteness, such as the recurring ritual of hair straightening, whiteness
can never be fully achieved. The body remembers and the "pasas" always
return, as Yetsaida notes: "If I sweat, the waves will flow again into their
original curls."[46] Miss Kety surely knows that the treatments she offers are
only temporary "remedies." Her beauty parlor nonetheless serves as a place
of solidarity and safety for these multiply marginalized women. At the end
of "Broken Strand," Miss Kety sends Yetsaida off with conditioner "para
que no andes por ahí con tanta hebra rota" [so you don't go around with so
many broken strands]. ("Hebra rota" 64).[47] This is a fitting admonition for
a young Afro-Latina in a society that works to render her silent and invisible. The story itself resists this disappearance, creating a narrative space of
remembrance where the "broken strands" of Afro-Latina history can begin to
be repaired.

PAIN AND PLEASURE: THE AFRO-LATINA
BODY AS ARCHIVE

While "Broken Strand" presents a somewhat indirect critique of the impact
of slavery on the present, *Fe en disfraz* probes much deeper into the legacy
of trauma that marks the history of Afro-Latinx communities. The novel is

narrated by Martín Tirado, a Puerto Rican historian who describes himself
and his fellow historians as "tan blancos como los pergaminos con los que nos
rodeamos" [as white as the parchments with which we surround ourselves].[48]
His wide nose, however, suggests a somewhat ambiguous racial identity,
although "esa información se ha perdido en el olvido" [that information has
been lost, forgotten].[49] He is preoccupied with his whiteness, which he refers
to as a kind of wound.[50] Martín is creating digital archives at the University of
Chicago when he meets Fe Verdejo, an esteemed Afro-Venezuelan historian
specializing in female slaves of seventeenth- and eighteenth-century Latin
America. Martín portrays Fe in poetic terms: "De [piel] tan oscura, a veces,
no se lograba ver la definición de su rostro, que parecía hecho de una madera
pulidísima. . . . Blanco y negro era su hábito, como el de una monja. Ese fue el
primer disfraz que le conocí. Disfraz de historiadora." [With skin so dark that
at times you couldn't see the definition of her face, which seemed to be made
of highly polished wood. . . . Her habit was black and white, like a nun's. That
was the first disguise of hers that I saw. The disguise of a historian.][51]

Martín begins to develop digital illustrations to accompany historical
archives that Fe has discovered, specifically documents and testimonials of
female slaves who sought legal protection from the abuses of their owners.
This work becomes a highly eroticized obsession for Martín, who finds himself aroused by the detailed scenes of sexual violence that Fe's materials document. The leitmotif of disguises develops further through Fe's acquisition
of a silk dress worn in society by Francisca "Xica" da Silva, an eighteenth-
century slave whose wealthy Brazilian owner married her. The first time Fe
examines the dress, which was given to her by the nuns in whose convent it
had been stored for years, she discovers that underneath the layers of rich fab-
ric and lace is an elaborate harness made of metal and leather. After the close
of the exhibition in Chicago in which Fe displays the dress along with other
artifacts from Latin American female slaves, she can't resist the impulse to
try it on. In so doing, Fe subjects her body to the same painful cuts, scratches,
and eventual scarring that Xica da Silva (and perhaps her descendants) would
have experienced. When Fe and Martín become lovers, this dress is an integral part of their ritualistic (and sadomasochistic) sexual encounters.

The purpose driving the Chicago exhibition and Fe's research is clear: to
tell the stories of the innumerable voiceless female slaves who have been
omitted from official Latin American history. She relates to Martín how her
discovery of the documents was utterly unexpected since other than the memoir of Cuban former slave Juan Manzano and Miguel Barnet's *Cimarrón*, no
slave narratives in Spanish have been found, much less narratives of female
slaves. But then, almost magically, Fe begins to find documents that had
been assumed to be nonexistent.[52] Whereas in the United States the WPA

Slave Narratives project (1936–1938) gathered more than two thousand testimonials of former slaves, no such historical recuperation took place in Latin America. In "La vivencia de la esclavitud: Nota bibliográfica sobre testimonios y autobiografías de esclavos afroamericanos," historian L. Arturo Arnalte confirms this absence of any first-person historical record of Latin American slaves, declaring that in the former Spanish colonies there was never any effort made to compile testimonials similar to those of the United States.[53] This is striking evidence of the silencing power of Intersectionality; the confluence of female slaves' identities as women, Blacks, and Latinas works to effectively erase them from the historical archives.

Fe, however, seeks to give these Afro-Latinas their rightful place in history. As Martín observes, every story/history needs a narrator to present the facts.[54] A telling feature of *Fe en disfraz* is that Fe herself has practically no voice in the text; she narrates only one of the novel's twenty-four chapters. This narrative absence highlights the disjointed, fragmented unnarratability of the trauma of slavery. For even in a novel about silenced Black women, the one voice that assumes authority and in fact owns the narrative is that of a white male. In the author's note at the end of the novel, Santos-Febres alludes to the impossibility of any such coherent narrative from the perspective of enslaved persons. She describes *Fe en disfraz* as a novel about memory, "de la herida que es recordar" [about the wound that is remembering] and admits that the text is based on false, falsified, or rewritten documents, with remnants of slaves' declarations that she gathered from multiple primary and secondary sources that she reorganized, translated, or invented.[55] Martín is surprised and disturbed by the invisibility of these enslaved women. As he reads the documents and testimonials that Fe is researching, he begins to recall other texts that he had read earlier without paying much attention, about infamous yet rarely named women: Malintzín (the "traitor"), Saartjie (the "Hottentot Venus"), Kitihawa (the Native American wife of Jean Baptiste du Sable and mother of his children), "centenares de indias, negras y mulatas paridoras de hipogrifos mestizos" [hundreds of Indians, Black women, and mulatas who gave birth to mixed-race hippogriffs].[56] A case that is of particular interest to Fe is that of Xica da Silva, who attempted to legitimize her daughters (by João Fernándes de Oliveira) by presenting them to society. However, none of them could be legally married, so they remained "mujeres ilegales, de las que viven entre susurros, de las que nadie nombra" [illegal women, the kind that live among whispers and that no one names].[57] Martín is unable to find visual images of the slaves, something that would show their faces or physical characteristics, and Fe tells him that no such images exist. She offers to send him testimonials that describe a few slaves, but she warns him that "Están llenas de prejuicios, carecen de objetividad . . . Las palabras son elusivas. Mejor es ver, tocar" [They are filled with prejudices and lack objectivity . . . Words are elusive. It's better to see, to touch].[58]

Fe's reference to touch alludes to the physicality and violence intrinsic to the slave trade, aspects from which Martín had been able to maintain a historian's distance until he began working with her. Faced with incontrovertible evidence, he is forced to confront the magnitude of the sexual violence wrought against innumerable anonymous enslaved women, whose very skin tells their story.[59] This telling is made doubly difficult by the fact that Black women have historically been sexualized in ways that discredit their claims of rape, as Crenshaw has argued. One of the testimonials that Fe discovers corroborates this image of the hypersexual Black woman. The wife of a slave owner describes the scene of her husband raping a female slave as "él pinchándole la carne, mordiéndole los pechos y ella gritando como las 'callejeras de la calle, como acostumbran las que son de su clase [. . .] las negras, personas sujetas a servidumbre, viles, de baja suerte, atrevidas y desvergonzadas'" [him pinching her flesh, biting her nipples, and her screaming like a 'streetwalker, like women of her class are accustomed to do . . . Black women, women subjected to servitude, vile, down on their luck, bold and shameless].[60] Yet for Fe, these slaves are more than anonymous victims despite their apparent powerlessness. By telling their stories, she shows that their bodies are an alternate archive, discredited as official historical sources yet the bearers of important truths nonetheless. She celebrates her collaboration with Martín because it has enabled her to expose the mute struggle between female slave and master, a struggle that parallels the battle between the world of reason and the world of the body.[61] In this world, history lives through physical features, scars, and memories that are archived in bodies and minds.[62]

It is at this intersection of body and mind that the force of postmemory can be perceived. As Martín observes the intensity of Fe's dedication to her project, he begins to understand the degree to which she feels connected to her enslaved ancestors (and how, in turn, this connection implicates him): "La leía, desdoblada bajo los nombres de sus ancestros femeninos escogidos –Xica, Petrona, Mariana––. Todas, Fe, y yo, esclavo de sus esclavas y de mi deseo" [I read her, extended under the names of her chosen feminine ancestors––Xica, Petrona, Mariana––. All of them, Fe, and I, a slave of her slaves and of my desire].[63] Fe surprises Martín with her observation that these slaves would have looked like her. He ponders the possibility that Fe might have the same complexión and body as a tormented slave of two hundred years ago, "Que el objeto de su estudio estuviera tan cerca de su piel" [That her object of study might be so close to her own skin].[64] This notion of time collapsing on itself recurs throughout the novel, as history is transported into the present through postmemory.[65] The most intense and disquieting sexual encounters between Fe and Martín occur each year on October 31, a date that is significant for its association with pagan ritual and the pagan concept of time. Martín notes that according to pagan beliefs, each year on this day a gap or hole opens up in time such that past, present, and future merge.[66] He narrates the last of these Halloween/Samhain meetings with Fe in future tense, underscoring the fusion of what is to come with past and present:

> Se convertirá . . . en todas esas mujeres negras, trasplantadas por un extraño curso del azar (y de la Historia) a ese traje, a esa otra piel. La veré también como Fe Verdejo, la insigne historiadora, esclava de su tormento.

> [She will become . . . all those Black women, transplanted by a strange stroke of fate (and History) into that dress, that other skin. I will also see her as Fe Verdejo, distinguished historian, slave of her torment.][67]

Through this imagined encounter, Martín seems to finally comprehend the degree to which Fe embodies and is haunted by the history of her ancestors.

Fe is thus a survivor of intergenerational trauma whose present is unmistakably marked by the legacy of slavery, from which she is several generations removed. Nirit Gradwohl Pisano refers to the original victims of trauma as "ghosts" in an article entitled "Ghosts in the Mirror: A Granddaughter of Holocaust Survivors Reflects the Faces of History." Gradwohl Pisano asks, "In what way is trauma transmitted intergenerationally across families and entire communities? Can future generations heal the pain of a past they did not personally endure?"[68] Through interviews with third-generation descendants of Holocaust survivors, she explores the ways that history may be unconsciously reenacted by future generations. Fe, however, reenacts history literally each time she puts on Xica da Silva's dress to have sex with Martín. Wearing the dress with its harness tightly fastened, she subjects her body to the pain and injury that its leather straps and metal stays inflict: "con cada caricia, la piel de Fe recibía un mordisco del arnés, que levantaba en una nueva herida" [with each caress, Fe's skin received a bite from the harness that resulted in a new injury].[69] Fe seems acutely aware of the historical trauma through which the identities of millions of enslaved people were effectively erased, trauma that now weighs upon her:

> Mi piel era el mapa de mis ancestros. Todos desnudos, sin blasones ni banderas que los identificaran; marcados por el olvido o, apenas, por cicatrices tribales, cadenas y por las huellas del carimbo sobre el lomo.

> [My skin was the map of my ancestors. All of them naked, without badges or banners to identify them; marked by oblivion, or perhaps by tribal scars, chains, and the traces of the branding iron on their backs.][70]

This passage forcefully captures the impact of what I have called intersectional postmemory. The scars on Fe's body and the ancestral memory that they evoke are uniquely connected to her Afro-Latina identity. Because Fe lacks a narrative voice, we have no access to her inner thoughts, yet it is apparent that she yearns to be liberated from the trauma of historical oppression. "Sácame de aquí" [Get me out of here],[71] she implores Martín; and he begins to understand that "bajo el disfraz, su piel rasgada por alambres cuenta una misma historia –la repetida, la inmutable—. Su piel ansía más ardor. Ansía liberarse en el ardor; botar la complejidad de su sangre" [underneath the disguise, her skin torn by the wires tells the same story/history –repeated, unchangeable—. Her skin longs for more burning pain. She longs to free herself in the pain; to spill the complexity of her blood].[72] The elegant gown with its agony-inducing harness becomes a powerful symbol of the legacy of slavery that is the inheritance of Black women in the Americas.

In both *Fe en disfraz* and "Broken Strand," pain and pleasure are inextricably linked: the pain of hair straightening juxtaposed with the pleasure of feeling beautiful and seen; pain from the straps and wires of the dress' harness juxtaposed with intense sexual pleasure. In both texts, scars feature prominently as evidence of past trauma. Martín observes that Fe's wide hips are crisscrossed by scores of small cuts, scratches from the harness, scars like a strange alphabet on her skin.[73] This "strange alphabet" inscribed on Fe's body and the map of burns covering Miss Kety's forearm are both to some degree self-inflicted, leading us to speculate as to why Santos-Febres's characters subject themselves to so much pain. Saidiya Hartman suggests that at least some Afro-descendants view pain (in the form of journeys "back" to Africa) as a necessary part of coming to terms with the devastation of slavery. She expresses some skepticism when she asks, "Is pain the guarantee of compensation? . . . Is it enough that these acts of commemoration rescue the unnamed and unaccounted for from obscurity and oblivion?"[74] Telling the stories of enslaved women—"the unnamed and unaccounted for"—and their Afro-Latina descendants cannot change history, but it can rewrite history, drawing upon the alternate archive of the body as source. Martín is unable to erase the memory of Fe's bruised and bloodied flesh.[75] This is precisely what the writing of Mayra Santos-Febres achieves for her readers as well, for her works offer unforgettable images of the bruised and bloodied history of Afro-Latinas.

In the final passage of *Fe en disfraz*, Martín imagines Fe demanding that he tear the dress off her body and destroy it, while "en la memoria de mi dueña, sonarán latigazos y carimbos. Se desvanecerán cicatrices y humillaciones. Entonces, Fe, liberada, entenderá" [in my lady's memory, lashes and brandings will sound. Scars and humiliations will vanish. Then Fe, liberated, will understand].[76] This hopeful image of Fe being freed from her ancestral pain and trauma is appealing. It is also problematic, however, insofar as she is liberated by the hands of a white man, and her story is told from the perspective of a traditional patriarchal writer of history. Ultimately this scene and the novel itself reflect the racial and gender hierarchies through which Afro-Latinas continue to be subjected to multiple oppressions. In "Broken Strand," likewise, Intersectionality is woven into the story as the characters struggle against unattainable standards of whiteness, violence wrought by the men in their lives, and seemingly inescapable poverty. As Saidiya Hartman asserts in "The Time of Slavery," "history is an injury that has yet to cease happening."[77] Nevertheless, Fe Verdejo's successful creation of a historical narrative that foregrounds "her" slaves and indeed Santos Febres's creation of *Fe en disfraz* and "Broken Strand" are triumphs of postmemorial work—small yet far-reaching acts of historical repair.

BIBLIOGRAPHY

Ali, Shahrazad. *The Blackman's Guide to Understanding the Blackwoman.* Self-published, 1989.

Araujo, Ana Lucia. *Slavery in the Age of Memory: Engaging the Past.* London: Bloomsbury Academic, 2021.

Arce, Chrissy B. "La fe disfrazada y la complicidad del deseo." In *Lección errante: Mayra Santos-Febres y el Caribe contemporáneo*, edited by Nadia V. Celis and Juan Pablo Rivera, 226–46. San Juan, PR: Editorial Isla Negra, 2011.

Arnalte Barrera, L. Arturo. "La vivencia de la esclavitud: nota bibliográfica sobre testimonios y autobiografías de esclavos afroamericanos." *Cuadernos de historia contemporánea* 12 (1990): 231–44. https://revistas.ucm.es/index.php/CHCO/article/view/CHCO9090110231A.

Barbre, Claude. Foreword. In *The Ethics of Remembering and the Consequences of Forgetting: Essays on Trauma, History, and Memory*, edited by Michael O'Loughlin. Washington, DC: Rowman & Littlefield, 2014.

Celis, Nadia V., and Juan Pablo Rivera, eds. *Lección errante: Mayra Santos-Febres y el Caribe contemporáneo.* San Juan, PR: Editorial Isla Negra, 2011.

Charles, Marilyn. Afterword. In *The Ethics of Remembering and the Consequences of Forgetting: Essays on Trauma, History, and Memory*, edited by Michael O'Loughlin. Washington, DC: Rowman & Littlefield, 2014.

Crenshaw, Kimberlé. "Mapping the Margins: Intersectionality, Identity Politics, and Violence against Women of Color." *Stanford Law Review* 43, no. 6 (July 1991): 1241–99.

Dawney, Leila, and Timothy J. Huzar. "Introduction: The Legacies and Limits of *The Body in Pain.*" *Body & Society* 25, no. 3 (2019): 3–21.

Gradwohl Pisano, Nirit. "Ghosts in the Mirror: A Granddaughter of Holocaust Survivors Reflects the Faces of History." In *The Ethics of Remembering and the*

Consequences of Forgetting: Essays on Trauma, History, and Memory, edited by Michael O'Loughlin. Washington, DC: Rowman & Littlefield, 2014.

Gutiérrez Aguilera, María Selina. "Mujeres esclavas bajo la autoridad femenina: entre dóciles y rebeldes (Buenos Aires, siglo XVIII)." *Historia y memoria* 12 (January–June 2016): 121–55.

Hartman, Saidiya. *Lose Your Mother: A Journey Along the Atlantic Slave Route*. New York: Farrar, Straus and Giroux, 2007.

———. "The Time of Slavery." *The South Atlantic Quarterly* 101, no. 4 (Fall 2002): 757–77.

Hirsch, Marianne. "The Generation of Postmemory." *Poetics Today* 29, no. 1 (2008): 103–28.

Hirsch, Marianne, and Leo Spitzer. "Small Acts of Repair: The Unclaimed Legacy of the Romanian Holocaust." In *Memory Unbound: Tracing the Dynamics of Memory Studies*, edited by Lucy Bond, Stef Craps and Pieter Vermeulen. Brooklyn, NY: Berghahn Books, 2017. https://doi.org/10.2307/j.ctvswx786.

Molloy, Silvia. *At Face Value: Autobiographical Writing in Spanish America*. New York: Cambridge University Press, 1991.

Moraga, Cherríe, and Gloria Anzaldúa, eds. *This Bridge Called My Back: Writings by Radical Women of Color*. Latham, NY: Kitchen Table: Women of Color Press, 1981.

O'Leary, Denyse. "Epigenetic Change: Lamarck, Wake Up, You're Wanted in the Conference Room!" *Evolution News*, August 25, 2015. https://evolutionnews.org /2015/08/epigenetic_chan/.

O'Loughlin, Michael, ed. *The Ethics of Remembering and the Consequences of Forgetting: Essays on Trauma, History, and Memory*. Washington, DC: Rowman & Littlefield, 2014.

Rosner, Elizabeth. *Survivor Café: The Legacy of Trauma and the Labyrinth of Memory*. Berkeley, CA: Counterpoint Press, 2017.

Santos-Febres, Mayra. "Broken Strand." In *Urban Oracles*. Translated by Nathan Budoff and Lydia Platón Lázaro, 1–8. Cambridge, MA: Brookline Books, 1997.

———. *Fe en disfraz*. Doral, FL: Alfaguara, 2009.

———. "Hebra rota." In *Pez de vidrio y otros cuentos*, 57–64. San Juan, PR: Ediciones Huracán, 1996.

———. *Sobre piel y papel*. San Juan, PR: Ediciones Callejón, 2005.

Sharpe, Christina. *In the Wake: On Blackness and Being*. Durham, NC: Duke University Press, 2016.

NOTES

1. I have two small but evident scars on my right hand: one, a smooth circle atop my first knuckle; the other a thin, jagged line that wraps part way around my index finger. I remember clearly how I sustained each of these scars. The smooth, round one was caused by an errant drop of boiling caramelized sugar that landed on my hand as my twentysomething self was making flan for friends. The jagged scar is older; at age seven, I convinced my mother that I was indeed capable of carving a jack-o-lantern.

Instead, I slashed my finger and spent Halloween in the emergency room. These scars are part of my personal history. I remember how I got each scar, how old I was, where I was living, and I'm reminded of these "historical facts" every time I look at my scars. They are the aftereffects of (admittedly mild) trauma—a burn, a cut—and the ensuing process of healing that leaves a permanent mark. The scars are history inscribed on my body, and as such, they are part of the story of who I am.

2. Saidiya Hartman, *Lose Your Mother: A Journey Along the Atlantic Slave Route* (New York: Farrar, Straus and Giroux, 2007).

3. Christina Sharpe, *In the Wake: On Blackness and Being* (Durham, NC: Duke University Press, 2016), 12.

4. The stories in *Urban Oracles* are translations of stories from Santos-Febres's 1996 collection *Pez de vidrio y otros cuentos*. *Fe en disfraz* has yet to be translated. All translated quotes from this novel are my translations.

5. Kimberlé Crenshaw, "Mapping the Margins: Intersectionality, Identity Politics, and Violence against Women of Color," *Stanford Law Review* 43, no. 6 (July 1991): 1242.

6. Crenshaw, "Mapping," 1242.

7. "Trauma-informed practice" is an approach that is increasingly used in therapy, social and human services, and legal practice. Cathy Caruth, author of *Unclaimed Experience: Trauma, Narrative, and History* (originally published in 1996), is often credited with founding the field of trauma studies.

8. Marilyn Charles, "Afterword," in *The Ethics of Remembering and the Consequences of Forgetting: Essays on Trauma, History, and Memory*, ed. Michael O'Loughlin (Washington, DC: Rowman & Littlefield, 2014).

9. Claude Barbre, "Foreword," in *The Ethics of Remembering and the Consequences of Forgetting: Essays on Trauma, History, and Memory*, ed. Michael O'Loughlin (Washington, DC: Rowman & Littlefield, 2014).

10. Silvia Molloy, *At Face Value: Autobiographical Writing in Spanish America* (New York: Cambridge University Press, 1991), 46.

11. Mayra Santos-Febres, *Sobre piel y papel* (San Juan, PR: Ediciones Callejón, 2005), 93 (my translation). Santos-Febres's notion of these other forms of knowledge, of wisdom and memory harbored in the body, resonates with the "theory in the flesh" based on "the physical realities of [women's] lives" proposed by Cherríe Moraga and Gloria Anzaldúa in *This Bridge Called My Back: Writings by Radical Women of Color* (Latham, NY: Kitchen Table: Women of Color Press, 1981), 23.

12. Chrissy B. Arce, "La fe disfrazada y la complicidad del deseo," in *Lección errante: Mayra Santos-Febres y el Caribe contemporáneo*, ed. Nadia V. Celis and Juan Pablo Rivera (San Juan, PR: Editorial Isla Negra, 2011), 240–41 (my translation).

13. In "Epigenetic Change: Lamarck, Wake Up, You're Wanted in the Conference Room!," Denyse O'Leary describes epigenetic inheritance as "the systems and processes by which genes' expression can be altered . . . by specific, predictable, repeatable, and researchable events—and then inherited in the altered state." The memories that Rosner studies may be a form of what geneticists call transgenerational epigenetic inheritance.

14. Elizabeth Rosner, *Survivor Café: The Legacy of Trauma and the Labyrinth of Memory* (Berkeley, CA: Counterpoint Press, 2017), 6.

15. Marianne Hirsch, "The Generation of Postmemory," *Poetics Today* 29, no. 1 (2008), 103.

16. Marianne Hirsch and Leo Spitzer, "Small Acts of Repair: The Unclaimed Legacy of the Romanian Holocaust," in *Memory Unbound: Tracing the Dynamics of Memory Studies*, ed. Lucy Bond, Stef Craps, and Pieter Vermeulen (Brooklyn, NY: Berghahn Books, 2017), 88.

17. Charles, "Afterword."

18. Hartman, "The Time of Slavery," *The South Atlantic Quarterly* 101, no. 4 (Fall 2002), 767.

19. Crenshaw, "Mapping," 1244.

20. Crenshaw, "Mapping," 1297.

21. Crenshaw, "Mapping," 1297.

22. Crenshaw, "Mapping," 1271. In a study entitled "Mujeres esclavas bajo la autoridad femenina: entre dóciles y rebeldes (Buenos Aires, siglo XVIII)," historian María Selina Gutiérrez Aguilera summarizes this perspective in relation to female slaves: "La mujer esclava estaba estigmatizada socialmente por su 'apetitosa y lujuriosa sexualidad,' tan atrayente como condenada por el mismo hombre blanco. Al mismo tiempo, la esclava era considerada como un objeto sexual" [Female slaves were socially stigmatized for their "hearty and lustful sexuality," both attractive to and condemned by white men. At the same time, the female slave was considered a sexual object] (133; my translation).

23. Crenshaw, "Mapping," 1271.

24. María Selina Gutiérrez Aguilera, "Mujeres esclavas bajo la autoridad femenina: entre dóciles y rebeldes (Buenos Aires, siglo XVIII)," *Historia y memoria* 12 (January–June 2016), 149 (my translation).

25. Arce, "La fe disfrazada," 229 (my translation).

26. Hartman, "The Time," 771.

27. Mayra Santos-Febres, "Broken Strand," in *Urban Oracles*, translated by Nathan Budoff and Lydia Platón Lázaro (Cambridge, MA: Brookline Books, 1997), 2.

28. Ibid., 1.

29. Ibid., 3.

30. Ibid., 3.

31. Ibid., 3–4.

32. Ibid., 3.

33. Ibid., 6 (my emphasis).

34. Crenshaw, "Mapping," 1242.

35. Santos-Febres, "Broken," 4.

36. Shahrazad Ali, *The Blackman's Guide to Understanding the Blackwoman* (Self-published, 1989), 169.

37. Crenshaw describes *The Blackman's Guide* as a "stridently antifeminist tract" ("Mapping," 1253) and concludes that Ali's premise is "that patriarchy is beneficial for the Black community, and that it must be strengthened through coercive means if necessary" ("Mapping," 1254).

38. Santos-Febres, "Broken," 7.

39. Ibid., 3.

40. Ibid., 1.

41. Hartman, *Lose Your Mother*, 85.

42. Santos-Febres, "Broken," 7.

43. Ibid., 5.

44. Ana Lucia Araujo, *Slavery in the Age of Memory: Engaging the Past* (London: Bloomsbury Academic, 2021), 7. Araujo attributes the formation of such social hierarchies to racialization, that is, "constructed racial models in operation in the Americas" that identified people of European descent as whites (7).

45. Santos-Febres, "Broken," 6.

46. Ibid., 2.

47. Santos-Febres, "Hebra rota," in *Pez de vidrio y otros cuentos* (San Juan, PR: Ediciones Huracán, 1996), 64. Here I have chosen to provide my own translation of the original Spanish. In the English edition, "hebra rota" is translated as "split ends," which fails to capture the important connotation of broken strands.

48. Mayra Santos-Febres, *Fe en disfraz* (Doral, FL: Alfaguara, 2009), 17.

49. Santos-Febres, *Fe*, 19.

50. Ibid., 20.

51. Ibid., 34.

52. Ibid., 23.

53. L. Arturo Arnalte Barrera, "La vivencia de la esclavitud: nota bibliográfica sobre testimonios y autobiografías de esclavos afroamericanos," *Cuadernos de historia contemporánea* 12 (1990), 235–36. As the novel suggests, Manzano's 1835 *Autobiografía de un esclavo* and Barnet's *Biografía de un cimarrón* (1966) are the notable exceptions.

54. Santos-Febres, *Fe*, 81.

55. Ibid., 117.

56. Ibid., 46.

57. Ibid., 78.

58. Ibid., 52.

59. Ibid., 46.

60. Ibid., 28.

61. Ibid., 74–75.

62. An entire scholarly discipline has emerged around the body, largely stemming from Elaine Scarry's influential 1985 work, *The Body in Pain: The Making and Unmaking of the World* (Oxford University Press). Scarry's wide-ranging study foregrounds the unnarratability of physical pain, insofar as pain is so difficult to describe that it can in fact destroy language. The journal *Body & Society*, founded in 1995, publishes scholarship with diverse theoretical approaches to body studies. The 2019 special issue of this journal is titled "The Legacies and Limits of *The Body in Pain*" and features essays that wrestle with Scarry's arguments and the controversies that they have generated. In the introduction to this issue, the editors assert that "Since its publication in 1985, Elaine Scarry's *The Body in Pain* has become a seminal text in the study of embodiment. . . . Divisive, powerful and elegant, the text has been

central in the shaping of approaches to embodiment over the past 30 years" (3). Representative texts from the field of body studies include Dorothy Roberts, *Killing the Black Body: Race, Reproduction, and the Meaning of Liberty* (Vintage, 1998); Lázaro Lima, *The Latino Body: Crisis Identities in American Literary and Cultural Memory* (NYU Press, 2007); and George Yancy, *Black Bodies, White Gazes: The Continuing Significance of Race* (Rowman & Littlefield, 2016).

63. Santos-Febres, *Fe*, 45.

64. Ibid., 53.

65. In several instances, Martín seems to actually sense the elasticity of time. He observes that "El tiempo se ha detenido" [time has stopped] (14) and "Vivo . . . suspendido en el tiempo" [I live . . . suspended in time] (17). He eventually discerns "*la summa contradictio*: el tiempo no existe y todo lo que existe es tiempo" [the *summa contradictio*: time does not exist, and all that exists is time] (92).

66. Santos-Febres, *Fe*, 106.

67. Ibid., 113.

68. Nirit Gradwohl Pisano, "Ghosts in the Mirror: A Granddaughter of Holocaust Survivors Reflects the Faces of History," in *The Ethics of Remembering and the Consequences of Forgetting: Essays on Trauma, History, and Memory*, ed. Michael O'Loughlin (Washington, DC: Rowman & Littlefield, 2014).

69. Santos-Febres, *Fe*, 57.

70. Ibid., 89.

71. Ibid., 102.

72. Ibid., 114.

73. Ibid., 110.

74. Hartman, "The Time," 772–73.

75. Santos-Febres, *Fe*, 68.

76. Ibid., 114–15.

77. Hartman, "The Time," 772.

Chapter 9

Afro-Mexican Women in the Northern Frontier

Subalternity, Agency, and Power Dynamics in the Seventeenth Century

Brenda Romero

INTRODUCTION

In *La esclava de Juana Inés*,[1] writer Ignacio Casas transports readers to Mexico City, capital of New Spain, in the seventeenth century. This 2019 novel narrates what could have been the life of Yara, a Black slave owned by celebrated poet Sor Juana Inés de la Cruz. Through this fictional protagonist, Casas attempts to reconstruct the overlooked experiences of Afro-descendant women in colonial Mexico. The names and stories of real-life individuals like Yara, oppressed by slavery, racism, and patriarchy, have been largely forgotten. Records from the Spanish Inquisition represent one of the very few exceptions where New Spain's Black population is taken into consideration. That type of colonial church archive brings light to the lives of those who have been historically marginalized, ignored, and left out of the official Mexican narrative. This chapter delves into the thirty-five confessions and accusations compiled by Alonso de Benavides, Commissary of the Holy Office, during his visit to Cuencamé—currently part of the Mexican state of Durango—in 1625 and 1626.[2] In these inquisitorial files, Afro-Mexican women acquire a voice and lose their anonymity. The firsthand accounts found in Benavides's collected testimonies provide a rare glimpse into New

Spain's northern frontier, a space where these subaltern women gain agency and participate in the complex power dynamics of their society.

The field of Latin American Studies has systemically relegated Afro-Latinx voices to relative silence. In the Mexican context, the invisibility of its Black population is deeply rooted in the country's colonial past, a period when African slaves and their descendants where demoted to the bottom of the intricate racial hierarchy known as Sistema de Castas. According to that classification system imposed in the Spanish American colonies, individuals with more Spanish—White—blood were at the top of the racial pyramid while those with a higher percentage of African—Black—blood were at the bottom. When investigating the first generations of Afro-Mexicans, the bulk of published works have relied on primary texts from Mexico City and other colonial metropolitan areas, including Puebla and the port of Veracuz.[3] As Peter Wade points out in "Estudios Afrodescendientes en Latinoamérica: racismo y mestizaje,"[4] this academic area has been characterized by a partiality of research because only certain geographical areas or time periods have been studied. In contrast, my purpose with this investigation is to explore sources and informants from the periphery. This research endeavor focuses on Afro-Mexican women living near the northern frontier of Colonial Mexico—then New Spain—during the early seventeenth century. Statements given by and about Black women during Benavides's visit are examined and interpreted to identify the ways in which they manipulated their circumstances to overcome their subaltern position and acquire an active role in the society of Cuencamé. By rescuing the voices and stories of a variety of Afro-Mexican women—*negras*, *mulatas*, *criollas*, and *ladinas*—this analysis contradicts their historical invisibility and reveals the complexities of northern Colonial Mexican society.

The Afro-descendant women who speak and participate in the tales of Benavides's inquisitorial portfolio inhabited a space and time ruled by strict gender and race politics. The colonial society imposed by Spaniards in the Americas mimicked the patriarchal order that prevailed in the Iberian Peninsula, where women were confined to the domestic sphere and assigned a passive role. In terms of racial dynamics, African slaves brought to the Spanish colonies to supplement the Indigenous labor force, as well as their descendants, were considered racially inferior but also—being neither part of the colonizers nor the colonized—became perpetual outcasts. Given the plurality of systems of oppression that affected Black women in Colonial Mexico, this exploration is framed by the notion of Intersectionality, a concept coined by Kimberlé Crenshaw[5] and recently revisited by Patricia Collins.[6] As Crenshaw explains, feminist and anti-racist approaches further marginalize Black women by focusing only on the circumstances of White women and Black men, respectively. On the other hand, Intersectionality departs from a "single-axis framework" to recognize "the multi-dimensionality of Black women's experience."[7] In other words, the subjects studied here are not regarded merely as women or as Black individuals, but rather as Black women subjugated by both patriarchy and racism.

In a broader sense, Collins states that "one way of conceptualizing Intersectionality is to see it as a methodology for decolonizing knowledge,"[8] as a means to allow those who have been oppressed by multiple power structures to become epistemic agents. In the case of Mexico, even though Black slaves and personal servants began arriving to the territory in 1519,[9] when Hernan Cortés first landed in Veracruz, and it is estimated that "before 1640 more Africans than Spaniards came to New Spain,"[10] it was not until the mid-twentieth century that the first study of Mexico's African ancestry was published. Gonzalo Aguirre Beltrán's *La población negra de México,* issued in 1946 and considered the foundation of Afro-Mexican studies, provides valuable information, but similarly to the few works that followed, Black Mexicans are portrayed as objects of study rather than active contributors to Mexico's past and present.[11] Blackness and African heritage were mostly depicted as exotic additions to the mainstream mestizo society, as those "early efforts focused on Black religion, dance, linguistics, and other cultural forms."[12] In contrast, this analysis of Benavides's inquisitorial files acknowledges the voices of Afro-Mexican women living in Cuencamé in the early seventeenth century and centers on their role as narrators and protagonists of their own stories.

THE NORTHERN FRONTIER

After the Conquest of Mexico (1519–1521), Spanish efforts in terms of settlement, exploitation, and evangelization remained mostly in the geographical region commonly labeled as Mesoamerica. The area between Mexico City, capital of New Spain, and Veracruz, the main port to the Atlantic, became the core of the new colony. While expeditions to the south, toward Guatemala and Honduras, took place immediately after the fall of Tenochtitlan, journeying to the north was delayed. As Ignacio del Río explains in *Estudios históricos sobre la formación del norte de México,*[13] the main reason for the slow exploration of the Mexican North was the lack of established towns and agriculture in the zone. The majority of indigenous groups of the region, collectively called Chichimecs, were hunters and gatherers with a nomadic lifestyle. Without a reliable source of food, Spanish explorers and conquistadors were discouraged to travel north. One exception was Nuño de Guzmán, who in 1529 "ventured into crossing the Sierra Madre Occidental [mountain range] towards the present-day territories of the state of Durango."[14] As Río recounts, the ambitious Spaniard could not fulfill his wish to establish and govern a new northern province that would expand from coast to coast because most of his men perished during the trek due to starvation. Alvar Núñez Cabeza de Vaca and his three fellow shipwreck survivors—two Spaniards and one Black servant—were other early voyagers of the Mexican North. As we know from his recollections published under the title of *Naufragios*,[15] the four men were found near San Miguel de Culiacán in 1536, after traveling through a large area covering parts of what is now Florida, Texas, Tamaulipas, and Nuevo León for eight years. Even though this journey was accidental, and the participants' main objective was mere survival, Cabeza de Vaca's account provides the earliest description of that region and its inhabitants.

The turning point for northern Mexico happened in 1546, when Juan de Tolosa's expedition found silver in La Bufa hill, which resulted in Zacatecas quickly becoming a prosperous mining city.[16] According to Río, this metal-extracting boom caused a multiethnic migration to the north. While Spanish colonizers managed mining, commercial, governmental, and religious activities, African slaves and free Blacks were mostly employed as domestic servants. Mesoamerican natives, who arrived in large numbers, worked as wage-earning employees in the mines. For the latter, earning a salary was an incentive to leave their places of origin in Central Mexico, where the *encomienda* and *repartimiento* systems were the norm. The Real of Zacatecas—Real being the title given to mining districts—was the first of many other mining towns that emerged in the region. As the colonized area kept expanding and more villages were founded, the vast northern region was divided into various provinces: Nueva Galicia, Nueva Vizcaya, Nuevo León, and Nuevo México.

Among the mining towns in Nueva Vizcaya—the area now covering the Mexican states of Durango, Chihuahua, and parts of Sonora, Sinaloa, and Coahuila—was the Real of Cuencamé, the epicenter of our study. After traveling through the area between 1602 and 1605, Catholic priest Alonso de la Mota y Escobar wrote his *Descripción geográfica de los reinos de Nueva Galicia, Nueva Vizcaya, y Nuevo León*.[17] Among other things, he mentions that Cuencamé, founded in 1601, had "a big hill with countless mines containing a large number of metals" and "more than one hundred Spaniards, between miners and neighboring merchants, besides many others coming and going," which "made this Real one of the most populated in the whole Vizcaya."[18] Mota explains that the town also had a church, a Franciscan monastery, ten milling haciendas, and an adjacent scanty settlement—*poblesuelo*—of Chichimecs. He describes the climate and natural environment of Cuencamé as hot, grim—*enfermo*—, and in short supply of water.

Mota's *Descripción* includes very specific details about Cuencamé and the entire province of Nueva Vizcaya. We learn that the Mapimí area was abundant in fruit trees, San Juan del Río grew white grapes suitable to make wine, Cacaria had ponds with sardines and catfish, San Bartolomé cultivated corn and wheat, Caxco had several cattle barns, and people in Cuencamé stored their water in barrels. He dedicates more lines to the village of Durango, smaller than Cuencamé but designated as capital of Nueva Vizcaya. The priest tells us that fifty Spaniards lived in this principal village, which had four streets, houses made out of adobe, and fifteen stores selling all sorts of clothing. This cleric also states that in Durango "the common services for the [Spanish] residents [were] provided by [B]lack men and women, enslaved [M]ulatto men and women, and some free colored people" and that in total there were "about eighty slaves."[19] Knowing that in Durango there were eighty slaves working for fifty Spaniards is very useful data. While Mota does not specify the size of the Black population in his description of other settlements of Nueva Vizcaya or in Cuencamé—a town then with one hundred Spanish inhabitants—we can estimate a comparable ratio as in Durango. Thus, it is feasible to determine that since its foundation, the Real of Cuencamé had a substantial Black presence.

ALONSO DE BENAVIDES AND THE INQUISITION

According to the biographical sketch provided by George Hammond, Alonso de Benavides was born in the Azores Islands and arrived in New Spain in 1598.[20] After becoming a Franciscan friar in Mexico City, he performed various duties for the Catholic Church and the Holy Office of the Inquisition in Puebla and Veracruz. In 1625 and 1626, while on his way to New Mexico, Benavides made a pause in Cuencamé to collect confessions and accusations from the inhabitants of that northern settlement. That was the first official visit of the Holy Office to this town.

New Spain's Inquisition, founded in 1571, was an institution associated with secrecy, torture, and harsh punishments. As José Toribio Medina explains in his *Historia del tribunal del Santo Oficio de la Inquisición en México*,[21] the wide variety of sentences imposed by New Spain's Holy Office for religious transgressions included fines, imprisonment, wearing a penitential garment—*sambenito*—for an extended period of time, lashes, forced exile, and execution. Large public ceremonies that often culminated with the slaying of major offenders were called autos de fée. Medina describes Mexico's first auto de fée in detail. He explains that during this initial inquisitorial outdoors ritual, which took place in Mexico City in 1574, seventy-one individuals were judged and sentenced. This solemn event that began at seven in the morning and continued until six in the evening was attended by a large crowd, besides many others who watched the gloomy spectacle from windows and roofs. In addition to serving as public trials, these theatrical ceremonies were deliberately organized by the Inquisition to instill fear and detract potential future wrongdoers.

While the apprehension toward

the Inquisition was palpable in the metropolitan areas of the viceroyalty of New Spain, remote settlements in the northern frontier like the newly established towns of Nueva Vizcaya, did not have a permanent presence of this religious policing entity. For the Indigenous population, considered too new in the Christian faith and therefore not subjected to the Inquisition, this did not have significant consequences. However, the lack of monitoring by the Holy Office was meaningful for Blacks and Whites living in the Mexican North. Without the Inquisition's continuous censorship, the society of Cuencamé, similarly to other towns in the region, fostered a permissive environment where residents could enjoy a more unrestricted lifestyle. Benavides' inquisitorial files reveal the limited contact that the people of Cuencamé had with the Holy Office. Some collected confessions and accusations allude to infractions occurred years before his visit and a few involve individuals already deceased. In addition, Benavides himself indicates in his introductory note to this testimonial dossier that some of the accused where not interviewed because "their location was unknown or because they were in isolated areas and could not be reached."[22] The remoteness and inaccessibility of new settlements like Cuencamé provided its inhabitants, including Afro-Mexican women, with opportunities for movement and expression unfeasible in larger Colonial urban areas.

AFRO-MEXICAN WOMEN IN CUENCAMÉ

Of the thirty-five individuals interviewed by Alonso de Benavides during his visit to Cuencamé in 1625 and 1626, eight were of African descent: seven women and one man. In addition to those seven Afro-Mexican women who met with the inquisitor, there were five others mentioned in the collected testimonies. Hence, these files provide us with an insight into the lives of twelve Black women living in the periphery of Colonial Mexico. Despite their common African heritage, there were important differences among this group of female residents of Cuencamé. To refer to their racial classification, Benavides distinguishes them as Black or Mulatto—*negra or mulata.* Occasionally, the friar uses the word *morena*—dark skinned—as a synonym to Black. That is the case of Leonor de Guzmán, who on the top of her file is listed as "Black slave" but in the record of her testimony is identified as "a dark-skinned woman who calls herself Leonor."[23] When referring to the racial hierarchy known as Sistema de Castas, Douglas Cope explains in *The Limits of Racial Domination: Plebeian Society in Colonial Mexico City, 1660–1720* that "at its most extreme, this model distinguished more than forty racial categories, though few of these had any practical significance."[24] Depending on the percentage of Black blood, Afro-descendants could be labeled by specifically devised terms like *morisco, lobo*, or *alborozado* but in reality, mixed-Blacks were usually identified with the generic designation of Mulatto. This seems to be the case in Benavides's portfolio, where the only racial labels employed for Afro-Mexicans are Black or Mulatto.

Place of birth and language skills were other elements that differentiated Black women in Colonial Mexico. Those born on the African continent were usually identified merely by referring to their skin color or bondage status. These women were called *negras* or *esclavas*—Black women or female slaves. However, if an African slave had arrived in Mexico or another Spanish colony at an early age and therefore was fluent in the Spanish language, she was also classified as a ladina.[25] For instance, in his testimony to the Inquisition, captain Bernave Peres de Arriola accuses her slave Ana, "who came from Guinea as a child and is now ladina,"[26] of eating meat during Lent. It was significant for the Holy Office to specify the language skills of an Afro-Mexican woman, whether she was an accuser or being accused. A testimony given by someone with limited Spanish proficiency could be put into question because the informant could have misunderstood a conversation or failed to correctly convey her story to the inquisitor. On the other hand, an alleged transgressor could say that due to her poor language skills she was not aware of certain rules of the Catholic faith or that her words were misinterpreted by the accuser. For this reason, in his files, Benavides states whether a Black woman being interviewed or discussed was a ladina or not. Another label employed to refer to Black Mexican women was criolla. In this case, this term was used to refer to those who were born in the colonies, but as Herman Bennett mentions in *Colonial Blackness: A History of Afro-Mexico*, "a key aspect of the term was reference to customs" as it was assumed that "from birth, criollos were familiar with the Christian commonwealth and its customs."[27] The designations of ladina or criolla were not employed when referring to *mulatas* because due to their mixed race they were presumed to be born in the colonies and speak the Spanish language.

All Afro-Mexican women in Benavides's files have Spanish names: Juana, María, Leonor, Francisca, etc., with the most common being Ana, a name given to four of the twelve Black women present in Benavides's documents. As Cope indicates in his explanation about names among non-Spaniards in Colonial Mexico, "Black slaves were forced to abandon their African names" and many "had no 'official' last name until they were forced to choose one when they first married."[28] In the community of Cuencamé we encounter a variety of situations. Most Afro-Mexican women in these confessions and accusations—seven out of twelve—are only identified by their first name, while three have last names of their own, and two others took their master's last name. Of those listed with last names different than their master, it is possible that they adopted such name at the time of marriage or that they took it from a previous owner.

While White individuals, Spanish or Mexican-born, specify their age in Benavides's collected confessions and accusations, a common denominator among all Afro-Mexican women is their uncertain age. Elite individuals of this inquisitorial dossier include Francisco Alvarez from Gibraltar, Spain, listed as a twenty-seven-year-old man and doña Maria de Leguisiamo from Mexico City, listed as a thirty-five-year-old woman. In contrast, the complex circumstances surrounding Afro-Mexicans—some born in another continent, many not knowing their parents or siblings, and the lack of documentation of their birth—made it difficult for them to know their age. For that reason, Benavides estimates the age of Afro-Mexican women who testify before him. For instance, when he interviews Ana, "a dark-skinned woman from the village of Culiacán, slave of Marcos Rico," Benavides states that she is of "over forty years of age."[29] Similarly, when referring to Cathalina, a slave owned by Diego de Gusman, she is listed as "ladina, of about thirty years of age."[30] Overall, a majority of Afro-Mexican women interviewed or mentioned in Benavides's files, like Cathalina, are described as individuals of approximately thirty years of age.

SUBALTERNITY, AGENCY, AND POWER DYNAMICS

Afro-Mexican women living in northern New Spain in the early seventeenth century were oppressed by multiple systems of power. Race, gender, enslavement status, place of birth, and language skills all played a role in their intersectional marginalization. While one might assume that their opportunity for expression and action was extremely limited, the thirty-five inquisitorial files collected in Cuencamé reveal the opposite. We encounter Black women who in contrast to their male counterparts—only one Afro-Mexican man testified during Benavides's visit—take advantage of the opportunity to have a voice and lose their anonymity. During the inquisitor's stay in Cuencamé, some Black women—including forty-year-old Ana mentioned above—are called to testify for being accused or witnesses of an alleged transgression, but others voluntarily appear in front of the Holy Office. For instance, the record of the interview conducted on September 1, 1625, indicates that Geronima de Porras, "a [M]ulatto slave woman owned by captain Martin Ruis de Zavala, arrived without being called and swore to tell the truth."[31] According to the file, she came to Benavides to make an accusation of sorcery against a "*negra criolla* named Maria, slave of Manuel de Roxas."[32] In her testimony, Geronima explains that Maria bragged about knowing how to use a type of grass to attract or even kill men.

Geronima's declaration provides an example of an Afro-Mexican woman who overcomes her subalternity to gain agency and participate in the power dynamics of Cuencamé. While slaves were dehumanized and perceived as merchandise, in this account Geronima self-creates her personhood and establishes her authority. As stated in the file, she describes herself as a thirty-year-old woman who works at a mining hacienda. She also indicates being "married to a slave from the mentioned hacienda named Juan de la Peña."[33] When talking about the accusation against Ana, Geronima explains that her motivation to testify was—as a good Christian—"to clear her consciousness and not due to hatred."[34] Thus, by portraying herself as a Christian woman living under the sacred institution of matrimony, Geronima is rescinding the usual objectivization of slaves and gaining authority as a reliable informant for the Inquisition. She is neither silent nor passive because, as indicated by Benavides, she reached out to the Holy Office on her own accord. Unlike Ana, a sinful slave involved with witchcraft, Geronima's moral superiority gives her the capacity to be an accuser. In fact, according to the testimony, she scolded Ana after hearing about her sorcery schemes. Geronima de Porras consciously portrays herself as a respectable resident of Cuencamé and undertakes a position of power.

The patriarchal structure imposed by Spaniards in the colonies constricted women to the domestic sphere. This characteristic was particularly true for Afro-Mexican women, who mostly worked as household servants. However, this confinement was not an impediment for the Black women of Cuencamé. As Benavides's files reveal, the domestic realm—especially the kitchen— became a main stage for expression and agency. From the testimony given by Leonor, Diego de Gusman's slave, we learn that it was common for Black servants working for different families to meet and interact at each other's households. When talking about another Afro-Mexican woman named Maria, Leonor explains that "she would come many times to the house . . . and have conversations with her and her *compañeras*."[35] The use of the word *compañeras*, female companions, suggests a sense of camaraderie among Afro-Mexican women. Leonor's testimony provides more detail about these exchanges by stating that such conversations would take place while they all "sat in the kitchen."[36] Hence, we can view the kitchen as a shared space where Afro-Mexican women could interact with those outside their household, build relationships with each other, and gain a better understanding of their role in Cuencamé's society.

For Ana, a ladina slave accused of a variety of religious offenses by four different people, the domestic sphere represented a site of rebellion and empowerment. It was inside her master's home, and very often in the kitchen, where she committed the alleged transgressions. Ana's offenses include eating meat during Lent, refusing to learn Catholic prayers, not kneeling when sacred artifacts paraded on her street, destroying religious images, and purposely killing her newborn baby during labor while invoking the devil. Four accusers came forward to speak about this Black woman's wrongdoings: her master captain Bernave Peres de Arriola, his wife doña Maria de Velastigui, a Black criolla slave also named Ana, and a Black ladino slave criollo from Brazil named Manuel. Despite the severity of some of Ana's charges, the sporadic presence of the Holy Office in northern Mexico and the remoteness of the Cuencamé area made it very difficult for transgressors to be prosecuted. Thus, it is very likely that Ana was not punished by the Inquisition, as it would have certainly happened—perhaps during an auto-da-fé—in Mexico City or other metropolitan areas in New Spain.

For reasons unknown to us, Ana was not interviewed during Benavides's visit. However, the four testimonies against her provide us with a glimpse into the life of this defiant Afro-Mexican woman. We learn from the accusation made by her owner that Ana, of about thirty years of age and fluent in the Spanish language, was originally from Guinea and belonged to Luis Hernandez Escudero, a resident of the town of Parras, before arriving to Cuencamé. Geographical wandering was often part of the life of a slave. In Ana's case, we can speculate that after being captured in her native Guinea at a very young age, she made the treacherous trip across the Atlantic aboard a slave ship. We do not know if after arriving in Veracruz, Mexico's main port, she was sold to Escudero or someone else, but at some point in her life, Ana had to travel halfway across New Spain to the northern town of Parras and later to Cuencamé. The drastic changes experienced by Ana throughout her life were the result of decisions made by others. Therefore, it is not entirely surprising that as an adult woman living in a remote area without the constant presence of the Inquisition, she refuses to follow orders and adopts a rebellious attitude. As Susan M. Socolow explains in *The Women of Colonial Latin America*, "slaves, in addition to their labor, were a capital asset"[37] because the children of a female slave immediately became properties of her master. Ana's young age and potential future offspring—additional slaves to keep or sell—probably carried more weight for Arriola and his wife than Ana's unruly conduct. Thus, she continued to serve in their house despite her appalling conduct.

Ana's accusers refer to various incidents occurred in Arriola and Velastigui's home. Some testimonies discuss episodes where they found Ana in the kitchen either cooking or eating meat during Lent. On one occasion, when she was reprimanded about it by Manuel, a male slave in the house, Ana is quoted to say: "Leave me alone, I am hungry!"[38] Also in the kitchen, which had a window overlooking the street, Ana is accused of refusing to kneel when the Blessed Sacrament—which in the Catholic faith represents the flesh and blood of Christ—made a stop outside their house while parading around town. According to Maria de Velastigui's testimony, when she questioned Ana for not kneeling in front of the Blessed Sacrament like everybody else, the accused slave responded: "Why do I need to worship it? Don't you see what I am doing?"[39] and she kept washing the dishes. Even though some of the statements report that Ana was punished by her masters for her wrongdoings, it is evident that those punishments—which one informant describes as being burnt with iron pieces—did not discourage her from continuing her defiant behavior. The declaration given by the other female slave in the house—Ana criolla—indicates that when the inculpated woman was threatened with being accused to the Inquisition, she "responded in an arrogant manner: What do I care about the Holy Office, what Holy Office?"[40] Ana was not afraid of her owners, other slaves, or even the Inquisition. Her recurring bold comments corroborate that the Mexican North enjoyed a less regulated environment in comparison to the colonial metropolis, and that for Afro-Mexican women like Ana, that represented an opportunity for empowerment.

In addition to their work as household servants, the Black women of Cuencamé performed other roles within the domestic sphere. Their high degree of expertise in certain matters placed them in a distinctive position within the female culture of the town. Two of the twelve Afro-Mexican women participating in Benavides's portfolio are identified as midwives, and according to the episodes that involve them—one occurring during a Spanish woman's delivery and another one while an Indigenous woman was in labor—they were trusted with the birth of children from all social ranks. Benavides's inquisitorial files also show that it was common for Afro-Mexicans to be sought after by elite women to provide magical remedies for relationship issues. That is evident in the accusations made against Cuencamé residents Juana de la Rocha and her mother Mariana Sanches. According to various testimonies, for a period of five or six years, twenty-two-year-old Juana had been physically abused by her husband, Sebastian Fernandes. Among other attempts to improve the situation, Juana and her mother received help from two Afro-Mexican women. One declaration states that a Black slave named Francisca—already deceased at the time of Benavides's visit—gave Juana some roots to grind and put in her husband's hot chocolate, while another testimony indicates that a Mulatto slave named Ana provided some worms for Sanches to mix into tortillas for her abusive son-in-law. Even though Juana and her mother were socially privileged women, they had to rely on their slaves' knowledge to try to manage this domestic violence situation. These episodes demonstrate that Afro-Mexican women played an active role and were certainly not invisible in the society of Cuencamé. As Bristol explains in his study about central New Spain, "Afro-Mexican practitioners gained power and authority, at times manifested by fear and at other times manifested as respect."[41] In the examples from Cuencamé, women of all socioeconomic and racial backgrounds dealing with critical situations such as childbirth or domestic violence perceived Black slaves as knowledgeable and capable of ameliorating their circumstances.

Although the private space—the home and particularly the kitchen—became a site of expression and agency for some Afro-Mexican women in Cuencamé, others, like Maria, a Black slave owned by Manuel de Roxas, acted in the public sphere. Maria's story, which involves crossdressing, bullfighting, and witchcraft, is perhaps the most fascinating tale in Benavides's dossier. We learn from the two testimonies recorded against her that less than a year prior to the inquisitor's visit, Maria and an unnamed Mulatto woman ran away to the town of San Luis. There the two dressed like men and participated in a bullfighting event. Both had a drawing of the devil on their feet so "when the bull was ready to charge them, he would turn back."[42] In fact, Maria and her companion were so successful with the spears that they received a prize at the bullfighting ring of San Luis. The women—still wearing male clothing—later went to a cave where they performed an act of sorcery using herbs, a lizard, and a snake. In the eyes of the society of Cuencamé and the Inquisition, these two women broke many rules. However, as discussed in the article "A Colonial Cross-Dresser (Mexico, 1796),"[43] while cross-dressing was punished by the Holy Office when the transgressor was male—understood as a sign of homosexuality—, female cross-dressers were rarely prosecuted. Thus, wearing male clothing was not perceived as women's sexual abnormality but rather just as a disguise. Maria and her fellow runaway took advantage of the bare trails and isolation of settlements in the Mexican North to escape from their masters, and in Maria's case to also be "fugitive of her husband."[44] They seized the opportunity to not only gain physical freedom but also, by wearing male clothing, they evaded the patriarchal constraints imposed to women. They were able to successfully pretend being free Black men, travel between towns, and even have a stellar performance at a bullfighting event, an occasion of utmost display of bravery and strength.

As Joan Cameron Bristol discusses in detail in *Christians, Blasphemers, and Witches: Afro-Mexican Ritual Practice in the Seventeenth Century*, "colonial residents felt that God, the saints, the devil, and other supernatural forces were involved in their daily lives"[45] and Cuencamé was not an exception. The two testimonies in Benavides's portfolio that accuse these fugitive Afro-Mexican women indicate that in addition to the witchcraft ritual that took place in the cave—which had the purpose of attracting men—Maria and her companion were involved in other acts of sorcery. According to one informant, the Mulatto woman that traveled with Maria was knowledgeable in making love potions, including one with a "cooked and toasted leech, combined with the female blood of the month"[46] that should be mixed in the man's hot chocolate. Even though this type of concoctions were fiercely censured by the Inquisition and those involved were prosecuted, they were common and perhaps more openly discussed in the society of Cuencamé due to the lack of supervision from the Holy Office. Among the wide array of items that were mentioned in various declarations as secret ingredients used by men and women of all races and socioeconomic ranks to attract those of the opposite sex were: herbs, fingernail clippings, the paw of a chameleon, placenta, amniotic sac, and menstrual blood. For other purposes, such as to have good luck in card games, to cure a malady, to cause someone's death, or to tame an abusive husband—case mentioned above—the people of Cuencamé employed a variety of magical ingredients like cockroaches, dirt, roots, donkey brains, worms, frog drool, human hair, and rooster feathers. Besides hot chocolate, which seemed to be the most common method of delivery, other mixtures were put in tortillas, bread, or cake. While remedies of this kind were present in all of New Spain, the geographical remoteness of Cuencamé, as well as sporadic presence of the Inquisition, allowed for these practices to be more prevalent and public than in Colonial metropolitan areas.

CONCLUSION

The earliest files from Cuencamé's civil registry, the entity in charge of issuing official documents such as birth, marriage, and death certificates, date from 1867.[47] By then, the region was no longer part of New Spain but rather of independent Mexico. In terms of Catholic Church records, which during the colonial period were the most prominent pieces of personal documentation, the preserved archives from this town only go back to 1694.[48] One single severely damaged page from 1656, with what appears to be Catholic marriage records, makes us infer that older files were destroyed, either accidentally or intentionally. Therefore, Benavides's files collected in 1625 and 1626—roughly twenty years after the foundation of the Real de Cuencamé—provides a rare glimpse into the early seventeenth-century society of this northern settlement. For the Inquisition, these testimonies were collected to investigate religious offenses, but by reading between the lines of these thirty-five personal narratives we can visualize the human geography of this town. Cuencamé was a thriving society where individuals from different social ranks and racial identities interacted. The inquisitorial file dated

October 4th, 1625—the case of a woman accused of asking a midwife for the newborn's amniotic sac with the intention of performing an act of sorcery—exemplifies this complex social dynamic. That record is an accusation made by Juana, a Black slave and midwife, against Ysabel Marin, a Spanish widow, about an episode that occurred while a third female participant, an Indigenous woman, was giving birth. The interactions and various roles played by these female residents, each one from a different social status and racial group, problematize the established hierarchies of Cuencamé.

Through Benavides's dossier we can envision the overall diversity among of the inhabitants of this town. In addition to mining, which spurred the growth of Mexico's northern region, the files mention individuals with very different occupations. Among the male residents and visitors of Cuencamé we find vendors, captains, soldiers, mayors, attorneys, carpenters, scribes, cowboys, doctors, tailors, priests, farmers, shepherds, and even a puppeteer. In terms of the birthplaces of men and women mentioned and interviewed, besides slaves from Guinea, Brazil and the Mexican town of Culiacán, the dossier makes reference to individuals—most likely White—from Cádiz, Tenerife, and other islands in Spain, Portugal, France, as well as people from nearby and faraway places in New Spain, including Mexico City, Guadalajara, Saltillo, Zacatecas, Parras, Guadiana, Sombrerete, Nombre de Dios, and Mapimí. Despite its newness and remote location, Cuencamé was a diverse and vibrant town.

By focusing on the voices and stories of Afro-Mexican women in the testimonies collected by Alonso de Benavides in 1625 and 1626 we are able to unveil a neglected part of the history of Cuencamé, which is also the case in other Mexican towns in the northern frontier. In present-day Mexico, Blackness and African heritage are topics mainly associated with the Costa Chica region and the states of Guerrero and Veracruz. That coastal area is perceived as an atypical location where Afro-descendants did not disappear as it is presumed to have happened in the rest of Mexico. As we see in Benavides's files, the Mexican North had a strong Black presence from the early years and, as we discussed above, Afro-Mexican women were vital participants of the society of Cuencamé. Despite racism, patriarchy, and their enslavement status, the Black women of this colonial town manipulated the circumstances to gain agency and overcome their intersectional oppression. The descendants of these *negras*, *mulatas*, *ladinas*, and *criollas*—many of them probably still residing in the area—might ignore their African heritage. As Jorge Delgadillo explains in his study "La desaparición de los afrodescendientes de Guadalajara: cambio identitario, demografía y ciudadanía, 1793–1823,"[49] a variety of factors, including right to citizenship after emancipation and social prejudice, motivated Afro-Mexicans to hide their racial background and self-identify as mestizo. As it happened in Guadalajara, it is likely that in Cuencamé and other Mexican towns, African ancestry was intentionally suppressed by many individuals and eventually forgotten by the subsequent generations.

BIBLIOGRAPHY

Aguirre Beltrán, Gonzalo. *La población negra de México. Estudio etnohistórico.* Mexico: Ediciones Fuente Cultural, 1946.
Bakewell, P. J. *Silver Mining and Society in Colonial Mexico, Zacatecas 1546–1700.* Cambridge: Cambridge University Press, 2010.
Bennett, Herman. *Colonial Blackness: A History of Afro-Mexico.* Bloomington: Indiana University Press, 2009.
Bristol, Joan Cameron. *Christians, Blasphemers, and Witches: Afro-Mexican Ritual Practice in the Seventeenth Century.* Albuquerque: University of New Mexico Press, 2007.
———. "From Curing to Witchcraft: Afro-Mexicans and the Mediation of Authority." *Journal of Colonialism and Colonial History* 7, no.1 (Spring 2006).
Casas, Ignacio. *La esclava de Juana Inés.* Mexico: Grijalbo, 2019.
Collins, Patricia. *Intersectionality as Critical Social Theory.* Durham: Duke University Press, 2019.
Cope, Douglas. *The Limits of Racial Domination: Plebeian Society in Colonial Mexico City, 1660–1720.* Madison: The University of Wisconsin Press, 1984.
Crenshaw, Kimberlé. "Demarginalizing the Intersection of Race and Sex: A Black Feminist Critique of Antidiscrimination Doctrine, Feminist Theory and Antiracist Politics." *University of Chicago Legal Forum*, no. 1 (1989): 139–67.
———. "Mapping the Margins: Intersectionality, Identity Politics, and Violence Against Women of Color." *Stanford Law Review* 43, no. 6 (July 1991): 1241–1299.
Delgadillo, Jorge E. "La desaparición de los afrodescendientes de Guadalajara: cambio identitario, demografía y ciudadanía, 1793–1823." (paper presented at LASA Virtual Conference 2020, May 13–16, 2020).
Díaz Casas, María Camila, and María Elisa Velázquez, "Estudios Afromexicanos: Una revisión historiográfica y antropológica." *Tabula Rasa*, no. 27 (July–December 2017): 221–48.
Fuente, Alejandro de la, and George Reid Andrews. "The Making of a Field: Afro-Latin American Studies." *Afro-Latin American Studies: An Introduction.* Cambridge: Cambridge University Press, 2018: 1–24.
Germeten, Nicole von. "Juan Roque's Donation of a House to the Zape Confraternity, Mexico City, 1623." *Afro-Latino Voices: Narratives from the Early Modern Ibero-Atlantic World, 1550–1812.* Edited by Kathryn McKnight and Leo Garofalo. Indianapolis: Hackett Publishing Company, 2009: 83–104.
Green, Debra. "African Mexicans in Spanish Slave Societies in America: A Critical Location of Sources." *Journal of Black Studies* 40, no. 4 (March 2010): 683–99.
Hammond, George P. "Biography of Benavides." *Fray Alonso de Benavides' Revised Memorial of 1634.* Albuquerque: The University of New Mexico Press, 1945.

Jaffary, Nora E., and Jane E. Mangan. "A Colonial Cross-Dresser (Mexico, 1796)." *Women in Colonial Latin America, 1526 to 1806: Texts and Contexts*. Indianapolis: Hackett Publishing Company, 2018: 214–23.

"Mexico, Durango, Catholic Church Records, 1604–1985, Cuencamé, San Antonio de Padua." *FamilySearch*, accessed on July 17, 2021, https://www.familysearch .org/ark:/61903/3:1:S3HY-DRBS-B5F?i=312&wc=3PZ6ZNL%3A107796301 %2C107796302%2C112011401%3Fcc%3D1554576&cc=1554576.

"Mexico, Durango, Civil Registration, 1861–1995, Cuencamé," FamilySearch, accessed on June 24, 2021, https://www.familysearch.org/ark:/61903/3:1:33S7 -95LN-9C3Y?wc=MDY5-VT5&cc=1916235.

Mota y Escobar, D. Alonso de la. "Descripción geográfica de los reinos de Nueva Galicia, Nueva Vizcaya y Nuevo León." *Anales del Instituto Nacional de Antropología e Historia*, no. 45 (1963): 287–364.

Núñez Cabeza de Vaca, Alvar. *Naufragios*. Valladolid, 1555.

Río, Ignacio del. *Estudios históricos sobre la formación del norte de México*. Mexico: UNAM, 2009.

Rivera, Viridiana, and Jerry Craddock. *Alonso de Benavides, Commissary of the Holy Office, Received Accusations and Confessions Cuencamé, 1625–1626*. Berkeley: UC Berkeley, 2020.

Socolow, Susan M. *The Women of Colonial Latin America*. Cambridge: Cambridge University Press, 2000.

Toribio Medina, José. *Historia del Tribunal del Santo Oficio de la Inquisición en México*. Habana: Imprenta Elzeviriana, 1905.

Wade, Peter. "Estudios afrodescendientes en Latinoamérica: racismo y mestizaje." *Tabula Rasa*, no. 27 (July–December 2017): 23–44.

NOTES

1. Casas, Ignacio. *La esclava de Juana Inés* (Grijalbo, 2019).

2. These files were recently transcribed and published in: Viridiana Rivera and Jerry Craddock, *Alonso de Benavides, Commissary of the Holy Office, Received Accusations and Confessions Cuencamé, 1625–1626* (UC Berkeley: 2020). All translations from these files are mine.

3. See: María Camila Díaz Casas and María Elisa Velázquez, "Estudios Afromexicanos: Una revisión historiográfica y antropológica," *Tabula Rasa*, no.27 (July–December 2017): 221–48.

4. Peter Wade, "Estudios afrodescendientes en Latinoamérica: racismo y mestizaje," *Tabula Rasa*, no. 27 (July–December 2017): 23–44.

5. Kimberlé Crenshaw, "Demarginalizing the Intersection of Race and Sex: A Black Feminist Critique of Antidiscrimination Doctrine, Feminist Theory and Antiracist Politics," *University of Chicago Legal Forum*, no. 1 (1989): 139–67. And Kimberlée Crenshaw, "Mapping the Margins: Intersectionality, Identity Politics, and Violence Against Women of Color," *Stanford Law Review* 43, no. 6 (July 1991): 1241–99.

6. Patricia Collins, *Intersectionality as Critical Social Theory (Duke University Press, 2019).*

7. Crenshaw, "Demarginalizing," 139–40.

8. Collins, *Intersectionality*, 144.

9. Gonzalo Aguirre Beltrán, *La población negra de México. Estudio etnohistórico* (Ediciones Fuente Cultural, 1946).

10. Nicole von Germeten, "Juan Roque's Donation of a House to the Zape Confraternity, Mexico City, 1623," *Afro-Latino Voices: Narratives from the Early Modern Ibero-Atlantic World, 1550–1812*, Eds. Kathryn McKnight and Leo Garofalo (Hackett Publishing Company, 2009): 83–104.

11. For an extensive review of published works about Afro-Mexicans, see Debra Green, "African Mexicans in Spanish Slave Societies in America: A Critical Location of Sources," *Journal of Black Studies* 40, no. 4 (March 2010): 683–99.

12. Alejandro de la Fuente and George Reid Andrews, "The Making of a Field: Afro-Latin American Studies," *Afro-Latin American Studies: An Introduction,*(Cambridge University Press, 2018): 1–24.

13. Ignacio del Río, *Estudios históricos sobre la formación del norte de México* (UNAM: 2009).

14. Río, *Estudios históricos*, 9. Unless otherwise noted, all translations from sources in Spanish are mine.

15. Alvar Núñez Cabeza de Vaca, *Naufragios* (Valladolid, 1555).

16. P. J. Bakewell, *Silver Mining and Society in Colonial Mexico, Zacatecas 1546–1700* (Cambridge University Press, 2010).

17. D. Alonso de la Mota y Escobar, "Descripción geográfica de los reinos de Nueva Galicia, Nueva Vizcaya y Nuevo León," *Anales del Instituto Nacional de Antropología e Historia*, no. 45 (1963): 287–364.

18. Mota y Escobar, "Descripción geográfica," 355–56.

19. Mota y Escobar, "Descripción geográfica," 354.

20. George P. Hammond, "Biography of Benavides," *Fray Alonso de Benavides' Revised Memorial of 1634* (The University of New Mexico Press, 1945).

21. José Toribio Medina, *Historia del Tribunal del Santo Oficio de la Inquisición en México* (Imprenta Elzeviriana, 1905).

22. Rivera and Craddock, *Alonso de Benavides,* 6.

23. Ibid., 31.

24. Douglas Cope, *The Limits of Racial Domination: Plebeian Society in Colonial Mexico City, 1660–1720* (The University of Wisconsin Press, 1984).

25. In other parts of New Spain, the term *bozal* was used to designate slaves from Guinea who did not speak Spanish or Portuguese. See: Herman Bennett, *Colonial Blackness: A History of Afro-Mexico* (Indiana University Press, 2009).

26. Rivera and Craddock, *Alonso de Benavides,* 74.

27. Bennett, *Colonial Blackness*, 105.

28. Cope, *The Limits,* 63.

29. Rivera and Craddock, *Alonso de Benavides,* 75.

30. Ibid., 34.

31. Ibid., 30.

32. Ibid., 30.

33. Ibid., 30.

34. Ibid., 31.

35. Ibid., 32.

36. Ibid., 32.

37. Susan M. Socolow, *The Women of Colonial Latin America* (Cambridge University Press, 2000), 132.

38. Rivera and Craddock, *Alonso de Benavides*, 79.

39. Ibid., 77.

40. Ibid., 76.

41. Joan Cameron Bristol, "From Curing to Witchcraft: Afro-Mexicans and the Mediation of Authority," *Journal of Colonialism and Colonial History* 7, no.1 (Spring 2006).

42. Rivera and Craddock, *Alonso de Benavides*, 32.

43. Nora E. Jaffary and Jane E. Mangan, "A Colonial Cross-Dresser (Mexico, 1796)," *Women in Colonial Latin America, 1526 to 1806: Texts and Contexts,*(Hackett Publishing Company, 2018): 214–23.

44. Rivera and Craddock, *Alonso de Benavides*, 33.

45. Joan Cameron Bristol, *Christians, Blasphemers, and Witches: Afro-Mexican Ritual Practice in the Seventeenth Century* (University of New Mexico Press, 2007), 16.

46. Rivera and Craddock, *Alonso de Benavides*, 33.

47. "Mexico, Durango, Civil Registration, 1861–1995, Cuencamé," FamilySearch, accessed on June 24, 2021, https://www.familysearch.org/ark:/61903/3:1:33S7-95LN -9C3Y?wc=MDY5-VT5&cc=1916235.

48. "Mexico, Durango, Catholic Church Records, 1604–1985, Cuencamé, San Antonio de Padua," *FamilySearch*, accessed on July 17, 2021, https://www.familysearch .org/ark:/61903/3:1:S3HY-DRBS-B5F?i=312&wc=3PZ6-ZNL%3A107796301 %2C107796302%2C112011401%3Fcc%3D1554576&cc=1554576.

49. Jorge E. Delgadillo, "La desaparición de los afrodescendientes de Guadalajara: cambio identitario, demografía y ciudadanía, 1793–1823," (paper presented at LASA Virtual Conference 2020, May 13–16, 2020).

Chapter 10

Blurring Genres, Blurring Borders

Contemporary Poetic Memoirs of Afro-Dominicanas in the United States

Melissa Castillo Planas

For Afro-Dominican poet, playwright, performer, award winning author and podcast host Jasminne Mendez skin has multiple meanings. As she points out in her poem "(W)hole" from her mixed genre memoir *Night-Blooming Jasmin(n)e* (2018), it is "the organ of the body allowed to take up the most space."[1] Unlike many, this is not something Mendez can take for granted. As a Black woman who also lives with chronic illness (lupus and scleroderma), her skin does not just affect her treatment in the world, it can also be a measure of her health. She explores the multiple meanings of skin early on in the memoir in the essay "Skin Score." Significantly, the majority of the essay describes her experiences with race as she maneuvers between white, Black, and Latinx worlds in San Antonio, Texas, where she was partially raised and then in Houston, Texas, where she attended college and later settled. She details advocating and directing an all-Black play in high school, her mother's nickname for her "wild" hair, dating a Sikh man in college, and being misread and subtly insulted by a Mexican woman who can't grapple with a Black Latina. However, it ends with a visit to a doctor shortly after her diagnosis of scleroderma where she is given a "skin score" to indicate the severity of her illness, an illness which has no clear cause and no cure. As she reflects on what would become a lifelong battle, Mendez asks, "Was scleroderma my body's way of keeping score of all the insults, racial slurs, bullying and micro-aggressions I had chosen to repress? And if it took years of painful experiences and rejection for my skin to form this shield and scleroderma to manifest, how long would it take and what would it take to shed this thick-ened skin and start anew?"[2]

Amanda Alcántara asks a similar question in her mixed-genre prose, poem, and photography piece "Mulata contemporánea searching for autonomy" from her book *Chula* (2019). Alcántara is a writer and journalist who was born in the United States but raised in the Dominican Republic until the age of fifteen. Her mixed-genre memoir charts, among many other themes, her relationship to a body that has been racialized and sexualized in often ter-rifying ways. Prior to the poem, she inserts a selfie and an artist statement in which she traces some of the historical roots of this treatment and why she must reclaim her sexuality. She writes:

> I read that during the colonial era, they sent pictures of mixed-race women from el Caribe back to Europe. They called them mulatas. Their bodies, their faces, their features—they used these to make people interested in coming to the New World.
>
> So, the settlers came.
>
> And when I go to el Caribe, many times they call me the same thing they called those women.
>
> Can I clean the oppression off? Can I rewrite the history of el Caribe, the history of colonization? Can I rewrite the history of my body?[3]

Both Alcántara and Mendez explore how their bodies are archives of their experiences as racialized women. More importantly, both use their books as a way to rewrite their experiences not only in ways that empower themselves and their communities, but also critique an archive that does not consider their stories.

Daring to Write: Contemporary Narratives by Dominican Women (2016), edited by Erika M. Martinez, brought together twenty-four narratives writ-ten by Dominican women and women of Dominican descent living in the United States, demonstrating a new spotlight on the work of Dominicanas after decades of literary neglect. Fiction and nonfiction by writers like Angie Cruz, Nelly Rosario, Sophia Quintero, and others reflect the emergence of a strong female narrative in the Dominican diaspora. Meanwhile, recent pub-lications by Elizabeth Acevedo and Peggy Robles-Alvarado represent a new Dominican American poetic voice. Amid this literary renaissance, within the past five years, Afro-Dominicanas Jasminne Mendez and Amanda Alcántara have each published books exploring a different genre, or rather blend of genres that I am calling "poetic memoir." Blending themes of race, heri-tage, and ancestral knowledge in poetics alongside narratives about family, upbringing, and personal challenges, *Night-Blooming Jasmin(n)e* (2018), and *Chula* (2019) reflect a new and exciting form of Afro-Dominican expression. Although poetic memoirs are not novel in Latinx literary history, the exploration of this blurred genre by Mendez and Alcántara as a form of Afro-Dominican women's writing in the diaspora that also addresses what have often been considered taboo topics offers a new opening into the personal and literary lives of Afro-Dominicanas in the United States. Employing a Black Latina feminist praxis, this chapter discusses these two texts by Mendez and Alcántara in order to explore the possibilities of embodied memoir writing and poetics for contemporary Afro-Dominican women in the diaspora. For both, these multigenre works represent a new archive of stories not often told even in Latinx communities, stories that celebrate the Afro-Latina body as site of transformative knowledge.

PERIPHERALIZED LITERATURE: CENTERING AFRO-DOMINICANAS IN POETRY & SCHOLARSHIP

Afro-Dominican women writers find themselves on the periphery of the US and Latinx Literary canon. As Yomaira C. Figueroa-Vásquez describes, "In the United States, we find Latinx literature juxtaposed to canonical and popular Anglo texts but rarely taken seriously as sources of study, and continually subordinated by white supremacist markets and logics. The work produced by Afro-Latinx writers are often overlooked both in the Caribbean and in the United States."[4] Figueroa-Vásquez's choice of the term "periphery" highlights how Afro-Latinx literature is sidelined further within an already marginalized Latinx field.[5] For Dominican and especially Afro-Dominican writers, this results in what Lorgia García-Peña has termed "the footnote condition that mutes Dominican plurality."[6] In a similar turn, Omaris Zamora's 2016 dissertation, "(Trance)formations of an AfroLatina: Embodied Archives of Blackness and Womanhood in Transnational Dominican Women's Narratives," begins by addressing how Afro-Latina experiences have been left out of both Black and Latina feminist theory. According to Zamora, "Black feminist theory lacks a transnational context and an afro-diasporic approach that acknowledges the multiplicities of blackness (Collins; Crenshaw; Davis; Combahee). Furthermore, Latina/ Chicana feminist theory maintains blackness parenthetical and invisible in favor of a Latinidad that is primarily mestiza (Anzaldúa)."[7] Thus following Figueroa-Vásquez, García-Peña and Zamora, this chapter seeks to center an Afro-Latina poetics and feminist theory that have often been overlooked.[8]

Within a specifically Dominican context, Dixa Ramirez's *Colonial Phantoms: Belonging and Refusal in the Dominican Americas, from the 19th Century to the Present,* offers the potent term "ghosting" to reflect the treatment of the Dominican Republic in scholarship on "colonial modernity in the Americas, the African diaspora, geographic displacement (e.g., migration and exile), and international divisions of labor."[9] In her powerful revision of Latinx studies and African Diaspora studies, Ramirez centers Afro-Dominican writers, artists, and performers, especially women, in order to counter this erasure of gendered and racialized Dominicans. Significantly, she does this across centuries beginning with the whitening of Salomé Ureña as a function of her anointment as the "muse of the nation."[10] Through an exploration of the poet's image, Ramírez adds complexity and history to Dominican racial identities that US-based scholars, García-Peña points out, have long misunderstood and oversimplified.[11, 12] In highlighting Afro-Dominican creatives, from Salomé Ureña to singers in the diaspora like Amara la Negra and Maluca Mala, Ramirez presents an alternative genealogy and archive of *Dominicanidad* to which I add Amanda Alcántara and Jasminne Mendez.

In their introduction to the 2015 special issue on Black Dominican studies in *The Black Scholar*, editors Raj Chetty and Amaury Rodríguez, present a rich array of scholarship that not only deepens this conversation on Dominican racial identity, but also adds the impact of other struggles including patriarchy, heteronormativity, and imperialism.[13] For example, in her article in the issue, García-Peñã, presents a very nuanced understanding of race: "I argue Dominican blackness must also be understood in terms of movement—as a vaivén—that is, as a trans-local concept very much linked to historical, cultural and political continuities."[14] She elaborates on this complexity in *The Borders of Dominicanidad: Race, Nation, and Archives of Contradiction* (2016) with several important and useful terms. The first is called contra*dictions* which she defines as "stories, narratives, and speech acts—that go against the hegemonic version of national identity."[15] The second, is a presentation of what performance artist and poet Josephina Báez describes as the space or experience of "El Nié," often translated as "neither here nor there."[16] Here again, García-Peña's explanation is illuminating: "El Nié signifies not the border space that the subject inhabits—Anzaldúa's the barbwire—but rather the body that carries the violent borders that deter them from entering the nation, from access to full citizenship and from public, cultural, historical, and political representation."[17] The third and final concept she terms "translating blackness," which García-Peña employs to understand the various negotiations made as "El Níe"—the body—moves through various spaces. From mixing genres to their presentation of themes, both Alcántara and Mendez, contradict hegemonic ideas of Afro-Dominican womanhood. Whether from a life in transit between the Dominican Republic and the United States as in Alcántara's case, or from a life largely in Texas where Latinx culture is often synonymous with Mexican as in Mendez's case, both texts are largely centered around their embodied experiences—what it means to be sexualized, what it means to be racialized, what it means to live with disability. These authors "translate blackness" in various ways throughout their books as they negotiate with a world that does not accept their full Afro-Dominican womanhood. Thus, within this context, I see Mendez's and Alcántara's embodied texts as direct responses to this forced peripheralization through a refusal to adhere to traditional genre forms that don't suit narratives about sexual assault, self-harm, disability, or infertility in addition to questions of identity, belonging and race that encompass their complete and complexly intersectional realities.

Omaris Z. Zamora's previously mentioned 2016 dissertation may be the first (and if not, certainly one of the few) that focuses specifically on Afro-Dominican women's narratives, and as such, her scholarship is an excellent complement to García-Peña's theorizations in terms of her development of an Afro-Latina feminist epistemology that centers the body as archive.[18] Zamora theorizes around the term "(trance)formation" to explore identities that are "transnational, transformative, and transient."[19] In tracing Afro-Dominican women's (trance)formations, she both centers the body as the site of knowledge production and dissemination, while also acknowledging the violence this process entails as women develop multiple attachments and performance practices to fully represent their subjectivities.[20] In this way, she levels a forceful critique at a US-centric Black intersectional feminism that has not reckoned with the complexities of transnationalism.[21] Thus, guided by Zamora and García-Peña, this essay offers an exploration of Alcántara and Mendez as part of an embodied archive in transit.

EMBODIED POETRY, MEMOIR POETICS: MIXED GENRE AS AFRO-DOMINICANA INTERSECTIONALITY

Latinas have long turned to the various permutations (autobiography, memoir, testimonio, autohistoria, etc.) of what Norma E. Cantú has called "life writing" as an important source of knowledge production. According to Cantú, it is because Latinas have not traditionally been included in the national canon, that they are frequent innovators of traditional genres. Cantú elaborates,

> but my use of the term "life-writing" allows for an expansion that includes blended genre works, transgeneric works, and testimonio. Because it also allows for a discussion of what it means for a people who have traditionally not had the resources or access to inserting their life story into the national fabric, or into

the hegemonic literary canon, life-writing explodes the boundaries of the more traditional genres.[22]

As such, works by Afro-Latinas who are even further marginalized, miscategorized, or overlooked, are ripe for this type of genre-bending work I highlight as "poetic memoir."

Here, Jasminne Mendez's reflection on the writing of both *Night-Blooming Jasmin(n)e* (2018) and *Island of Dreams* (2013) as mixed-genre memoir essays and poems is instructive:

> For me writing in mixed genre is all about intersectionality. I hold many identities, Black, Latina, daughter of immigrants, military brat, bilingual, disabled, woman, etc., etc., etc., so intersectional form/mixed genre is what makes the most sense to me. In truth this started because I was simply writing about personal topics in multiple genres and in order to encompass the totality of my experience and the stories that I wanted to tell it made sense to include both of the poems and the essays into both of those collections. It's also because there are some things that I need more words than what poetry affords in order to tell that story and its truth and I'm able to also retreat to poetry when there are personal subjects or topics that are often difficult to broach head-on. I also knew I wanted to honor the ways in which both Black and Latinx cultures have told stories in our past. . . . Our ancestral storytelling ways are not confined by "genre"- we have and always will tell stories using our ENTIRE selves, our entire experiences, all the tools we have at our disposal which include poetry, song, dance, narrative, dramatic arts, visual art etc. I didn't want to shy away from that.[23]

Mendez's reflection, like the collections she references, echo key interventions made by both García-Peña and Zamora about anti-hegemonic narratives and embodied writing.

In developing an Afro-Latina feminist epistemology, Zamora does not shy away from using her own experience as an Afro-Dominican woman. She begins her dissertation with an original poem and memoir that highlights her perspective growing up in Chicago where her "*dominicanidad* is invisible or misread at best"[24] and her experience both within and outside US contexts and borders. Thus, as she explores the idea of an embodied archive, "or place where memories are kept,"[25] throughout the text she also presents her own personal creative archive alongside her scholarship. Of course, this mixture of scholarly theory, memoir, and poetry is not unique—Zamora is well versed in Gloria Anzaldúa's work and what she called autohistoria-teoría. Nevertheless, her dialogue with a Chicana feminist framework is specific: "Ultimately, to try to read AfroLatina women's bodies within a Chicano/Latino and Black feminist framework is to recognize that this body is at times in transgression."[26] Her engagement with Anzaldúa and other Chicanas like Cherrí Moraga's (1981) "theory in the flesh" both reflects the possibilities and limitations of these theories for Black Latina bodies.

Rather, Zamora, Garcia-Peña, Mendez, and Alcántara continue the important work of building an Afro-Latina narrative archive that centers their transnational experiences and embodied memories found in earlier publications such the *Afro-Latin@ Reader* (2010) and *Woman Warriors of the Afro-Latina Diaspora* (2012), a volume that specifically choose to focus on "life stories."[27] Significantly, here again, bodies, memory, and movement are on display in essays like Ana-Maurine Lara's "Bodies and Memories: Afro-Latina Identities in Motion" in which she reflects on her relationship to her body within different contexts and experiences of racialization. Lara writes, "As Afro-Latinas in the world, we are constantly negotiating others' assumptions about where our bodies and our memories overlap, where our Blackness/negritud begins and our Latina-ness end."[28] What Ramirez's work delving back into the nineteenth century demonstrates, is that Dominican women's racial identities have long been far more complex then self-perception, but rather influenced by US and European imperial power structures.

Given this context, perhaps it is not a surprise that Afro-Dominican writer, performance artist, director, actress, and educator Josefina Báez has developed her own theoretical framework called "Performance Autology," a teachable philosophy of performance connected to El Nié. At the center of this philosophy is a process of introspection that fully incorporates the body through a globally inspired set of physical practices including yoga, world dance, herbs, Chinese calligraphy, and more, all aimed at mind-body balance.[29] The ultimate goal is the creation of an authentic work of art through a process that is "both healing and joyful in the ever-changing AS IS."[30] Combining a process of introspection with joy and creativity, Mendez and Alcántara like Báez before them produce unique autoethnographic texts[31] that are both road maps and provocations.

MULATA AUTONOMY: OWNING YOUR ARCHIVE IN AMANDA ALCÁNTARA'S *CHULA*

In the "Intro" to *Chula*, Amanda Alcántara presents her nontraditional migration story—she was born in the United States and then raised in the Dominican Republic until the age of fifteen when she moved to West New York, New Jersey. In describing her early attempts to fit in and "assimilate" to her new surroundings[32] and then later rekindle her relationship to the Dominican Republic, Alcántara describes complex feelings of loss, suffering, and joy. Her experience reflects what Josefina Báez (who Alcántara thanks in her introduction) as a "Domincanyork"[33] has described as the "flagless nation" of "El Nié."[34] As García-Peña points out, there are various identifications—Dominicanyork, *rayano, dominicano,* Afro-Dominican, *dominicanos ausentes*—that have come to make up Dominicanidad across nations but from these often marginalized subjectivities also comes possibility. On the one hand, Alcántara, as an Afro-Dominicana *ausente*, to particularize García-Peña's term, has experienced exactly the type of ostracism described in *Borders of Dominicanidad*: "Dominicans who migrate to the United States are 'racexiles'; they are expunged from the Dominican nation because of their race yet they remain inadmissible in the United States for the same reason."[35] On the other hand, it is from this discomfort of El Nié that authors like Alcántara are also able to find a "poetics of dominicanidad ausente" in which "the contra*dictions* of dominicanidad are embraced and redefined, allowing the Dominican subject to emerge as an agent of his or her own history and identity/ies, finding hope, harmony, and even bliss within this very uncomfortable space of contra*diction*."[36] As if responding directly to García-Peña's intervention, Alcántara's introduction lays out several significant goals for *Chula.* In a response to a world that she is well aware attempts to exclude her[37] and her narrative, in *Chula,* Alcántara is the main character and historian of her own archive.

Everything about *Chula* reflects Alcántara's quest to take full ownership of her story. A mixture of episodic memoir, journal entries from throughout her life, photographs, and poems, the book is organized by emotion rather than chronology. Already imbued with music from reggaeton to salsa to bolero, the book, especially the poetry, is rhythmic and not surprisingly, Alcántara has described writing poems to beats she found online.[38] This musicality was central to Alcántara's vision of the book which she compares as more similar to creating an album than a memoir: "To me, it was more like writing, more like creating, an album then writing a book because I wanted to mix different kinds of genres. Some genres, some writing pieces, may not even be like a genre."[39] Likewise, Alcántara takes full command of her language choices moving unapologetically between English and Spanish and incorporating slang and terms particular to the Dominican diaspora. Her commitment and confidence in all of these artistic choices also resulted in one more: to publish independently. She both wanted to get the work out quickly and have full creative control.[40] In this way, Alcántara took full ownership of her history and identities, presenting an archive of memories selected and curated to her tastes.

In the first section (of two), Alcántara interweaves memoir, poems, and journal entries form her teenage years, that present her experience at various points in her life surrounding issues of race, traditional gender roles, sexual harassment and assault, sexuality, and disordered eating among other topics. What is striking about these texts is that while these experiences may vary across time periods and even national spaces, a common thread is how Alcántara is racialized and sexualized in a way that sends a message that she is not in control of her body, that her body is not hers to own or dictate. When she is sexually assaulted by a boy her age at eight or nine, she reflects, "But cuz he's a boy, he didn't need a dream. He had permission to do it in real life. And he didn't even need consent."[41] During a college semester abroad in Paris, she is threatened by a French man who is offended by her interest in women: "This was my first sexual encounter with a woman and here was this guy already threatening me by saying that I needed a man."[42] In a harrowing end to the section, Alcántara details years of terrifying stalking and harassment by her cousin's husband, to which her mother responds, "Es parte de ser mujer."[43] All of these experiences, are of course in addition to the highly sexualized catcalling she was on the receiving end of from a young age while simultaneously being called a "puta" (by both men and women) for showing any interest in sexual expression or exploration.

Omaris Zamora powerfully describes life in a sexualized *and* racialized body:

> The presumption that Black Latina girls are always willing has haunted us for centuries. It is this seduction of the church forced on to our black bodies and subjectivities that led me to believe that as a child and teenager I was always on the wrong side of both biblical and social "law." Because of my blackness there was no such thing as innocence granted to me—hence, I had to pray harder, fast longer, and look for the holy spirit to possess me. We Black children are always guilty. Black Caribbean or Dominican girls, in particular, are thought of as willful: *agenta, voluntariosa, chivirica*. These words in Dominican Spanish resonate with Sara Ahmed's notion of "willful subjects": we, Black Latina girls, are already deemed guilty and deviant—we are too "fresh" for our age. We accept the charge without our consent in a geopolitical landscape that has positioned us with an unacceptable agency and yet always available for others' perusing and consumption—both in the Dominican Republic and in Dominican diaspora communities.[44]

Although Alcántara was not raised in a strict religious household herself and her mother was not allowed to have the body of Christ during Catholic mass due to her divorce, she, like Zamora, received the message that to be anything but virginal was to be impure, and that this responsibility lay entirely on her shoulders as a source of temptation to men who can't help themselves and are never guilty.

Significantly, interwoven in horrifying descriptions of harassment and assault are also Alcántara's efforts, from an early age, to take ownership back of her body. For example, in considering her unsuccessful attempt as a teen to lose her virginity before her move to the United States, she writes, "I think wanting to lose my virginity became about rejecting what I had been told and taking ownership over an intrinsic part of me. Quise controlar la única cosa que me pertenecía: mi cuerpo y mis decisions sobre mi cuerpo. Everything else, like where my body would live, was out of my hands."[45] In her revision of a traditional memoir genre, Alcántara's interspersed poems often joyfully celebrate her agency over these harmful gendered messages and the voice she has developed to dictate her narrative. In an untitled poem that invites you to imagine a reggaetón beat in the background, she introduces herself as "La palabrista/La que se hacía llamar Radical Latina" unwilling to be silenced.[46] Acknowledging the realities of violence against women of color, she writes, "Me prefieren muerta porque mi boca es muy grande pa sus ideas vendidas."[47]

For Alcántara, taking ownership of her body is complicated and it must be done repeatedly and forcefully as she negotiates various spaces. In a gorgeous poem in which Alcántara connects language to an Afro-indigenous matrilineal history of resistance[48] she addresses white men who fetishize her body: "My mama is the OG your white Mami is the original thief."[49] Meanwhile, she is also critical of the harmful gendered messages she received around her body and sexuality within her own Dominican communities. According to Alcántara, "Dominican culture is riddled with these secretos a voces: things that everyone knows are happening, yet no one discusses."[50] What Alcántara points out is sometimes these messages come from what is not said, for example in the ways women are expected to accept catcalling, harassment and rape culture. A similar comment can be made of the silence around the treatment of Afro-Dominicanas, another area she explores in the book.

Alcántara's responses to racism, sexism and other forms of societal control especially within Dominican communities are the contra*dictions* to what is both said and unsaid in *Chula*. The title itself is a metaphor for the complexity of an Afro-Domincana *ausente* and the poetics those identities produce. In her review of the book, Nuyorican-Dominican American poet Peggy Robles-Alvarado, outlines the multilayered meanings of the word *Chula*, which can be as much epithet as compliment.[51] This is of course, Alcántara's exact intention: "The word chula can mean something very beautiful; I think it can also mean something very sexual and very sexy. I also think it can be derogatory. Even the word is a little complicated and I'm okay with that. I want it to be that."[52] Similarly, another term which can be seen as derogatory in some of her Dominican contexts is self-identifying as "Negra," which Alcántara does throughout the text. As the darkest among her mother, father, and sister she has had to navigate the Blackness of her body that is often rejected by her own family. She navigates "pelo malo" and "pelo bueno" categorizations that deem her acceptable but an Afro-Dominican man she is dating unacceptable. Alcántara writes: "He is everything they wish I already wasn't. And everything they don't want us to be."[53] Thus, in *Chula*

Amanda Alcántara embraces the contra*dictions* in her unapologetically Afro-Dominican women's story, one she anchors by opening section 2 with the previously mentioned poetic and photographic intervention.

Of course, that's what she's been doing all along in various ways, putting a journal entry from her sixteen-year-old self who feels like she has "about 6 extra pounds"[54] in conversation with a poem titled, "An ode to my stretch marks,"[55] with a memoir piece in which she describes developing an eating disorder.[56] In "Mulata contemporánea," however, she takes this exercise further by embracing identities she has been told not to embrace and performing these identities until they are internalized. Calling social media likes, "los catcalls modernos,"[57] Alcántara prints a series of photographs of herself relishing her sexuality and sexiness while also celebrating her Blackness. Although her journey is not over—other writing in this section, for example detail self-harm and problematic psychiatrists who only contribute to Latina stereotypes[58] - Alcántara makes clear that exploring these contra*dictions* of El Nié are crucial to her well-being. According to the author, "It's about autonomy of ourselves and our bodies. That's the feeling that I want to convey. It's about owning every part of my story and every part of who I am unapologetically. It's a celebration of my inner child."[59] By ending *Chula* with her first entry in a brand-new diary at age fifteen, she signals the importance of writing as resistance, as a way to control her narrative and take ownership of a body that is racialized, sexualized, and sought to be owned. It is an act of survival and of joy.

AFRO-DOMINICAN EMBODIED WRITING: DISABILITY AND RECLAMATION IN JASMINNE MENDEZ'S NIGHT-BLOOMING JASMIN(N)E

In "(Trance)formations of an AfroLatina: Embodied Archives of Blackness and Womanhood in Transnational Dominican Women's Narratives," Omaris Zamora makes a clear connection between embodied memoir and Afro-Dominican women's narratives. She writes, "I argue that bodies and archival memory are linked to form an embodied archive, or place where memories are kept. The body becomes the place in which experiences are recorded and/or engrained."[60] For Afro-Dominican women who are racialized and sexualized both within and outside their communities, their bodies can be reminders of sexual assault, racism and other traumatic experiences. Amanda Alcántara's embodied writing in *Chula,* then serves as one example of the creation of an alternative archive, one where she is not silenced or disregarded, but one she curates and stars in.

Jasminne Mendez does similar work in *Night-Blooming Jasmin(n)e* although her experience and archive look and feel much different from Alcántara's. Born to immigrant parents and raised in cities without major Dominican communities (for example Clarksville, Tennessee; San Antonio, Texas), Mendez was not able to visit the Dominican Republic until the age of nineteen.[61] Additionally, Mendez's relationship to her body is greatly affected after being diagnosed with an autoimmune disease at twenty-two and struggling with infertility, which she reminds, is also considered a disease.[62] As a result, much of the book details her struggle with both the physical and mental effects of understanding disability as another one of her intersectional identities while also continuing to move forward as a wife, mother, daughter, writer, performer, creator, educator, and more.

This new "layer of complexity" as Mendez describes her experience with illness and identity, is not one that is disconnected from her Afro-Latinidad. Mendez reflects:

> I learned a lot about epigenetics and generational trauma while writing this book. I realized that the diseases that had manifested themselves in my body, had a lot to do with the trauma I had inherited from my ancestors as well as the years of micro-aggressions, racism, and sexism that I faced as a woman of color in America. The journey of writing and organizing this book was my way of trying to make sense of all of that. When did the disease really begin? What triggered it? How did my other identities influence or affect the evolution and management of the disease? I also learned a lot about and personally experienced medical racism and sexism and I wanted to explore that in the book.[63]

Thus, in addition to anecdotes, vignettes, poems, and essays about traditional gender expectations, family dynamics, Dominican identity, immigration, and race which were at the heart of her first collection *Island of Dreams* (2013), in *Night-Blooming Jasmin(n)e,* she shows how these issues are negotiated in a whole new set of contexts such as the medical industry.[64] Through it all, Mendez's archive of life writing rejects a white-dominant literary point of view that already marginalizes Afro-Latinidad and disability while also refusing the silences and expectations of her own community around motherhood and illness. To achieve this, Mendez not only has to make peace with her body and all that it has been through, but also create a new language and genre that accurately captures her experience.

Night-Blooming Jasmin(n)e is divided in five sections, each of which oscillate between prose and poetry in order explore aspects of her identity and experience. The first section "Spanish Jasmin(n)e," establish the importance of her identity as an independent Afro-Latina creative against the pressure she feels as the daughter of immigrants to achieve recognizable markers of success. It is also during this time period that she is first diagnosed with scleroderma and must try to grapple with how her life will change. As with the section shared in the opening of this article, Mendez continues to connect her bodily experience living with illness to her encounters moving through these new medical worlds as a Black woman. Of the many consequences of scleroderma, perhaps one of the most devastating is the way it begins to affect her hands, a main tool of a writer. Yet support groups are often little comfort as her reality as a woman of color is not recognized: "Because I was also usually one of only two women of color in the room, this added to the burden of feeling like an outsider in a place where I was supposed to feel like everyone else."[65] This feeling of not been seen as a three-dimensional person but rather just as a medical specimen creates a great deal of disconnect for Mendez as she describes in the poem "Exam Table": "remind yourself you are human/even if this won't change/the weather or the results."[66] Here, Mendez describes the embodied trauma of having to reconnect with yourself and your body given a new descriptor: disabled.

These issues are compounded further in "Red Jasmin(n)e" in which Mendez explores her relationship to motherhood given that her illnesses make conception not only difficult but extremely risky. It is in this time period that Mendez also suffers a miscarriage. Although she informs us that one in four pregnancies end in miscarriage, the silence around an issue that affects so many women mean that Mendez must grapple with a lack of language for this devastating loss. It also means Mendez must create her own: "There is no word in English or Spanish for a parent who has lost a child. There is no word in English or Spanish for a woman who once was pregnant and suddenly is not. One in four pregnancies end in a miscarriage. We named our child Baby M so we had a name for our grief, a word for our loss" (82). These silences and silencing continue as Mendez journeys into the world of fertility clinics, which she describes as shrouded in obscurity and ostracism. As a woman, and especially as a Latina, she is meant to feel ashamed and at fault. She is taught to stay silent: "We let this silence fill the room and our wombs. We let this silence hold us because our stories were silenced. Silence did not need an explanation. Silence was the sound of sorrow and solace. Our silence was a moment of grace for our grieving bodies."[67] Again, Mendez's writing demonstrates an embodied archive filled with stories often only passed along in whispers and sayings. Giving multiple meanings to the color red, Mendez describes the first time she wore red lipstick after her miscarriage at age twenty-seven due to the message that "Red lipstick is for cualquieras . . . Whores" (99). Like her writing, wearing red lipstick reflects Mendez's evolving relationship with her body as well as the development of a language of grief and empowerment. Mendez writes,

Before twenty-seven, red frightened me. I was afraid of "el qué dirán," of what others would say. Of what Mami would say. Of what everyone would think. But eventually, I realized that if I was strong enough to survive the loss of a child in my womb, then I was woman enough to be dangerous. Woman enough to wear the color of blood and fire without fear and without trepidation.[68]

Although a seemingly small moment, this act of wearing red lipstick reflects a physical manifestation of her healing.

The third section, "Summer Jasmin(n)e" introduces the metaphor of hunger to explore her desires—both said and unsaid—in a way that also continues the development of her own language and archive of her experiences. While in the section's opening poem "Gluttony: Undigested," for example Mendez describes being consumed by medical exams and procedures: "the doctors swallow my face/their eyes like tar seeping/through the cracks of city pavements,"[69] it also concludes with the declaration of her desire: "Survival is not enough."[70] Unfortunately, as the poem "Hunger" describes, at this point Mendez is trapped in a series of "Little *white* lies" including "I feel fine," "I'm not black, I'm Latina," and "I don't want to get pregnant right now."[71] Again, the physical experience colludes with her language. At some points during her illness she loses her languages (especially Spanish) and ability to put together thoughts the way she yearns to, while over the years she also describes becoming fluent in medicine.[72] All of the English medical language affects her fluency in Spanish, and as a result in part of coming to terms with chronic illness, is fighting for her mother tongue. "These languages shaped my memories," Mendez reflects. "I needed my Spanish and my English to remember me, the me I was before."[73]

Although Mendez does accept that she can never go back to life before scleroderma and lupus,[74] part of considering her personal history also includes returning to painful histories of racism and colonialism. In the fourth section "Winter Jasmin(n)e," Mendez describes the loss of 60 percent of the use of her right dominant hand,[75] alongside the genocide enacted upon Haitians by the dictator Rafael Trujillo. As she faces a partial finger amputation, she evokes the violence of lost Haitian lives deemed "too black" and therefore expendable.[76] As a Black disabled woman, daughter of immigrants, of course, Mendez is also treated as expendable whether in still predominantly white literary circles or the medical world where she is reduced to the ailments of her body of which she is not deemed expert. However, as Mendez warns, that does not mean those stories go away: "I got rid of the pain, but its memory still remains."[77]

Jasminne Mendez concludes her powerful collection with a final section "True Jasmin(n)e" composed of pieces all beginning with the letter H—"Hope, (W)Hole, Health, Home, Haima, Hostility, Heridas, Heroine"—through which she describes what it means to fully take ownership of her own body and most importantly, its healing. As Mendez describes, "I didn't want my life or my health to be in anyone else's hands. I was not anyone else's problem to fix. I knew then that my body and spirit weren't broken, just tired. That night, I washed my hair and scrubbed my scalp until I no longer felt any shame. I vowed to find a way to heal myself."[78] For Mendez this journey includes reconnecting to her body via yoga, advocating for herself, taking ownership of her medical choices, and telling her story. In her review of the book, Molly Dooley Appel aptly sums up this journey:

> Mendez both loses and finds herself in the languages of her body—English, Spanish, music, medicine—and in the process, she maps a new territory of how her body speaks itself into being. The beauty of Night-Blooming Jasmin(n)e is in the way it stages a specifically Afro-Latinx feminist resistance to the erasures of Western knowledge, misogyny, and colonialism.[79]

Appel is right. *Night-Blooming Jasmin(n)e* is a map, but it is also a living embodied achieve of an Afro-Dominican woman's survival, resistance, and most importantly, joy.

"I AM THE LIGHT": BEYOND SURVIVAL IN AFRO-DOMINICAN WOMEN'S NARRATIVES

Near the end of *Night-Blooming Jasmin(n)e,* Mendez realizes that only she can heal herself. "I am the Light" she writes.[80] Reflecting on the book, Mendez says, "Much of what this book is about is silence and language. How women (and especially women of color) are silenced, how the language we have been given cannot adequately capture our pain, our experiences, or the trauma our bodies have endured."[81] These words strongly evoke Alcántara's project in *Chula* as well. Facing the multiple modes in which they have been silenced, marginalized, and otherized, Alcántara and Mendez develop their own language and narrative forms to fully and unapologetically tell their stories. These Afro-Dominican women's poetic memoirs powerfully contradict hegemonic narratives both within and outside their communities in ways that center the embodied experiences of Black Latina women.

Although both Amanda Alcántara and Jasminne Mendez invoke the language of survival, their ultimate resistance as Afro-Dominicanas in the diaspora is their journey toward joy. Whether it is in the sexy selfies or rhythmic reggaetón-infused poems of Alcántara's *Chula,* or Jasminne Mendez's realization that she is the only light her flower needs to blossom, for both these women, survival is not enough. True healing must include the immense pleasure of accepting all the aspects of their identities and the bodies that have housed them. And while they're stories are unique, their books chart a road map of how to create a work that fits one's personal history, especially if that work needs to break artificial boundaries of genre and language not made with women of color in mind. As Alcántara imagines her reader: "I hope that they can identify with it, but parts of it I hope that they don't identify with. I want them to know that no matter how complicated their story is they can also heal. All of our healing journeys are very different and to embrace their individuality. Whatever else they get from the book, please do. I want them to be badasses, too."[82] As such, these poetic memoirs act as personal archives that celebrate their journeys, while also contributing to a growing body of poetics of Afro-dominicanidad ausente written by women. And for all those who may never have felt seen, perhaps Alcántara and Mendez will inspire them to curate and write their own archive of Afro-Dominican womanhood too.

BIBLIOGRAPHY

Alcántara, Amanda. 2019. *Chula.* Amanda Alcántara.

Anzaldúa, Gloria. 2007. *Borderlands/La Frontera: The New Mestiza.* San Francisco: Aunt Lute Books.

Anzaldúa, Gloria, and Cherríe Moraga, eds. 1981. *This Bridge Called My Back.* Watertown: Persephone Press.

Appel, Molly Dooley. 2019. "Jasminne Méndez, Night-Blooming Jasmin(n)e: Personal Essays and Poetry." *Chiricú Journal* 4, no. 1 (Fall): 218–19.

Báez, Josefina. 2018. "Inner Dance. Outer Joy. Autology. A Route." In *Theatre and Cartographies of Power: Repositioning the Latina/o Americas,* edited by Analola Santana and Jimmy A. Noriega, 184–86. Carbondale: Southern Illinois University Press.

Candelario. Ginetta E. B. 2007. *Black Behind the Ears: Dominican Racial Identity from Museums to Beauty Shops.* Durham, NC: Duke University Press.

Cantú, Norma E. 2013. "Memoir, Autobiography, Testimonio." In *The Routledge Companion to Latino/a Literature,* edited by Suzanne Bost, and Frances R. Aparicio, 310–22. New York: Routledge.

Castillo-Garsow, Melissa, ed. 2017. *¡Manteca!: An Anthology of Afro-Latin@ Poets.* Houston: Arte Público Press.

Chetty, Raj, and Amaury Rodríguez. 2015. "Introduction: The Challenge and Promise of Dominican Black Studies." *The Black Scholar* 45, no. 2 (Spring): 1–9.

Contreras Schwartz, Leslie. 2019. "Jasminne Mendez In Conversation With Leslie Contreras Schwartz." *American Microreviews & Interviews,* 45 (September). http://www.americanmicroreviews.com/jasminne-mendez-interview.

DeCosta-Willis, Miriam, ed. 2003. *Daughters of the Diaspora: Afro-Hispanic Writers.* Kingston: Ian Randle Publishers.

Fernández, Stacy. 2019. "Amanda Alcántara Wanted to Tell an Untraditional Dominican Story, So She Decided to Self-Publish." *Remezcla,* March 21, 2019. https://remezcla.com/features/culture/amanda-alcantara-chula/.

Figueroa-Vásquez, Yomaira C. 2020. *Decolonizing Diasporas: Radical Mappings of Afro-Atlantic Literature.* Evanston: Northwestern University Press.

García-Peña, Lorgia. 2016. *The Borders of Dominicanidad: Race, Nation and Archives of Contradiction.* Durham: Duke University Press.

———. 2015. "Translating Blackness: Dominicans Negotiating Race and Belonging." *The Black Scholar* 45, no. 2 (Spring): 10–20.

Jiménez Román, Miriam, and Juan Flores, eds. 2010. *The Afro-Latin@ Reader: History and Culture in the United States.* Durham, NC: Duke University Press.

Lara, Ana-Maurine. 2012. "Bodies and Memories: Afro-Latina Identities in Motion." In *Woman Warriors of the Afro-Latina Diaspora,* edited by Marta Moreno Vega, Marianieves Alba and Yvette Modestin. Houston: Arte Público Press.

Martinez, Erika. 2016. *Daring to Write: Contemporary Narratives by Dominican Women.* Athens: University of Georgia Press.

Martinez, Janel. 2019. "Amanda Alcántara Speaks for Dominican Women with 'Chula.'" *HipLatina,* March 25, 2019. https://hiplatina.com/chula-amanda -alcantara/.

Mendez, Jasminne. 2013. *Island of Dreams.* Moorpark: Floricanto Press.

———. 2018. *Night-Blooming Jasmin(n)e: Personal Essays and Poetry.* Houston: Arte Público Press.

———. Email Interview. Aug. 29, 2021.

Morena Vega, Marta, Marianieves Alba, and Yvette Modestin, eds. 2012. *Woman Warriors of the Afro-Latina Diaspora.* Houston: Arte Público Press.

Mota, Jennifer. 2019. "How Amanda Alcántára's Intimate Journal of Poems and Stories, Chula, Embraces Caribeñx Culture." *People en Español,* May 1, 2019. https://esus.noticias.yahoo.com/amanda-alcant-ra-intimate-journal-160256577 .html.

Peña, Daniel. 2018. "Inking Well: An Interview With Jasminne Mendez." *Ploughshares,* April 2, 2018. https://blog.pshares.org/inking-well-an-interview -with-jasminne-mendez/.

Ramirez, Dixa. 2018. *Colonial Phantoms: Belonging and Refusal in the Dominican Americas from the 19th Century to the Present.* New York: New York University Press.

Ricourt, Milagros. 2016. *The Dominican Racial Imaginary.* New Brunswick: Rutgers University Press.

Rivera-Rideau, Petra R., Jennifer A. Jones, and Tianna Paschel, eds. 2016. *Afro-Latin@s in Movement: Critical Approaches to Blackness and Transnationalism in the Americas.* New York: Palgrave Macmillan.

Robles-Alvarado, Peggy. 2019. "Entre Lenguas Y Vidas: Book Review Of Chula By Amanda Alcántara." *Queen Mob's Teahouse,* Oct. 18, 2019. https://queenmobs .com/2019/10/entre-lenguas-y-vidas-book-review-of-chula-by-amanda-alcantara/.

Spry, Tami. 2001. "Performing Autoethnography: An Embodied Methodological Praxis." *Qualitative Inquiry* 7, no. 6 (December): 706–32.

Zamora, Omaris Z. 2020. "Black Latina Girlhood Poetics of the Body: Church, Sexuality and Dispossession." *Post 45,* Jan. 21, 2020. https://post45.org/2020/01/black-latina-girlhood-poetics-of-the-body-church-sexuality-and-dispossession/.

———. 2016. "(Trance)formations of an AfroLatina: Embodied Archives of Blackness and Womanhood in Transnational Dominican Women's Narratives." PhD diss., University of Texas at Austin.

NOTES

1. Jasminne Mendez, *Night-Blooming Jasmin(n)e: Personal Essays and Poetry* (Houston: Arte Público Press, 2018), 186.

2. Ibid., 53.

3. Amanda Alcántara, *Chula* (Amanda Alcántara, 2019): 67.

4. Yomaira C Figueroa-Vásquez, *Decolonizing Diasporas: Radical Mappings of Afro-Atlantic Literature* (Evanston: Northwestern University Press, 2020), 5.

5. Ibid.

6. Lorgia, García-Peña, *The Borders of Dominicanidad: Race, Nation and Archives of Contradiction* (Durham: Duke University Press, 2016), 5.

7. Omaris Zamora, "(Trance)formations of an AfroLatina: Embodied Archives of Blackness and Womanhood in Transnational Dominican Women's Narratives" (PhD diss., University of Texas at Austin, 2016), vi.

8. In addition to Figueora-Vásquez, García-Peña, and Zamora, I am of course indebted to Miriam Jiménez Román who alongside Juan Flores are foundational to the field through their 2007 *The Afro-Latin@ Reader* which featured a section specifically dedicated to Afro-Latinas. Other significant scholarship that specifically address the Afro-Latina experience include Petra R. Rivera-Rideau, Jennifer A. Jones and Tianna Paschel's edited volume *Afro-Latin@s in Movement: Critical Approaches to Blackness and Transnationalism in the Americas* (2016); and Ginetta E. B. Candelario's *Black Behind the Ears: Dominican Racial Identity from Museums to Beauty Shop* (2007). Likewise, I am grateful for literary volumes such as Miriam DeCosta-Willis, eds., *Daughters of the Diaspora: Afro-Hispanic Writers* (2003); Marta Morena Vega, Marinieves Alba, and Yevette Modestin's *Woman Warriors of the Afro-Latina Diaspora* (2012); and the women I was able to publish in the volume I edited, *¡Manteca!: An Anthology of Afro-Latin@ Poets* (2017).

9. Dixa Ramirez, *Colonial Phantoms: Belonging and Refusal in the Dominican Americas from the 19th Century to the Present* (New York: New York University Press, 2018), 5.

10. Ibid., 38.

11. Lorgia García-Peña, "Translating Blackness: Dominicans Negotiating Race and Belonging," *The Black Scholar* 45, no. 2 (Spring 2016): 17–18. According to García-Peña, "Thus, confronted with a US racialization that is very much linked to the open wound of slavery and Jim Crow as foundational experiences of the nation, US diasporic Dominicans find that blackness provides a language for confronting their new place in their host nation while interpellating the historical oppression back

home. It is not then that Dominicans 'find out they are black' when they migrate to the United States, as Moya Pons suggested, but rather, that in the United States Dominicans find a political language from which to articulate their own experience of racialization, oppression, disenfranchisement, and silencing—a process that allows them to build alliances with other oppressed communities around the world."

12. See Milagros Ricourt, *The Dominican Racial Imaginary* (New Brunswick: Rutgers University Press, 2016).

13. Raj Chetty and Amaury Rodríguez, "Introduction: The Challenge and Promise of Dominican Black Studies," *The Black Scholar* 45, no. 2 (Spring 2015): 7.

14. García-Peña, "Translating Blackness," 11.

15. García-Peña, *The Borders of Dominicanidad, 2.*

16. Ibid., 4.

17. Ibid.

18. Zamora, "(Trance)formations of an AfroLatina," 23.

19. Ibid., 54.

20. Ibid., vii.

21. Ibid., 41.

22. Norma E. Cantú, "Memoir, Autobiography, Testimonio," in *The Routledge Companion to Latino/a Literature*, ed. Suzanne Bost, and Frances R. Aparicio (New York: Routledge, 2013), 312.

23. Jasminne Mendez, Email Interview, Aug. 29, 2021.

24. Zamora, "(Trance)formations of an AfroLatina," 8.

25. Ibid., 18.

26. Ibid., 54.

27. Marta Morena Vega, Marianieves Alba and Yvette Modestin, eds., *Woman Warriors of the Afro-Latina Diaspora* (Houston: Arte Público Press, 2012), ix.

28. Ana-Maurine Lara, "Bodies and Memories: Afro-Latina Identities in Motion," in *Woman Warriors of the Afro-Latina Diaspora,* eds. Marta Moreno Vega, Marianieves Alba and Yvette Modestin (Houston: Arte Público Press, 2012), 30.

29. Josefina Báez, "Inner Dance. Outer Joy. Autology. A Route," in *Theatre and Cartographies of Power: Repositioning the Latina/o Americas, eds. Analola Santana and Jimmy A. Noriega (Carbondale: Southern Illinois University Press, 2018), 184.*

30. Ibid., 185.

31. Tami Spry (2001) defines autoethnography as "a self-narrative that critiques the situatedness of self with others in social contexts. Autoethnography is both a method and a text of diverse interdisciplinary praxes" (706).

32. Alcántara, *Chula,* 8.

33. García-Peña (2016) provides the history of the term: "The term 'Dominicanyork' was originally coined in the early 1970s by young Dominican men who played sports on US teams, particularly basketball. However, in the early 1980s, following a transnational media campaign that portrayed Dominicans living in the United States as drug dealers and criminals, Dominicanyork became synonymous with undesirable, lower-class, criminal, sellout and corrupt. Lately, many diasporic artists have begun to reappropriate the term" (172).

34. García-Peña, *Borders of Dominicanidad,* 4.

35. Ibid., 173.

36. Ibid.

37. Alcántara writes, "En un mundo donde me dicen que soy marginal, aquí recuerdo que mi centro so yo" (9).

38. Stacy Fernández, "Amanda Alcántara Wanted to Tell an Untraditional Dominican Story, So She Decided to Self-Publish," *Remezcla,* March 21, 2019, https://remezcla.com/features/culture/amanda-alcantara-chula/.

39. Janel Martinez, "Amanda Alcántara Speaks for Dominican Women with 'Chula,'" *HipLatina,* March 25, 2019, https://hiplatina.com/chula-amanda-alcantara/.

40. Jennifer Mota, "How Amanda Alcantára's Intimate Journal of Poems and Stories, Chula, Embraces Caribeñx Culture," *People en Español,* May 1, 2019. https://esus.noticias.yahoo.com/amanda-alcant-ra-intimate-journal-160256577.html

41. Alcántara, *Chula, 25.*

42. Ibid., 47.

43. Ibid., 65.

44. Omaris Zamora, "Black Latina Girlhood Poetics of the Body: Church, Sexuality and Dispossession," *Post 45*, Jan. 21, 2020, https://post45.org/2020/01/black-latina-girlhood-poetics-of-the-body-church-sexuality-and-dispossession/.

45. Alcántara, *Chula,* 39.

46. Ibid., 17.

47. Ibid.

48. She opens with, "My Spanish is an Afroindigenous creolized Cibaeo song which my buelita sang as if it was her favorite bolero" (27).

49. Alcántara, *Chula,* 28.

50. Ibid., 48.

51. Peggy Robles-Alvarado, "Entre Lenguas Y Vidas: Book Review Of Chula By Amanda Alcántara," *Queen Mob's Teahouse,* Oct. 18, 2019, https://queenmobs.com/2019/10/entre-lenguas-y-vidas-book-review-of-chula-by-amanda-alcantara/.

52. Martinez, "Amanda Alcántara Speaks."

53. Alcántara, *Chula, 55.*

54. Ibid., 30.

55. Ibid., 31.

56. Ibid., 49.

57. Ibid., 76.

58. Alcántara describes working with a psychiatrist who gives her a medication and reduces her sex drive. The psychiatrist responds, "You're a Latina, so sexy, maybe it's good that it goes down from 95% to like 85" (86).

59. Martinez, "Amanda Alcántara Speaks."

60. Zamora, ""(Trance)formations of an AfroLatina,"18.

61. Jasminne Mendez, *Island of Dreams* (Moorpark: Floricanto Press, 2013), 10, 94.

62. Leslie Contreras Schwartz, "Jasminne Mendez in Conversation with Leslie Contreras Schwartz," *American Microreviews & Interviews,* 45 (September 2019), http://www.americanmicroreviews.com/jasminne-mendez-interview.

63. Ibid.

64. Notably, although Mendez describes beginning *Island of Dreams* and *Night-Blooming Jasmin(n)e* at the same time, they form a sort of companion in publication. According to Mendez, "I do see *Night-Blooming* in some ways has a sequel to *Island of Dreams*. I actually started writing both of those at the same time and they were at one point meant to be one big memoir. But then I realized that I needed to write *Island of Dreams* before I could actually tackle *Night-Blooming* in its totality. I always say that it took me 10 years to write *Night-Blooming* because it did. I had conceived of that book when I was first diagnosed (2007, published in 2018) but I wasn't ready to write it fully because it didn't have an ending and I didn't know where my disease was going or would take me so I just wrote until enough had happened to make it a book with an ending. And with the third memoir that I have coming out in 2022 (another YA memoir) I would say is the prequel to *Island of Dreams* and it was originally supposed to be a part of *Night-Blooming Jasmin(n)e* but was removed in revisions (email interview, Aug. 29, 2021).

65. Mendez, *Night-Blooming Jasmin(n)e,* 71.

66. Ibid., 13.

67. Ibid., 106.

68. Ibid., 99.

69. Ibid., 109.

70. Ibid.

71. Ibid., 110.

72. Daniel Peña, "Inking Well: An Interview With Jasminne Mendez," *Ploughshares,* April 2, 2018, https://blog.pshares.org/inking-well-an-interview-with-jasminne-mendez/.

73. Mendez, *Night-Blooming Jasmin(n)e,* 150.

74. In an interview with Leslie Contreras Schwartz, Mendez reflects, "My chronic illness isn't just about me and grieving the loss of who I was and who I will never be, it's also about my family and how they grieved the loss of the Jasminne they once knew. It took me a long time to finally understand that we were all grieving that loss and that we all had to do it in our time and in our own ways.

75. Mendez, *Night-Blooming Jasmin(n)e,* 168.

76. Ibid., 157.

77. Ibid., 159.

78. Ibid., 182.

79. Molly Dooley Appel, "Jasminne Méndez, Night-Blooming Jasmin(n)e: Personal Essays and Poetry," *Chiricú Journal* 4, no. 1 (Fall 2019): 219.

80. Mendez, *Night-Blooming Jasmin(n)e,* 184.

81. Contreras Schwartz, "Jasminne Mendez in Conversation."

82. Martinez, "Amanda Alcántara Speaks."

Chapter 11

Papi's Bridge

Toward a New Diasporic Dominican Identity in Clap When You Land

Keturah Nichols

On November 12, 2001, two months and one day after the September 11th attacks, American Airlines Flight 587 bound for Santo Domingo took off at 09:16 in the morning. Minutes later it crashed in Belle Harbor, Queens, New York, killing all 260 people on the flight as well as five people on the ground. This is the second-deadliest aviation accident in US history; however, it seems to have fallen from both the collective and cultural memory of the country. Most of the passengers on the flight were of Dominican descent and the event had a substantial impact on the Dominican and Dominican American communities. In light of the harsh realities of US life after 9/11, I contend that this disaster has fallen out of the wider US cultural and collective memory because these passengers were not viewed as American, or American enough, to be collectively grieved. Mourning the dead, who came from a migrant community of color, did not serve the anti-terror political agenda of the time.

Clap When You Land (2020), a novel in verse by Afro-Dominican American poet Elizabeth Acevedo, reminds readers of this event. It is the story of two half sisters, Camino and Yahaira Rios, who connect following a plane crash that results in their father's death. They discover that he had been traveling back and forth between New York City and the Dominican Republic to juggle his two secret families and his two daughters. Upon learning of each other's existence, they are drawn into each other's lives where they uncover layer upon layer of secrets and gain a deeper understanding of both their father's past and their connection to each other. Acevedo switches between the perspectives of the two girls, allowing the reader an intimate view of each girl's innermost thoughts, their relationships with their father, their respective environments, and the dreams each one hopes to achieve. The girls' Papi is at the center of the story, and although absent, the reader feels his presence. As the girls navigate their loss from their respective locations, they deal with the related issues of grief, mourning, and inheritance. Considering the complicated familial relations and the international context of their stories, the novel also addresses themes of sisterhood, identity, community, and diaspora.

In the following analysis, I exemplify ways Dominicans throughout the diaspora shape narratives of survival, memory, and visibility in a world dominated by anti-Blackness. I argue that by decentering patriarchy and the male voice, the main characters Camino and Yahaira enact a gendered reconciliation of Dominican diasporic identity. Through the reconstruction of their father's identity, they navigate their own racialization and invisibility to write themselves and the American Airlines Flight 587 tragedy into a transnational diasporic narrative. I mobilize a collective memory framework to create an archival space for remembering racialized bodies in the wake of disaster and beyond that carve out space for transnational citizens in a multicultural republic. This study bases itself on selective sympathy in disaster remembrance and how notions of citizenship and national identity affect which events deserve recognition.

First, I examine what the greater American public's lack of remembrance and sympathy demonstrates about the limited citizenship held by passengers on AA Flight 587 and concurrently the Dominican American community left to grieve them. Then, I interrogate alternative modes of mourning and memorialization as they appear within the context of the novel. Finally, I deconstruct the patriarchal order within the text and the invisible borders of national identity for diasporic citizens that allow for a new transnational Dominican consciousness.

American Airlines Flight 587 has been largely overlooked and understudied outside of the areas of mechanics, engineering, and flight techniques. My analysis focuses on this tragedy and its relative absence from archives. The study concentrates on ways Black Dominicans mobilize and memorialize themselves in a society that doesn't prioritize them. By narrativizing the events Acevedo makes space and place for this accident, the subsequent retelling draws attention to the question of whose lives matter. It tests the limits of American identity where it meets the Dominican diaspora. Black history and Black tragedies are often viewed as separate from national and Western history.[1] Shining light on these stories brings them to a wider public outside of the community. It also delves into the racial calculus used to prioritize some tragedies over others. It questions which lives or deaths garner attention and invite collective mourning outside of the affected communities.

Acevedo's traumatic account questions how an accident of this proportion would have been remembered if it hadn't immediately followed 9/11. How does social media affect our looking back on the past? In today's society where Instagram, Facebook, and Twitter are mobilized as sites of memory and action by groups like BLM, these sites combat dominant narratives and make space for invisibilized tragedies by showing, "how the shaping and reshaping of collective memory is political—and part of cultural history."[2] Counter memorials on social networking sites dialogue with major media's coverage of events and affect both, "our collective and cultural identities."[3] Throughout this tragic tale, Acevedo shows the key role family and community play in reconstructing scenes from the past and imagining new futures. This chapter extends prior collective and media memory studies by focusing on social media as a site of memory and as a living archive. It highlights how these platforms extend known areas of collective memory outside of the family, local community, and religious institution and expand exponentially over the web. It further goes into how this shapes our visions of the lost and how, for members of communities like that of the Dominican diaspora, reciprocal interchange is central to remembrance.

Scholars of Dominican history and identity agree on the importance of the international exchange of culture between Dominicans on the mainland and abroad. Transnationalism and diaspora can be used interchangeably to navigate the different positionalities inhabited by Dominican subjects in different places. Death complicates this by forcing an interrogation of race, gender, and nationality in mediatized grieving and both public and private memorialization. This chapter enters the discussion of Black mourning and memorialization, Dominicanidad, citizenship, and transnational identities. I dialogue with Christina Sharpe (2016) on Black death as well as Silvio Torres Saillant (2010) and Lorgia Garcia Peña (2016) on Dominicanidad and citizenship. My text builds on Camilla Stevens's (2017) intervention on Dominican identity and performance by analyzing the transnational identities created within the Acevedo text and how the poetic form allows questions of citizenship and identity to be negotiated. I contribute to this body of scholarship by focusing on the gendered, generational exchange that produces a type of citizenship between the spaces, neither here nor there, but in both places at once.

How did this incident affect Dominican memorialization at home and abroad? Traditional mourning and commemoration occur in funerary practices, sites of memorialization, and more recently in online memorials. These rites are culturally based and reflect characteristics of the person or persons who have passed as well as that of the communities mourning them. National tragedies, be they disasters, accidents, or acts of war, are marked, and remembered culturally through holidays and memorials. In the case of AA Flight 587, while the community grieved, the rest of the world moved on. Five years after the accident a memorial was dedicated in Belle Harbor and a year later many of the unidentified human remains were entombed in four mausoleum crypts at the site. Each year a memorial service is held at this monument, but more widely the discussion of this event has fizzled out.

Acevedo employs young adult fiction to reflect on her community's cultural memory surrounding this great loss of life from an underrepresented viewpoint. Revisiting the crash highlights the limited coverage the story received and its disappearance from public memory. Acevedo's research revealed secrets that came to light in the wake of this tragedy and this novel in verse captures a part of this reality. She situates the reader in the communities facing this loss, Dominicans on the island and in the diaspora, and in the minds of two young girls learning to deal with it, the realities of their situations, and the historical discourses that produce these outcomes. Human is understood through a white masculine lens, Afro-Latinx adolescence is a positionality where "Blackness disrupts the figure of the child."[4]

Her novel prompted a revisiting and re-remembering of the past for many, but what was the catalyst for collective amnesia of such a huge loss? An American Airlines memorandum containing details about those lost in this accident reveals that of the 260 passengers and crew members 176 had US nationality. Sixty-eight people were from the Dominican Republic and the remaining seven passengers were from other countries. While 65 percent of the passengers were born in the United States or held US citizenship 90 percent of the passengers were of Dominican descent.[5] Would this dual ethnic and national allegiance or foreign citizenship cause the government and media to give less attention to this disaster? In situations such as these, it falls to the community and loved ones to create space for remembering those lost. This tragedy came in the wake of another, and the memory of this event was relegated to that space. In the aftermath of 9/11, a flight with 90 percent Dominican passengers was not given the same level of care and attention as the former tragedy. Following these terror attacks rhetorical and discursive strategies were employed by the state and disseminated through media to mark certain bodies as American or other. The category of other was subdivided into racialized and gendered groupings focusing on those deemed as warranting surveillance and detainment, specifically those bodies marked as terrorists. Additionally, those who were viewed as a threat to conservative American values were targeted, namely the LGBTQ community. A flight that was largely composed of migrants and their descendants and that was not targeted by extremist violence fell outside of the scope of the national project.[6] In both cases, the book, and the actual incident, the victims of these disasters were treated unequally. Echoing the words of Fatou Diama "if they were Whites, the whole Earth should be shaking now. Instead, it's Black and Arabs who are dying and their lives are cheaper."[7] The lives lost on that flight were treated as if they mattered less. Race and ethnicity undoubtedly played a role in the reception of these events. At a time when the country was uniting as one, Black and Brown bodies were continuously otherized and excluded. The way the system is organized around white supremacy doesn't see the importance of racialized lives that exist in the wake.

Citizenship can be understood as membership and participation in a demarcated political and geographic state. Although it gives this type of status, "it further separates as Mary K. Bloodsworth-Lugo and Carmen R. Lugo-Lugo describe."[8] Varying classes of citizenship form a hierarchical system wherein the differential status of different subjects is reflected in unequal media treatment. Not all traumas or instances of death are viewed as newsworthy and when certain cases are reported they often do not receive the same treatment and care, as Butler observes in her concept of grievable and ungrievable lives. In *Frames of War: When Is Life Grievable?* (2016), she asserts that "consideration for the differential distribution of precariousness and grievability constitutes an alternative to those models of multiculturalism that presuppose the nation-state as the exclusive frame of reference."[9] This challenge to recognizing the equality of human life accounts for the necropolitical policies of the state that reify exclusionary discourses of nation and man. These deaths are described by Morse as those, "whose deaths are acknowledged and treated as morally flawed and those whose deaths make no ethical solicitation."[10] Not covering deaths and glossing over them sends a message that these lives are viewed as less desirable, less important, and outside of the realm of citizen/human that deserves public mourning. When facing the loss of a loved one under these circumstances, collective reconstructions are often a recourse that allows affected members of marginalized groups to reenvision and remember moments in time and traits of that individual. Both Camino's and Yahaira's remembrances of their father will join with those of others who knew him to create a fuller picture of him. They recall both the good and the bad, his lies and deceit, but also his love. Papi was a soul divided; neither daughter got to know him as a whole man. They experienced the work in progress that was a life spent trying to bridge the divide across the ocean.

Employing a collective memory framework built upon a series of flashbacks it is possible to reconstruct Papi's identity in his absence. He is a major character due to and perhaps despite the fact he dies at the outset of the story. His daughters' memories and impressions of him allow the reader to paint a mental picture of him and to better understand him. The author includes poems from each girl's perspective, providing a detailed character sketch. Through these homages to their father, it is possible to recreate parts of his identity. Though both girls have unique voices, the two voices begin to meld in these descriptions. The girls characterize their father in what could be classified as response poetry. Both poems start with the same idea and similar phrasing. They seemingly respond to one another maintaining the same rhythm, rhyme scheme, and form; together they sketch a fuller image of Papi. Yahaira begins "All I want / Is Papi back" while Camino says, "All I want / Is my father back."[11] Both verses evoke a sense of nostalgia; he will never be with them again. In this case, as Butler states, "a full "recovery" of Papi "is impossible, one for whom the irrecoverable becomes, paradoxically, the condition of a new political agency."[12] Papi's death marks a complete loss; it is impossible to return to a time and place where he is still alive. The pain of his death is compounded by the violence surrounding it. The lives lost have been rendered anonymous, commodified, and tagged with a commensurate amount of money. Though this violence harms, it also produces new possibilities for his daughters. The new agency previously mentioned is not Papi's but rather part of the legacy he leaves to his two daughters. It is after his death that the girls really come into their own by retracing his route and reconnecting these two halves of diaspora and family. It is due to his loss that the girls learn of each other and can form their own relationship with each other and in relation to his memory. When they shift their focus from his lies and deceit to the possibilities this new kinship tie produces for them, they succeed in drawing the two sides of his life and ultimately island and diaspora closer together.

In these two poems, they humanize the memories they hold of him. They go on to describe his "booming laugh."[13] Both girls mention his "angry bellow."[14] Yahaira remembers his "rapid Spanish" and Camino is drawn to his "mixed up English."[15] His vocalizations are depicted as sonorous, and he dominates his first language in a different way than his second. They talk about "his eyes that misted over" when he prayed or danced in Camino's experience or when he listened to his favorite songs in Yahaira's.[16] While they noted several of their father's traits and things he loved, they also recall how he spread himself so thinly across the Atlantic. He left pieces of himself in both places, from the "República Dominicana"[17] to "New York City."[18] Papi embodies diasporic living and nostalgic looking back. He is constantly caught in the in-between, longing for home in the motherland while creating a new home in his chosen country. The back-and-forth in the poems reflects his continuous journeys between the two nations. Like Papi, it symbolizes and incomplete crossing and a yet to be reconciled diasporic identity.

Each of the intertwined poems captures a shared desire to have their father back alive, well, and whole. They end by highlighting this impossibility with the words, "But I can't bundle" up all the "pieces of him" he has left scattered about, "To make anything, anyone/resembling him."[19] They acknowledge that they can't rebuild him from what is left behind. The image created in the reader's imaginary approximates who he truly was but could never stand in for the whole. Papi is trapped in between while his daughters stand for the Dominican Republic and the diaspora. They share more than they think: ancestry, culture, this loss, the subsequent erasure, and finally the remembrance and storytelling that keeps this incident from being forgotten. Through the girls' memories and rapprochement, they can form an affective and embodied bridge across the ocean. They inherit his positionality in the in-between, a condition they embody and employ to expose "citizenship" for its limitations. Their positionalities as racialized double diasporic women negotiating their identities within what Kimberlé Crenshaw describes as "intersecting patterns of racism and sexism provide them a unique perspective to problematize our understanding of community and belonging."[20] Full citizenship is predicated on sociohistorical discourses that multiply marginalize and deny humanity to Black peoples still treated as fungible.

In writing their father into memory, they are engaging in conversation with one another without ever having officially met each other. Due to the transnational exchange facilitated by their father on his travels, they are both shaping him and being shaped by these exchanges. Reciprocal give-and-take produces commonalities between two girls who have never met each other but share an ancestral and diasporic connection that is shaped by transnational exchange. They are products of this back-and-forth, as Camilla Stevens affirms in *Aquí and Alla* "The households, social webs, economic ventures, political activities, and cultural tastes of Dominicans both aquí and allá link and mutually constitute an influence one another."[21] Outside of theater and performance, diaspora affects both mainland and overseas communities and their negotiations of identities. In his journeys back-and-forth Papi imparts little cultural elements to each daughter. He gives them a bit of each nation and a bit of himself.

He was notably Afro-Dominican; he was their mirror; his features can be seen in both of their faces. He also holds great importance for his family. He was "Papi, the big hot boiling sun/we all looked to for light."[22] He isn't only central to the story but also at the center of their lives. He held their communities together while maintaining their distance, and he binds Yahaira and Camino in bonds of kinship.

MEMORIALIZATION SITES

In her book *In the Wake: On Blackness and Being* (2016) Christina Sharpe asks "What does it mean to defend the dead? To tend to the Black dead and dying: to tend to the Black person, to Black people, always living in the push toward our death?"[23] The two physical rites held for Papi exemplify care for the dead. The family holds a wake for him in New York as well as a ceremony for him in Sosúa. The communities practice care in the memorials left for him, and in the remembrances, readers witness throughout the entire tale.

Writing this book is another way of defending and tending to those people whose lives were lost in this transnational tragedy. Acevedo remembers and memorializes the dead through her writing. Like the ceremonial performances in the book, it helps them along their way while also caring for those who have been left behind.

Physical memorials are a traditional way of remembering lost loved ones. One is erected in Yano's honor outside of his billiards bar in NYC. It is composed of small mementos and images in homage to his memory. Acevedo describes it:

> there's a blown-up picture
> of Papi smiling,
> holding a glass (of what I imagine / is whiskey) out to the camera.[24]

She pays particular attention to the items other mourners have left behind. She mentions the "Flower wreaths, so many flowers" in addition to

> A lottery ticket,
> a bottle of shoeshine polish,
> a small Dominican flag,
> a baseball card of Robinson Canó,
> a little figurine of a man dressed in red and black.[25]

Each item that was left behind shows a connection to Papi and his life. They highlight different aspects of this identity. Some of the items are easily decipherable and expected such as the flowers and the Dominican flag. Others like the figurine can only be understood by people with connections to syncretic African spirituality.

Religion provides a lens into Papi's double life and the two different roles he played in each setting. His varying religious practices make cracks in his story but ultimately serve to paint a fuller picture of him. Camino and Tia are followers of Afro-Caribbean spirituality. They have an altar in their home and perform ceremonies and rituals for the horasanta. The saints are very present in their lives, but Yahaira has no frame of reference for this. She calls the religious practice "voodoo" and observes the altar as an outsider.[26] She has no memory of her father in relation to this faith.

In contrast, Camino remembers her father as a faithful man who carried religious beads with him while he was on the island. Yahaira struggles to reconcile what she knows of her father with the reality of his secret lives. She says:

> I can't imagine my father kneeling
> or praying at the foot of this altar. & yet,

> I think about the silver coin he always carried in his pocket
> & how its twin sits on the altar here.[27]

That silver coin reveals his faith; it is a symbol of a specific Santo, or Misterio, who is later confirmed through Yahaira's own recollections:

> I think about how he would always say something
> About San Anthony, & isn't that the statue by the door?
> My father hid this part of himself tight inside his pockets,
> But it still slipped through the stitching I just never paid
> Attention.[28]

The offerings left on the altar paired with the placement of the statue and the mention of Saint Anthony suggest that the statue by the door is Eleguá/Papa Legba. In Santeria, he is the orisha of "roads, crossroads, and thresholds" and is also frequently syncretized with Saint Anthony of Padua.[29] Followers of 21 Divisions know him as being syncretized with Saint Anthony; he is a gatekeeper; he opens doors and highlights paths.[30] Camino's name is Spanish for path; she draws the link between the two. Their father kept his two worlds completely apart, but a single coin slipped through and links his two lives. Though he doesn't practice his religion in New York, he keeps it close to his body. He may be physically away from his homeland, but he carries a piece of it with him constantly.

Similarly to how the items left at Papi's memorials evidence the different way people are grieving him offline; there is an online outpouring of grief as well. Collective grieving on social networking sites is another unmediated archive of stories surrounding the deceased. People's posts can affect how the person who has passed is perceived, but also mark their relation to said person and more broadly the degrees of separation between various people in their lives. The intersection between online and offline memorialization is crucial in this novel. Both sites of remembrance serve to redress the lack of care given by wider American society, media, and government. In the context of the story, social networking sites serve to connect Yano's two daughters, but the physical burial of his body is what draws them together in the flesh. Camino encounters Yahaira's Facebook profile when she notices a profile picture marking a person in mourning. It is due to the social outpouring of love and remembrance in posts on her half sister's wall that she is finally able to ascertain that she has found the right person. She says,

> I am about to quit when I see a profile
> but the picture is only a black box, & the date
> my father died.
> Although the profile is private,

> I can see some other posts, including condolence messages.
> "Tio Yano was a great man. He's in heaven now, RIP,"
> a boy named Wilson has written.
> "I will always miss Pops,"
> writes a girl named Andrea.[31]

Although Yahaira has curated her profile and maintains a certain level of privacy regarding her own posts, other people's posts about her father are visible and allow people outside of her communal network to interact and engage with this online memorialization. Camino chooses to privately message Yahaira but ensures her own connection to their father will be visible. She

> press[es] the message button.
> I write a quick sentence & press Send before I can stop myself.
> There is no way she can't know who I am once she sees it."[32]

Camino consciously frames how she wants both the message and herself to be received. She wants her half sister to know and acknowledge who she is and their connection. She ensures that she will be recognized as her father's daughter through her profile picture. She

> isn't alone in the photo;
> she is in a red bathing suit, my father's arm
> thrown around her shoulders
> as they laugh in the sunlight.[33]

This photo can be viewed "as a method of communicating attendance and presence, not just to the family of the deceased, but to one's wider social network."[34] Camino is signaling presence and relationship, not only for her sister but for all who see. She employs social media to reinsert herself into the narrative.

She correctly says, "I deserve to know & be known."[35] She uses her agency to enter into her sister's life. She claims space for her own grief, and her feelings of anger and betrayal. She attempts to right a wrong that so many had overlooked. Yahaira's initial response of fear and anger is warranted and she too contemplates her agency in how to address her sister's message. She thinks

> I could delete the message.
> I should delete the message
> but instead, she responds and presents herself to her sister in her
> own way.[36]

The revelation of their relationship makes it evident that the families knew about each other, only the daughters that were kept in the dark. The girls employ their agency by engaging in secret online communication, planning a meeting, and forging a relationship. The families are upholding hegemonic discourses of identity and belonging, but the girls' secret communications allow them to subvert the roles and relationships that had been established for them to recreate their own futures. Their father's two memorial services link them:

> Papi will have two funerals.
> Papi will have two ceremonies.
> Papi will be mourned in two countries.
> Papi will be said goodbye to here & there.
> Papi has two lives.
> Papi has two daughters.
> Papi was a man split in two,
> Playing a game against himself.
> But the Problem with that
> Is that to win, you also always lose.[37]

He was a man divided in two. He attempted to hold both countries and families within himself but ultimately failed. His betrayal of his two wives and his daughters reinforces invisible barriers between the mainland and the diaspora. He maintains rhetorical ideologies about ethnicity, nationality, and identity. Maintaining his secret depends on keeping these two sides of the diaspora apart.

His daughters call themselves Papi's mirrors, marking both their physical similarities to him and the personality traits each has picked up from him. Like him, both long for the other side of their transnational bond. They feel a sense of nostalgia for the other half of the diaspora. Acevedo evades the expected nostalgia for an impossible return by splitting the story between the two different sites. Here and there blur and blend into one another and through their mourning they reestablish their sisterly ties. Communal virtual sites of memory serve to keep this story alive though his death, among the many others who passed on this flight, has faded from the attention of the larger public and of the media. The author reflects on media memory: "the systematic exploration of collective pasts that are narrated by the media, through the use of the media, and about the media" to discuss how the power of the press affects cultural and collective memory.[38] In the section titled "Forty days after" the text speaks to the slow disappearance from mainstream media. Through her fictional lens, Acevedo explores the notion of living and dying and how a major issue in the New York and mainland Dominican community was minimized by the American mainstream media. Following two months and a day after 9/11, US media attention was not given to this situation to the same extent. Yahaira observes that while:

> The rest of the world has moved on
> To bigger & juicier news;
> So many of us here seem suspended
> In time, still waiting for more
> Information, still hoping
> This is a nightmare we'll wake from.[39]

While this community grieves, the rest of the world moves on. Christina Sharpe defines "the wake" as "the conceptual frame of and for living blackness in the diaspora in the still-unfolding aftermaths of Atlantic chattel slavery."[40] In thinking about the living legacy of the transatlantic slave trade she offers additional insight into why these racialized bodies were treated as if they mattered less. This framework for viewing contemporary Black life is marked by an ever-present past and universally internalized. It essentially relegates Black peoples to the Fanonian "zone of non-being,"[41] where Black peoples are socially dead, and it is that figurative denial and exclusion that removes them from the liberal idea of human. Black adolescents are similarly denied their innocence and humanity.

On the topic of humanity, Alexander Weheliye dialogues with Hortense Spillers and Sylvia Wynters to address the pitfalls of Western philosophical ideas of "Man." He understands racialization as a project comprised of different sociopolitical processes that divide people into categories of "full humans, not-quite-humans, and nonhumans, then blackness designates a changing system of unequal power structures that apportion and delimit which humans can lay claim to full human status and which humans cannot."[42] Various mechanisms of the state bar othered subjects, notably Black peoples, from full humanity. Black girlhood lies at the intersections of multiple marginalizations; thus, the girls in the novel are doubly and triply denied their humanity.

Like Weheliye, Katherine McKittrick troubles our understanding of human through Wynter's interventions. In *Demonic Grounds* she states Western conceptions of humanity are limited, writing, "the fullness of human ontologies, which have been curtailed by what she describes as an over representation of Man (Western bourgeois Man) as if it/he were the only available mode of complete humanness."[43] Colonization and contact with indigenous and African peoples ruptured the original understanding of man and necessitated the creation of other categories or rather "abolishing Man once and for all."[44] This would serve as a true route to liberation, equality, and equity. In the preface to *Precarious Lives* (2004), Judith Butler states, "Some lives are grievable, and others are not; the differential allocation of grievability that decides what kind of subject is and must be grieved, and which kind of subject must not, operates to produce and maintain certain exclusionary conceptions of who is normatively human: what counts as a livable life and a grievable death."[45] Racialization is clearly a factor in this mathematics of mournability. Proximity to whiteness and Western understanding of goodness factor into who is an acceptable victim.

In addressing anti-Blackness on the island of Hispaniola and in Dominican diasporic culture it is necessary to avoid oversimplification of racial views under a US hypodescent model of Black and white. As Lorgia Garcia-Peña affirms being, "'black' does not exist as an ethnically distinguished category in the Dominican Republic the way it does in the United States, being black (prieto, Haitian, or rayano) there inhibits social mobility through civic, political, and economic exclusion."[46] Although she implies that there is a differentiation in how Blackness is perceived in each country, racialization's social effects are felt in similar ways.[47] Despite that, it is equally important to note the influence of US anti-Blackness in the reading of Dominicanidad and the treatment of this accident. The lack of media coverage of this tragedy is a violence against that community. As Matos correctly asserts "History, memory and fiction represent absences in different ways."[48] History silences and erases, memory is fallible, but the strength of fiction lies in how it can fill these gaps. Building a new archive rectifies these purposeful silences. It gives voice to previously silenced voices and stories.

DOMINICANIDAD

Through the reconstruction of their father's identity, both daughters seek to legitimize their own identities. Yahaira questions her Dominicanidad, as a person who was born and raised off the island. She is cognizant of her position in the diaspora and says, "I was raised so damn Dominican."[49] She enumerates her cultural connections to the island to further cement herself as Dominican enough. Here Acevedo problematizes ideas of legitimacy. She questions

> Can you be from a place
> You have never been?
> You can find the island stamped all over me,
> But what would the island find if I was there?
> Can you claim a home that does not know you,
> Much less claim you as its own?[50]

What legitimizes one's national or ethnic connections? They transcend the limits associated with citizenship, stated here as the protections and benefits granted by your allegiance to a particular nation. Like Yahaira, Camino also questions her place in the world. She calls herself, "American-adjacent."[51] She benefits from her father's US residency and the money he sends back, but she is not of that society. US imperialism and paternalism are still present in contemporary Dominican society, and she is the product of her island country. She calls her home, "a playground place," an exclusive place, where even at home she is subjected to a type of second-class citizenship behind the foreigners who, "threaten to disappear us in a single gulp."[52] It isn't only resources that are exploited, but also the women who are objectified and turned into playthings,

> Even the women, girls like me,
> Our mothers & tías, our bodies
> Are branded jungle gyms
> for the foreign male gaze.[53]

The complex relationship between the United States and the Dominican Republic is made metaphor by El Cero, a character who mediates machista patriarchal relationships by pimping young Dominican women to foreign men. The exploitation of resources is juxtaposed with the sexual exploitation of these women and knowing at the end of the day there's no difference between the two,

> Sand & soil & sinew & smiles;
> All bartered. & who reaps? Who eats?
> Not us. Not me.[54]

These same questions of legitimacy the girls explore apply to the passengers on the flight. Many of them held dual connections to the United States and the Dominican Republic. They were considered American enough to participate in the economy, but were they viewed as American enough to be grieved.

MEMORIALIZATION

Although Papi attempted to hold his connections to two countries and two families in his body, his attempts to compartmentalize these two sides of his life and maintain them through deceit led to failure. Nevertheless, his two daughters, Yahaira and Camino, succeed in enacting a gendered reconciliation of Dominican diasporic identity through the collective reconstruction of their father's memory, the simultaneous interrogation of Dominicanidad and US citizenship, and ultimately by uniting as a feminine collective to destroy the embodiment of patriarchy, El Cero. Papi worked within the existing systems and he upheld them through his actions. He paid El Cero off rather than challenging him. He was complicit in the patriarchal system that sought to destroy his daughters and keep them apart. El Cero personifies this hetero-patriarchal system. Taking him down is only possible when the women stand together and though it is only one battle it has emboldened them and prepared them for the ones to come.

The novel encapsulates where history, erasure, memory, trauma, and violence meet fiction. Acevedo problematizes the idea that there is a correct medium for approaching historical trauma. Shining light on past events and memories, even in a loose representation, adds to the archive and establishes presence. In the same manner that the girls insert themselves into each other's lives, this book inserts itself into the vacuum left by society overlooking this tragedy. The overwhelming silence on behalf of the US national media creates a need for texts like these. Beyond representing the past, they encourage readers to think and view happenings from an insider's perspective. These narratives fill silences in the historic account and simultaneously provoke more questions than they answer. Are the people who lost their lives on this flight considered citizens? How does race play into who we view as citizens? Who we mourn as our own? In an Audible interview with Edwin de la Cruz, Elizabeth Acevedo confirms some of the questions she raises with this text, "What was the work of supplying dignity for the people who were lost on that flight? And can we keep doing that 20 years later? Do we still remember?" She states she was inspired to write this book text by a real event that seriously affected her community. Coming in the wake of 9/11 it affected an already vulnerable New York community that hadn't yet finished processing that devastating event. In the author's note, Acevedo recalls, "how little this crash was remembered when it was determined the cause was not terrorism. How quickly the news coverage trickled off, how it seemed the larger societal memory had moved on, even though the collective memory of my community was still wrestling with this loss."[55] She states that the purpose of this book stemmed from a desire "to remember." She "wanted a larger narrative that commemorated that moment in time."[56] The American Airlines crash wasn't given sufficient attention by the US media and twenty years after this tragedy, Acevedo's book text breathes life back into the story. While this fictional retelling is set in contemporary times and has diverging storylines it all centers back to the main theme of loss and how it disrupts the present. Loss doesn't remain in the past, but rather continuously makes itself present in different ways. The characters in the book see their father in themselves, in other family members, in places, and in activities they love. The sisters admit

"We look just like him."[57] They are their father's mirrors in different shades of Brown and Black. He left Yahaira with his chess skills and Camino with a love and talent for swimming. Their memory of past events is forever marked by the circumstances in which they happened and upon repetition and annotation from other people who experienced the same event the reader is given a broader picture of the past.

While the book refers to Facebook, it hadn't yet been invented in 2001. Collectively, the world watched the World Trade Center fall, and in US society this moment is marked and signaled by the phrase "Never Forget" which appears online each year on the anniversary of the attacks. Nowadays social networking sites have become a ground for expressing feelings of collective loss and grief interactively. Social media allows users a virtual community online and is a place where people eulogize friends, family members, and even strangers upon their deaths. Different features like memories allow users to look back on virtual moments they've shared with their online friends. This is referenced in the text, but the glaring difference is that it still shows a disconnect between certain tragedies and others. Does it change how we construct our communal memories? It makes them more public and shrinks the gap between reported history and our own recollections of the past. This text exists in the borderlands between history and memory and highlights the difference and the link between the two. History is an archive of memories that have been taken as fact and fiction is a narrative shaped by the imagination that is often inspired by real events. Acevedo problematizes the idea that there is a correct medium for approaching historical trauma. She doesn't approach this topic from a historical or journalistic point of view, rather she imagines it in verse in the perspective of and for young adults.

The link between history, memory, and media has changed the landscape of how we remember, are remembered, and how we mourn and grieve. When fellow citizens, mass media, and government fail to adequately address instances of Black death and suffering, members of communities turn to themselves to grieve their lost loved ones and to ensure they will not be forgotten. As Sharp asserts, "Living in the wake on a global level means living the disastrous time and effects of continued marked migrations, Mediterranean and Caribbean disasters, trans-American and -African migration, structural adjustment imposed by the International Monetary Fund that continues imperialisms/colonialisms, and more."[58] The characters in this book exist within the wake, they experience the microaggressions and larger violence that mark the lives of Black people throughout the diaspora. They live in a place where the past continuously affects their daily lives, they practice acts of wake work in caring for their family and friends. *Clap When You Land* is an unforgettable book and experience that artfully expresses the complex feelings of loss, pain, anger, and wonder at losing a father and finding a sister. It confronts

Black death in several situations and questions whose lives matter. Acevedo memorializes the real lives lost in a tragic accident and enacts the same ethics of care her characters practice in service to her community. This novel helps keep the memory of this tragedy alive and depicts a new agency for the young female protagonists.

The tale narrates the rekindling of family ties to create a small community in solidarity. These characters revisit and remember the past. Collective memory simply serves as a tool to navigate a story that is full of grief and pain to find that in the midst of it all there is some joy. By resituating a similar plane crash at a different time Acevedo imagines how the crash could have been responded to if it hadn't happened so soon after 9/11. She follows current media trends in our twenty-four-hour news cycle that move from one sensational event to the next before the public grows bored. News media and social media go hand in hand as both have changed dramatically in the past twenty years.

In presenting two sisters in two different parts of the Americas Acevedo questions our understanding of citizenship. The novel shines a light on the limits of the US model, particularly when it comes to transnational communities that are continually in movement. Showing the lack of care provided by the United States forces a remembrance, but also deconstructs what is accepted as true and impartial. The partiality of US and Western media shines out in which incidents they choose to cover, *Charlie Hebdo* instead of Beirut. By exposing who is truly considered American it shows exclusion along racial and ethnic lines. This book simultaneously reinserts this tale into the American narrative while challenging it. The protagonist cannot be contained by one nation. How do you memorialize within three different narratives of memorialization to belonging?

The final images of the novel situate the reader at a crossroads between two nations and two sides of diaspora. Looking back, Camino presents the reader with an image of Tia. The focus of this backward glance is not on what she left behind, but rather what has shaped her. Tia is described as a mountain and personifies the island. She is permanent; she is home. Camino is a product of Tia's upbringing and knows she remains for when Camino returns. At this moment Camino is like water, she ebbs and flows in the in-between and when joined with her sister they mark a new development in transnational identity. The final section switches seamlessly between their perspectives, but ends with an image of togetherness, "It ends not with us in the sky or the water,/but together/on solid earth/safely grounded."[59] Mainland Dominicanidad unites with the diaspora to show that both are shaped by the other. Gendered acts of agency are employed to reconnect and reconcile. They demonstrate only when both halves of diaspora come together are they truly whole and form the bridge of a new diasporic identity.

BIBLIOGRAPHY

Acevedo, Elizabeth E. *Clap When You Land*. Harper Teen, 2020.

Beaman, Jean. "Citizenship as Cultural: Towards a Theory of Cultural Citizenship." *Sociology Compass*, 10 (2016): 849–57.

Bloodsworth-Lugo, Mary K., and Carmen R. Lugo-Lugo. *Containing (UN)American Bodies: Race, Sexuality, and Post-9/11 Constructions of Citizenship*. Amsterdam: Editions Rodopi B.V., 2010.

Butler, Judith P. *Frames of War: When Is Life Grievable?* London: Verso, 2016.

Butler, Judith. *Precarious Lives: The Powers of Mourning and Violence*, Verso, London, 2004.

Crenshaw, Kimberlée. "Mapping the Margins: Intersectionality, Identity Politics, and Violence against Women of Color." *Stanford Law Review* 43, no. 6 (1991): 1241. https://doi.org/10.2307/1229039.

De la Cruz, Edwin. "The Unflinching Honesty in Elizabeth Acevedo's 'Clap When You Land.'" (August 10, 2020) https://www.audible.com/blog/interview /the-unflinching-honesty-in-elizabeth-acevedos-clap-when-you-land, Elizabeth Acevedo interviewee, Audible, inc.

Fanon, Frantz. *Black Skin, White Masks*. New York: Grove Press, 1952.

García-Peña, Lorgia. *The Borders of Dominicanidad*. Duke University Press, 2016. Kindle.

Leyh, Brianne McGonigle. "Imperatives of the Present: Black Lives Matter and the Politics of Memory and Memorialization." *Netherlands Quarterly of Human Rights* 38, no. 4 (2020): 239–45. https://doi.org/10.1177/0924051920967541.

Matos, Sergio. "History, Memory and Fiction: What Boundaries?." *História da Historiografia*. (2015). 8. 10.15848/hh.v0i17.930.

McKittrick, Katherine. *Demonic Grounds Black Women and the Cartographies of Struggle*. University of Minnesota Press, 2006.

Meese, James, Martin Gibbs, Marcus Carter, Michael Arnold, Bjorn Nansen, & Tamara Kohn. "Selfies| Selfies at Funerals: Mourning and Presencing on Social Media Platforms." *International Journal of Communication* [Online], 9 (2015): 14. Web. 7 May 2021

Morse, Tal. "The Construction of Grievable Death: Toward an Analytical Framework for the Study of Mediatized Death." *European Journal of Cultural Studies* 21, no. 2, (Apr. 2018), pp. 242–58, doi: 10.1177/1367549416656858.

Olmos, Margarite Fernández, and Lizabeth Paravisini-Gebert. *Creole Religions of the Caribbean: An Introduction from Vodou and Santeria to Obeah and Espiritismo*. New York University Press, 2011.

On Media Memory: Collective Memory in a New Media Age, edited by M. Neiger, et al., Palgrave Macmillan UK, 2011. *ProQuest Ebook Central*, https://ebookcentral -proquest-com.ezproxy.lib.utexas.edu/lib/utxa/detail.action?docID=713277.

Salva, Hector. *The 21 Divisions: Mysteries and Magic of Dominican Voodoo.* (2020) Weiser Books.

Sharpe, Christina. *In the Wake*. Duke University Press, 2016. Kindle.

Stevens, Camilla. *Aqui and Alla: Transnational Dominican Theater*. United States, University of Pittsburgh Press, 2019.

Torres-Saillant, Silvio. "The Tribulations of Blackness: Stages in Dominican Racial Identity." *Latin American Perspectives* 25, no. 3, (1998), pp. 126–46. *JSTOR*, www .jstor.org/stable/2634170.

Torres-Saillant, Silvio. *Introduction to Dominican Blackness*, CUNY Dominican Studies Institute, 2010

Weheliye, Alexander G. *Habeas Viscus: Racializing Assemblages, Biopolitics, and Black Feminist Theories of the Human*. Duke University Press, 2014.

NOTES

1. Christina Sharpe. *In the Wake: On Blackness and Being*. (Duke University Press. Kindle Edition. 2016).

2. Bryan McGonigle Leyh. "Imperatives of the Present: Black Lives Matter and the politics of memory and memorialization." 243.

3. Ibid.

4. Christina Sharpe. *In the Wake: On Blackness and Being*. (Duke University Press. Kindle Edition. 2016) 97.

5. CBSnews.com Staff, "Flight 587 Passenger List," CBS News, November 14, 2001, https://www.cbsnews.com/news/flight-587-passenger-list/.

6. Mary K. Bloodsworth-Lugo and Carmen R. Lugo-Lugo, *Containing (un)American Bodies: Race, Sexuality, and Post-9/11 Constructions of Citizenship*, (2010).

7. Christina Sharpe, *In the Wake: On Blackness and Being*, (2016). 72.

8. Jean Beaman, "Citizenship as cultural: Towards a theory of cultural citizenship." *Sociology Compass*, 10 (2016): 850.

9. Judith Butler. *Frames of War: When Is Life Grievable* (2016). 31.

10. Tal Morse, "The Construction of Grievable Death: Toward an Analytical Framework for the Study of Mediatized Death." *European Journal of Cultural Studies* 21, no. 2, (Apr. 2018), pp. 243, doi:10.1177/1367549416656858.

11. Ibid.

12. Judith Butler, *Precarious Life: The Power of Mourning and Violence* (2004).

13. Elizabeth Acevedo, *Clap When You Land* (Harper Teen, 2020). 267.

14. Ibid.

15. Ibid., 267, 286.

16. Ibid.

17. Ibid., 268.

18. Ibid., 286.

19. Ibid., 286–87.

20. Kimberlé Crenshaw. "Mapping the Margins." 1243.

21. Camilla Stevens, *Aqui and Alla: Transnational Dominican Theater*. (United States, University of Pittsburgh Press, 2019), 5.

22. Elizabeth Acevedo, *Clap When You Land* (Harper Teen, 2020). 139.

23. Christina Sharpe, *In the Wake* (2016). 10.

24. Elizabeth Acevedo, *Clap When You Land* (Harper Teen, 2020). 171.

25. Ibid., 172.

26. Elizabeth Acevedo, *Clap When You Land* (Harper Teen, 2020). 365.

27. Ibid.

28. Ibid., 366.

29. Margarite Fernández Olmos and Lizabeth Paravisini-Gebert. *Creole Religions of the Caribbean: An Introduction from Vodou and Santería to Obeah and Espiritismo.* (New York University Press, 2011). 47.

30. Hector Salva. *The 21 Divisions: Mysteries and Magic of Dominican Voodoo.* (2020) Weiser Books.

31. Elizabeth Acevedo, *Clap When You Land* (Harper Teen, 2020). 222.

32. Ibid.

33. Ibid., 235–36.

34. James Meese, Martin Gibbs, Marcus Carter, Michael Arnold, Bjorn Nansen, & Tamara Kohn. "Selfies| Selfies at Funerals: Mourning and Presencing on Social Media Platforms." *International Journal of Communication* [Online], 9 (2015): 14. Web. 1827.

35. Elizabeth Acevedo, *Clap When You Land* (Harper Teen, 2020). 223.

36. Ibid., 247.

37. Ibid., 285.

38. *On Media Memory: Collective Memory in a New Media Age*, edited by M. Neiger, et al., Palgrave Macmillan UK, 2011.

39. Elizabeth Acevedo, *Clap When You Land* (Harper Teen, 2020). 269.

40. Christina Sharpe, *In the Wake: On Blackness and Being* (2016). 2.

41. Frantz Fanon, *Black Skin, White Masks.*

42. Alexander Weheliye. *Habeas Viscus.*12.

43. Katherine McKittrick. *Demonic Grounds.* 123.

44. Ibid., 22.

45. Judith Butler. *Precarious Life: The Power of Mourning and Violence* (2004). xiv–xv.

46. Lorgia García-Peña. *The Borders of Dominicanidad.* Duke University Press, 2016. Kindle, 2.

47. See Silvio Torres-Saillant for reading on Dominican "deracialized consciousness."

48. Sergio Matos. "History, Memory and Fiction: What Boundaries?" *História da Historiografia* (2015). 432.

49. Elizabeth Acevedo, *Clap When You Land* (Harper Teen, 2020). 97.

50. Ibid.

51. Ibid., 108.

52. Ibid, 160.

53. Ibid.

54. Ibid., 160.

55. Edwin de la Cruz, "The Unflinching Honesty in Elizabeth Acevedo's 'Clap When You Land.'" (August 10, 2020).

56. Ibid.

57. Elizabeth Acevedo, *Clap When You Land* (Harper Teen, 2020). 326.
58. Christina Sharpe, *In the Wake: On Blackness and Being* (2016). 15.
59. Elizabeth Acevedo, *Clap When You Land* (Harper Teen, 2020). 417.

Index

About the Contributors

Algris Xiomara Aldeano Vásquez is a Black woman who was born and raised in the village of Santa María la Antigua, located in the province of Darién, Panamá. She completed all her elementary and secondary studies in Panama before emigrating to the United States. She earned a bachelor's at Norfolk State University and a master's at Howard University, where she is currently a lecturer in Spanish. She has written *Bunde y bullerengue: Literatura oral popular de mi tierra, Darién* (2010); *Bunde and Bullerengue: Popular Oral Literature from My Native Region, Darién* (2011); and in conjunction with Ian Isidore Smart, *Cosas casi jamás contadas: A New Cultural Reader for the Fourth Semester of College Spanish* (2007).

Jamie Lee Andreson holds a PhD in anthropology and history from the University of Michigan and is currently a postdoctoral scholar with the Africana Research Center at Penn State University. She completed an MA in ethnic and African studies from Pós-Afro, UFBA, and is the author of *Ruth Landes e a Cidade das Mulheres: uma releitura da antropologia do candomblé* (Editora UFBA, 2019). Her research employs historical and ethnographic methods to address debates on matriarchy, gender, and race in the Afro-Brazilian religion Candomblé by centering Black priestesses as political actors and intergenerational leaders who have shaped the meanings of African heritage in Brazil.

Concetta Bondi is a Spanish lecturer at Arizona State University (Phoenix, Arizona). Originally from Canada, she received her master's degree in Hispanic Studies from McGill University, Montreal, and her PhD in Chicanx Studies from Arizona State University. Her research interests include Mexican American/Chicanx studies and their relation to architecture, art, and literature. The proud daughter of an immigrant family and product of a mixture of cultures, her research explores the relationship between space, place, and identity formation in the Borderlands.

Yoiseth Patricia Cabarcas is an AfroColombian educator. She is currently a PhD student in literature at the Technological University of Pereira, Colombia. She is an active member of the Red Elegguá and of the research group in Regional Studies in Literature and Culture, specifically in Literature and Social Context line. Her research interest focuses on the field of Afro-Latin American Studies and everything that has to do with the role of Black women as a prime mover of memory, inheritance, and resistance.

Natasha Carrizosa is a poet, writer, and speaker. Her work is deeply rooted in her childhood and life experiences. Raised as the daughter of a fierce African American mother and Mexican father, her writing reflects the dichotomy of these two rich cultures. She is author of "mexicafricana," "heavy light," and "crown." Her work has been published in *¡Manteca! An Anthology of Afro-Latino Poets*, *CONTRA: Texas Poets Speak Out*, *raising mothers*, and *R2: The Rice Review* (Rice University). She has performed her work and conducted workshops for audiences in Madrid, Paris, Saint Lucia, New York, Houston, New Mexico, and countless other cities.

Meaghan Jeanne Coogan is a PhD student in the Romance Studies Department at UNC Chapel Hill. Her research focuses on Afro-diasporic literary, cultural, and artistic expression in the Hispanophone and Francophone Caribbean and how coloniality manifests itself through pathways of migration between the Caribbean and its former colonial powers and current neocolonial powers. She has worked as grant writer for the forthcoming film *Antes de que nos olviden*, a fiction film exploring racialized and gendered violence and women's resistance to said violence. In 2020 she received a FLAS fellowship to study Haitian Creole at Duke University.

Karen S. Christian is professor of Spanish at California Polytechnic State University, where she teaches Caribbean, Latin American, and Latinx literatures and cultures. She is the author of *Show and Tell: Identity as Performance in U.S. Latina/o Fiction* (1997) and has published articles on Cuban and Cuban American narrative, Latinx literature, and service learning in Latinx immigrant communities. Recent publications include "'Who and what are you?': Tracing the Middle Passage in Afro-Latinx Writing" (*Label Me Latina/o*, Summer 2020); "Trauma in the Caribbean: Postmemory and the Persistence of History in Latinx Literature" (*Studies in American Culture*, Spring 2020); and "Weaving a Larger Web: Cuban American Writing in the Latin@ Narrative" (*Latino Studies*, 2017). Her current research focuses on (post)memory, trauma, race, and identity in contemporary Latinx fiction. Dr. Christian received the Cal Poly Distinguished Teaching Award for 2015–2016.

Renata Dorneles Lima is a Brazilian educator. She holds a master's degree in Hispanic-American Literature and is currently pursuing a doctorate in Hispanic-American Literature at the Universidade Federal do Rio de Janeiro. Her research tackles the production of Black poets in Latin America and the spoken word. She is coordinator of NEAB, a group of Afro-Brazilian studies for the promotion of the history, culture and politics of the Black Brazilian population and in diaspora.

Yesenia Escobar Espitia is an Afrocolombian educator, writer, and lawyer. She holds a master's degree in literary studies at Universidad Nacional de Colombia and is studying for a PhD in Spanish at Temple University. She is an active member of Red Elegguá, a Colombian NGO interested in researching and fostering an anti-racist education based on the study of Africa and the African diaspora. Her academic work has been combined with a sensitive poetry and narrative that reaches children as well as adults.

Lesley Feracho is Associate Professor of Spanish in the Department of Romance Languages at the University of Georgia and the Associate Director of the Institute of African American Studies. Her current research and publications examine transnational, literary, and cultural texts of women writers of African descent from the Hispanophone and Lusophone Americas. Her first book, *Linking the Americas: Race, Hybrid Discourses and the Reformulation of Feminine Identity*, was published by SUNY Press in 2005.

Lindsay Gary graduated with a BA in history and minors in dance and business administration, and with an MA in history and an MPA in public policy. In 2018 she was selected as a Mellon Scholar in African American History at the Library Company of Philadelphia. She obtained her Graduate Certificate in African American Studies and is a recipient of the Molefi Kete Asante Founder's Award.

Kerry Green is a Spanish Graduate Associate at Arizona State University where she is also pursuing a PhD in Spanish in Latin American literature and culture in the School of International Letters and Cultures. She previously acquired her Spanish MA with a concentration in both literature and linguistics at San Diego State University and her bachelor's degree in Spanish at the University of Tennessee. Having grown up in Brazil with Honduran parents and being born in United States, she quickly realized how each country shaped her in becoming who she is today. For this reason, her research focuses on identity in the twenty-first century, particularly of women and marginalized groups. She takes a particular interest in the presence of Afro-Latinx cultural productions and representations in short stories, photography, as well as films in Mexico, Brazil, and the United States. She plans to continue exploring how contemporary issues shape the identity of Black, indigenous, and people of color. Kerry intentionally seeks to apply her research in her classroom as well as looking for ways her knowledge can positively impact her immediate community.

Keturah Nichols is a PhD student in the department of Iberian and Latin American Literatures and Cultures at the University of Texas at Austin. Currently, she is studying Spanish and Portuguese literature and working on a portfolio in African and African Diaspora studies. She has a keen interest in the Caribbean, and her areas of focus include the intersections of race and gender in poetry and performance by Caribbean and US Latinx artists as well as Black activist work and international communities of solidarity. After receiving her BA in Romance languages from Washington and Lee University in 2012, she was awarded a Fulbright English teaching assistantship in brazil for the 2014 academic year. Upon her return, she completed her MA in Spanish and French at the University of Alabama.

Lillie Padilla is currently an Assistant Professor of Spanish at Sam Houston State University. She was born in Accra, Ghana. She received her PhD and MA in Spanish linguistics at Arizona State University, and her bachelor's degree in sociology and Spanish at the University of Ghana. Her research interests include Spanish language variation in Equatorial Guinea , heritage language pedagogy, and translation and interpretation curriculum development. Her work has been published in journals such as *Language Awareness*.

Melissa Castillo Planas is an Associate Professor of English at Lehman College in the Bronx, New York, and the CUNY Graduate Center PhD program in English specializing in Latinx Literature and Culture. She is the author of the poetry collection *Coatlicue Eats the Apple*, editor of the anthology, *¡Manteca!: An Anthology of Afro-Latin@ Poets*, coeditor of *La Verdad: An International Dialogue on Hip Hop Latinidades*, and coauthor of the novel *Pure Bronx.* Her most recent book project, with Rutgers University Press' new Global Race and Media series (March 2020), *A Mexican State of Mind: New York City and the New Borderlands of Culture,* examines the creative worlds and cultural productions of Mexican migrants in New York City. Her second book of poetry, *Chingona Rules*, was released with Finishing Line Press in September 2021.

Brenda Romero is an Assistant Professor of Spanish at the Department of World Languages and Literatures at California State University, Sacramento. She received a master's degree in Spanish and a PhD in Latin American

Literature from the University of Utah and was a faculty member at College of Saint Mary in Omaha, Nebraska. Her areas of expertise are Mexican studies and the colonial period. Her research focuses on the exploration of marginalized voices in literature and the interpretation of hybrid texts, including the study of the Nahua Codices. She was editor-in-chief for the *Utah Foreign Language Review* and has presented her research at numerous professional conferences in the United States and abroad. Her work has been published in various academic journals. In 2020 she was awarded the College of Arts and Letters Development Grant from Sacramento State University and she recently contributed to the anthology *Letras femeninas: escritoras mexicanas del siglo XX* published in Mexico. Besides teaching, Dr. Romero has extensive experience as an interpreter and translator.

Rosita Scerbo is an Assistant Professor of Afro-Hispanic Studies at Georgia State University. She has previously worked as an Assistant Professor of Afro-Latinx culture, Black studies, and women's, gender, and sexuality studies at Allegheny College. She received her PhD in Latin American and Latinx Literature and Visual Studies from Arizona State University. Dr. Scerbo is the author of the book *LATINAS EN LOS MÁRGENES. QueerARTivismo y TRANSdisciplinariedad: hacia una politización de la autobiografía visual de mujeres invisibles/LATINAS ON THE MARGINS. QueerARTivism and TRANSdisciplinarity: Towards a Politicization of the Visual Autobiography of Invisible Women* (Peter Lang, 2021) and of numerous book chapters and scholarly articles. Through her teaching, mentoring, service, and research she advocates for ethnic and racial minoritized communities and other underrepresented groups in the United States and Latin America. Her current publications and teaching endeavors focus on intersectional and transnational feminism, Afro-Latinx/diasporic literature and culture, and the Black woman experience in the Hispanic world.

www.ingramcontent.com/pod-product-compliance
Lightning Source LLC
Chambersburg PA
CBHW071845270326
41929CB00013B/2113